A History of Urban America

# A History of Urban America

## Second Edition

**CHARLES N. GLAAB**

University of Toledo

**A. THEODORE BROWN**

University of Wisconsin–Milwaukee

REVISION PREPARED BY CHARLES N. GLAAB

## Macmillan Publishing Co., Inc.

NEW YORK

Collier Macmillan Publishers

LONDON

Macmillan Publishing Co., Inc.
866 Third Avenue, New York, New York 10022

Collier Macmillan Canada, Ltd.

---

*Library of Congress Cataloging in Publication Data*

Glaab, Charles Nelson, (date)
  A history of urban America.

  Bibliography: p.
  Includes index.
    1. Cities and towns—United States. I. Brown,
Andrew Theodore, (date)      joint author. II. Title.
HT123.G56  1976       973'.09173'2       74–33097
ISBN 0–02–344110–0

---

Printing:  2 3 4 5 6 7 8                Year:  7 8 9 0 1 2

To the memory of
R. Richard Wohl

# Preface to the Second Edition

The first edition of *A History of Urban America* was not designed as a text-book in American urban history. In view of the state of knowledge in a then new field, to have tried to prepare one at the time Professor Brown and I wrote our study would have been presumptuous. We had in mind what we came to call "the synthesis," a group of essays essentially, organized around a few themes that had interested us in our years of working together in re-search and in teaching urban history courses. It grew to be a bit more than this in the writing, but we always understood that much of this vast new field was well beyond our measure. The book, however, did find use in the courses in urban history that had begun to proliferate in colleges and universities in the latter 1960s. In reviews and bibliographies, it has, to our gratitude, been assessed sympathetically, as an interpretative text, albeit one of modest dimen-sions. We came to accept the designation. This revision, however, has been undertaken reluctantly, for we never really changed our initial view that we had little talent for the writing of texts, and as the years passed, the book still continued to reflect in our eyes what we had wanted to say. On the other hand, despite the numerous excellent readers, collections of essays, and other works designed for courses that appeared after its publication, no other study seemed to go beyond what we had attempted. Because many seemed sincere when they said they had found our work useful as a guide to a subject we still thought important, we decided that a revision to bring the study up to date might be worthwhile.

This edition is essentially an expansion of the first. Only a handful of the original interpretations seemed to require modification, and only two or three of the changes that resulted represent a change of mind. Although the work is much longer, with five chapters added to the original ten, the present writer has scrupulously tried to keep to the book's design, and the earlier stated assumptions still hold. Although in general the work was rewritten page by page, I eventually decided to leave two chapters virtually intact, because they represented to me the more original products of a most congenial collabora-tion, and personally evoked the spirit of freer and happier, and I have no doubt better, times in the great world of learning. The additions vary in kind. Scholarship on subjects such as the history of colonial communities and of the lower classes in nineteenth-century cities permitted further ex-amples and illustrations as well as the addition of material on new topics related to those we had considered. In regard to some matters ignored in the original, although we recognized their importance, urban art and architecture for example, my competence over the years has been enlarged enough to permit a few more observations. I have not abandoned our earlier view that many subjects involving race and ethnicity customarily included within a rubric of urban history are more properly part of a national social history. Nevertheless, the extensive scholarship in recent years does make it possible to isolate urban dimensions of such matters, and these have now been included. Other topics often to be found in urban history courses, aspects of the history of labor for example, still seem to me so indirectly related to the process of urbanization that they are better examined from some other framework. The additions most difficult to justify are those involving the urban history of the past twenty-five or thirty years or so. Reading historians on their own times after several years of avoiding the task strongly reinforced the view, which we expressed in the preface to the first edition of our book, that the value of the historian's work diminishes as it approaches the present. But inquiry into current matters seems customary in topical history courses, and I decided to plunge in, convinced that I could hardly do worse than those I was reading. In the latter portions of the study, I have tried, seemingly in contradiction to some current practice in the craft, to indicate the tentative and often personal character of most judgments and interpretations of present-day affairs.

I regret deeply that my friend A. Theodore Brown, who to his credit has always followed more exact and demanding pursuits than my own, could not participate in this revision. He would not agree with many things I have added, and should not be held accountable for them. But I doubt that he will be disturbed to find them under his name. A true Jeffersonian, he has never believed in revealed or received truth; he has always accepted the diversity of minds and recognized merit in all opinion founded on reason. As a defender of the democracy of learning, he would not care to be praised as the exceptional man he is—a good companion nonpareil in the exploration of the urbane, and an intellectual aristocrat who showed many of us ill-educated country bumpkins and denizens of the city streets that wisdom and beauty are to be found in art, history, and literature. Both of us and our friends know how much I and this study owe to him. I would only add that if a sense of respect for reason and civility remain here, it is largely his doing.

Obviously I have drawn on the work of many scholars, and I have tried to acknowledge as much of this as was feasible. But any such attempt was bound to be inadequate, and I hope that my colleagues, who have so graciously acknowledged my work in the past, will understand. Three of my graduate students, David M. Rich, Dennis J. Signorovitch, and Ivan M. Tribe, supplied assistance of various kinds in a manner that I thought had disappeared from the academy. My wife Mary, freed at long last from some of the demanding tasks of child rearing, helped with a number of chores essential in preparing a manuscript, chores that I used to do for myself. I am grateful for the assistance and for the pleasure of her company.

C. N. G.

# Preface to the First Edition

The word *urban* has come in our day to have almost the value of a talisman in academic as well as political life. It lends an air of serious and informed concern to discourse in which it appears. And yet, other than the fact that *urban* has somehow to do with cities, there is little agreement in ordinary discussion on what it means. Sociologists, geographers, political scientists, and economists have in recent years subjected city and metropolitan phenomena to intensive examination from many points of view and are endeavoring to make analytical tools of such concepts as urbanization. Historians, although not characteristically seeking generalizations and definitions, have contributed substantially to our knowledge of cities. Still, there has been almost no effort to synthesize the historical evidence that has been discovered—to use urban growth as the organizing theme in a study of the American past and to try to discover the historical meaning of that useful but elusive adjective, *urban*.

This book is an attempt to do just that. Many themes relevant to American urban history have not been examined here. Nevertheless, the book reflects our views of the subject's coherence, developed during a combined experience of twenty years' teaching and research in urban history. Particularly, we have avoided subordination of the subject to the periodization and other conventional categories of national history; readers will find little mention of the Revolution and Early National Period, the Civil War and Reconstruction, or the Progressive Era. We feel strongly that more is learned about the social process of urbanization when it is regarded as an "independent variable," when it is allowed to reveal its own phases and is not stretched to a Procrustean framework which was constructed long before scholars took urban history seriously.

We have made no effort to treat developments since World War II in any comprehensive way. The rapidly proliferating data on recent urban expansion, which the nation's scholars, journalists, and administrators amass in their growing attention to the city and the metropolis, cannot yet be viewed synthetically. We believe also that there is a point—impossible to locate exactly —as our studies approach the present day, at which the usefulness of historians' work diminishes relative to the usefulness of contributions by other social scientists.

Although much that appears on the following pages rests upon our own conclusions developed during close study of original material, in a work of this kind the necessity for unsparing appropriation of the scholarship of others is obvious. Our colleagues will understand that adequate acknowledgment has not been possible, although we have tried to indicate those works from which our borrowing has been the heaviest.

We accept joint responsibility for the entire book. We wish to acknowledge special assistance generously extended by Lyle W. Dorsett, Catherine Goldsmith, and Eric E. Lampard, Shirley Darling and members of our departmental typing pool, and several graduate students in the Urban Affairs and Urban History programs at The University of Wisconsin–Milwaukee.

C. N. G.
A. T. B.

# Contents

# A History of Urban America

CHAPTER

# 1

# The Colonial Matrix

POPULAR understanding of our history has emphasized the transformation of America from a wilderness, to a land of farmers, to an urban society. This conception, like all group conceptions of a collective past, is partly true: one of the fundamental forces in American history has been rapid growth of population and the inexorable movement of people from farms and dispersed settlements to cities. Yet from the beginning there was an element in the American experience that can be called urban—the first settlers brought with them an emphasis on ordered communities and a loyalty to town that in a sense was as strong as their religious faith. The New England towns, as several studies of recent years have pointed out, were particularly influenced by a corporate, Utopian ideal—a belief that it was necessary for man to live in a stable, compact, organized society. It can be argued perhaps that this was not urban at all, that *urban* means specialization, diversity of experience, and freedom of choice. In this sense of *urban*, Boston emerged early as an urban place, but the other towns of New England and elsewhere represented something altogether different, places where the ideals of the tribe or the village persisted. It can also be argued that in America, urban, in contrast to what was urban in past times, was represented by the nineteenth-century city in which the emphasis on individual enterprise and private interest seemed, in practice, to deny explicitly the necessity of responsibility to any community, and that the colonial town became a part of a "world that we have lost." Yet in other ways the belief in the rational, organized community has always persisted in America, sometimes only as a memory of a path not taken, and the influence of the belief represents a special dimension of American history.

Regardless of whether one broadens the definition of urban to include the first compact settlements or whether one narrows it to centers with metropolitan characteristics, it is clear that from a very early date in the colonization of North America the British Crown fostered urban aspects of American society by encouraging its subjects in "the plantations" to organize towns and to arrange their farming and other extractive industries around these towns. In the seventeenth century, colonial governors were often instructed, as in one actual case, "to draw tradesmen and handicraftmen into towns." One of the governors of Virginia told the colonial assembly in 1680 to pass measures facilitating the organization of towns; the King, he said, "is resolved as soon as storehouses and conveniences can be provided, to prohibit ships trading here to land or unload but at certain fixed places." The imperial rulers saw advantages to themselves in fostering the Americans' dependence upon their colonial towns. In the view of these rulers, the American colonies were like all other colonies: sources of English wealth and sources also of administrative problems. Colonies were supposed to function so as to profit the Empire—or at least to profit the relatively small group that ran the Empire—and for this purpose they had to be controlled; the doings of the energetic colonists had to be overseen. This task of control could best be carried out if colonial life, and especially colonial economic life, was channeled through a limited number of focal points. At these points the imperial authorities could regulate trade and check illicit businesses. So the Crown encouraged, even required, the laying out and chartering of towns in its American possessions—as in the case of Burlington, in what is now New Jersey, late in the seventeenth century: "Not any thing being of greater efficiency to promote trade and business . . . than the indult of such privileges as may invite active and ingenious men to resort thither and coinhabit therein and adventure their stocks and estates upon the issue of Providence in the way of trade. . . ." Or, a few decades later on, in the case of Suffolk, Virginia: "Great numbers of people have lately settled themselves at and near a place called Constances warehouse . . . and . . . in case a town was laid out there, trade would be greatly encouraged." There is irony in the fact that the process by which town life, originally promoted partly in the interest of royal authority and imperial control, became the matrix of self-sustaining cultural life, business ambition, and political training in the colonies, all of which culminated in their secession from the British Empire. But that process occupied the better part of a century and three-quarters; people in the colonies were not generally aware of what was happening to them as their towns and later their cities flourished. Settlements designed originally to serve the needs of a mercantilist empire became agencies in its dissolution.*

To an extent, of course, the colonists needed no encouragement in starting town settlements. The civilization that shaped them, and which they represented when they reached the shore of the wilderness, was far past the stage where subsistence agriculture could play any significant part in it. The Virginia and New England pioneers came from an England whose political, social, and economic life depended upon connections and interactions which focused on London and the provincial cities. There, in the cities, goods were exchanged and ideas clashed; there wealth accumulated, power resided, and decisions

---

* *Mercantilism* signifies, broadly, the political economy of the early nationalist era. Although the term never represented a thoroughly consistent, agreed-upon theory, its leading propositions were that a country's economic power should be systematically mobilized in the interest of national (usually imperial) security, and that this was best accomplished by strictly controlling productive activity and trade to the end that hard money (gold and silver) would flow into the country rather than out of it. Colonies were sought as sources of raw materials and colonists were restricted in their access to finished products to the mother country.

were made. In their American enterprise the colonists would begin with closely-knit communities that would soon become towns. These towns would serve as markets, temples (in the sense that religious life would gather around them), and centers of political organization and control. The towns were essential to colonial life from the beginning. They were not called into existence by an earlier development of farming, but rather constituted the necessary positions from which agriculture and other activities, such as the fur trade, could spread inland without losing connection with the great world. Thus, the roots of American urbanization go back to the day of the first permanent settlement.

The Winthrops, Byrds, Livingstons, and those who accompanied them westward across the Atlantic Ocean, brought along notions of what towns were for and how people should live in them which still bore traces of the thought and custom of medieval Europe. Towns had appeared on the largely rural landscape of the Dark Ages and had grown at first almost as cracks in the social edifice of selfdom, manor, vassalage, and fealty. Although they were obviously very useful economically, and increasingly so as Western Europe arose from the patchwork efforts at organization that succeeded the fall of Rome, towns and townsfolk fitted uncomfortably into the localized and hierarchical arrangements of the earlier middle ages. Bit by bit, usually in the face of noble or clerical hostility, the people in the towns were able to defend their claims to varying measures of self-government and to such privileges of trading as they thought would be profitable. Thus, in a legal sense, towns became "bundles of privileges," or concessions which had been wrung from traditional authorities. This characteristic was carried over into the period when national states dominated political life; that is, the towns and cities of England, France, and other countries in Western Europe were groups of people, living close together, to whom the sovereign granted the privilege of holding a market, establishing a municipal court or constabulary, and other similar functions. In the sixteenth and seventeenth centuries, as the principles of English mercantalism became clarified, the "privileges" were dispensed more in the interests of control than of benevolence.

There was another good reason for the organization of towns, which also reflected the need to impose authority upon the doings of people who lived close together. Social disorder usually attended such assemblages of people and the force of police and legal regulation of behavior had to be made available to the more responsible inhabitants of an area. The Mayflower Compact is an example of what was necessary; the leaders of the Pilgrim expedition formally agreed "to covenant and combine ourselves together into a civil Body Politick, for our better Ordering and Preservation. . . ." Before leaving London, the migrants had picked up as volunteers what one of their principal men called "an undesirable lot," and hence they wanted to provide themselves with some kind of seemingly authoritative means of making and enforcing laws. This could be done on a voluntary basis, as among the settlers of New

England (and many other Americans after them) or the necessary stamp of legitimacy could come from the Crown. Thus, Elizabeth, New Jersey, was chartered in mid-eighteenth century, among other things, "for the promotion of good order and the establishment of a firm, certain, and peaceable government." Schenectady, New York, a bit later, reveals the same motive: "to prevent disorders and excesses because of the influx of so many strangers to this rapidly growing trading center."

While the building of towns was a crucial feature of American colonization, the towns were to be thought of as instruments of control—not as laboratories of democracy or experiments in individual freedom. Economic life was strictly regulated. Externally, the lines of trade were prescribed: it could be carried on only in English ships, which included English colonists' ships, and its most important components could be shipped only between the colonies (hinterland) and the mother country (metropolis). Internally the price and quality of goods was subject to public regulation, as were wages, profits, and the time and place of marketing—as well as who would be eligible to sell certain kinds of goods.

Regulations bore heavily on idleness. Individuals were legally responsible to work on public projects and even on private projects that were felt to be in the interest of the community. When, in 1644, three New Haven entrepreneurs proposed to deepen the channel of a creek, the authorities gave them four days of work from each male resident between the ages of sixteen and sixty. On another occasion, Newark offered three days of work from every able-bodied resident to assist anyone who undertook to set up a corn mill.

Social life was regulated similarly and sometimes as explicitly. When street plans for colonial towns were laid out on paper it was always understood that some of the future inhabitants would be wealthier and of higher social rank than others, and different areas were provided for spacious estates and more modest accommodations. In at least one case (Swansea, Massachusetts), the original plan specified areas for three denominated ranks. "Not only did this action receive the sanction of the townsmen," writes Thomas J. Wertenbaker, "but in after years committees were appointed to perpetuate these distinctions, or to promote and degrade persons from one rank to another." Laws provided that clothing must reflect the status of the person wearing it. Gentlemen and their ladies were allowed to wear lace, gold, and silver ornaments and items made of silk, which were forbidden to those in lower classes. The assignment of seats in churches was almost everywhere made on the basis of sharp and explicit class distinction, and anyone who tried to claim a seat not befitting his status was likely to be punished severely.

In this omnipresence of the regulating hand of government, the colonial towns mirrored arrangements in the mother country. But there were circumstances of colonial life, in this early period at least, that reinforced the idea that a high degree of social control was desirable. These towns, as Colonial and European writers often stressed, were placed on the edge of a wilderness of uncalculated extent. Separated by thousands of miles of dangerous ocean from their only source of outside assistance, the colonists confronted the unknown strength of Indians and competing empires as well as the threatening and all-encompassing forest which dwarfed their tiny settlements. John Winthrop of Massachusetts Bay, often charged with undue preference for authoritarianism in the governing of his colony, explained the need for social control. "It is to be feared," he wrote, "that many [creep] out at a broken wall. For such as come together into a wilderness, where are nothing but wild beasts and beast-like men, and there confederate together in civil and church estate, whereby they do—implicitly at least—bind themselves to support each other and all of them that society . . . whereof they are members, how they can break from this . . . is hard to find . . . Ask thy conscience if thou wouldst have plucked up thy estates and brought thy family three thousand miles, if thou hadst expected that all, or most, would [forsake] thee there?" In a much different environment, Captain John Smith had already found it necessary to impose the severest kind of dictatorial control on his infant Jamestown settlement in the simple interest of its survival.

Physical necessity, then, along with the political and military nature of mercantilism, helps explain the closely regulated character of life in the first generation or two of most of the colonial cities. But beyond these considerations, certain values of urban life were believed to inhere in the regulating, the planning, of communities. When John Winthrop, in his famous lay sermon of 1630, delivered aboard the flagship *Arabella,* which was bringing his Puritan followers to the New World, summed up his views as "Wee shall be as a City upon a Hill," he meant partly that the Puritan experiment would be a "City of God," in accord with the Gospel of Matthew, a place where man would serve God as He had intended. But as Darrett B. Rutman has demonstrated in his study of Boston, Winthrop also had in mind a city in a literal, physical sense, a place where arrangements involving land, property, and status would be planned and organized around a central community institution, the church. William Penn planned carefully for the growth of his Philadelphia project, which he laid out in 1682. Existing plans for the reconstruction of London influenced him and Surveyor-General Captain Thomas Holme in drawing up the physical design of Philadelphia. But from the very choice of its classical name, Utopian impulses also guided Penn's thoughts. Streets were to form a gridiron pattern, but five spacious squares interrupted the monotony, providing pleasure grounds and space for civic and religious centers. Residential streets were fifty feet wide and stately trees arose along them soon after the turn of the century. One great artery (later called Market Street), one hundred feet wide, traversed the city and ended at the Delaware River. Everything was planned to assure comfortably compact settlement of which even the physical layout would encourage social organization and a vital community life. Penn could not abide the passionate land hunger which increasingly dispersed American settlements all over the landscape—land hunger (an important part of which was coming to be real estate hunger) which increasingly supported individualistic attitudes largely foreign to the seventeenth century. It might be added that the hunger and the attitudes also made it difficult for Penn to collect rents that were supposed to accrue to him from his colony project.

The importance of all this is not simply in Penn's physical vision of a "city beautiful." Cities, if properly built, represented the possibility of realizing important social values and Penn had these clearly in mind. A German pastor, who led his flock to Pennsylvania shortly after the colony had begun to flourish, remarked that Penn "will not give any man his portion separately, but all must dwell together in townships and towns, and this not without weighty reasons . . . the children can be kept at school and much more conveniently brought up well. Neighbors also can better offer each other loving and helpful hands and with united mouth can in public assemblies praise and extol the greatness of God." This insight into the notion of a city as a social organism to be carefully nourished and guided in its development for the benefit of the parts that made it up was more clearly expressed in Penn's plan for Philadelphia than elsewhere, but it was not really peculiar to him.

All of the colonial cities and towns were planned communities in origin; the idea that their growth might be shaped by individuals' interests in real estate speculation was to emerge only slowly. New Haven's street plan was set out on a scale almost as impressive as Philadelphia's: there was a common 825 feet square in the center of town with provision of space for meeting house, jail, school, and courthouse. Surrounding this square were eight others of the same dimensions, in which residential neighborhoods could be built. Much of the seeming confusion of Boston's streets, which can still frustrate the tourist, was actually the result of careful planning: the first proprietors took pains to follow the local topography when they sketched their plan, and then stuck to it.

The most impressive example of city planning after Philadelphia came with the establishment of Savannah, Georgia. Early in the eighteenth century, a well-to-do Englishman named James Oglethorpe became interested in prison reform. He began planning a New World colony where formerly imprisoned debtors might start life anew. In 1732 he and some associates got a charter from the King for the colony of Georgia. The first party was led by Oglethorpe himself, and it began by plotting out Savannah. On a good level site, about ten miles upstream from the mouth of the Savannah River, the founders outlined the town's limits in a large rectangle. Within the rectangle, house lots were grouped in square wards of forty each; a gridiron of main streets seventy-five feet wide, and others with half that width, divided the wards. Squares where the lines of the main streets intersected were mostly to be given over to churches and other public buildings. Around the outside of the rectangle there was a common, as the language of the plan has it, "for Convenience of Air"; around this common the next area was to be divided into five-acre garden plots, and outside the garden plots it was to be divided into forty-four-acre farms. It is not surprising that Savannah, thus imaginatively and pains-takingly founded, grew steadily; its population reached 3,000 by the 1770s, although the philanthropic impulse in Oglethorpe's plans had by then dropped out of view.

This widespread and often imaginative concern for city planning reflects the assumption, common to Britons and Americans in the seventeenth and eighteenth centuries, that civilized life is urban life and that personal develop-ment in any full sense is possible only to people who live in or near towns. Thus the main proprietor of the Carolinas, communicating with his agents in the colony in 1671, stressed the value of "the Planting of People in Townes"; this was "the Cheife thing that hath given New England soe much the ad-vantage over Virginia." Five years later he repeated the admonition: "for wee must assure you," he wrote on behalf of his associates, "that it is your and our Concerne very much to have some very good Towns in your Plantations for other wise you will not longe continue civilized or ever bee considerable or secure."

In colonial Virginia there were numerous legislative proposals to promote "cohabitation" in towns. On six occasions from 1655 to 1705, for example, the Virginia assembly passed laws to create port towns. But these efforts pro-duced little result. The authors of the pamphlet *The Present State of Virginia*, printed in 1727, lamented the colony's failure to progress as rapidly as it might have, owing to "want of towns, markets, and money." An earlier Vir-ginia writer, arguing the need for towns, referred to "well ordered Schools, in well governed Towns," "nurseries of learning and piety," and at one point postulated that "Christians (if they have Liberty) ought to live together in visible united societies, in cities, towns, or villages." A Massachusetts preacher in 1705 excoriated the impulse which led people to leave the city and move into the country. "By that means," he said, such individuals "bid defiance, not only to Religion, but to Civility itself." There was little doubt among the colonists that the town and the city was man's proper habitat.

To whatever extent their development was guided by planning, and what-ever they may have owed to British protection and British commerce, many communities in the American colonies were developing rapidly by the eigh-teenth century and several of them deserved the title of "city" by any reason-able usage current at that time. These were the important seaports, and their impressive growth testified to the vitality of the imperial partnership and to the role of these cities as channels of commerce governed according to mer-cantilist considerations. Boston, the first of them, numbered about 13,000 inhabitants by 1730. New York, which had amounted to very little as the Dutch outpost of New Amsterdam, had grown to something more than 8,000 once under the aegis of the British Empire, and there were already more than 11,000 Philadelphians, even though that community was less than half a cen-tury old. Norfolk, Charleston, and Providence also flourished around their busy ports. Some of the interior settlements showed signs of growth, but American colonial civilization continued to be mostly a maritime phenomenon; its cities arose on the shores of the ocean and faced outward, across the water toward the metropolitan mother country. Until a very late period in their development, these colonies each had more communication and connection with Britain than they had among themselves.

Still, within the process of growth itself, there were seeds of conflict. The leading colonial cities grew beyond a point, wherever it lay, where they could still function—or could still be made to function—as key pieces in the structure of a mercantilist empire. This came about for two reasons, and both are closely related, in turn, to social development in the cities. In the first place, ships owned and based in the colonial ports began searching out profitable trade areas outside of those permitted them by the Navigation Laws—mercantilism's operating code, as those laws may be called. Tentative and on a small scale at first, this kind of smuggling grew in importance until it had become almost systematized by the middle of the eighteenth century. In the second place, business might also be done in the other direction: westward. Here, in the unmapped expanse of continent that lay just over the back doorsteps, so to speak, of American city dwellers in the Colonial period, was the source of highly profitable trade in furs. Later on, it occurred to some enterprising men that the land in the interior could be converted into real estate: the colonists (perhaps in partnership with homeland English) could themselves plant colonies out there for the greater glory of the empire, and also for sizeable accretions to their own bank accounts. In other words, while the colonies radiated outwards from urban centers that faced east toward the empire as it existed in the seventeenth and eighteenth centuries, there was no obvious reason why they should restrict themselves to that direction. They could also face westward and capitalize upon resources to which the imagination of no man could set any limit.

These two developments both reached significant stages by the mid-eighteenth century, and both had come about because growth had complicated society in the colonial cities. Local elites had appeared in each of them: groups of merchants and landowners with fortunes which were considerable for the day, with ambitions which outran those fortunes, with increasing political and administrative experience, and with the firm conviction that they possessed the same rights and perquisites, the same claims to status and deference, as their counterparts in the mother country. In short, born in the hinterland of a mercantilist empire, these communities bred groups of men who began to think of themselves as imperialists in their own right, and of their communities as nascent metropolitan centers that might command hinterlands of their own. That such prospects absolutely contradicted the major propositions which the imperial rulers in London simply assumed as the basis for all their policy and action was true enough, although for a long time this was not evident to the colonists. When it did become evident, the colonists' only reaction was to question the validity of those propositions.

By that time, the colonial leaders had grown used not only to directing private business ventures on a large scale, whatever officials in England might think of their legality, but also to administering an increasingly complicated and challenging public life. As the colonial cities had grown on their expanding economic bases, their social and political characteristics had become more elaborate, and the problems which had to be met if large numbers of people were to live together closely, were more and more demanding. Public problems, in other words, were precipitated by growth; in dealing with them the colonists accumulated an impressive fund of administrative (or, more broadly, *political*) experience. In the same measure, their political ambitions extended.

The growth of each successful colonial town was nourished by one or more basic economic activities. The cluster of settlements in Plymouth and Massachusetts Bay colonies, for example, quickly found that fishing in the North Atlantic gave them a surplus product that they could trade (especially in the West Indies and later in southern Europe) for cash as well as for articles they needed—or which someone else needed—and would trade for, thus adding another transaction to what became a rather complicated pattern of commercial triangles. It led to shipbuilding in Marblehead, Salem, Boston, and other places in the area, both for the fishing fleets and the wider-flung maritime trade. This base industry required others to support it: rope-walks, foundries and forges, sail-making shops, and so on. The people who worked in all these establishments needed others to furnish food and clothing, cabinet work, and other carpentry. Growth in these circumstances took place rapidly. In 1650 when Boston was only twenty years old, an observer called it a "City-like towne," and wrote admiringly of the many buildings that were going up, "whose continuall enlargement presages some sumptuous city. The wonder of this Moderne Age that a few yeares should bring forth such great matters by so meane a handfulle. But now behold, in these very places where at their first landing the hideous Thickets in this place were such that Wolfes and Beares nurst up their young . . . the streets are full of Girles and Boies sporting up and downe."

New York City began as New Amsterdam, a fur trading post for the Dutch West India Company. Although it was situated at the finest natural harbor on the Atlantic coast, it was not especially profitable to the company and no effort was made to develop it. (The French, who had spotted and investigated the harbor before the Dutch, never showed any constructive interest in it at all.) The British took over the port in 1674, and shortly it began to grow. The fur trade interest remained and even increased, but it was joined by other activities as New York began to look like a growing colonial city. Flour milling especially became important in the local economy; New York began to export flour to the West Indies, and by the same token New Yorkers became increasingly interested in pushing out a wheat-growing hinterland around the city.

Norfolk, Virginia is another example of a city rising upon an economic base activity. Its municipal beginnings date from the 1720s, when it was organized as a result of the Crown's policy of trying to channel all commercial activity in the colonies through specified towns. Its first significant income derived from the export of naval stores—tar, pitch, and turpentine—to England. Then, as the neighboring colony of North Carolina began to attract farmers, residents of Norfolk discovered that their town could serve as the most convenient port for the newcomers: much of the Carolina coast was lined by sea islands so that ocean-going vessels could not reach it; produce was loaded onto special low-draft vessels and sent to Norfolk, at the southern end of Chesapeake Bay, there to be trans-shipped. (Norfolk merchants demonstrated a dramatic interest in this hinterland by helping to capture the pirate Blackbeard, who had made a hiding place out of the shallow water between the islands and the coast of North Carolina.) By the outbreak of the Revolution, Norfolk had flourished mostly on this business, to the extent that 6,000 people made their homes there.

Baltimore was perhaps the most spectacular example of the same process, and can be called the first "boom town" in America, although that phrase was not used until much later. In 1729 the colonial legislature granted a charter to a group of men who wanted to put a town on some land belonging to the powerful and wealthy Carroll family. This enterprise suffered the fate of most of the "towns" that were chartered in Maryland and Virginia primarily for the purpose of controlling the shipment of tobacco. The heavily indented Chesapeake Bay coast, with its many inlets and rivers which were simply narrow arms of the sea, made it easy for tobacco ships to sail directly to the wharves of the large plantations, thus escaping regulations in the towns. Early Baltimore languished; by mid-century only a very few ships had picked up any tobacco at the wharf, and there were not more than twenty-five houses scattered around on the town's land. At about this time, however, a pair of Scots, brothers named Stevenson, arrived on the scene. They saw what appeared to them to be good wheat-raising country in back of the town, which was being exploited very lightly. They wrote to a friend in Ireland to send over a ship to load flour; then they went around the countryside buying up all the wheat they could get. It was cheap, for no one knew of a market extending beyond the few people in Baltimore and the surrounding tobacco farms. A flour mill was hastily erected; the ship from Ireland arrived in due time, picked up its cargo, presumably for market in the West Indies, and the Stevensons had made a killing. Others were attracted by their success, and it was not long before other mills appeared, wheat farming extended farther and farther into the hinterland, a new wharf was built, and population began to grow. In 1763, Charles Carroll recognized the drift of events when he shifted 10,000 acres of his land to wheat growing, and by 1790 there were 13,000 people living where only a hundred or a hundred and fifty could have been found forty years earlier.

The economic bases of most of the colonial cities were secure by the end of the seventeenth century. Commerce was the most important element in each case, and it was at the outset a commerce closely related to imperial need and profit: masts and ships from New England towns, furs from New York and Philadelphia, pitch and turpentine from Norfolk and Charleston. Later, reaching large proportion in the eighteenth century, came the ominous African slave trade and the various exchanges that arose out of it—rum from New England ports to the African Gold Coast, slaves from there to the West Indies (or Sugar Islands, as they were called), and sugar from there back to New England. There were other patterns of maritime commerce; as the Sugar Islands developed their kind of monoculture, they had to be supplied from abroad with food that came increasingly from the middle colonies, later from Norfolk, and still later from Maryland as the city of Baltimore grew up after 1750.

Along with perfectly legal and highly profitable maritime trade, there developed more and more illegal, and also highly profitable, trade. The Navigation Acts would have been difficult to enforce in any case; the colonists needed money with which to buy British-made goods, and it put a strain on human nature to serve paying customers in the British Sugar Islands while ignoring potential paying customers in the islands belonging to France. Coupled with this was the fact that the British authorities made very little effort to enforce their trade regulations until the early 1760s. Some of the British understood that the illegal trade carried on by the colonists performed an economic function in supporting at least the northern colonies. Some of them felt, like Robert Walpole, that it was best not to stir up a hornet's nest by trying to enforce the trade laws.

That the Americans were smuggling at an increasing rate was generally known. As early as 1672, a complaint was made to the Privy Council that Massachusetts traders "boldly employ two or three hundred Sail of ships yearly, trading to and fro . . . and this without being under the restrictions of such laws as put our Merchants to vast charges." The complaint averred that by ignoring the Navigation Acts colonial shippers were able to undersell their British counterparts, a state of affairs which would, if not checked, provide "an infallible bait to all our Manufacturers to remove thither, where people trade with such advantage over their fellow subjects." Far from being checked, smuggling continued to flourish, reaching its most profitable proportions during wars, when many colonial merchants traded brazenly with the French enemy. In 1759 Thomas Penn reported to the Prime Minister the appearance of several new Philadelphia fortunes. These arose from illegal trade with the French West Indies. Philadelphia, Penn continued, was full of "shallops unloading these illegal cargoes . . . besides carrying provisions and ready money to the enemy." The people in this nefarious business included, in Penn's words, "a very great part of the principal merchants" of the City of Brotherly Love. In 1764, a colonial official said of New York City's merchants that "many of them have rose suddenly from the lowest rank of the People to considerable Fortunes, and chiefly by illicit Trade in the last War. They abhor every limitation of Trade . . . and therefore gladly go into every measure whereby they hope to have Trade free." The same sort of thing was going on elsewhere; John Hancock, one of Boston's "principal merchants," when he signed the Declaration of Independence owed the British customs authorities thousands of pounds sterling in unpaid tariffs and imposts. The significant point is that by the 1760s, an important part of the mercantile elite groups, which governed the colonial cities, depended upon smuggling for their continued prosperity. Even though the number of colonists directly involved in trade of any kind was small, still colonial life at its urban focal points was dependent to a considerable extent on smuggling.

Townspeople could also find opportunities in the other direction: inland. This began in a small way at an early date. By the time Boston was a generation old, Carl Bridenbaugh has written, "it had begun to extend its control into the back country, and to develop a metropolitan form of economy that was essentially modern." The other ports quickly developed interest in their surrounding areas, and each began to appear as the small metropolitan center of its own hinterland. This relationship meant that the port cities would shape the character of interior society. "Colonial America," as Julius Rubin has put it, "though certainly 90 per cent agricultural in an occupational sense, may also be described as 90 per cent urban in a cultural sense."

Concern for the hinterland also affected imperial relationships. By the middle of the eighteenth century, Philadelphians (and Virginians) were examining the possibility of planting large colonies, in the nature of real estate investments, west of the Appalachian mountain chain. Had they been able to carry any of these ideas through to fruition, the entire character of the imperial structure in North America would have changed. Benjamin Franklin understood this, and suggested (in an unguarded moment) that developing the American interior along these lines might make it desirable at some future date to move the capital of the British Empire across the ocean. As the British authorities also came to understand the implications of the colonists' developing western hinterlands, they looked with more and more suspicion upon the whole idea.

The opportunities that led American colonial merchants to look outside the Navigation Acts for trade, and to look beyond the confines of imperial land policy for real estate profits, thus placing more and more of them in opposition to the whole tenor of mercantilist imperial regulations, were rooted in city growth. The internal consequences of this growth were equally important to the development of autonomous community life in the colonies. As local populations grew, the problems of sanitation, fire protection, police, schooling, and—from a very early day—poverty arose. It was in their confrontation with these problems that the colonial cities developed political and administrative techniques that were fairly sophisticated in the world of the seventeenth and eighteenth centuries. Local leadership began to emerge from the problem-solving process, and the knowledge and experience were accumulated which would later make reasonable the demand for more freedom from metropolitan (British) regulation, and which would sustain political independence when the colonists reluctantly concluded that this was the only way they could escape the onerous regulations on which the mercantilist empire rested.

The story of fire protection illustrates a fairly consistent pattern in the genesis of community enterprises. The colonists brought with them from Europe community responsibility laws relating to the prevention of fire damage. These laws required each property holder to turn out on a fire signal and help quench the blaze. As towns grew into cities this arrangement became less and less adequate, and came to be largely replaced by volunteer fire companies. Bostonians led the way: in 1717, twenty leading citizens got together and agreed to attend every fire that broke out in the city, bringing with them sand, buckets, and other equipment to put it out. They called themselves the Boston Fire Society, and their idea spread rapidly to other towns and cities, with former Bostonian Benjamin Franklin organizing a volunteer company in his adopted Philadelphia. It is not surprising to find leading property owners in the forefront of this kind of work; their own monetary interests were served by it. Sometimes the wealthier among them supplied the companies with water-pumping equipment. In 1736, the richest man in Newport, Rhode Island, bought the best fire engine available at the time in England, had it shipped across the Atlantic, and gave it to the city outright. By the time of the Revolution, there were at least six volunteer fire companies in Philadelphia, several in Boston, and all of the leading communities had at least one.

The story is similar in the case of police protection. The traditional night watch, dating back to medieval times, was not sufficient security for life and property in a growing seaport. Here again, men of wealth made their own arrangements; sometimes they started out by taking turns at a nighttime police patrol themselves. It was not long, in any case, until they found it better to contribute money to a common fund out of which other men could be paid to do the patrolling. Here again, private interest and the community's general welfare overlapped. This curious mixture between public and private enterprise came to be a recurrent characteristic of American municipal development.

The problem of poverty also called forth responses which mingled public and private initiatives. That communities were collectively responsible for the poor who lived within their boundaries was an old proposition in English public law, formalized in the famous Statute of Artificers of 1562 and the Poor Law of 1601. The principle was that the poor had to be maintained out of local tax money; the burden might be lightened by requiring the recipients of this relief to work at publicly set wages, usually in private enterprises. The colonies either adopted these English laws or drew up for themselves others that closely resembled the earlier models in the homeland. In some cases public workhouses were established; Plymouth Colony had one by 1658 and within a century they were to be found in all the large colonial towns. Binding out (requiring the poor to work for enterprisers on contract) was another possibility. Both practices could be carried on together as in Boston, after its workhouse was put up in 1685. During the same period, towns and provincial authorities passed strict laws regulating immigration, in the hope of minimizing the tax burden that "sturdy beggars" represented, especially in bad times. Thus Bostonians were forbidden in 1636 to house strangers without official permission; three years later it was provided that any newcomers had to be able to name a permanent inhabitant as a kind of bond if he wished to remain in the city; in 1647 legislation forbade any inhabitant to sell or rent a dwelling or shop without official permission. In New Amsterdam-New York, in the seventeenth century, laws were promulgated to assure that the town authorities knew the name and the whereabouts of everyone who came into the city. In Newport, bond had to be posted for all newcomers before they could be admitted to the city. Beginning in 1705, Philadelphia adopted a set of regulations similar to those of New York City.

The problem of urban poverty intensified in the eighteenth century, owing in large part to extensive migration into the cities from abroad and the American countryside. In 1700 the New York City Council sounded a note, heard frequently thereafter, when it lamented that "the Crys of the poor & Impotent for want of Reliefe are Extreamly Grevious." According to Jackson Turner Main's statistical examination of the social structure of revolutionary America, one-third of the people in the northern colonies could be termed poor by the end of the Revolutionary period; by then the presence of poverty in cities had severely taxed municipal facilities. As early as the 1730s, poorhouses in the largest towns were filled, there was steady expansion of relief outside institutions, and by mid-eighteenth century relief costs constituted the largest municipal expenditure in cities such as New York and Boston. During the eighteenth century, again in accord with British precedent, there was considerable expansion of the activities of private charitable associations. Many of these organizations dealt with special groups such as Negroes, Indians, widows and orphans; others were concerned with such purposes as education, medical care, and religious instruction for the poor.

The assumption of responsibility for community problems by local governments and the restrictive measures that accompanied efforts to deal with them were characteristic of the mercantile ideals of early Colonial America. But gradually mercantile practices began to break down, and the erosion of these restrictions is of considerable importance. It testifies to the growth of the colonial communities—to their success as communities—which went beyond any seventeenth-century expectations and which ultimately made it impossible for them to find satisfactory places within imperial structure as it then existed. The prevailing labor shortage and the availability of land in all of the colonies, as Richard Morris has noted, made it certain that the system of strict internal regulation would be tried and also that it would not be as successful as in the mother country. Adam Smith estimated that, around the time of the

Revolution, average standards of living in the colonies were three times as high as in Britain itself. This made migration attractive to many people and presented a problem to the imperial rulers. After about 1700 they began to try to restrict the migration of skilled workers, but they knew also that some kinds of workmen (those familiar with naval stores, for example) had to be provided in the colonies. At about the same time, the authorities in the colonial cities started having second thoughts about the policy of exclusion. They found it more and more desirable to encourage the growth of local labor forces and made efforts to attract foreign workers.

This change represented a serious breach in the structure of mercantilist social control. At the same time a kind of society began to emerge in the colonies which was markedly different from the parent society in Britain. While the colonists were by no means thorough-going egalitarians, and while vast distinctions continued to separate the highest social ranks from the lowest, labor (including the lower-paid kinds of what would today be called "white collar" employment) had more respectability. This naturally accompanied more opportunity to rise economically in the colonies. The common assumption of polite society in Europe and England, as Carl Bridenbaugh has pointed out, was that labor, usually called "the mechanic arts," was mean or base. Plenty of colonists shared this assumption; but, as one of them had to concede in 1744, the lower house of the New Jersey colonial legislature "was chiefly composed of mechanicks and ignorant wretches; obstinate to the last degree." In Philadelphia, a commentator noted in 1772 that "the poorest labourer . . . thinks himself entitled to deliver his sentiments in matters of religion or politics with as much freedom as the gentleman or the scholar." He concluded that "there is less distinction among the citizens of Philadelphia than among those of any civilized city in the world. . . . For every man expects one day to be upon a footing with his wealthiest neighbor." Bridenbaugh has found that in New York between 1700 and 1776, two-fifths of those granted "the freedom of the city" were craftsmen such as leather workers and woodworkers. In Philadelphia in 1774, 30 per cent of those who had assessable property (real estate, slaves, servants, and livestock) were listed as craftsmen.

These figures reflect a high degree of social mobility, judged by the standards of European civilization at the time. Still, as the increase in public welfare demonstrated, many urban dwellers were excluded from the benefits of an expanding economy. James A. Henretta, in a pioneering study of people in colonial Boston, has found a substantial increase in the percentage of the propertyless between 1687 and 1771, a growing inequality in the distribution of wealth, and a particular concentration of wealth and power in the hands of a small mercantile elite. In all cities there was a substantial class of the "inferior sort": free and enslaved Negroes, Indians, indentured servants, and a fairly large number of badly-treated merchant seamen. This lower class group played a significant part in a number of anti-British incidents in cities before the Revolution. The Boston Massacre of 1770, for example, involved a battle, as John Adams observed, between British soldiers and "a motley rabble of saucy boys, negroes and molattoes, Irish teagues and outlandish jack tarrs." In New York City in 1774, fear that the lower classes might get out of control over the closing of the port of Boston produced one of the classic conservative statements in American political rhetoric. "The mob begin to reason," wrote Gouverneur Morris. "Poor reptiles! it is with them a vernal morning, they are struggling to cast off their winter's slough, they bask in the sunshine, and ere noon they will bite, depend upon it. . . . if the disputes with Britain continue, we . . . shall be under the dominion of a riotous mob."

The steady commercial expansion of the colonies, in addition to modifying the class structure of cities, tended also to disintegrate religious orthodoxy, at least as a means of social control. This was apparent even in 1663 to the Netherlands authorities in charge of New Amsterdam. Noting that the town had recently exiled a Quaker, they advised local officials to take great care in these matters: "although it is our cordial desire that similar and other sectarians might not be found there, yet as the contrary seems to be the case, we doubt very much if rigorous proceedings against them ought not to be discontinued except you intend to check and destroy your population, which however in the youth of your existence ought rather to be encouraged by all possible means." A few years earlier, a pious Bostonian protested that the city's merchants "would willingly have . . . the Commonwealth tolerate divers kinds of sinful opinions to intice men to come and sit down among us, that their purses might be filled with coyn, the civil Government with contention, and the Church of our Lord Christ with errors."

The spread of printing establishments and newspapers in the colonial cities suggests a cultural aspect of the growth that was sapping the basis of the mercantilist empire. The first printing press in British America was set up in Boston in 1639. It remained the only one for many years, but there were five presses in that city by 1715 and at least nine booksellers. By 1776 seven newspapers were published in Philadelphia, four in Boston, and at least one in every other colonial city. There are records of more than forty printers in Philadelphia between 1740 and 1776. Their significant social role has been described by Bridenbaugh: "Skilled craftsmen, they belonged by interest and training with the mechanics and artisans. The superior education that practice of their profession required made them important members of the growing middle class, and the widening market for their wares occasioned by the increasing literacy of their times brought them material prosperity that often placed them economically at the head of it."

Printing and the circulation of books and newspapers provide evidence of an intellectually vigorous culture growing up in the cities, and they were also associated with another important development: the rise of an inter-colonial culture. It continued to be true for more than a century after the planting of the colonies that each of the cities had more connection with the mother country than with its sister cities in the colonies. In 1704, a quick (and difficult) trip from Boston to New York took six days. But the printers and the newspaper editors, with Franklin playing a prominent part, led in a long series of agitations to improve communication, especially through the mails. This, along with the coasting trade, which was promoted especially by Philadelphia merchants, was essential to the emergence of any feeling of community between, say, residents of Boston and residents of Charleston. Here, in the relationships between the colonial cities, lay the seeds of a sense of nationality.

The newspaper, the pamphlet, the broadside, and other instruments of an expanding communications system also led to new forms of political action within cities that involved lower-class groups. In the first half of the eighteenth century, as Gary B. Nash and others have demonstrated, a "radical mode of politics" which encompassed, and to a degree exploited, lower-class aspirations developed in Boston, New York, Philadelphia, and probably other cities. Pennsylvania Governor William Keith in 1726 reflected this approach when, in order to gain control of the colonial assembly, he built a constituency among lower-class groups in Philadelphia, the "Rabble Butchers porters & Tagrags." The elite of the cities had no great sympathy for the lower classes but found it feasible in gaining power to use new organizations and innovations in communication to gain their support. Often this new style of politics led to sanctioning and utilizing mob action and violence—usually fairly carefully controlled—to foster political objectives. Class conflict was more intense in rural areas than in cities in Colonial America; American cities were more orderly than those of Europe. Still, attacks on unpopular leaders, unofficially permitted rioting, and the use of the mob by political elites reflected, in Nash's words, the "general abrasiveness of life in the eighteenth century and the frailty of law enforcement in the cities."

A degree of disorder and lawlessness of this kind had probably always been characteristic of urban life in the world. Colonial American cities were also typical in reflecting another fundamental role of the historical city—to serve as a center of culture. Only the accumulations of wealth created through urban-centered enterprise and concentrated populations made possible the establishment and support of art museums, public libraries, and scientific associations. By the end of the eighteenth century Boston had become the second largest publishing center in the British Empire. Philadelphia, the cultural capital of eighteenth-century America, may have seemed provincial when compared to London during a golden age, but it was nonetheless a city of cultivation and sophistication. The American Philosophical Society, founded there in 1743, numbered among its members several outstanding scientists of the Western world. Although its most notable painter, Benjamin West, deserted the city for London, Philadelphia became a kind of colonial Rome to which painters made pilgrimages to fulfill commissions or to visit the excellent collections in the city. Philadelphia was also of course the home of Benjamin Franklin, the "first civilized American" and one of the world's foremost scientists. Franklin, who fostered such local civic institutions as a hospital, a library, and a university was an exemplar of urban values and interests. An unknown poet's prophecy in 1740 that

> Europe shall mourn her ancient fame declined
> And Philadelphia be the Athens of mankind . . .

achieved a degree of fulfillment in the Philadelphia of Franklin, Benjamin Rush, David Rittenhouse, and Charles Willson Peale.

The cities had been called "nurseries of learning" and it is not surprising to find schools of various kinds proliferating in the commercial centers. Some of the founders of the colonies were, of course, profoundly interested in making education widely available for religious reasons. After 1647, each town in Massachusetts was required to have an elementary school. Penn tried to have the municipal government in Philadelphia provide for an educational system, but was unsuccessful. Another significant impulse that helped produce an impressive educational establishment in the colonial cities was commerce. This introduced a strong vocational element into the teaching which distinguished American education from the classical studies of the English upper classes. "The City," one man wrote of New York in 1713, "is so conveniently Situated for Trade and the Genius of the people are so inclined to merchandise, that they seek no other Education for their children than writing and Arithmetick." The practical approach, of which this writer did not fully approve, was quite consciously defended by others. "Thus instructed," wrote a Philadelphian about a proposal that emphasized subjects necessary for success in a mercantile calling, "youth will come out of this School fitted for learning any business, calling, or profession, except wherein [Latin and Greek] are required." The exceptions would have included law, the ministry, and very little else.

During the passing years of commercial prosperity and economic and cultural growth, urban society in the colonies developed a variety of forms of organization. The cities were not simply collections of individuals; instead, they were made up of groups that were interconnected in many ways, and this gave city life somewhat the character of a finely woven web of social and personal relationships. It meant that for almost any given purpose, the energies and talents of many people could be quickly combined and concentrated in the desired direction. A century's growth of voluntary associations, for example, gave the cities a degree of social versatility. From an early period in the 1700s, travelers commented on the plethora of clubs that they found: in New York the Hum Drum Club, in Philadelphia the Beefsteak Club, in Newport the Philosophical Club, in Annapolis the Tuesday Club, in Charleston the French Club—and many more in each of the cities. There are records of about fifty in Philadelphia during the twenty-five years before the Revolution. Some were devoted to special activities such as singing, debating, or discussion of shared hobbies or interests. New York City had a chamber of commerce from 1768;

Charleston organized one before the Revolution. Other associations were purely social, the members perhaps having dinner together once a month.

Even the purely social clubs were related to community interests, whether consciously or not: one traveler in 1744 was royally entertained at Newport's Philosophical Club, but observed that philosophy was not discussed: "they talked of privateering and the building of vessels." In most places the volunteer fire societies, of which there were six or seven in Philadelphia and eleven in New York City, added social functions to their practical ones; in Philadelphia some of the fire societies sponsored regular debates of public issues. Effective and quickly organized resistance to imperial policies after 1763 was made possible by just this kind of experience. Associational life also served to crystallize and mobilize public opinion. Philadelphia's delegates to the First Continental Congress, for example, called upon representatives of most of the clubs in the city to assist their deliberations on propositions to be submitted to the Congress.

We are not here concerned with the Revolution itself. The cities' experiences during the years 1775–1783 were various: Boston remained in American hands from the moment near the beginning of the war when General Gage abandoned it. New York was captured by the British in the same year Boston was evacuated by them, and it remained an occupied city until the end of the war. Philadelphia was captured, abandoned, recaptured, and abandoned yet again. An attack on Savannah permitted the British to overrun Georgia. Charleston fell to the British late in the war. Norfolk was held by the Americans, but their way of holding it was to make it useless to the British by burning it to the ground.

The particular fortunes of particular communities are less important than the changed environment of independence and how this change affected American urbanization. The change had no immediate effect upon that process. Certain restrictions upon business enterprise were removed; certain opportunities were opened. But the legal opportunity to colonize the West did not of itself produce colonization; and the legal opportunity to trade outside the limitations of the Navigation Acts did not necessarily make up for Americans' having lost their partnership in the world's most profitable empire. The demographic and technological forces that were beginning to accelerate the urbanization of the Western world were not affected by the Revolution. How the histories of communities on the American shore would be shaped by these forces rested on many contingencies.

New York City, for example, with its aggressive and already well organized businesss community, managed actually to capitalize on its occupation by the British during the Revolution. The presence of British troops meant that more hard money circulated there than anywhere else in the colonies. When the troops left in 1783, many American loyalists went with them from New York, and had to sell most of their possessions at sacrifice prices. It was not long before old enterprises revived and new ones joined them. Banking flourished at the southern end of Manhattan Island by the 1790s; merchants with large views were already risking their money in what would prove to be a lucrative trade from New York to Canton, China. Soon New Yorkers would be looking westward toward the vast interior of a continent, and planning to reach it with a canal to the Great Lakes, as their city came to surpass even Philadelphia in size and wealth.

Norfolk, Virginia exemplifies a different fate. Its wealth had come to be built on supplying the West Indies with food. After the Revolution, Britain's commercial regulations kept Americans—like other foreigners—out of the islands, or from time to time allowed them to trade there only under heavy and inconvenient restrictions. Norfolk's merchants dedicated themselves to the task of regaining the commerce that had been lost; they agitated at the nation's capital for diplomatic negotiations to secure re-entry of American ships into the ports of the Sugar Islands. As these almost continuous negotiations waxed and waned, the spirits of the Norfolk business community rose and fell. Finally, in 1830, the negotiations were successful, but by that time Norfolk could gain but little from the outcome; the Sugar Islands trade was no longer important. Meanwhile, other projects had been slighted; only belatedly did the Chesapeake port rally in support of railroad projects to connect with the interior, and then it was found that other interests had arisen in Richmond and Petersburg to prevent the realization of a unified transportation scheme radiating from Norfolk. Baltimore had seized much of what might have been Norfolk's hinterland, and the older city languished throughout the nineteenth century.

But, if the consequences of independence were problematic for particular cities, still the bearing of urban growth on American independence was obvious enough. The cities nurtured economic life so successfully as to feed economic ambition. The cities offered problems for solution by associated effort, thus stimulating the colonists to accumulate political experience—and political ambition. The cities were focal points for the development of a colonial culture, in which the life of the mind or spirit shaped itself to an American rather than to an imperial environment. In doing these things, the colonial cities were simply functioning as cities classically functioned: they were both matrix and evidence for the appearance of a civilization.

CHAPTER

# 2

# Cities in the New Nation

THE STORY of American urbanization as outlined by the statistics of growth has an interesting dialectical feature about it. The first settlements were, of course, towns, which made possible the subsequent growth of agricultural (and increasingly commercial) hinterlands. Consequently, in the early decades, town dwellers made up a *decreasing* percentage of the total population. The urban percentage continued to decrease for a longer period than might be supposed. As late as 1690, between nine and ten per cent of the American colonists could have been classified as urban. A century later, the first federal census revealed twenty-four places with more than 2,500 people living in them, but these people accounted for only 5.1 per cent of the population. For the next thirty years the proportion remained fairly stable, rising almost imperceptibly to about six per cent in 1800, to 7.3 in 1810, and then apparently dropping to 7.2 in 1820. (The figures in these early censuses are more convenient than those derived by the kind of guesswork required for the Colonial period, but it should be kept in mind that they are not reliable enough to support any very sophisticated statistical operations.) After 1820, the figure begins to rise significantly, as it has continued to do ever since; by 1830, it was back to where it had been 140 years earlier.

In other words, during the eighteenth century and the first two decades of the nineteenth, urbanization barely kept pace with the diffusion of hundred of thousands of settlers into the back country. To the extent that city growth represents specialization and therefore increasing productivity, the fall and leveling off of our figure suggests that no very important rise in average living standards took place during that period. One or two economists have concluded that the average American standard of living actually fell in the early 1800s, as westward-migrating throngs spread the country's stock of resources more and more thinly over a wide expanse of territory.

Leaving aside (and open) the question of how much generalizing the rather paltry handful of available statistics really allows, we can see, in the decease-increase curve, urbanization extending the territory that could be exploited by Western European—including American—commercial agencies, and then beginning to gather momentum as the results of commercial expansion began to accumulate. Total population continued to grow rapidly, increasing by about one-third during every decade between 1810 and 1860. But the urban population grew three times as fast as the total; by the later year about one-fifth of all Americans were living in places of 2,500 or more. Urbanization was particularly rapid in the period after 1840, as the urban proportion of the population increased by 92.1 and 75.4 per cent in the respective census decades, a rate unmatched before or since.

The percentage not only rose, but new and larger urban centers were appearing rapidly. In 1820, when one American in fourteen could be called an urbanite, one-third of these people lived in New York City and Philadelphia; the country contained only twelve cities with populations larger than 10,000, and these twelve accounted for over two-thirds of the city-dwelling total. By 1860, however, there were 101 such cities, including eight which had passed the 100,000 mark and one (New York plus its large suburb of Brooklyn) which exceeded a million.

How had this happened? In large part it was the local reflection of a world trend. Rapid and sustained urbanization is a recent phenomenon, reflecting technological progress and changes in forms of social organization: the steam engine, agricultural machinery, the nation-state, the joint-stock company and its descendant the corporation, developments in medical and sanitary practices that slowly cut away at the death rate, and so on. In 1800, it is estimated that perhaps three per cent of the world's inhabitants lived in places of more than 5,000 inhabitants. In the next century and a half, world population went up by 250 per cent, but the urban component went up by 2,600 per cent, so that the earlier three per cent has now become over thirty per cent. Great Britain, northwestern Europe, Japan, the United States, and more recently the Soviet Union—those places which have industrialized earliest—have simply been at the front of this world wide trend.

The figures tell only part of the story, and for our purposes it is not necessarily the most important part. As cities grew, their natures and functions in many cases changed. At the beginning of the nineteenth century, the sizeable cities of the United States were strung out along the coast; they were ports and reflected what George R. Taylor calls the "extractive–commercial" character of the American economy at that time. "The streets of every large city," in Taylor's apt phrase, "led down past the warehouses to the piers." These cities faced the sea and the maritime trade which had nurtured them. By the time of the Civil War, however, this could no longer be said. Maritime trade, indeed, was still directly or indirectly an important element in the life of the cities, but new cities had appeared deep in the continental interior and the older ones, the great seaports, had engaged in great metropolitan rivalries with one another to secure as much as possible of the commerce that came from the interior. Manufacturing had begun to influence the shape of many of the cities, accounting for the activities of ten per cent of the people in New York and Philadelphia, about seventeen per cent of those in Cincinnati, twenty-six per cent of those in Newark—not to mention a group of smaller New England river towns which lived entirely by manufacturing.

Horse-drawn buses dating from the 1830s, commuter train service from the 1840s, and street railways (still horse-drawn for another quarter-century) from the 1850s enabled the cities to encompass larger areas and to generate residential suburbs. Most larger American cities, those reaching 20,000 population or so, had developed clearly defined central business districts with a distinctive downtown pattern of economic and social life. Widespread town promoting and urban ambition had become characteristic of the optimistic, progress-minded culture which foreigners and natives alike often identified as "American."

Nor did American urbanization come unexpectedly upon a surprised people. Commercial journals such as *Niles' Weekly Register* in Baltimore, *Hunt's Merchants' Magazine* in New York, and later *De Bow's Review* in New Orleans had national circulation and constantly bemused their readers with glowing accounts of city growth, buttressed with endless statistics. A Bostonian writing in 1816 described at length the types of cities that were growing up in the young nation and analyzed quite accurately the rivalry between the port cities for commercial control over portions of the hinterland. New Orleans seemed to him certain to flourish with the settlement of the Mississippi Valley. Baltimore was "struggling with Philadelphia to obtain the preference of the western country." Philadelphia had begun to lose some of its business to New York, and had turned its attention to "the increase of the western country" and to a variety of manufacturing projects. New York, already anticipating its canal between the Hudson River and the Great Lakes, was "probably destined to become the greatest commercial emporium in the United States." Boston could profitably encourage the vigorous development of the New England region that was tributary to it. The writer's obvious enthusiasm for the metropolitan drama he described was by no means unusual in early America.

American growth is usually, and correctly, associated with the westward retreat of the "frontier," which represented not, as in Europe, a line marking the limit of opportunity within a country but rather a vast reservoir of unexploited resources. Only recently, however, has it been made clear that this very westward movement was made possible by urban impulses and, in Richard C. Wade's metaphor, "spearheaded" by townsmen hoping to convert strategic positions in the continental wilderness into cities, putting down checkerboarded streets with hotels and public buildings where Indian trails had run irregularly through the forest. Despite the importance in American culture of the myth of the independent yeoman farmer on his self-sufficient homestead, in reality, the American interior did not experience a stage of subsistence agriculture. From the beginning, economic development there was town-centered, tied to a trade and communication network which stimulated an urban, commercial outlook in both city and country dwellers. Interior America became a small-scale replica of the social and economic system of the seaboard region.

It is important then to discard the image of expanding agricultural settlement bringing towns along behind it. In the first English settlement of the
country, towns were the necessary bases from which the farmers could move
out and begin to subdue the new land to their purposes. Pittsburgh, St. Louis,
Louisville, and Cincinnati were all founded before there was any significant
farming in their respective areas. In the cases of all these except St. Louis,
Indians and the problem of military security alone would have dictated some
kind of concentrated settlement before agricultural development could safely
begin. George Washington noted the spot where the Allegheny and Mononga-
hela Rivers join to form the Ohio as an ideal one for a fort; he also belonged
to a company of land-speculating Virginians who proposed for a time to put
a town near the site. It was to be laid off, in the words of one of the group's
agents, "in squares of two acres each, every square to be divided into four
lots so that every lot may front two streets, if the ground will so admit, and
. . . all the streets [should] be of convenient width." French and British
authorities alike agreed with Washington on the military evaluation, and it
was first as Fort Duquesne and later as Fort Pitt, during the early stages of the
French and Indian War (1756–1763), that the settlement which became Pittsburgh first took shape. The settlement that was to become Louisville began
similarly, in 1778, as a military base set up by George Rogers Clark. Cincinnati,
while it was not originally a military post of any kind, became the site of a
temporarily important fort three years after its founding. Another example is
the town of Lexington, Kentucky, which began as a stockade against the
Indians in 1779, and rose by 1800 to become the biggest of these interior
places with a population of 1,500 and a reputation as "the Philadelphia of
Kentucky."

St. Louis was a somewhat special case among what were to become the
main inland cities, in that its original auspices were French. Early in the 1760s,
the most powerful fur traders in New Orleans began to explore the possibility
of establishing a central sub-station on the Mississippi River to coordinate and
supply their enterprises. They already had some up-river posts, but they were
about to lose the best two of these (Kaskaskia and Cahokia, both of which
had come to number over 1,500 inhabitants) because the French had surrendered to the British all claims to the east bank of the great river, on which
these posts were located. Their one substantial post on the west bank, Ste.
Genevieve, was not entirely satisfactory owing to the erratic behavior of the
river around its site. Several miles below the point where the Missouri River
enters the Mississippi, a party of men sent out by the New Orleans traders
found a limestone bluff that offered excellent possibilities, a place which, as
the chief of the party said, "might become, hereafter, one of the finest cities
in America." The following year, 1764, the construction of St. Louis began.
The settlement did not grow rapidly—but no one particularly wanted it to—
until a much later date. Nevertheless, here in the middle of an almost unpopulated continent there were by 1800 about a thousand people. St. Louis was

an administrative headquarters for the governing authorities, as well as a key point in the widespread fur-trading business.

Many, although by no means all, western towns began as forts, but at an early stage they became speculative enterprises, and the decisive questions in each case were whether or not the speculative enterprise would pay off, and whether in the process of paying off it would work itself into a growing regional economy. The answers depended partly on forces beyond the control of local residents. Once founded, the futures of places like Pittsburgh and Cincinnati depended upon the agricultural and commercial development of the areas that became the states of Kentucky, Ohio, and Indiana. This development, in turn, was critically affected by the Indian policy of the federal government, the land-disposal policies of the same government, arrangements for political organization of the territory (provided by the Northwest Ordinance of 1787), and finally, military success against the Indians during the War of 1812. The future of the interior towns depended also on the kind of use that could be made of the rivers which ran right past most of them. Thus Robert Fulton's successful development of the steamboat and its adaptation to inland river navigation (long before it was of any importance on the ocean) lifted the horizons for western city growth far above the level that slower means of transportation could have sustained.

There were ways, however, by which local enterprise or its absence could determine the success or failure of a town-promotion scheme. In the pre-steamboat period, endeavors in Pittsburgh, Cincinnati, and other towns to design and build more efficient river craft were examples of local efforts to serve hinterlands better and therefore more profitably. Between 1801 and 1816, the value of western goods shipped downstream to New Orleans rose from $3,700,000 to $8,000,000, partly because of such efforts.

Pittsburgh merchants, admirably situated to supply the rising tide of westward migration along the Ohio River, tried to furnish everything migrants needed. At first, the merchants brought these goods in from eastern seaports, especially Philadelphia and Baltimore. Increasingly, they began to manufacture many of them; foundries, nail and glass factories, and machine shops appeared; Pittsburgh was soon known as "the Birmingham of America." Here and in the other river towns merchants tried to supply credit to their customers, without which trade could not move in an area always short of hard cash, and trading companies often became fledgling banks. Town sites needed advertising, so local boosters imported presses and sometimes editors in order to establish newspapers—not for local information, but rather with an eye to eastern readers. Hotels had to be provided for the temporary accommodation of prospective investors and settlers. Fire and police protection, street grading, market and wharf supervision, and many other urban services were necessary, and on a rising scale, as the successful town enterprises grew.

Clearly, in addition to their private business activities, the promoters had to see to it that public authority functioned as efficiently as possible. It is not surprising, then, to find the leading merchants of a young city prominent in efforts to get legislative authorization from the state, in the form of charters, and, generally, to find these men directing political life. The day of the professional city politician was still far off. "Throughout the West," says Richard C. Wade, "the pattern was everywhere the same, with city-council lists reading like the local business directory."

Location, the course of events in the world outside, decisions made in eastern cities, and local ability and energy all went to determine whether a particular speculative town project would grow. Most projects did not. Hundreds of New Athenses, New Lisbons, Palermos—as well as a fantasy called the Town of America, expected to raise shimmering towers at the junction of the Ohio and Mississippi Rivers—remained little or nothing more than paper speculations. Sometimes they were designed simply to defraud the unwary; sometimes their surprised proprietors were bankrupted along with the others. One western observer during this period remarked that most town projects came to nothing and added that "it requires the united influence of many individuals and various interests and the concurrence of a diversity of circumstances, to give impulse to the healthy growth of a town." The American scenes in Charles Dickens's *Martin Chuzzlewit* give sharp, if satirical, insight into what happened more often than not in the course of town promotion.

The failure of Lexington is illustrative, for here was a place which progressed far beyond the merely speculative stage and which for several years had more of urbanity about it than any other place in the West. After the Indian threat subsided, a group of men got a land grant from the Virginia legislature (Kentucky was the western part of that state until 1791) for the purpose of putting up a town. They laid it out carefully in a gridiron pattern, reserving some sites for public purposes, and proceeded to advertise it. The rapid development of Tennessee and western Kentucky in the 1790s gave Lexington a solid economic base, outfitting the migrants who traveled overland. Farmers prospered in the surrounding Blue Grass region, marketing their surplus through Lexington. The town began to flourish culturally as well as in a business way; at the beginning of the nineteenth century its people, numbering just under 2,000, enjoyed a variety of amenities, including Transylvania, the first institution of higher learning west of the mountains. There were at least two newspapers, a monthly literary journal, a library, musical and debating societies, as well as several churches. The wealthier residents offered lavish hospitality.

Lexington continued to grow through the period of the War of 1812, its population reaching 5,200 in 1820. It added the profits of hemp manufacture to its commercial income, as other western towns began processing the raw produce of their immediate hinterlands. A branch of the Second Bank of the United States was located there. The local real estate market became livelier and land prices rose with each passing year. But continued success for Lexington was not in the cards. Depression hit there, as it hit the entire country, shortly after the war when the resumption of imports from Britain bankrupted thousands of American manufacturers and the inflation of real estate values reached a point as high as it could go. Lexington declined, just as a new force that was to benefit other western towns—the steamboat—came upon the scene. Its inland location now a serious competitive disadvantage, Lexington stopped growing and began to slide downhill economically, as business sought the river towns, especially Louisville. Projects for connecting with the river, first by turnpike and then by railroad, and a program designed to make Lexington a permanently great cultural center, all failed to arrest the decline. A visitor to the town in 1829, who had known its former prosperity, wrote that "it has degenerated beyond measure. . . . Where was once the dwelling of gayety and friendship, with every good and noble sentiment, was now a rusty and moss-grown mansion of ill nature and repulsive indifference." City-building was obviously a risky, uncertain business.

Still, as more and more river steamboats carried the West's rapidly increasing commerce, other towns of course did grow: the basis for urban life and function in Pittsburgh, Louisville, Cincinnati, Memphis, New Orleans, and other places, was apparently permanent. Increasing population meant that new states were carved out of the Northwest Territory; they needed state capitals, and Columbus, Indianapolis, and Jacksonville—later Springfield—were planted in the retreating wilderness to fulfill this need. To these were added the many county seats. A few town projects had initiated the attack upon the wilderness and their success had made the area accessible to thousands upon thousands of westward-moving farmers. This incursion, in turn, sustained a further expansion of urban civilization in the interior. In 1828 one observer caught the spirit of taming frontiers, reporting that "the stranger views here with wonder, the rapidity with which cities spring up in the forests; and with which barbarism retreats before the approach of art and civilization."

Urbanization also accompanied the American westward movement in the South, where slavery and the cotton plantation gave somewhat different characteristics to social and political life. Baltimore, Norfolk, and Charleston, of course, were English settlements antedating the Revolution. Baltimore continued its high rate of growth and indeed in the early decades of the nineteenth century hoped to surpass Philadelphia. Norfolk had not fulfilled expectations and grew only very slowly in the pre-Civil War period. Charleston, similarly, lost most of its earlier momentum, and though its population rose from 20,000 in 1820 to 40,000 in 1860, its rank among American cities dropped from fifth to twenty-second. Efforts by the city's business leaders to maintain a vital connection with a moving cotton hinterland were occasionally energetic and imaginative: early in the 1830s the longest railroad in the world ran between Charleston and Augusta. But these efforts were unavailing, and some of the more articulate residents developed a marked nostalgia for past greatness.

Far to the west, commanding the Mississippi River's delta, was the most spectacular urban success of the cotton South. New Orleans, from its founding by the French in 1718, had been a hot, sleepy, and somewhat unhealthy administrative center, to which the magnates of the fur trade added their homes and offices. The period of its rapid growth came after the War of 1812, as northern family farms and southern cotton plantations moved west and as towns along the Ohio River grew and funneled more and more produce down the great system of rivers. American names and American projects moved into New Orleans to crowd its hitherto French, and rather leisurely, culture. Warehousing and maritime shipping displaced the once important fur trade. Between 1810 and 1860, New Orleans's population grew from 17,000 to 168,000. In the 1840s, New Orleans's metropolitan position—which had obviously rested on the river trade—was threatened by railroads, which ultimately did divert much of the river trade into a west-to-east direction. Even so, concerned businessmen wanted to launch a railroad program of their own. They managed to have the Louisiana constitution changed so as to make financial subsidies to railroads easier, and also to remodel the city's charter in such a way as to improve greatly its credit rating—so, of course, that it, too, could help finance the railroad program. The lines were begun, and New Orleans remained the greatest city in the South. While Charlestonians may have mourned their city's disappearing grandeur, people in New Orleans experienced, as a native later reminisced, "an overweening confidence in the ability of the city to become speedily and without exertion the metropolis of America, if not eventually of the world."

Mobile was another southern port started by the French early in the eighteenth century which began to grow in response to dynamic business impulses initiated later by Americans. Its population, insignificant until 1819 when the United States bought the land in which it was located, came to 12,000 twenty years later and the population continued to grow with the flourishing cotton trade. Savannah became another growing southern city after the War of 1812. Sharply competitive commercial policies—at first maritime and later involving railroads—enabled it to command a profitable hinterland, to grow from 7,500 in 1820 to 11,000 in 1840, and to attract praise from a Northerner who found in Savannah "a spirit of enterprise that could honor any place in this country." Savannah's growth continued to be guided by the original plan set down by James Oglethorpe almost a century earlier. Consequently, it was probably the best example of urban design to be found in the United States during the first half of the nineteenth century. A British visitor not predisposed in favor of American city life favorably noted "no less than eighteen large squares, with grassplots and trees, in the very heart of the city, disposed at equal distances from each other in the greatest order; while every principal street is lined on each side with rows of trees, and some of the broader streets have also an avenue of trees running down their centre." Richmond, Virginia was yet another impressive southern city, with 38,000 residents by 1860. Here the manufacturing spirit was as prominent as in any northern city of comparable size: a large iron-making establishment and many tobacco factories early gave

Richmond, like Pittsburgh, the appearance of a phenomenon of the Industrial Revolution.

But even if the myth of the agrarian South must be discarded, as it obviously must be, still urbanization proceeded there in a less fruitful environment than elsewhere in the country. The relationship between slavery and urban-industrial growth cannot yet be clearly described, but it is certain that city life tended to lessen the rigidity of the peculiar institution. Slaves could more easily learn trades in the towns, they could congregate together to exchange news or plans or teach one another to read, they could and did hire themselves out to labor, absenting themselves for long periods from their owners. Whether or not these practices meant that slavery was disintegrating in the cities is more debatable. It is true that the slave population in the cities increased much less rapidly than the total slave population between 1820–1860, and in the last census decade before the Civil War, 1850–1860, actually declined. But, even in the latter decade, many individual cities, including the booming Border State cities, exhibited substantial increases in slave population. A recent statistical examination of slavery has permitted the argument that in general the urban demand for slaves rose in every decade between 1820 and 1860, but when slave prices rose to a certain point free labor was substituted, a change that could not readily be made on the plantation. Slaves in short, write Robert Fogel and Stanley L. Engerman, "were shifted from the cities to the countryside, not because the cities didn't want slaves, but because as slave prices rose, it was easier for the cities than the countryside to find acceptable, lower-cost alternatives to slave labor."

Still, this type of economic analysis suggests little about the broad cultural effects of the city on the authority of slavery as an institution. The extent to which Southern thought attached itself to slavery, and this increased noticeably after 1815, may tend to mark an ill-defined limit to the South's enthusiasm for urbanization. Certainly, in the South, the artisans and mechanics, so necessary to growing cities, found and often expressed a grievance in the threat to their own well-being which slave and free Negro competition offered. Similarly, it is not seriously disputed that while businessmen of all kinds flourished in the cotton South, they were never given as high a rank in the popular culture there—never became representative symbols of virtue, so to speak, held up to the young for emulation—as they were in northern and western cities. The battle over the cultural value of "enterprise" had only begun in the pre-Civil War south; in the northern cities it was won by the entrepreneurs even before it began.

In the early nineteenth century, western urbanization was one important index of national growth; another index was the dramatic growth of the metropolitan centers of the east coast. Between 1790, the year of the first federal census, and 1860 New York City's population went from 33,000 to about one million (this figure includes Brooklyn, which was actually a great suburb but still politically independent); Philadelphia's increased from 42,000 to slightly over half a million; Baltimore's from 13,500 to 212,000; and Boston's from 18,000 to 177,840. It is useful to think of the entire country as an expanding hinterland, with the great seaports encouraging the expansion and trying individually and competitively to draw to themselves as much as possible of the trade yielded by the hinterland. Abstractly, one might imagine each of the port cities carving out as large a part of the hinterland for itself as it could; the only trouble with this abstraction is that the sub-hinterlands of the several seaports overlapped geographically, with the rough exception of New England, which remained commercially subordinate to Boston. In fact, by mid-century, it is in a broad way accurate to say that, with the same exception, the entire country was the hinterland of New York City, with Philadelphia and Baltimore competing for that business which New York was simply not big enough to handle. The story of this metropolitan growth can best be organized around the roles of luck and enterprise in the sudden rise of New York, and around varying responses to this rise in the other cities.

In the first twenty years of United States history, Philadelphia and New York were, in that order, the two biggest cities in the country; among the eight or ten largest, Baltimore was growing most rapidly but was far behind the leaders. By the end of the second twenty years, New York was unchallenged as the biggest, and Philadelphia *was* being seriously challenged by Baltimore for second place. What lay behind these developments was, as has been suggested, the interplay of chance and policy.

New York's and Philadelphia's populations were about equal at the time of the War of 1812; the war injured both cities by disrupting their maritime trade. Its effects, and the commercial restrictions which preceded it, also encouraged manufacturing in some parts of the country, notably along the seaboard. Behind the protective wall of commercial exclusion and then war, Americans began to manufacture things that they had been importing from Britain. The war, however, had no sooner broken out than negotiations were begun to end it, and during its two and a half-year duration British manufacturers anxiously planned how to regain their lucrative American market. They resolved, quite deliberately, to sell their products for a time at a loss, if necessary, and as the hour for a peace treaty drew near they loaded ships with goods for the American market. When the negotiations were over and the peace was ratified, these ships sailed, most of them, into New York's harbor where the goods were unloaded and "dumped" on the market at unusually low prices. This policy succeeded admirably in bankrupting many American manufacturers. It also made New York particularly attractive to buyers from inland towns, who now went there in larger numbers, giving that port an obvious and fortuitous, if temporary, advantage over the others.

This was in 1815 and 1816, and the advantage could have been lost, had not certain other decisions made their effects felt. Some New Yorkers had been interested for years in cutting a water connection between the Hudson River and the Great Lakes; nature favored the Empire State with a combination of river courses and valleys that made possible something close to "the water level route," which a later railroad company has advertised. The whole matter was a political issue in the state, its fortunes identified with those of DeWitt Clinton. As Governor, Clinton pushed the canal project through the legislature with strong New York City backing. The state undertook what was for the period a staggering bond program, and in 1817 the digging began. The success story of the Erie Canal is well known. Some sections of the canal were in profitable operation even before 1825 when the whole route was opened; within a few years after that, canal tolls had paid off the entire original cost and were financing improvements along the line to handle business, which continued steadily to rise.

The success of the canal struck contemporaries so forcefully that canal programs were begun in many parts of the country where they proved to be much too expensive, even bringing some states close to financial disaster. The canal's success has struck later observers, when they have tried in retrospect to account for the supremacy of New York City. This is understandable, but it has also, according to one careful scholar, obscured much of the real explanation. Robert G. Albion has pointed out that in the first place, the full effect of the Erie Canal was not felt until after 1825, by which time New York had already taken a commanding lead over Philadelphia. In the second place, the canal stimulated exports more than imports, whereas the latter were more important for metropolitan supremacy than the former; New Orleans' ante-bellum export trade was often close to New York's in volume and value, and for a few years actually surpassed it, but New Orleans never threatened New York's commercial dominance. In the third place, a number of significant business decisions were taken at about the time construction of the Erie Canal was started, which were less spectacular but which, taken together, perhaps played a larger part in the long-run achievement.

One important policy had to do with the auction sale of merchandise. Instead of selling his goods to a British exporter who then sold them to an American importer, the British manufacturer could consign his shipment to an auctioneer on this side of the water, keeping title to his goods until they were sold here. Two middlemen were thus eliminated, and auction prices were usually the lowest a buyer could find. This irritated many of the importers, and in Philadelphia and Boston they managed to have certain legal inconveniences put in the way of auctions. In New York, however, legislation favorable to that mode of sale was secured in 1817 and 1818, in the hope that, as one leading auctioneer put it, "all the Atlantic cities [would] become tributary to New York." Again, the western storekeepers were encouraged to do their trading in the Empire City.

At almost the same time, another entrepreneurial innovation added to New York's commercial attractions: the institution of regularly scheduled shipping service (called "packet service") across the Atlantic Ocean. No one on either side of the ocean had done this before 1817, when four local Quaker merchants determined to try it. To many, it looked foolhardy to announce a sailing schedule months in advance, and to stick to it whether the ships had cargo or not. Nevertheless, late in December, New York papers announced that the Black Ball Line would begin trans-Atlantic packet service—both ways—in January. The advantages of regularity and dependability were apparent to shippers and importers, and the line succeeded, very quickly receiving the homage of extensive imitation. New Yorkers also developed their coastwise packet service all the way round to New Orleans.

They were still seeking out new trading areas, as in earlier days when China had beckoned to a few adventurous merchants. In the 1820s, Latin American countries, especially after they gained independence from Spain and Brazil, and also Cuba which remained in the Spanish Empire, attracted the attention of New Yorkers. Resident agents were sent into these countries. They made credit extensively available; the Latins were encouraged to borrow from them. New Yorkers were doing the same thing in the American South, traveling into the cotton country, establishing branch offices in southern cities, providing maritime insurance, and through the advantages that volume, European connections, and the profitability of their other enterprises gave them, establishing general financial control over much of the trade that went to other cities, especially New Orleans. By the 1840s and 1850s, when southern chambers of commerce began to seek escape from northern commercial power and to urge that the cotton trade go directly between their ports and Europe, it was too late for this to be anything more than a dream, a kind of business romanticism. A Norfolk editor summed up what had happened; in 1834 he wrote that "instead of being what its geographical position entitles it to be . . . [Norfolk] is reduced to the humiliating condition of waiting on the pampered aristocracy of New York." Norfolk's hopes of becoming a great port were gone, along with those of many another southern port, and "now, since the concentration of capital in the North, she has become a hewer of wood and drawer of water to the lordly merchants of the northern city." New York was at one corner of every trading triangle which touched the United States, and her metropolitan supremacy could have been destroyed only by a properly located earthquake.

The other main seaports gradually gave up the notion of overtaking New York City, but in a hinterland the size of the United States there was considerable trade left over for which they could compete. Philadelphians had experienced the troublesome competition of Baltimore from the first days after the Revolution, when Baltimore interests began building roads up into the Susquehanna Valley—cutting in behind Philadelphia and taking away some trade that had gone to that city. The Philadelphians responded with a road of their own, the Lancaster Turnpike, and then discovered that their rivals were considering a combination of canals and improvements to the Susquehanna River which would carry Pennsylvania trade south to Chesapeake Bay. Accordingly, Philadelphia began to develop a canal program of its own.

By the mid-1820s, however, the Erie Canal and New York's dramatic growth posed a more serious threat to Philadelphia's western connections, and plans were drawn up to meet it. One concerned resident wrote, "we observe our population daily diverging from our State. . . . We have beheld our markets neglected. . . . We have found that while we slept our *locks* have been shorn." About the same time, forty or fifty local business men, led by the economist and publicist Matthew Carey, organized the Pennsylvania Society for the Promotion of Internal Improvements in the Commonwealth. The Society began public agitation for a response to the Erie Canal; its members collected and circulated technical and financial data on transportation facilities —roads, canals, and railroads. As it happened, the British had just experimented successfully with the world's first commercial steam railroad line, the Stockton and Darlington. Interest arose in some quarters in the United States, and Philadelphians found themselves divided into a canal party and a railroad party on the question of how they should improve their connections with the trans-Appalachian West.

After lengthy and sometimes bitter public debate, in journals and newspapers, at meetings, in the city council and the state legislature, the canal party won. On their side was the great, if conservative, argument from experience: the Erie Canal seemed to prove the superiority of canals in general, while the value of railroads was speculative and "theoretic." What was wanted, one typical proponent of this view urged, was "something solid, the usefulness of which is not doubted, but tested by experience; such undertakings will always have *public confidence* to promote them."

Perhaps because of the quiet tempo of its Quaker-dominated business life, perhaps because of its defensive responses to Baltimore's commercial aggressiveness, Philadelphia had already the reputation of a rather conservative community. Whether or not the designation was accurate, the city (in this instance supplying leadership for the entire state) now deliberately rejected an innovation—the railroad—and proceeded to tie its hopes to a canal connection with Pittsburgh. There were, of course, the mountains to be dealt with; these were conquered by a series of winch-drawn cable cars on inclined planes. This fantastic combination of devices took seven years to build, cost more than $12,000,000 (almost double the cost of the Erie Canal), and never began to fulfill the hopes that had accompanied its progress. Within four years of its completion, a movement arose to replace it with a railroad, and in 1846 the Pennsylvania Railroad was chartered for precisely this purpose; it received large amounts of public aid as its construction advanced across the state. The whole experience was disappointing. The project not only lost money but delayed Philadelphia's western rail connections. One businessman wrote in 1852 that many of his associates had become disheartened, and "some of our most astute and enterprising merchants removed to New York."

In Baltimore the story was quite different. Interest in the Stockton and Darlington experiment arose very early, and a project to build a railroad was carefully and quietly organized by a few of the city's leading men. When matured, the proposal was presented to the public in urgent terms: "whilst the Cities of Philadelphia and New York are making such great and efficient exertion to draw to themselves the trade of the West, . . . Baltimore must soon lose the comparatively small portion which remains to her . . . should she remain inactive." After a favorable eye-witness account of the British railroad, this small group of men decided quickly against a canal, formed a committee to get a charter for a Baltimore and Ohio Railroad company, organized the company, and began construction—with both state and municipal aid—all within about two years. Significantly, the Baltimore group knew it was taking a risk. In its own words, "the stock of information upon the general subject of railroads . . . is admitted to be not very extensive," but the risk was accepted. The Baltimore and Ohio Railroad did not, indeed, push Baltimore ahead of Philadelphia, but it did narrow the gap between them and rivet the city into third place, which it held until Chicago edged it out after the Civil War.

Boston's response was different again. Bostonians were urged in familiar terms to do something: "if we sleep much longer, Boston will sink, in a commercial view, into comparative oblivion." How could the city cut through the hills of western Massachusetts and connect with the Erie Canal at Albany, thus tapping at least some of the rich canal trade that was going on down to New York? The business community began considering the problem at the same time as this happened in Philadelphia and Baltimore, in 1825 and 1826. Time passed; a few experiments were made with short railroads; and finally, after ten years of consideration, a railroad across Massachusetts was begun. There was much less rush about the project, and apparently less anxiety about the relative advantages of other cities.

For one thing, Bostonians were doing well enough superintending the industrialization of New England. This process had its tentative beginnings in the years just before the War of 1812, as already noted. The westward movement took its toll from New England, as its citizens moved west toward better farming land or else moved into growing cities, while some areas experienced urban as well as agricultural decline. At the end of the Revolution, Connecticut had nine towns with populations of over six thousand, but by 1820 only three —New Haven, Hartford, and Bridgeport—had as many as five thousand inhabitants. This decline probably reflected a concentration of population in the new factory towns, as those who did not move west sought jobs in the factories. As late as 1860, half the product of American industry came from a rectangular area on the map whose corners were Hartford, Lowell, New York City, and Wilmington.

Boston capitalists did not, of course, found all of the mills and factories that dotted the New England landscape by mid-century, but they were very active, and frequently helped finance enterprises in which they did not otherwise participate. One group, calling itself the Boston Associates, which by

1850 controlled about half the city's banking and insurance capital and about a third of the railroad mileage in Massachusetts, had for several decades put much of its money into industrial enterprises. They went about looking for water-power sites, buying them up, and erecting mills of various kinds. Thus, in 1823, the Boston and Springfield Manufacturing Company, a Boston Associates concern, bought a waterfall site where it began to manufacture both textiles and textile machinery; the town of Chicopee, Massachusetts grew up around the mills. Again, in the later 1840s, the Associates paid $300,000 for land and water rights where a railroad had been built along one of Massachusetts' many turbulent streams. In 1851, their first mills were opened here and the factory town of Holyoke appeared on the map.

During the earlier stages in the growth of these new towns, the Boston Associates endeavored to put up housing for employees, as well as retail stores, churches, and schools. The most famous project along these lines was the provision at Lowell, Massachusetts of a complete set of social institutions (and regulations) for the young New England girls who were recruited to work in the mills there. The backers had to do this in order to attract employees, but it fitted in well enough with ideas about well-regulated communities which they derived in part from older New England traditions of orderly social life. In the later nineteenth century the opprobrious term "company town" would have been applied to these projects, but in their historical context they did reflect an effort to control the development of the industrial revolution in the interests of community life. It was hoped that the establishment of manufacturing communities in rural settings would make it possible for Americans to avoid the abuses of the European industrial cities, which had horrified Francis Lowell on his travel abroad. When the protecting, if paternalistic, hand was withdrawn it is highly questionable that the factory towns became better places to live.

Beginning in the late 1840s, and continuing in subsequent years, the labor force for these mills came to be recruited increasingly among poverty-stricken French Canadians rather than New England farmers' daughters. Barriers of language and religion between these workers and the factory owners perhaps diluted the latter's sense of responsibility for their operatives. A flood of Irish immigration, providing abundant cheap labor, combined with financial reverses in the late 1850s to complete the destruction of the planned social-control systems in the factory towns. But the mills remained and the towns continued to grow. They confronted Americans for the first time with large urban concentrations made up mostly of industrial workers.

Despite the significance of the New England manufacturing towns as a foreshadowing of the American future, until after the Civil War commerce and trade rather than manufacturing sustained the growth of larger cities. It is true that in the period after 1840 a foundation was laid for the large-scale manufacturing that led to a surge of urbanization in the latter part of the nineteenth century, but as Allen Pred has demonstrated, there were numerous

obstacles—involving the level of technology, the forms of business organization, the availability of power, and the shortage of a labor supply—that limited
efforts to develop factory-centered manufacturing systems during the first half
of the century. Particularly significant was an economic factor related to the
success of the commercially based cities: the tendency of merchants who
held the limited investment capital available to invest in activities related to
their sector of the economy—transportation projects and particularly urban
construction and real estate. Profits from successful real estate speculations—
so fundamental in shaping the character of American urban development—
could be spectacular even in the period before the great growth of cities.
Some streets in New York had front-lot values of $1,000 per foot by 1823;
the total assessed value of real estate in the city increased from $50 million in
that year to over $76 million in 1829, to more than $104 million in 1833, and
to over $253 million in 1836. Baltimore and Boston experienced similar rises.
In the less populous western cities such as Cincinnati, chances for enormous
profits were also evident. As an example, a lot purchased for $2 in 1790 was
resold in 1804 for $800. A small part of it was sold for $2,500 in 1814, for
$4,000 in 1817, and for $6,000 in 1819. The same segment was sold and
repurchased in 1828 for $15,000, and another even smaller piece of the origi-
nal lot was rented in 1839 at a rate of $2,000 annually. From this time on, the
frenzied urban concentration on real estate profits seemed to many critics—
including, for example, Henry George in his influential study of *Progress and
Poverty*—the source not only of the problems of the city but of many of the
problems of American society in general.

The Bostonians—to return to their position during the years of New York's
surge forward—were also profiting from the China trade and from the western
railroad projects in which some of them became increasingly interested. They
seemed to be less concerned than their Philadelphia contemporaries about
"losing out." One of them, in fact, noted in his diary that "some think the
city is large enough and do not want to increase it."

In the competition between the seaports for western hinterlands some suggestive points emerge. There was the more or less conscious adoption of
metropolitan goals: the delineation of hoped-for trading areas and the elab-
oration of strategies to gain them. In this process some kind of public con-
sensus had to be achieved if only because the transportation schemes required
considerable public financing and other legislation. Consequently, notions of
the "general interest" emerged in debates about the proper competitive
course to pursue; the railroad or the canal was desired, or was talked about
as desired, not just by this or that group of aggressive Baltimore or Philadelphia
businessmen but by "Baltimore" or "Philadelphia." In this way the cities acquired public images, indicating that they possessed one or another set of
individual characteristics. Philadelphia was frequently characterized as conservative; its business leaders, one English traveler asserted, "do not conduct
their business in the same *dashing* style which is done in some commercial

cities, but confine themselves within bonds and secure what they gain." New Yorkers, on the other hand, were said (by a Baltimorean) to "*deserve* success for their enterprise. There is a good spirit among the citizens to advance the business of New York. Let it be imitated—not envied."

This kind of city rivalry was to be repeated many times and in every part of the country; it always took the same forms and was expressed in the same sort of community personification. The community's general interest crystallized around a project conceived to stimulate growth, and the community's character was cast in terms of the success of its businessmen. Much of the pushing, aggressive spirit that attracted the attention of every observant foreign traveler in the United States during the nineteenth century stemmed from these efforts to foster city growth in thousands of places from New York to San Francisco.

As the great seaports sought more and more western trade, their activities speeded western development. Baltimore's railroad, Philadelphia's misfortune with the "main line" to Pittsburgh and later its railroad, and New York's Erie Canal (and later *its* railroad as well) all made it possible for western agriculture to expand and necessitated more urban establishments in the interior. The Erie Canal, especially, opened up a whole new region tributary to the Great Lakes and triggered the growth of a new urban complex on the shores of the lakes. It also launched a program of internal improvements throughout the Old Northwest Territory that produced frenzied town-booming of both river and lake town sites. This period of intense rivalry demonstrated the close connection between municipal government and local business leaders; the struggles among these competing communities, as Harry N. Schieber observes, were "marked by intense ambitions, deeply rooted fear of failure, and ingenious employment of the instruments of political and economic leverage at the disposal of urban leaders." In Ohio the movement for construction of a canal between Lake Erie and the Ohio River, which resulted in a legislative canal program in 1825, set off a series of minor town rivalries between such places as Piketon and Chillicothe in the Scioto Valley; between Cleveland and Sandusky for control of the headship of the Ohio Canal; among Zanesville, Dresden, and Marietta in the Muskingum Valley; and among a cluster of towns, including Toledo, Maumee, Perrysburg, and Manhattan, along a short stretch of the Maumee Valley. Similar rivalries occurred in Illinois and Indiana; they continued throughout the whole Northwest Territory during the period of railroad-building that followed. The inevitable failure of most of these competing transportation projects dashed the hopes of many communities and left a legacy of opposition to public support of internal improvements in the latter part of the nineteenth century.

During this period, from the late 1820s on, the successful cities of the Great Lakes region, beginning with Buffalo and continuing westward to Duluth, grew faster than the older river towns and came to eclipse them in size. Just as on the Ohio Valley frontier, towns were established around the Great

Lakes far in advance of any agricultural development in the area, although their growth, of course, had to proceed along with that development. This process—towns, followed by exploitation of an area's agricultural (or mineral) resources, and this in turn accompanied by rapid urban expansion—was repeated from east to west along the lakes about a generation after it had been exhibited in the rise of the river towns. Those towns had established themselves between the 1790s and the 1820s. In the lake region, the period ran from the 1820s into the 1850s, the second phase in the growth of what later Americans would call the Middle West.

Cleveland, Ohio is one example, although it was laid out as a town much earlier than most of the lake cities. In 1796, shortly after a company had been organized in Connecticut to dispose of lands reserved for that state and located in the Northwest Territory (and also shortly after the Indians in the Ohio country had been defeated in the battle of Fallen Timbers), a party representing the company and led by Moses Cleaveland chose the site of the future town. At the mouth of the Cuyahoga River they found high and level ground on either bank and a shoreline offering a fine potential harbor. Cleaveland chose the heights on the Cuyahoga's east bank, and saw that a plan was drawn up. The plan centered around a commodious public square, from which wide thoroughfares led off through rectangles of numbered lots to the limits of the projected town. Although changes were made in the layout on a few later occasions, its form, by now somewhat shadowy, can be discerned on any street map of the present-day city.

Time passed and little happened. In 1810, the fourteen-year-old town's population was just fifty-seven; in 1815 it was not over a hundred and fifty, and only two of the ten streets originally on the plan were actually cleared. Then a road was completed linking Cleveland with the Ohio River; in 1818 the first Great Lakes steamboat called at the little port; in the late 1820s the harbor was improved at federal government expense, and a canal between Cleveland and the Ohio River was built. By 1830 there were about a thousand Clevelanders, and they had among them two newspapers, a school house, a church, a courthouse, and a steam sawmill.

The effect of the Erie Canal's completion now began to be felt; ships became more numerous in the harbor and population mounted to 6,000 in 1840, and to 17,000 in 1850. The next year, the first railroad entered Cleveland, from the south, and marked the beginning of even more rapid growth. Cleveland businessmen began to build up an iron industry; at first they used relatively low-grade ores that could be found in Ohio, but by the 1850s they were looking as far afield as northern Wisconsin, and several of them were vitally concerned in the events that led to the cutting of the Soo Canal between Lakes Michigan and Superior in 1855. Cleveland had already become an industrial city.

Detroit was officially older than Cleveland; like New Orleans and St. Louis, its founding dated from the days when Frenchmen still hoped to dominate

North America. By the end of the eighteenth century, about 2,500 people lived in Detroit and were legally under the American flag. In all important respects, however, the place was still a rather sizeable fur-trade settlement, the inhabitants of which felt much closer to Canada than to the United States. With the creation of Michigan Territory in 1805, Detroit became a political center, but in the same year it was almost completely destroyed by fire. This proved to be a watershed in its history; it was rebuilt according to a completely new plan, which probably borrowed some features from L'Enfant's proposals for the nation's capital, and began to become an American city in its leading social, cultural, and political characteristics.

Still, the land around it was not popular with settlers and did not fill up; early maps printed the words "interminable swamp" across the southern part of Michigan Territory. Life in the city suffered another disaster when British forces defeated the Americans in the area in 1813, and during the rest of the War of 1812 Detroit was garrisoned by the British. Not until after the war was over and after the Erie Canal was completed did the city's urban prospects begin to seem at all impressive. Then, as lake commerce began to grow, Detroit's location along the narrow connection between Erie and Huron began to return dividends. Detroiters could outfit the migrants who now began to interest themselves in Michigan land; they also sent Michigan's growing agricultural surplus back east in lake ships. Detroit's population, which was 1,400 in 1820 and still only 2,200 in 1830, reached 9,000 in 1840 and 21,000 in 1850.

By that time it had begun to appear that another lake port, younger than either Cleveland or Detroit, was likely to surpass both in every quantitative way. Although Chicago was a young city, not incorporated until 1833, interest in its site was very old indeed. Joliet and Marquette had noted as early as 1673 an easy passage between Lake Michigan and the Illinois River, running over the spot where the city would later appear. A few attempts to establish a Jesuit mission there seem to have failed, but a fur trading post did take root and later a United States fort was set up to protect it. The fort had to be surrendered during the War of 1812, however, and the entire white community—which numbered ninety-six at the time—was massacred by Indians.

But the location seemed an important one for Americans to try to hold; the fort was rebuilt after the war, and a government fur trading post was set up there. Meanwhile the idea of a canal connecting Lake Michigan with the Illinois River (and thus with the Gulf of Mexico), conceived first for its military value, had attracted the attention of highly placed people. They included John C. Calhoun who, as Secretary of War, began in 1819 to urge Congress to provide for such a canal. It did so in 1827 by granting to the State of Illinois alternate sections of land along the proposed route. Two years later, the state legislature established a Canal Commission; twenty more years were to pass before the canal was usable.

In the meantime, the commission laid out a town at each end of its canal line, Ottawa on the south, Chicago on the north, and proceeded to advertise its holdings in order to get enough money to begin digging the canal. Land sales were sluggish for a year or two; a couple of eighty-acre lots went for a hundred dollars each. Then came the brief flurry of Black Hawk's War, 1830–1832—the Indians' last effort to reclaim their land east of the Mississippi River —which brought a good many soldiers into what had been the almost unknown lands of northern Illinois and southern Wisconsin Territory. This publicity, along with a gathering "boom" period in the nation's economy and the influence of the Erie Canal, suddenly created intense speculative interest in the Illinois canal and in the town at its northern end.

What this could mean to a town's growth is best shown by a few examples. In 1833, the county officials began to sell the school lands—the income, of course, to be used for educational purposes. Sale of 576 acres in that year brought in just under $40,000: about $75.00 per acre. But in 1837, just three and a-half years later, three small lots in the school tract sold for $7,500. In 1830, 126 lots in the Canal Commission's town of Chicago sold for an average price of $35.00 each; four years later, lots on South Water Street were bringing $3,500 each. The next year, a local real estate firm sold a tract, which had cost it $5,000, to some New York buyers for $80,000. One forty-acre plot was bought on January 2, 1835 for $4,000, and sold on April 10, for $10,000. As the real estate boom neared its climax, early in 1837, daily advances in land values of 20 and 25 per cent were not unusual.

All of this naturally attracted attention to Chicago, and its population swelled. There came the inevitable crash, in 1837, but by now enough people had sunk their fortunes (including their credit) in Chicago's prospects to give the place a nucleus of leaders who fought to sustain its growth. One of its first mayors, for example, was William Ogden, who had come in representing a group of wealthy New York investors. Throughout the depression that followed the speculative real estate inflation, Ogden and several associates busied themselves in pushing plank roads out from Chicago into its immediate farming hinterland. They agitated for harbor improvements as more and more lake ships sailed as far west as the southern end of Lake Michigan. By the mid-1840s, they were organizing railroad companies and seeking lines west into a lead-mining area around Galena, Illinois, and east to Detroit and Buffalo, and ultimately to New York City. They arranged for street-grading, for hotel-building, and for social amenities including churches—Ogden, a devout Presbyterian, contributed money to help build a Catholic church, no doubt on the grounds that by so doing he was helping the city to grow. Curiously, the canal project which had launched Chicago's career, went ahead only slowly and intermittently. Not opened until 1848, it had little direct effect upon the city's growth; its presence, as a project, may have done no more than help to sustain hope, during a dark period in 1837 and after, that the city would amount to something in the future.

Like Cleveland, Chicago quickly sought and found an industrial base for its economic growth. In the 1840s, meat-packing began to loom large among the businesses of Chicagoans; and in 1847 Cyrus McCormick moved his agricultural implement factory from Virginia to the city at the tip of Lake Michigan. These beginnings, coupled with the complete success of Chicago's railroad planning, secured the city's place on the American metropolitan scene. By the outbreak of the Civil War its growth was a phenomenon discussed in the counting rooms of New York and in the drawing rooms of London and Paris.

Seventy miles or so to the north, along the western shore of the lake, a similar urban drama unfolded at almost the same time, on a somewhat smaller scale. Here, where the Milwaukee River enters the lake, there had been another small community of French, Indians, and halfbreeds, with the slow tempo of its life dictated by the fur trade. It did not have a fort, and there was apparently no attempt to establish any religious institution there before the appearance of the city of Milwaukee. During the early 1830s, as the Indians were driven out of the area and the Territory of Wisconsin advanced toward statehood, men began to arrive looking for promising land speculations.

One of these was named Morgan L. Martin, who was a member of the Territory's governing council, and he formed a partnership with the director of the shrinking fur-trade business, Solomon Juneau. Martin went to Washington and lobbied for legislative favors, especially affecting land disposal, while Juneau and his brother remained on the spot and began filling out pre-emption claims to as much of the land around the river mouth as they could file for (it would cost them $1.25 per acre). Martin also called the attention of easterners to his promising site, and the Juneaus began to lay out streets and prepare for newcomers.

About the same time another hopeful speculator arrived in the person of Byron Kilbourn, who was the federal government surveyor for the district. He too had a partner, one Micajah T. Williams, who happened to be Surveyor-General for Michigan Territory before Wisconsin Territory was separated from it. Since Juneau had pre-empted most of the land east of the river, Kilbourn concentrated on the southwest side, and very quickly two competing speculative interests were both doing what they could do to attract settlement. A month before government land sales opened in the district, *all* the land within two miles of the mouth of the Milwaukee River had been pre-empted! Soon a real estate boom began, and the inflation of values proceeded much as it had in Chicago, with quarter-acre lots selling for $600. The depression broke up this activity, but again there had been enough solid investment along with it to create the basis for a flourishing lake port in the 1840s and 1850s. Much of the early history of Milwaukee revolved around fierce rivalry between the Martin-Juneau and Williams-Kilbourn groups; they got together in 1846 in order to secure a municipal charter that would enable them to provide basic urban services for the rapidly growing community.

Although there were important differences between these lake towns, and between them and the older river towns, certain comparable features appear in their growth. Speculation aroused interest and drew money to the towns;

the towns then sought commercial empires and later industrial bases to sustain themselves. In doing this, these communities aligned their public interests, or general welfares, with the growth of their surrounding areas. A Milwaukee editor in 1846 remarked that it was "clearly to the interest of our . . . businessmen generally to unite upon some plan for extending and improving the roads leading to Milwaukee." In almost the same terms, one of his Cleveland counterparts was urging, three years later: "let us, like the wise Cincinnati merchants, spend liberally for these roads and . . . arouse our farmers and everybody to the importance of increasing our facility for trade and travel and thus make Cleveland the center of a large region." They also strove to provide amenities for domestic community life, though probably none of the cities in the interior did as well in this line as Lexington, Kentucky had done in its halcyon days. Their efforts meant that American expansion was largely a function of urban expansion, and that the civilization that pushed the edge of wilderness always toward the Pacific drew its impulses from cities.

In this era of promotion, rivalry, and the search for wealth through real estate, the colonial view that it was imperative to plan and to maintain the good community seemed often to have disappeared from the American urban scene. But this time of town-booming was also the time of New Harmony, Brook Farm, and Oneida—a period when Utopian visions flourished in scores of religious and economic experiments in communal living. In part, these communities represented a rejection of the greed and materialism of industrial capitalism and, indirectly, of the city; yet the same broad cultural impulses that led to the Utopian colonies were also present in the growing cities themselves. These impulses did not of course result in plans to ensure the good life for all citizens. But the continuing emphasis on establishing traditional institutions to advance arts and letters, and on building the structures and monuments that serve as symbols and visible tokens of civilization, indicated that the nineteenth-century American city was still something more than a site where the enterprising could make money.

The history of Washington, D. C. during its early years provides illustration of the interplay of urban ideals—of visions of civilization and the city as creative achievement—and speculative economic activity. Always present in the planning of the capital was the conception that the city should embody the grand ideals of the republic, that it should be designed to convey the greatness of a powerful nation of the future, that it should be conceived as a "permanent seat of empire." Yet from the start the efforts of promoters and speculators to take advantage of the opportunities in a new city hampered efforts to realize the design, and it was a hundred years before Washington partially became what its founders hoped it would be.

Locating the permanent seat of the national government had occasioned sporadic debate for seven years after the treaty of peace was signed with the British in 1783. The constitution adopted in 1789 authorized Congress to govern whatever site, not exceeding ten miles square, might be selected. In

1790, Congress passed the Residence Act, providing that the President should choose a location somewhere along a specified stretch of the Potomac River; he was also to choose three commissioners, along with surveyors, charged with responsibility to prepare the capital for occupation by the end of 1800. Early in 1791, the President selected a location adjacent to Georgetown and named the commissioners; he appointed Andrew Ellicott to survey the boundaries and Major Pierre Charles L'Enfant to prepare drawings of sites which might be convenient for public buildings. L'Enfant, born in France in 1754, had been educated as an engineer and architect; he had volunteered for military service with the American revolutionaries and bore wounds received in their cause. He soon acquired a reputation as a designer of buildings, and when New York City was chosen as the first seat of the federal government, L'Enfant was picked to remodel the city hall into a national capitol. Ambitious, idealistic, and possessed of vision, he wrote President Washington offering to plan a permanent capital city; he urged that the plan "be drawn on such a scale as to leave room for that aggrandisement and embellishment which the increase of the wealth of the nation will permit it to pursue at any period, however remote." L'Enfant stressed "magnificent distances": broad avenues radiating from central squares, leaving great empty spaces which could only be filled in as the city grew up to his plan. There was a brief conflict between L'Enfant and Jefferson, who favored a compact rectangular plan. But Jefferson yielded, and the Frenchman developed his grandiose ideas for the next year and a half with little hindrance, although Washington added a few modifications of his own as the planning went on. Capacious squares to be adorned with statutes and obelisks, sites for educational institutions, a broad garden-lined boulevard along the river, five large fountains—even a plan to divert the river, making it flow toward the capitol whence it would be routed over a forty-foot waterfall and back to its original course—all of these went onto the increasingly detailed maps that L'Enfant prepared.

Planning, as L'Enfant undertook it, was a slow process, whereas the President, the commissioners, and others wished quickly to start selling some of the government's land in the District of Columbia. Otherwise, the privately owned land there would be offered and bought for building purposes in the new city, and the government's revenue would suffer accordingly. L'Enfant refused to produce a properly engraved plat which could be distributed to advertise land sales, for he feared that hasty real estate promotion would impair the integrity of his plan. He also balked at accepting the supervisory authority of the three commissioners. A series of increasingly ill-tempered disputes led to his dismissal in 1792. He was then consulted by Hamilton on the latter's projected industrial town at Paterson, New Jersey, and later designed a great house in Philadelphia for the famous banker, Robert Morris. L'Enfant had never learned to take care of his own financial affairs, however, and his pride had induced him to refuse compensation for some of his works. In the early 1800s, Benjamin H. Latrobe, another architect and urban engineer, described his French predecessor as almost starving; L'Enfant and his dog walked through the streets of the slowly rising capital city each day, while governmental parsimony, the momentum of real estate development, and the ideas of other urban designers eroded detail after detail of his original plan. He died in 1825 on the state of a Maryland farmer who had offered him a home.

Meanwhile, efforts to establish an economic and financial foundation for the city had foundered. The auction of lots in 1792, which had been the source of L'Enfant's dismissal, was a failure. The commissioners were forced to sell lots at reduced prices to a syndicate which then went on to gain control of about a third of the available lots in the city. The syndicate over-extended itself and went bankrupt in 1797, leaving Washington with a number of unfinished houses and the reputation as a bad place for investors. In the early years of the nineteenth century, city leaders were continually involved in transportation and manufacturing projects, none of them really successful, that might provide an economic base for growth. Not until after the Civil War, with the great expansion of government, did Washington become an economic success through the industry of government. And it was only late in the century, in response to the typical problems of growth characteristic of the commercial, manufacturing cities, that Washington began to emerge not only as Jefferson's "symbol of national ideals as evocative of patriotism as the flag" but also, to a continually urbanizing society, as a symbol of the city as an embodiment of civilization.

CHAPTER

# 3

# The City in American Thought
## 1790–1850

D
URING the early years of the American nation, reaction to the
country's rapidly growing cities was inconsistent and often contradictory. Most prominently, perhaps, the city seemed to threaten decay
in the ideals of an agricultural republic; a formal doctrine of political anti-
urbanism, to which successful candidates had to pay a greater or lesser measure of homage, persisted long after we had become an urbanized nation.
The American literary tradition, even as it established its independence from
Europe, inherited old prejudices against the city. Strains of Hebraic agrarianism
in Christian thought, which pictured the city as the home of vanity, carnal
lust, and conspiracy, often gave an anti-urban cast to American religious writing. Yet to assume from these manifestations of ideology that nineteenth-
century Americans were overwhelmingly hostile to the city and to urban values
is to oversimplify grossly the complexities and ambivalences of popular
thought. The easy assertion, made frequently by students of contemporary
American culture, of a basically anti-urban tradition does not stand the test
of historical analysis.

A number of sentiments and interests that are sometimes overlooked influenced early nineteenth-century attitudes toward cities and their meaning in
American life. Sectional considerations, for example, often determined the
character of any such inquiry. Spokesmen of the South and West might attack
the cities of the eastern seaboard as the seats of national evil and corruption,
yet defend their own cities as representing the highest ideals of a republican
civilization. The ante-bellum South, for example, is often portrayed as a bastion
of agrarianism, yet a number of southern writers during the period were arguing the need for great commercial capitals in the region to free the southern
economy from financial control in northeastern cities. Those who reflected on
the meaning of America might attack features of national development associated in a general way with the city, such as the factory or the machine,
yet vigorously defend some other aspect of urban life, such as the cultural
opportunities presented by the city environment. The metropolises of the
eastern seaboard might represent all that was evil in Old Europe; those of
smaller size, particularly the cities of the West, might, as part of the same
statement, represent all that was virtuous in the American experiment. The

question of when a city reached a stage of growth at which it was transmuted from splendor to decay was never subjected to analysis. Nor was there much effort to distinguish between types of cities, between the commercial and manufacturing, for example. Concepts of "city" and "urban" were, in short, sufficiently vague to serve a variety of sometimes contradictory purposes. Even those who saw great social dangers in the rise of cities still regarded them as one of the best indicators of the country's material growth. And in nineteenth-century America, only an occasional isolated figure—Thoreau, for example—questioned the view that material growth meant progress.

The formal expression of opposition to cities owed much to the influence of Thomas Jefferson and the political tradition he left to the nation. Although Jefferson's reflections that bear directly on the city are limited, a vague anti-urbanism pervades his entire defense of agriculture and the farmer, and occasionally his view becomes explicit. In his early *Notes on Virginia,* written in 1784, he asserted in one of his most famous dicta that those who labored in the earth were the chosen people of God. "The mobs of great cities," he continued, "add just so much to support of pure government as sores do to the strength of the human body." During his travels in Europe from 1784 to 1789, Jefferson was greatly interested in the architecture of European cities and systematically collected city plans as guides for building the new American capital. But he reacted unfavorably to the "empty bustle" of European cities, and unlike his countryman Benjamin Franklin, responded to the pleasures of Paris with the traditional distaste of the American Puritan.

Over-all, Jefferson's experience abroad reinforced his belief that cities represented a threat to American values. "I think our governments will remain virtuous for many centuries," he wrote to James Madison in 1787, "as long as they are chiefly agricultural; and this will be as long as there shall be vacant lands in any part of America. When they get piled upon one another in large cities, as in Europe, they will become corrupt as in Europe." In a comment to Benjamin Rush in 1800 on yellow fever epidemics, Jefferson supplied his most bitter observation on the American city. "When great evils happen," he wrote, "I am in the habit of looking out for what good may arise from them as consolations to us, and Providence has in fact so established the order of things, as most evils are the means of producing some good. The yellow fever will discourage the growth of great cities in our nation, and I view great cities as pestilential to the morals, the health and the liberties of man. True, they nourish some of the elegant arts, but the useful ones can thrive elsewhere, and less perfection in the others, with more health, virtue and freedom, would be my choice."

But practical man that he was, Jefferson could never act on the proposition that plagues should not be fought, even though theoretically they might have a beneficial influence in destroying cities; in fact, as president he formulated plans explicitly intended to check the spread of yellow fever. In similar fashion, Jefferson accommodated his ideology to the political and economic implications of urban life. Late in his career, he recognized that, as a result of the developments stimulated by the Embargo Act of his own Administration and by the War of 1812, the United States had to become a manufacturing nation. In one of his frequently cited pronouncements he declared in 1816 that "we must now place the manufacturer by the side of the agriculturist." Jefferson recognized that manufacturing meant cities and the rise of a propertyless working class, but the realities of international life permitted no other course.

Despite this realization, Jefferson never abandoned his deeply-rooted hostility to the city and the city dweller. At the age of eighty, writing in a vein similar to that of *Notes on Virginia* thirty years earlier, he found city life offering "more painful objects of vice and wretchedness" as well as more opportunities for wasting time. New York seemed a "Cloacina of all the depravities of human nature." Philadelphia was little different. In contrast, life in rural Virginia was orderly, rational, moral, and affectionate.

After 1820, large American cities, which grew in part through the manufacturing Jefferson had feared, became fixtures on the American scene, and the "urban mobs" that constituted a threat to republicanism were part of the political constituency. Accordingly, political leaders influenced by the Jeffersonian tradition were forced to confront his anti-urbanism. Some, such as John Taylor of Caroline, author of that classical defense of rural values *Arator*, simply continued to express and to refine a pure Jeffersonianism. Others tried to adjust the old truths to the new realities of city and industry.

Attempts at reconciling urbanization to the principles of agrarianism were perhaps most evident in New York, a state which by the 1820s had acquired many of the features of a modern capitalist economy. In the fight over suffrage extension during the 1821 constitutional convention, conservative Federalist spokesmen chided Democratic delegates for their abandonment of their leader's principles. Would not suffrage extension spread the content of urban sores through the whole body politic, Elisha Williams asked, and expose the yeomen interest to the will of the "ring streaked and speckled population of our large towns and cities, comprising people of every kindred and tongue?" "These cities," he warned, "are filled with men too rich, or too poor to fraternize with the yeomen of the country." By the 1830s many Democratic leaders were willing to adjust their principles and put the urban workman by the side of the Jeffersonian yeoman. Amasa Walker, a radical Jacksonian, argued in 1833 that "great cities are not *necessarily*, as the proverb says, 'great sores.' " A time would come, he predicted, when they would be "great fountains of healthful moral influence, sending forth streams that shall fertilize and bless the land." Another Jacksonian leader, the ex-New England Federalist Theodore Sedgwick II, argued that the reputation of cities did not involve a moral question at all but simply an economic one. Do something about people sleeping in cellars and garrets and living in holes and dens, clean up the filthy streets, provide the means of cleanliness and health: then the city, he asserted, would assume its place as the site of opportunity and no longer be a social problem.

That this kind of accommodation to the city involved difficulties was demonstrated in the editorials of the *Democratic Review,* founded in 1837 as an organ of Jeffersonianism. In its initial statement of principles the journal emphasized that the city often operated as an anti-democratic force in society. It was in the city that wealth accumulated, luxury unfolded its corrupting tendencies, and social divisions grew. It was here also that the mercantile classes, and their allies in the law and the ministry, worked against the democratic movement. Two years later, the *Review* noted that unfortunately the New York Democracy did better in the metropolis than in outlying parts of the state, and confessed that the suffrages of the country were to be preferred to those of the city. The atmosphere of competition and emulation in the city and the lack of leisure to reflect were not conducive to a proper independence of mind in a voter. "In the city," the editorial writer observed, "men move in masses. They catch the current opinion of the hour from their class, and from those public organs of the press on which they are accustomed to depend for their daily supply of superficial thought—for their morning dose of mental stimulus, in those flaming appeals to their passions, their interests, or their vanity, which it is the vocation of the latter daily to administer. . . . They are like men in a troubled crowd, swept hither and thither by the current of the huge mass, with a force which the individual can rarely nerve himself to stem. Individuality in fact loses itself, almost of necessity, in the constant pressure of surrounding example, of the general habit and tone of society, and in the contagious excitements which rapidly chase each other in their successive sway over the multitudinous aggregate of minds."

Such views of urban life would be frequently expressed in another century —and would be up to date in a contemporary magazine. The writer's "troubled crowd" does not really differ much from the "lonely crowd" of our own time. But in the 1830s and 1840s this kind of analysis seldom shaped the character of political dialogue. Although politics sometimes reflected divergent views of the American future, these were not expressed in terms of city and country as opposed social environments. And ordinarily the city, along with the machine and the factory, was accepted as a part of American progress. An 1852 orator commemorating Jefferson could, for example, praise all the Jeffersonian principles and yet still provide a vision of America's urban future: "May her villages which are fast becoming towns, her towns which are rapidly growing to cities, and her chief cities which are each one by itself, bidding hopefully yet to surpass in population a Pekin and a Canton; in enterprise and power, a London and a Paris; in art and intellectual and moral renown, an ancient Athens and Rome combined; finally exceed in every commendable respect, all the past achievements of men down to the discovery of the Western Continents."

It was only as the position of the farmer and of agriculture began perceptibly to decline, that Jeffersonian anti-urbanism reasserted itself as part of the rationale of an economic group losing its power in a changing society. Agricultural journals after 1850 began to fill their columns with proclamations against the city. A writer to the *Prairie Farmer* of Chicago typically asserted that the pursuits of agriculture "are so connected with everything around us which tends to enlighten and enoble the mind, improve the condition of society, and promote the common welfare—and its influences have so direct a bearing in all its ramifications, upon individual and national felicity, that it would seem as if a man must come from some other planet who could find anything to say in its disparagement." City life, he went on, *"crushes, enslaves, and ruins so many thousands of our young men,* who are insensibly made the victims of *dissipation,* of *reckless* speculation, and of ultimate crime." In his reminiscences, a Michigan pioneer emphasized another aspect of the Jeffersonian view of the city which was frequently expressed as the century wore on. In his part of the country, he wrote, "a sturdy race of honest and patriotic men grow to counterbalance the effeminancy and wickedness of the old cities of the east. But for this, ruin and decay would have long since marked the gradual downfall of our great republic. There is today more leaven of salvation right here by the lonely shores of the mighty waters of Lake Michigan, than in all the borders of all the cities of the corrupt civilization of the older east. The wide extent of our country is the conservative influence that will save it from the fate of the ruined dynasties of the old world for ages yet to come."

These kinds of anti-urban sentiments helped to sustain the farmer movements of the late nineteenth century. "The great cities rest upon our broad and fertile prairies," said William Jennings Bryan in his famous Cross of Gold speech, which provided a prelude to the last important political effort seriously based on the Jeffersonian vision of America. "Burn down your cities and leave our farms, and your cities will spring up again as if by magic; but destroy our farms, and the grass will grow in the streets of every city in the country."

But Bryan lost. It is doubtful that the anti-urbanism that was part of the agricultural fundamentalism of the late nineteenth century ever in any precise way reflected community ideology toward the city. The formality and rigor of the agricultural attack on the city might alone indicate that the argument provided a defense of self-interest, not a collective response to perceived circumstances.

The often superficial city-country argument that influenced the character of political debate reflected deeper strains in American and Western thought. Thomas Jefferson's view of the city rested on assumptions about man and the world that at least went back to Virgil's *Georgics;* it owed much directly to Adam Smith, who had found "unnaturalness and dependence" to be the urban dweller's vices and had argued that "to cultivate the ground was the natural destination of man." Enlightenment rationalism and eighteenth-century Romanticism, although the latter developed in part as a reaction to the former, both posited a natural man created in a fixed image, not a social being whose nature was modifiable and partly determined by the workings of institutions. In much early nineteenth-century thought, European as well as American, the city was looked upon as an artificial institution that might be corruptive of the elemental man.

The Transcendentalist philosopher, Ralph Waldo Emerson, held to such a conception. Emerson's view of the universe differed radically from Jefferson's, but his view of the city was similar. The city, Emerson argued, was the source of "Understanding," the essentially empty knowledge of empirical science; the country was the school of "Reason," the higher truth of intuition and vision. Like Jefferson, Emerson recognized the value of cities in providing such educational agencies as the opera, the museum, the library, and the lecture. But the city was also artificial; it denied man's creative facilities. The true test of a civilization was the kind of man the country turned out. And a choice between city and country was necessary. "I wish to have rural strength and religion for my children, and I wish city facility and polish. I find with chagrin that I cannot have both." Although he was not altogether consistent, Emerson fundamentally chose the country. He wrote to Thomas Carlyle in 1840: "I always seem to suffer some loss of faith on entering cities. They are great conspiracies; the parties are all maskers, who have taken mutual oaths of silence not to betray each other's secret and each to keep the other's madness in countenance." In a late essay on farming and the farmer Emerson went further: "That uncorrupted behavior which we admire in animals and in young children belongs to him, to the hunter, the sailor—the man who lives in the presence of Nature. Cities force growth and make men talkative and entertaining, but they make them artificial."

In one of the most famous passages of his works, Emerson argues the need of man to return to the woods. There "man casts off his years, as the snake his slough, and at what period soever of life is always a child." It was in the woods that one could return to reasons and faith. There one could become the celebrated "Transparent eyeball" seeing all, becoming a part and parcel of God, loving "uncontained and immortal beauty." There all the associations of the city became mere trifles. "In the wilderness," Emerson wrote, "I find something more dear and connate than in streets or villages. In the tranquil landscape, and especially in the distant line of horizon, man beholds somewhat as beautiful as his own nature."

In American literature of the early and mid-nineteenth century, Emerson's metaphysical view of the unnatural city became part of a more general indictment of the city and of urban life. As Morton and Lucia White have demonstrated in their pioneering study of the intellectual and the city, the American literary tradition has often been an anti-urban one. A dominant theme in the important fiction of the period is that of America as the lost Eden. The city becomes the symbol of the fall from grace of the land and its people. Particularly as manufacturing becomes important, the city serves to represent materialism, commercialism, corruption, and the evil influences of Old Europe.

This kind of symbolic use of the city extends back past Emerson at least to the first important American novel, Charles Brockden Brown's *Arthur Mervyn* published in 1799. Brown uses Philadelphia during the yellow fever epidemic of 1793 as a setting that represents the reality of evil in the world; the dark and ominous, plague-filled city is entered by the young country hero, Arthur Mervyn, fled from, and returned to with fascination. As R. W. B. Lewis has pointed out, Mervyn is the first of the American Adams—the innocent who matures through knowledge of evil but aches for the freedom of his past. In Brown's novel, the city is specifically the vehicle of the hero's maturation; Arthur Mervyn is continually aware, as he puts it, of the "contrariety that exists between the city and country."

Melville, Hawthorne, and Poe, as the Whites observe, all had "bad dreams of the city." Their characters are attracted to the city but fearful of its effects. Melville's *Pierre,* for example, is a hero with the "choice fate to have been born and nurtured in the country, surrounded by scenery whose uncommon loveliness was the perfect mould of a delicate and poetic mind," and who is defeated by the heartlessness and commercialism of New York. In general, the three authors' bad dreams are of the European city—of London, Liverpool, Paris, or Rome—but there is usually present an implied warning that the evil may reach America's shores.

Lewis, in his analysis, has examined Hawthorne's frequent symbolic use of the city, the "frantic shuffling" between city and country in novel after novel. The two environments, to Hawthorne, represent a moral choice between freedom and restraint. Thoreau found the choice simple—retreat to the woods. Hawthorne, Lewis notes, perceived the complexities in this decision: "He acknowledged the dependence of the individual, for nourishment, upon organized society (the city), and he believed that it was imperative 'to open up an intercourse with the world.' But he knew that the city could destroy as well as nourish and was apt to destroy the person most in need of nourishment. And although he was responsive to the attractions of the open air and to the appeal of the forest, he also understood the grounds for Puritan distrust of the forest. He retained that distrust as part of the symbol. In the forest, possibility was unbounded; but just because of that, evil inclination was unchecked, and witches could flourish there."

Hawthorne's tale of an Utopian colony, *The Blithedale Romance,* based to a degree on the author's experience at the famous Brook Farm, addresses itself directly to the problem of community. The book provides a good example of the way in which city and country were used as symbols in the mid-nineteenth-century novel. The book's hero, Miles Coverdale, who has decided to join the Blithedale experiment, feels regret as he leaves his comfortable bachelor rooms, his cigars, and his claret. But as the party of colonists starts out in a snowstorm he becomes aware of the oppressive force of buildings on all sides and "the old conventionalism" of the city—the smoke in the air and the tramping feet of passers-by that destroy the freshness of nature. Coverdale feels a sense of release as they leave the city and find better air to breathe. "Air that had not been breathed once and again! Air that had not been spoken into words of falsehood, formality and error, like all the air of the dusky city!"

At Blithedale, Coverdale experiences a degree of regeneration, but at the end of an unhappy summer, he realizes that the communitarian experiment represents merely another form of conventionalism and feels compelled to return to the city. He is immediately aware again of its smoke, cruelty, and conventionalism. But he finds satisfaction in the city's sounds and impressions. "Whatever had been my taste for solitude and natural scenery, yet the thick, foggy, stifled element of cities, the entangled life of many men together, sordid as it was, and empty of the beautiful, took quite as strenuous a hold upon my mind. I felt as if there could never be enough of it." In an extended passage, Coverdale describes the sounds of the city—the stir of the hotel, the noise of the pavements, a marching band going by, fire engines, church bells, applause from a nearby public hall. "All of this was just as valuable in its way," Coverdale concludes, "as the sighing of the breeze among the birch-trees" at Blithedale.

Throughout Hawthorne's work there is fascination with the city, but always coupled with the realization that the features that make it fascinating are those that make it dangerous. As one of his latter thoughts on the matter, he suggests in *The Marble Faun* that "all towns should be made capable of purification by fire, or of decay within each half-century . . . we may build almost immortal habitations, it is true; but we cannot keep them from growing old, musty, unwholesome, dreary, full of deathscents, ghosts and murder stains."

Themes of the evil city, elevated to the level of literature in the work of Melville, Hawthorne, or Poe, also served more popular writers of fiction. Sensational works on the sinful metropolises of America began to find a wide market as early as the 1840s. Osgood Bradbury in his *The Belle of the Bowery* (1846) and *Female Depravity, or, the House of Death* (1852) developed, in near pornographic fashion, the story of the innocent country girl who is led into evil ways in the city. The latter book has as a main character the intriguing Henry Luroff, who had "seduced more girls from the country than any other young man in the city." Edward Z. C. Judson in *The B'Hoys of New York* (1849) presented the complementary topic—the "green countryman" corrupted by the city's evil women. Under his pseudonym, Ned Buntline, Judson was later to popularize another genre of sensational American writing, the dime-novel Western. Often vice was portrayed attractively in these works on the city, as in *The Gamblers' League or the Trials of a Country Maid* (1857). The book tells the story of two New York confidence men and their tool, the beautiful Arabella, who was forced to live a life of sin with one of them. The depraved Arabella develops special talents for ensnaring innocent victims from the country and lives luxuriously as a result.

Written at a similar level and often centering on the same themes were alleged guidebooks that revealed the mysteries and sins of American cities.

One of the earliest writers of these exposés of urban life, which became particularly popular in the years after the Civil War, was a *New York Tribune*
journalist, George G. Foster. In two books collecting his columns—*New York
in Slices by an Experienced Carver* (1849) and *New York by Gas-Light: With
Here and There a Streak of Sunshine* (1850)—Foster presented most of the
themes and topics that were later to become standard in the genre. Here the
reader encounters the gullible country lad seduced and robbed by the painted
streetwalkers; the symbolic area of complete degradation—in this case the
notorious Five Points district, which ordinarily served the purpose in writings
about New York; the invidious comments on the city's "races," the Jewish,
Negro, and Irish. Here also is the prostitute's confession: "Princess Anna,"
once an innocent country girl, seduced and abandoned by a city boy, exploited
by the clergy, and now steadily drifting downward to the lower depths; contrasts between the luxurious sexual immorality of the upper classes and the
sordid life of the poor; and Wall Street as a collection of temples to Mammon.

Often works of this type have been dismissed as lurid anti-urban tracts,
designed to appeal to the prejudices of rural and small-town America. There
is much that is lurid and much that is anti-urban in Foster's accounts. Yet his
reaction to the city is more complex than simple hostility. Running through
both books is the theme that the American city as it stands may be evil but
that potentially it is the site of the good community and the locale for the
fruition of Christian society. In *New York in Slices,* he states the theme explicitly: "A great city is the highest result of human civilization. Here the Soul,
that most perfect and godlike of all created things, the essence and spirit of
the visible world has put forth all its most wonderful energies. . . . Yes—man
in isolation, or thinly gathered in feeble neighborhoods and scattered villages,
is powerless to accomplish great works or to fulfill the mission of his race.
It is only in a large city, where some hundreds of thousands combine their
various powers, that the human mind can efficiently stamp itself on every
thing by which it is surrounded—can transmute the insensible earth to a fit
temple and dwelling place for immortal spirits."

These pious sentiments, which were often a part of the better known later
exposés, can perhaps be dismissed frequently as window dressing for prurient
sensationalism. Still, they were common sentiments expressed in a variety of
contexts. The notion of the city as an arena where American society could
either move toward a higher good or descend toward evil informs much of
the pre-Civil War writing about the meaning of the city in American life. It
is to be found, for example, in the first important demographic analysis of the
United States. George Tucker, a Jeffersonian politician who became Professor
of Moral Philosophy at the University of Virginia when it opened in 1825,
examined the census returns from 1790 to 1840 and speculated on their meaning in a significant but little-known work entitled *Progress of the United States
in Population and Wealth,* published in 1843. His compilations demonstrated
that towns and cities were clearly growing at a much faster rate than the

country as a whole and that this trend would continue in the future. Tucker was uncertain, however, as to what would be the effect of this development on American society. "The growth of cities," he wrote in a passage widely quoted in contemporary sources, "commonly marks the progress of intelligence and the arts, measures the sum of social enjoyment, and always implies mental activity, which is sometimes healthy and useful, sometimes distempered and pernicious. If these congregations of men diminish some of the comforts of life, they augment others: if they are less favourable to health than the country, they also provide better defences against disease, and better means of cure. From causes both physical and moral, they are less favourable to the multiplication of the species. In the eyes of the moralist, cities afford a wider field both for virtue and vice: and they are more prone to innovation, whether for good or evil."

The early religious studies of the city in America offered a related view—that the city could serve as the testing ground for the faith of a Christian. Amory D. Mayo in *Symbols of the Capital; or Civilization in New York,* published in 1859, established a pattern for the clerical examinations of American life, another genre which later in the hands of such figures as Josiah Strong and William T. Stead was to find a wide popular market. Mayo attacked the city with all the conventional romantic and agrarian arguments. The struggle for success in the city scarred the bodies and twisted the minds of both successes and failures. "All dangers of the town," he wrote, "may be summed up in this: that here, withdrawn from the blessed influence of Nature, and set face to face against humanity, man loses his own nature and becomes a new and artificial creature—an unhuman cog in a social machinery that works like a fate, and cheats him of his true culture as a soul. The most unnatural fashions and habits, the strangest eccentricities of intellect, the wildest and most pernicious theories in social morals, and the most appalling and incurable barbarism, are the legitimate growth of city life."

Yet Mayo understood the appeal and the reality of the city. He saw young people flocking there and being challenged by the experience. If they survived the ordeal, he thought their faith and character would unquestionably be strengthened. Moreover, an ideal city, a monument to Christian principles, was conceivable if there were only a way of removing the poor and the exploiters of the poor. "But, we cannot build cities 'to order,'" he wrote in a more realistic vein, "they are and will be huge receptacles for all varieties of humanity, and represent the worst as surely as the best in our American character. All the teacher of Christianity can do is to take men and women in towns as he finds them, and in spite of disheartening influences, keep on forever warning, instructing and inspiring to virtue."

Numerous nineteenth-century clergymen who became aware of the problems of the eastern cities had realized that the American city was here to stay and was not necessarily a threat to the good community. One of the more optimistic spokesmen of this point of view was Joseph Tuckerman, a Unitarian minister in Boston who pioneered community programs of social welfare in the United States. Tuckerman consistently argued that cities were not inherently un-Christian. With effort, he asserted, they could be made the centers of the "purest and highest religious and moral influences of the highest intellectual culture, and of the greatest advancement of the arts and sciences, and that the most vigorous growth of all the Christian virtues may be made a characteristic of cities." The most famous national spokesman of Unitarianism, William E. Channing, a friend and Harvard classmate of Tuckerman's, argued that American cities could become the metropolises of world civilization if individuals in the cities would face up to their responsibilities for the health and welfare of the poor. In eulogizing Tuckerman, Channing reflected his own as well as Tuckerman's view of the city when he wrote that it "became his deliberate conviction and one which he often repeated, that great cities need not be haunts of vice and poverty; that . . . there were now intelligence, virtue and piety enough, could they be brought into united action, to give a new intellectual and moral life to the more neglected classes of society. In this faith he acted, toiled, suffered and died."

The religious argument, that the city could represent Christian good but that the American city, with its extremes of wealth and poverty, its materialism and its exploitation contradicted Christian principles, worked its way into a substantial body of pre-Civil War writing about urban life. It received typical statement, for example, in an 1857 governmental investigation of the slums of New York. The writers argued that man was a gregarious creature who yearned for neighborhood. Theorists of all ages had conceived of noble cities. Even the Bible had "coupled the forms of earthly splendor with the more spiritual excellences of a New Jerusalem." The city could be the site of "intellectual and moral beatitude." If desolate nature was "symbolical of savage or barbarous life," then its opposite ought to be found where art, luxury, and industry existed in profusion. "Yet here," the report continued, "in reality, where pleasure wreathes perennial flowers, and magnificence runs wild with varied forms; here, in sad refutation of Utopian speculation, the leper crouches in dumb despair, the beggar crawls in abject misery, the toiler starves, the robber prowls, and the tenant-house—home of all those outcast beings—rises in squalid deformity, to mock civilization with its foul malaria, its poison-breeding influences, its death-dealing associations."

A number of questions, then, were part of the early nineteenth-century dialogue on the American city and its relationship to the American future. Did the city, with its extremes of wealth and poverty, its spiritual impoverishment, its greed and oppression, constitute an overwhelming threat to the Christian community, or did the existence of these problems of urban life provide a way of strengthening Christian ideals? In a broader sense, was the city, in Christian eschatology, really Sodom and Gommorah or the New Jerusalem, the "city on a hill?" Were the growing cities part of a new economic pattern that would undermine the foundations of republican government? Could man,

a creature of nature, comprehend his place in the universe while restricted by
an essentially artificial environment?

Underlying these and related social and philosophical questions, however,
was a scientific conception—the city was essentially unhealthy, a dangerous
type of environment that threatened man's physical existence. Observation
tended to lend support to this conception, for it was largely city dwellers who
were struck down by the frequent, dreaded nineteenth-century plagues of
cholera, yellow fever, and other epidemic disease. Ebenezer Hazard, who had
survived the Philadelphia yellow fever epidemic of 1793 in spite of the massive
bloodletting prescribed by his physician, expressed a view that was to be
echoed many times in the next fifty or sixty years when he observed that the
plague might teach the country a lesson and check the "prevailing taste for
enlarging Philadelphia, and crowding so many human beings together on so
small a part of earth."

These ecological views related closely to prevailing medical theories concerning the nature of disease. Not until the 1880s was the germ theory of
disease generally accepted in the United States, and before that time many
diseases, particularly those that were epidemic in nature, were regarded not
as entities but as dynamic conditions whose manifestations varied in terms
of a range of moral, climatic, and environmental factors. This type of etiology
generally supported the view that the city provided an unwholesome, unnatural atmosphere for human life. Miasmas which induced both physical and
moral disease (and the two were not rigorously demarcated) were frequently
associated with an urban environment.

Nineteenth-century novelists conceived of the city as representing a danger
to the soul of man or to his society, but they also feared the city in a physical
sense—as the source of dangerous contaminating exhalations. When Hawthorne's Miles Coverdale, for example, finds "better air to breath" upon leaving the smoke-filled city, he is in part employing metaphor—but only in
part. The same point could be made of Jefferson's observations on cities as
"pestilential" or as "sores," which have too commonly been construed simply
as comments on political or economic matters. The city as "cancer," a metaphor still frequently employed, has its roots in this kind of nineteenth-century
biological theory. Jefferson's friend, the distinguished scientist and physician,
Benjamin Rush, a firm believer in miasmatic theories of disease, made the
point of the physical danger of cities explicit in a letter to Jefferson: "I consider them in the same light that I do abscesses on the human body, viz., as
reservoirs of all the impurities of a community."

In a little-noted aspect of his Presidential career, Jefferson devised a plan
to remove disease-causing vapors from American cities. He outlined his proposal after the acquisition of New Orleans from the French. "Such a constitution of atmosphere being requisite to originate [yellow fever] as is generated
in low, close, and ill-cleansed parts of town, I have supposed it practicable to
prevent its generation by building our cities on a more open plan. Take, for

instance, the chequer board for a plan. Let the black squares only be building ones, and the white ones be left open, in turf and trees. Every square of house will be surrounded by four open squares, and every house will front an open square. The atmosphere of such a town would be like that of the country, insusceptible of the miasmata which produce yellow fever. I have accordingly proposed that the enlargement of the city of New Orleans, which must immediately take place, shall be on this plan. But it is only in the case of enlargements to be made, or of cities to be built, that this means of prevention can be employed." There is no evidence that the scheme was ever applied to New Orleans. But the town of Jeffersonville, Indiana, later to be eclipsed by Louisville across the river in Kentucky, was initially plotted in the fashion Jefferson suggested, and the original plan for Jackson, Mississippi also followed his design. In both cases, the open squares offered too great a temptation as building sites for the system to endure longer than very briefly.

Until the 1860s, when it was recognized that epidemics could be combatted through systematic community programs of sanitation, each year of plague brought warnings to abandon the unhealthy cities. In 1849, for example, a physician wrote that the siege of cholera that year could be considered one of the "greatest *reforms* the world has ever known," for it might teach Americans "to forsake large cities . . . to choose the country's wholesome air with its quietude and competence." The first investigations of housing and other problems of urban life in America emphasized that the city sapped the moral and physical vigor of its residents. The famous 1845 report of John H. Griscom, a New York physician and pioneer in the public health movement, argued that the foul air of New York caused an individual's blood to become burdened with impurities, preventing it from imparting to the "system the qualities demanded by nature for the due maintenance of health and strength." All that was necessary to demonstrate this, the report argued, was a stroll in the country. The contrast between an atmosphere filled with "animal and vegetable exhalations" and the air of grassy plains, rivers, and mountains needed "no epicurean lungs to detect." The "superior corporeal activity" and the mental stimulation imparted by these latter surroundings provided "prima facie proofs" of the country's superiority.

Although efforts to introduce trees and parks into the city—which became a well-organized movement in the 1840s and 1850s—rested in part on a formalized enthusiasm for nature aroused by the romantic writings of John Ruskin, William Cullen Bryant, Andrew Jackson Downing, and others, fundamental also to the movement was the view that the city was inherently unhealthy and that parks and trees would bring it closer to the state of the country. Parks would serve as "lungs" or "ventilators," and both terms were used often, absorbing or dispelling the impurities created by the urban environment. A physician writing about the 1849 cholera epidemic speculated that the principal cause was insufficient electricity in the air, a result of the unnatural congestion of cities. Accordingly, the answer to epidemics was clear: "If cities must exist let many and large spaces be devoted to parks, and let all the streets on each side of the way be lined with trees, with two or three trees to every building, so that the people may be supplied with electricity and oxygen in abundance from Nature's own laboratory." Regardless of the particular environmental theory of disease advanced, parks were viewed as an urban public health measure of fundamental importance. In gaining support for New York's Central Park and the other large urban parks that followed, considerations of health often proved more important than did arguments stressing the aesthetic or philosophical value of bringing the countryside to the city.

The notion of an individual city as an organic structure subject to inevitable decay because of its production of pervasive disease-producing vapors absorbed many writers about the American future in the early and mid-nineteenth century. Reflecting on the past urban history of the world, a commentator in *De Bow's Review* noted that great cities had always declined. Babylon, Nineveh, Memphis, Tyre, and Carthage had been succeeded by Pekin, Canton, Constantinople, Naples, Vienna, Madrid, London, and Paris. The fate of ancient cities was now being prepared for the present world capitals. "Most of these great cities," he wrote, "are, in their oldest portions, exhibiting signs of decay. Like ancient trees, while at the heart they are wasting away, they add circle to circle of outward growth; now gaining in progress of growth on the measure of interior decay, and again failing to increase outwardly as the interior portions waste away." This decay was chiefly the result of exhalations of a great city caused by the accumulation of filth at its interior. Would American cities face the same fate? The author thought not. The next great metropolises, he predicted, would be located in the interior valley of America. Because of the pattern of the magnificent Mississippi River system, the natural impurities that led to deterioration of a city could be safely carried away. A long life could thus be predicted for the future great cities of the United States.

If the city as a place to live was viewed as inherently unhealthy, the desirability of the city as an institution for the promotion of economic activity was seldom questioned. Along with the telegraph, the railroad, and the factory, the growing city by the 1830s was looked upon as a certain token of American progress toward a magnificent future. From Christopher Columbus on, the New World had in part meant wealth; the city had always been an important symbol of America as the land of material opportunity. The nineteenth-century immigrant's vision of New York with its streets paved with gold continued a traditional cultural attitude as old as the seven cities of Cibola sought by the Spanish explorers. Moreover, the rationale that developed in defense and explanation of American capitalistic expansion had the city as one of its principal elements. We read Thoreau today and are moved by his prophetic remonstration against American materialism, against the city, the machine, and the factory. Yet in his own time people were more likely to read the poetic tributes to the telegraph, the iron horse, or the country's magnificent thriving cities to be found in their commercial magazines or local newspapers. Although the anti-urban philosophers and novelists of the nineteenth century intrigue the contemporary mind, the defenders and prophets of the material city perhaps reflect more exactly the early popular view of the city.

Much of the favorable writing about early nineteenth-century urban growth grew out of the city rivalries of the period and stressed geographical theories of city location and development. Generally present in these discussions was a formal viewpoint that could be termed the *doctrine of natural advantages*: great cities were located and grew because of the influence of a variety of deterministic geographic influences involving river connections, distances, raw materials, and climate. Human enterprise was not entirely ruled out of the calculation; potentially great cities with all the natural advantages in the world might presumably fail through lack of enlightened effort by local leaders. But until well into the railroad era it was accepted that the forces of geography fundamentally determined the success or failure of attempts to build great cities.

This meant that a proper study of geography would enable a student to predict the future of urban growth in America. Prophecy was a salient part of the doctrine of natural advantages, and DeWitt Clinton's exuberant vision of New York's destiny expressed in 1825 was unusual only in that it proved largely to be true. The city, he declared, "will, in course of time become the granary of the world, the emporium of commerce, the seat of manufactures, the focus of great moneyed operations, and the concentrating point of vast, disposable, and accumulating capitals, which will stimulate, enliven, extend, and reward the exertions of human labour and ingenuity, in all their processes and exhibitions. And, before the revolution of a century, the whole island of Manhattan, covered with habitations and replenished with a dense population, will constitute one vast city." Statements like this accompanied American city building for another century.

In the early nineteenth century the American West, not the urbanizing Northeast, sustained the hopes of those who wished the United States to remain an agrarian republic. Yet, ironically, it was the American West that also spawned the most elaborate visions of an urban future for the nation. Just as historians long failed to recognize town and city building as a force in the economic development of the West, interpreters of the character of our national culture in their concern with the myths arising from struggle with the wilderness have tended to overlook the impact of a western urban experience on American thought. Those who saw American progress in material growth often perceived the West as an eventual land of magnificent cities. From the first days of settlement across the Appalachian Mountains, every region of the West had its newspaper editor, hired promoter, or local intellectual predicting greatness for a primitive hamlet or perhaps a city that existed only on its promoter's map. Writing in 1815, Daniel Drake, the frontier physician and long-time promoter of Cincinnati, admitted it might seem visionary and boastful to speak of cities in the West. Yet, Drake argued that if one became familiar with the natural advantages of the region, it would be apparent that the primitive villages on the banks of the Ohio and Mississippi would attain the position of "populous and magnificent cities." The magnificent river transportation system of the interior, the fertility of the soil, and the region's bountiful resources betokened enormous population growth. Of all the great cities destined to develop along the Ohio, Drake predicted that Cincinnati with its unparalleled natural advantages was destined to be the foremost.

At each successive stage of westward movement, similar claims were made for other western cities. With more obvious justification than in many communities, St. Louis writers worked out the doctrine of natural advantages in elaborate detail. Located near an unrivalled confluence of rivers at a key point on the great central waterway, the Mississippi, St. Louis struck many observers as nature's favorite. The city, the British traveler Alexander Mackay wrote near mid-century, "occupies as it were the central point, from which the great natural highways of the Union diverge in different directions. The different radii which spring from it bring it into contact with a vast circumference. The Missouri connects it with the Rocky Mountains, the Ohio with the Alleghenies, the Upper Mississippi with the Great Lakes, the lower with the ocean. It is destined soon to become the great internal *entrepôt* of the country."

Farther to the west Albert Richardson, the journalist and western traveler, wrote a few years later of the "New Babylons" springing up along the Missouri and Kansas rivers on the fringe of settlement. Each of these, he said, had beautifully lithographed maps showing magnificent city development and railroads converging from all directions. In many cases, however, not a single habitation had actually been built at the site. Richardson warned immigrants and investors to turn "deaf ears to plausible theorists with elaborate maps, who prove geographically, climatically, and statistically that the great city *must* spring up in some new locality."

Although the doctrine of natural advantages, utilized to justify prophecies of urban greatness for aspiring villages and towns, often represented little more than a narrow boosterism, in the hands of many western writers it was developed into an involved theory of city location and growth. In 1851 an obscure Cincinnatian named S. H. Goodin seized on the theory of gravitation to try to prove that his city was destined to be a great metropolis. Describing a process by which circles of varying-sized urban settlements formed according to the fundamental law of centralization, he concluded that ultimately the competition of cities in the third circle would create a great central city in mid-America, which would have all the others as "satellites or outposts."

A number of threads of nineteenth-century thought were woven into the presentation of these theories: a geopolitical emphasis on the importance of central land masses in a society's development, the old geographical-historical idea that great cities are inevitably located along the major rivers of the world, and the view that mankind moves ever westward. In addition, these reflections were always informed by a vision of an urban future for the nation.

Particularly influential in shaping the outlook of the western urban writers was the German geographer and explorer, Alexander von Humboldt, whose multi-volume study of the universe entitled *Cosmos* was widely circulated in the United States in an English translation. Humboldt argued that nature determined the patterns of development of all society. He emphasized the importance of the continual movement of the peoples of the world along an isothermal zone where yearly temperature conditions were most favorable for civilization. Cities, he argued, would form at intervals within this favored habitat. These views and several related concepts advanced by Humboldt provided the foundation for much of the mid-nineteenth-century speculation about the urban future of the West.

The American popularizer of Humboldt and one of the more significant of the western urban prophets was the explorer, military adventurer, and land speculator, William Gilpin (1813–1894). Gilpin participated fully in the frontier experience. He first arrived in the West as a young army recruiting officer during the Second Seminole War, became active in politics in St. Louis, participated in the early efforts of Oregon settlers to organize the territory, and after a year in Washington, spent noisily advocating America's manifest destiny, participated in Stephen Kearny's expedition to New Mexico during the Mexican War. After the war he again became active in politics, early supported the Republican party in Missouri, became territorial governor of Colorado in 1861, and late in his life made a fortune from land speculation in Colorado. All the while, he was speaking and writing about the West; his articles of the 1850s, later collected in a book first called *The Central Gold Region* and later *The Mission of the North American People,* won him national recognition as a spokesman of the West.

Gilpin's erudite but tangled writings are made up in large part of detailed topographical description, but running through them all is a version of Humboldt's geographical determinism. Gilpin adopted Humboldt's conception of the Isothermal Zodiac, an undulating belt of land around the globe where climate was most favorable for man. Within this zone, and there only, Gilpin asserted, the great civilizations of the world had flourished. Upon the Axis of Intensity, running through the heart of the Isothermal Zodiac, the migratory movements of the human masses had pressed. Near this line of favorable median temperature, men had constructed the world's primary cities, the "foci from which had radiated intellectual activity and power."

Gilpin further asserted that North America was a vast bowl that focussed all forces to the center and led to a harmonious pattern of social development. The continent was a "symmetrical and sublime" geographic unit, the Mississippi Valley its dominant center. "The Great Basin of the Mississippi is the amphitheatre of the world," he wrote; "here is supremely, indeed, the most magnificent dwelling marked out by God for man's abode."

These geographical conceptions emphasizing population movement westward and the concentration of wealth and power in the interior of the nation could easily be fitted to a rationale justifying the future of the cities of the West. They were continually used in this fashion, and Gilpin himself in several instances made the necessary applications. As a resident of Independence, Missouri during the 1840s, he had formulated a plan to make an area of land near the small frontier community into "Centropolis," the preeminent city of the mid-continent. Although Gilpin had a magnificent map prepared that showed the national capital and national observatory located in the heart of a great city embracing an area of over a hundred square miles, the speculative scheme proved a complete failure and left Gilpin in debt for a number of years.

As part of this promotional venture, Gilpin in 1853 had advanced an explicit theory of city location to justify Independence's claim to urban greatness. His articles on the subject incorporated many of the geographical arguments that were a part of the doctrine of natural advantages prevalent in western urban writing, as well as his own version of Humboldt. Independence, Gilpin asserted, occupied a key point on the zodiac of the westward movement. Throughout history man had erected the world's cities along great navigable rivers, the Ganges, Nile, or Danube, which ran through broad fertile basins. A physical law locating emporiums a hundred leagues apart had operated along the rivers of North America. Gilpin argued that if a reader were to make even a slight inspection of a map of the river system of the world, such as Humboldt had prepared, his eyes would immediately be drawn to the portion of the Missouri River running east from the mouth of the Kansas to St. Louis, and he would see that Independence, because of its location at the western end of this natural throughway, was destined to be the next great American metropolis. St. Louis and Independence, he wrote, "stand out upon the face of the continent like eyes in the human head." No mere works of man could alter the rise of Independence to metropolis. "The peculiar configuration of the continent," he declared, "and its rivers and plains make these *two* natural *focal* points. This will not be interfered with by any railroads or any other public works which may be constructed by arts, as these latter are successful and permanent only when they conform with the water grades of nature and the natural laws which condense society."

At the time Gilpin wrote, numerous railroads were being projected west of the Mississippi River, and this had to be taken into account in any prediction about the future location of great cities in mid-America. Although it was soon to be conclusively demonstrated that railroads could be built virtually anywhere, decisely altering natural patterns of city location, prophecy lagged far behind technology, and spokesmen for aspiring communities generally argued that railroads would always be bound by the logic of river course and natural physical channels of trade and communication. In advancing the claims of Independence, Gilpin projected a great north-south railroad to run from Independence to Galveston and the Gulf of Mexico, which, he asserted, would conform to the pattern of continental forces. Advancing a common point of view that persisted in western promotional writing until late in the century, he argued that such a line would prove to be the means by which the West escaped the exploitation of the East.

In the late 1850s after the failure of his project, Gilpin abandoned his interest in Independence and moved the *"site* for the central city of the 'Basin of the Mississippi' " a few miles west to Kansas City, which by that time had clearly eclipsed Independence as the regional city. "There must be a great city here," Gilpin concluded, "such as antiquity built at the head of the Mediterranean and named Jerusalem, Tyre, Alexandria, and Constantinople; such as our own people name New York, New Orleans, San Francisco, St. Louis." A few years later, he found that the pioneer population moving ever westward along the Axis of Intensity had again begun to condense itself in force. The settlers had chosen Denver, a "focal point of impregnable power in the topographical configuration of the continent." Ultimately, Gilpin argued, Denver would also become the gateway for eastward migration along the Axis of Intensity toward the world's vital center, the Mississippi Valley. In the 1850s and 1860s, Gilpin was considered a leading authority on the West. His kind of vision of the great cities of the West, as fanciful as his notions seem, supported the hopes of hundreds of ambitious promoters in the towns and hamlets of the region.

Jesup W. Scott (1799–1873), who ranks with Gilpin as a student of early western cities, was influenced by a similar view of the significance of interior geography. In the late 1840s and 1850s, at roughly the same time Gilpin was winning prominence, Scott wrote a series of widely circulated articles designed to show that the future urban population of the United States would be concentrated in the Mississippi Valley and Great Lakes regions. Gilpin had been influenced by town boosting on the Missouri-Kansas border; Scott was the product of an earlier urban frontier. He came west to the booming Maumee Valley of Ohio in the 1830s at a time when twelve villages and paper town sites along a fifteen mile stretch of river were competing to become the metropolis of the lake region. The Panic of 1837 ended this boom brought on by interior canal building and nearly wiped out Scott. But after several years of newspaper work and land speculation, he eventually made a fortune from a key holding of downtown Toledo real estate that he had purchased at an early date.

In his writings, published in the widely known *Hunt's Merchants' Magazine* and *De Bow's Review,* Scott consistently advanced an urban interpretation of the westward movement. The rise of the city, he argued, was the fundamental economic development occurring in the West. It had not attracted sufficient attention; the country's "best minds" had tended to ignore it; yet surely, he asserted, the rapidity of the growth of cities was "among the most remarkable phenomena of human progress." Finding the natural laws that impelled mankind toward an urban society should in fact be a primary aim of the student of the United States.

Like Gilpin, Scott stressed the geographic unity of the interior of North America in shaping the growth of cities. "The centre of power, numerical, political, economical, and social," he wrote, "is . . . indubitably, on its steady march from the Atlantic border toward the interior of the continent. That it will find a resting place somewhere, in its broad interior plain, seems as inevitable as the continued movement of the earth on its axis." Scott argued that Europeans and their descendants in the United States had too closely associated great cities with "salt, sea and commerce"; the interior of America for too long had been thought of as a land of gloomy forests and desert prairies. People perhaps acknowledged in the abstract the potentialities of a vast transportation system of rivers, lakes, and railroads, supplemented by canals and macadamized highways, but had only begun to recognize by the 1840s how the locomotive and the steamboat were actually creating easy interior commerce and stimulating the growth of interior cities.

Substantial portions of many of Scott's articles consisted of elaborate population projections, both for the region as a whole and for individual cities, designed to show the future growth of urban population in the West. Although his methods of handling statistics were crude, Scott ranks among the first important American students of demography. In 1843, he set the pattern for his later calculations when he predicted that by 1890 the great interior valley would have a total population of 48 million, with 35 million people in cities. By this date the Atlantic slope would have grown only to a 21 million total; Canada and the region west of the Rocky Mountains would have respective totals of five and two million. These figures clearly indicated the future dominance of the interior cities of America, Scott asserted, particularly because he felt that he had been unduly generous in assigning the number of people that would still be required in agriculture. Although Scott's statistics become more and more detailed over the years, his projections were always shaped to demonstrate the same trend—the inevitable rise to dominance of the cities of the West over those of the eastern seaboard. In an 1854 article, for example, he estimated the population of the great central plain—which he defined to include portions of Canada and the American Southwest—at 15 million, seven-eighths of this population on farms. He counted 600,000 people living in the cities and towns that bordered on the Great Lakes and the St. Lawrence River; the Mississippi and Mobile river basins added urban population of 800,000. Natural increase for the region could be calculated at 800,000 a year. Owing to technological advances in agriculture, most of this growth would be absorbed in the interior cities, particularly in those located along the Great Lakes.

By the late 1840s, the Great Lakes cities performed a key function in Scott's calculations. He argued that although the cost of railroad transportation would steadily decline, commerce on the waterways would always be less expensive than overland commerce. The future great cities, therefore, would be located at strategic positions along the Great Lakes, where the interior railroad system would join lakes and rivers. Although over the years he had picked a number of cities as the site of the future great metropolis of the interior, by the 1850s he had narrowed the rivals for supremacy down to Chicago and Toledo—the holders of the "keys of commerce, soon to become immense between the great rivers and lakes of the continent." The "great manufacturing hives of the North American plain" would also come as naturally to these two sites as "teeth in the mouth of an infant child." In his later years, he became increasingly interested in Humboldt's geography and built his arguments more explicitly upon geographical determinism. On the great interior plain of North America, he predicted in one of his last pieces, "will grow up the greatest aggregation, the greatest nation, the noblest empire of man, and the greatest city."

Scott was convinced that the growth of cities was the most vital and most progressive aspect of American development. If one is to sustain the thesis that American intellectual energies have been directed against the city, it is necessary to rule out the influence of a host of lesser popular writers like Scott who viewed the nineteenth-century city as the exemplar of American progress. "All people take pride in their cities," he wrote in 1848. "In them naturally concentrate the great minds and the great wealth of the nation. There the arts that adorn life are cultivated, and from them flows out the knowledge that gives its current of thought to the national mind." The western urban writers, and probably a goodly proportion of all Americans at mid-century, would have agreed with these sentiments.

CHAPTER

# 4

# The Urban Milieu: Everyday Life, 1800–1865

FOREIGN travelers who visited early nineteenth-century American cities were impressed by their bright, airy appearance and the absence of the decaying congested districts to be found in the cities of Europe. English visitors often compared American cities to the larger villages they knew at home. Even New York, in spite of its rapid growth during the early part of the century, shared in this evaluation. "No dark alleys, whose confined and noisome atmosphere marks the presence of a dense and suffering population," the Utopian reformer Frances Wright wrote of America's largest city in 1821, "no hovels, in whose ruined garrets, or dank and gloomy cellars crowd the wretched victims of vice and leisure, whose penury drives to despair, ere she open them to the grave."

Yet by this date the view that American cities were different was already illusory. Travelers, although they often visited some symbolic area of sin and degradation, tended to ignore the poorer residential areas of cities. In the last decade of the eighteenth century large-scale immigration to such places as New York, which grew by more than 80 per cent, and Baltimore, which doubled its population, led to considerable congestion and intensified the problem of poverty that had always existed in American cities. Periodic depressions intensified the hardship and distress of many urban dwellers. As early as 1815, slums had begun to take root on a half-dozen streets or so around Chatham Square on the lower east side of New York City. By this time Boston also had begun to develop districts inhabited by a class of urban poor; to local reformers like Joseph Tuckerman this circumstance seemed to represent a transfer of the abuses of Old Europe to the New World. In the years of great urban growth and industrialization after 1830, eastern seaboard cities rapidly acquired the characteristics associated with the manufacturing cities of Europe. Within a decade and a half after Frances Wright wrote, visitors to New York were noting the presence of precisely the things she had found absent—misery, filth, and overcrowding. Areas such as the notorious Five Points district had become standard symbols of the evil city.

As early as the 1830s, New York had also acquired its reputation as the city of frenetic hustle and bustle. Asa Greene, a New York physician, newspaperman, and literary figure, noted in his 1837 commentary on the city that to cross Broadway "you must button your coat tight about you, see that your shoes are secure at the heels, settle your hat firmly on your head, look up street and down street, at the self-same moment, to see what carts and carriages are upon you, and then run for your life. We daily see persons waiting at the crossing place for some minutes, before they can find an opening, and a chance to get over, between the omnibuses, coaches, and other vehicles, that are constantly dashing up and down the street; and after waiting thus long, deem themselves exceedingly fortunate if they can get over with sound bones and a whole skin."

No other nineteenth-century city was quite like New York, nor for that matter were any two city environments entirely similar. In physical appearance, early nineteenth-century cities had more personal character than they did later on. Baltimore and Philadelphia were distinguished by rowhouses and stoops; Savannah had its attractive park squares, Charleston its gracious verandas. Nationality influences—French in New Orleans, German in Philadelphia, Dutch in New York, or English in Baltimore—contributed to distinctive architectural patterns. But already building methods and the technology of municipal services were making cities more alike. In 1819, Benjamin Latrobe, architect and designer of municipal water systems, made this point in his diary, noting that the standards of Baltimore and Philadelphia were diluting the French influence in New Orleans. "We shall introduce many grand and profitable improvements," he wrote, "but they shall take the place of much elegance, ease, and some convenience." The general acceptance of Georgian architecture and the use of balloon-frame construction broke down regional diversity in houses and other buildings. By the 1840s travelers found a monotonous similarity in the appearance of American cities, particularly those that had been newly built in the West.

Although cities were coming to look more alike, visitors still noted striking sectional differences in the kind of urban environment they represented. By the 1830s signs of decay were evident in the southern seaboard cities tied to a plantation economy; in contrast, the interior river towns of the South such as Louisville and Memphis had begun to boom and were viewed as seats of opportunity. Pittsburgh early in the century had already acquired its reputation as the "large workshop" of America. The towns and cities of the West consistently seemed to represent American progress and the conquest of a hostile wilderness. To virtually all travelers, such places as Chicago, Cincinnati, and St. Louis presented a picture, as Alexander Mackay wrote of the latter, of "bustle, enterprise, and activity." Because of their warmer climate, southern cities were often portrayed as especially unhealthy, and there was evidence to support this view. The cholera epidemic of 1833 nearly destroyed the small thriving city of Maysville, Kentucky and New Orleans had the highest death rate of any city in the union. In spite of this, New Orleans was frequently labelled the most cosmopolitan and urbane of American cities. The indefatigable English traveler, James Buckingham, for example, thought the city's St. Charles Hotel had no equal in beauty any-where in the world. He commented that New Orleans' fine restaurants, its concerts, balls, operas, and masquerades, in fact its whole mode of life, merited comparison with Paris.

These sectional contrasts were often extended to cities in the same region, New Orleans and Charleston, for example, or even to neighbors as in the case of Chicago and Milwaukee. To Frederika Bremer, the Swedish novelist who visited the West in 1850, Chicago was "one of the most miserable and ugly cities" that she had seen in America. People had apparently come there, she observed, "to trade, to make money, and not to live." Milwaukee, on the other hand, appeared to be "a splendid city" that "grows and extends her-self every day," increasing "with all its might."

Although most American cities before 1850 escaped the congestion of the growing slums of New York and Boston, all of them shared a number of unpleasant features. Because streets were paved only in a few sections of larger cities, mud was always present in rainy weather. Joshua T. Smith in an 1837 journal provided a comment echoed in virtually every account of western cities but also customary in those of the eastern metropolises. "One characteristic of Detroit should have been noticed before—its *mud*. It is the common topic of conversation & exceeds credibility—After a little rain the cart wheels sink literally up to the axle-tree in the filth—*No single* street in the town is paved or lighted—This of course adds to the numerous advan-tages of which the city has to boast." This omnipresent condition gave rise to the famous tall tale of American folklore: a citizen offers help to a man embedded to his neck in a mud hole on a city thoroughfare. "No need to worry," replies the unfortunate, "I have a horse underneath me." In addition to mud, there was refuse and garbage clogging the streets; in all parts of the country, bands of hogs protected as scavengers roamed about town, a condition that usually aroused protest only when children were attacked. Frances Trollope, in her famous account of America's domestic manners, found it "decidedly unpleasant" to live in Cincinnati surrounded by herds of "unsavory animals" but admitted the necessity of their "Herculean service." Without them, she observed, streets would soon be choked with filth in every stage of decomposition. Many southern cities, Charleston for example, protected turkey buzzards by law because of their scavenging. Because of objections to their smell, other southern cities such as Norfolk used wander-ing herds of cattle, and many small towns placed their faith in goats, geese, and "ravenous dogs."

In the 1830s and 1840s, New York was often considered the showcase city of America—the exemplar of growth, change, and progress in the new so-ciety. Local residents were proud of its role, but not until past mid-century did the community do much to make the city presentable. Diarist George Templeton Strong wrote in 1839 that New York was "one huge pigsty" but that a prudent farmer would avoid putting his pigs into it for fear they might catch the plague. In 1844 the editor of the *New World* made the same point: "That our streets have been horrible enough in times past no one denies, but they are now . . . more abominably filthy than ever; they are too foul to serve as the styes for the hogs which perambulate them. . . . The offal and filth, of which there are loads thrown from the houses in defiance of an ordinance which is never enforced, is scraped up with the usual deposits of mud and manure into big heaps and left *for weeks together* on the sides of the street." With the extensive use of horses in cities, the disposal of manure was a serious and continual urban concern. Because of the general inefficiency of the scavenging system, manure often simply accumulated, turning streets into cesspools in wet weather; in dry weather "pulverized horse dung" was a principal source of dust in the air. Not until after the establishment of the New York Metropolitan Board of Health in 1866 was there reasonably systematic and permanent clean-up of the city. As part of this program, hogs were finally eliminated from the city's streets.

The absence of adequate sewage facilities also contributed to the unpleasantness and unhealthiness of urban life in the nineteenth century. Before 1850 methods of removing waste were still chiefly those of the country, even in larger cities. Privies or water closets emptied into vaults or cesspools, and the waste material soaked into the soil or was hauled away as receptacles became filled. Kitchen waste was run into the street and left to evaporate or was led off by open drains to watercourses. Ditches provided for this purpose often carried urine and fecal matter as well as house slop, because privy facilities were often hopelessly inadequate in the congested districts of cities. A Cincinnati board of health report of 1865 told of a two-story tenement which housed 102 people for whom only one privy had been provided. When a municipal department of sewers was created in New York in 1849, only 70 miles of sewers had been built. Eight years later the mileage had grown to 158 for 500 miles of city streets, still leaving three-fourths of the city, including most of the slum areas, without facilities.

Inadequate sanitation, a laissez-faire governmental tradition which made measures of public control difficult, and erroneous beliefs about the causes of disease contributed to one of the most serious problems facing the nineteenth-century urban dweller—epidemic. Diseases, particularly those spread through water contamination, flourished in the congested districts of cities; outbreaks of typhoid, dysentery, and typhus were continual. In addition, there was the most dreaded plague of all—cholera—which struck the United States with force in 1832, 1849, and 1866. Cholera becomes epidemic largely through water contamination, but neither its cause nor etiology was known at the time. The disease was particularly terrifying, with symptoms comparable to those of arsenic poisoning. Its spectacular presence led city dwellers to question the fundamental character of American society. Initially, cholera was interpreted as a scourge of God, a punishment for national sins, which would strike those who were filthy, intemperate, and immoral. Accordingly, many spokesmen of the urban upper classes accepted as natural its depredations among immigrants in congested slums. John Pintard, the aristocratic founder of the New York Historical Society, reflected the views of his segment of society when he wrote to his daughter that the 1832 epidemic was "exclusively confined to the lower classes of intemperate dissolute & filthy people huddled together like swine in their polluted habitations." He argued that the epidemic could not be coped with; it would simply have to run its course. "Those sickened must be cured or die off, & being chiefly of the very scum of the city, the quicker the dispatch the sooner the malady will cease."

Not until 1883 was the micro-organism that caused cholera isolated; until that time there was debate over the nature of the disease and how it was transmitted. But by the time of the 1866 epidemic, the social and moralistic explanations of the disease that had earlier been common were no longer generally accepted. It was recognized that the disease was specific and contagious, that it struck both rich and poor, both moral and immoral. New York's success in checking the epidemic through a vigorous program of sanitation reinforced the conviction that cholera could be prevented through public-health measures and that communities had the duty to make this effort. The Metropolitan Board of Health organized in response to the epidemic had power to deal with problems of quarantine and urban sanitation. It instituted systematic street cleaning, the removal of 160,000 tons of manure from vacant lots, control of butchering and tanning in residential areas, disinfection of privies, and the burning of personal belongings of cholera victims. The Board's success led within a few years to the establishment of similar agencies in other large American cities and marked a beginning stage of the modern urban public-health movement.

An equally serious plague that struck the early American city was yellow fever, a virus disease transmitted by a variety of mosquito. Although its cause was not directly related to the unsanitary conditions of cities as was the case with cholera, fetid pools of water to be found within most cities did provide excellent breeding places for the disease-carrying insect. Those who argued, as many did, that yellow fever was the result of locally created miasmas urged the necessity of cleaning up the cities. Although their explanation was wrong, their program when adopted helped to check the spread of the disease. Accordingly, yellow fever was controlled to some extent long before its etiology was established in the twentieth century.

Yellow fever appeared frequently in the eighteenth-century American towns; it struck Philadelphia, then America's largest city, with unusual intensity in 1793. Over 4,000 deaths, a figure which represented almost 10 per cent of the city's population, were attributed to the disease. Business and government in what was then the national capital came to a halt as over half the residents fled to the countryside. A Philadelphia citizens' group reflected the concern about urban life that epidemics evoked, when it observed that "if the fever shall become an annual visitant, our cities must be abandoned, commerce will desert our coasts, and we, the citizens of this great metropolis, shall all of us, suffer much distress, and a great proportion of us be reduced to absolute ruin." Other cities faced the dreaded plague before the decade was over—Baltimore and New Haven in 1794, New York, Baltimore, and Norfolk in 1795. The 1798 Philadelphia epidemic was nearly as serious as that of five years earlier; New York with 2,000 deaths was hit again as were Boston and seven smaller port cities. In 1799 yellow fever continued its ravages of the decade with visitations to Philadelphia, New York, and Boston.

For reasons not clearly known, yellow fever generally disappeared from northern cities after 1825. Sanitation measures had some effect, but changing trade patterns with the West Indies and changing weather patterns may also have contributed to this outcome. Yellow fever continued to be one of the serious problems of the South. A major epidemic struck New Orleans in 1847, leaving over 2,000 dead. This attack, though, hardly compared with the epidemic five years later when, during one hot week in late August, yellow fever claimed 1,365 victims in the city, and for the whole summer the death toll stood at 8,000.

During the early nineteenth century such endemic diseases as malaria and consumption killed many more city dwellers than yellow fever and cholera. But it was the presence of plague that produced speculation about the nature of the American urban environment and contributed to efforts to change it. Although spokesmen for contagion always remained vocal, the view that decaying filth and the resultant miasma in the atmosphere caused epidemics gained ground in medical thinking toward the middle of the century.

Mortality statistics, which for the first time had begun to be systematically compiled, lent support to the view that the rising death rate might be simply the result of urban congestion. In New York City, for example, the crude death rate rose from one death per 46.5 persons in 1810 to one in 29 in 1859. The rate there showed a particularly significant rise in the decade from 1845 through 1854. Other large cities demonstrated a similar alarming tendency. Awareness of the unhealthiness of the city contributed to the view that community energies had to be directed toward alleviating the conditions that caused squalor, overcrowding, and decay. This conviction often rested on an unsound environmentalist theory of disease, but it still led to programs that improved the health of cities and the quality of the life to be lived in them. The New Orleans Board of Health, arguing unsuccessfully for enlarged power in 1849, expressed the sentiment that cities were here to stay and that their problems would have to be met through community action. "If large cities have been denominated the 'graves of mankind,' " its report declared, "it has been with too much reason, both reason and calculation sanction it, but still they should not be unnecessarily so; it is perfectly apparent in this investigating age, what has made them so, and that they proceed from causes that are in a great measure removable. Were there not great social and intellectual advantages from them (as well as pecuniary) men would not willingly, with the knowledge of these facts, thus multiply the sources of their own mortality, by congregating together, and it is well known that the population of many cities is maintained by immigration alone; but it is a poor compliment to an intelligent, rich and free people, that the love of thrift is stronger than all the numberless enjoyments which health produces."

In the 1830s George Templeton Strong, an aristocratic New York lawyer whose magnificent diary records the rise of a metropolis, accepted the views of his class that the poor became ill because of their moral derelictions. Yet, reflecting a general change in attitude among the urban elite, Strong, by the time of the 1866 cholera epidemic, was willing to argue that the whole community was responsible for the presence of the disease through allowing "poisonous rookeries" to exist in New York. "It is shameful," he wrote, "that men, women, and children should be permitted to live in such holes as thousands of them occupy this night in the city." The change of attitude among the urban upper classes not only contributed to the institution of public-health programs but also led to more general efforts to make cities livable for all classes.

As cities grew rapidly in the nineteenth century, there were also changes in community attitudes toward the long-standing urban problem of poverty. Colonial cities had established relief programs in accord with the British poor-law tradition that there were deserving poor in all times and places and that their assistance was a responsibility of local government. Christian humanitarianism had dictated also that the individual should give alms to the poor. But under the impact of extensive migration into cities beginning in the 1790s these attitudes hardened, and there was increasing emphasis on the Puritan view that poverty was the result of individual moral failing. John K. Alexander has labeled late nineteenth-century Philadelphia the "City of Brotherly Fear" because of the divisiveness that arose from concern about the growth of a "dangerous" class of "indigent" and "vicious" poor. A report of an 1809 investigation by the New York Humane Society into the "sources of vice and misery" in New York City nowhere mentioned economic causes. "By a just and inflexible law of Providence," the report declared, "misery is ordained to be the companion and the punishment of vice." The New York Society for the Prevention of Pauperism, which functioned between 1817 and 1823, emphasized in its report of 1819 the need for active programs of character-building and moral reform. Pauperism became a term used to describe the kind of poverty that resulted from individual dereliction and moral failure. It could be eliminated, the report argued, only "by inculcating religion, morality, sobriety, and industry, and by diffusing useful knowledge among the indigent and laboring people."

The rise of a distinct class of poor in the eastern cities was often attributed to immigration; European nations were accused of exporting their problems to the New World and destroying the classless paradise. The *New England Magazine* in an 1834 article found the Irish who came in gangs responsible for the growing urban pauperism. "The consequence is, that they almost invariably continue gregarious, and will not assimilate with the rest of the inhabitants. They do not dispose themselves over our western savannahs, or fell the broad forests which stretch between us and the Pacific, but they nest together in thickly-settled places, and constitute, with some praiseworthy exceptions, the most corrupt, the most debased, and the most brutally ignorant portion of the population of large cities." Philip Hone, a former mayor of New York City and a long-time civic leader, expressed a customary view of the problem in relationship to urban society. "Our good city of New York," he recorded in his diary in 1847, "has already arrived at the state of society to be found in the large cities of Europe; overburdened with population, and where the two extremes of costly luxury in living, expensive establishments, and improvident waste are presented in daily and hourly contrast with squalid misery and hopeless destitution. The state of things has been hastened in our case by the constant stream of European paupers arriving upon the shores of this land of promise. . . . If we had none but our own poor to take care of, we should get along tolerably well; we could find employment for them, and individual charity, aiding the public institutions, might save us from the sights of woe with which we are assailed in the streets, and the pressing applications which beset us in the retirement of our own houses." The presence of large numbers of newly arrived immigrants in American cities was a principal cause of the growth of a strong, organized anti-foreign movement throughout the country in the depression period of 1837–1843. The nativist Know-Nothing Party, which became important in the 1850s, directed much of its energy against the European immigrant who remained in the eastern city.

Although poverty might be considered the result of individual failing, particularly of the immigrant, the problem did exist and it was necessary for city leaders to try to deal with it in some fashion. The ideas and policies of Thomas Chalmers, a minister in Glasgow, Scotland who worked against the policy of providing outdoor relief to the able-bodied, influenced the character of American programs. The New York Society for the Prevention of Pauperism was concerned with providing institutional relief, as were similar agencies organized in Boston and Philadelphia.

The approach adopted by these early agencies is illustrated in the Baltimore experiment. In 1820, seventy-two city leaders, who had felt the pressure of heavy contributions to private charities during the hard times following the Panic of 1819, organized the Baltimore Society for the Prevention of Pauperism. The organization isolated the four "most obstrusive causes of pauperism" —excessive drinking, lotteries, houses of prostitution, and the types of charitable institutions that fostered the notion that something could be gotten for nothing. To counteract these forces, the Sociey emphasized the necessity for moral reform—to be achieved mainly by removing temptation from the citizenry. The Society's attempt to serve as a "moral police" for the city and to restrict the liquor traffic aroused opposition. Its opponents denounced a system designed to erect an "inquisitorial power" in Baltimore, terming the Society a "foundation of a fanatic and gloomy despotism." Answering these charges, a leader of the Society reaffirmed the individualistic ethic that influenced so much of the nineteenth-century program to deal with urban poverty. "In this country," he wrote, "the sober and able-bodied, if industriously disposed, cannot long want employment. They cannot, but by their own folly and vices, long remain indigent. Correct these vices, whether they are cherished by the bagnio or grog-shop, and you will prevent the consequent evils." Recovery from the depression, which had altogether been ignored as a cause of distress, ended the activities of the Baltimore society. But the point of view it had expressed continued to be influential; much of the justification for the temperance crusade that swept over the country in the years after 1825, for example, rested on its principles.

The official statements justifying early nineteenth-century poverty programs emphasized a concept of moral police as a means of social order. But in practice many of the people who worked in the slums—those in New York in the 1820s, for example—were quite practical in their approach, emphasizing such programs as the organization of schools, churches, savings banks, and asylums. Moreover, many religious-minded poverty reformers gradually changed their minds about the sources of urban pauperism. Joseph Tuckerman supplies the most striking example. His "ministry at large," a kind of city mission for the poor organized in the period of depression following the Panic of 1819, was based on the principle that the answer to urban pauperism lay in individual spiritual regeneration. But as a result of his investigations of the poor in their homes and his growing awareness of their everyday problems, Tuckerman became interested in a great many practical programs that involved wages, housing, education, and the delinquency of children. Although he never abandoned an individualistic explanation of poverty, he argued that the community had collective responsibilities to the poor and that to some extent at least these obligations could be met only through legislation. His experiments in defining categories of the poor and in coordinating charitable programs won him a reputation on both sides of the Atlantic as a pioneer of philanthropy.

Many of Tuckerman's views of scientific philanthropy were in accord with a new approach toward social problems that evolved in the Jacksonian period—the "discovery of asylum," as David Rothman has termed it. The flourishing of a movement to found such institutions as penitentiaries, insane asylums, reform schools, and almshouses was based on the secular outlook that the discipline and order of an institution, managed according to the best scientific principles, could restore, train, or rehabilitate a wayward individual. Tuckerman was active in organizing Massachusetts' almshouse program. In a report on the matter, he argued that the "well ordered" and "well regulated" almshouse would provide the sense of discipline necessary for an individual to rise from pauperism.

Another leading charity worker of the early nineteenth century, Robert M. Hartley, who was responsible for the organization of the New York Association for Improving the Condition of the Poor in 1843, underwent changes of viewpoint comparably to Tuckerman. Beginning as a deeply religious tract-distributor and temperance worker, Hartley became convinced that concern with the material welfare of the poor would have to accompany concern with their spiritual welfare. As secretary of the Association for over thirty years, he worked for the coordination of independent charities and pioneered housing reform. But like Tuckerman he remained an intensely religious man with a firm belief in pietism and the conviction that pauperism was evidence of one's moral state. Louis M. Pease, a leader in New York's Five Points House of Industry, recognized early that before the poor could be expected to profit from reading tracts or listening to lectures on morality, it was necessary to provide them with regular jobs. Increasing community awareness of a collective responsibility to the poor led to a more efficient organization of private charities and the passage of legislation providing an institutional base for governmental relief. In addition, some measure of protection was provided to European immigrants who had begun to arrive at America's shores in great numbers in the 1830s.

The New York Association led by Hartley made clear in its annual report of 1846 that if poverty in the city was to be reduced and the morals of the poor improved, tenement reform was essential, for improvement of environmental conditions lay "at the basis of other reforms." But this emphasis on practical programs aimed at changing social conditions and alleviating specific abuses did not mean the abandonment of earlier principles. Environmentalism and moralism existed side by side in the pronouncements of the same agency and in the justifications of the same man. The reformers moved toward practical programs, but they worked within a Christian tradition; Carroll Smith Rosenberg has found in the social welfare movement of this era "a peculiar mixture of pragmatism, moral self-assurance, and pious commitment," "a very American and not completely ignoble compound." Well into the twentieth century, after social welfare was thoroughly secularized and professionalized, leaders of public and private charitable enterprises would still speak of their task as one of regeneration of the sinful individual.

The United States has traditionally been thought of as a refuge for Europe's downtrodden and oppressed who were welcomed and immediately launched out on a better life. To a considerable extent, this view represents a false social myth. The lot of the individual immigrant who came to American cities in the early nineteenth century was a particularly hard one. If he survived the voyage with its dangers of typhus, dysentery, and malnutrition, he faced exploitation on his arrival at an eastern port from a host of sharp operators —bond brokers, runners for forwarding companies, and boarding-house owners and agents. New York, where a high proportion of immigrants entered the United States, was a rapidly growing city in the 1830s. Immigrants could find employment in the burgeoning factories of lower Manhattan Island, and many of them remained in the city. Long and narrow Manhattan Island was not geographically suitable for the kind of rapid growth it experienced. Land values jumped, and considerable overcrowding took place early at the island's lower end. Those who could afford to moved northward. Houses were converted to tenements, and the profits made in this fashion stimulated the building of new tenements. Front and rear buildings on the same lot created an intricate array of dark foul courts and alleys in several sections of the city. The intense housing shortage caused basements, attics, and lofts to be rented. As a measure of the resulting congestion, the density of the seven lower wards of Manhattan increased from 94.5 to 163.5 persons per acre in the period from 1820 to 1850. In 1843, a survey found 7,196 people living underground in New York. Within seven years, as immigration expanded during the decade, the cellar-dwelling population of the city had increased to 29,000. By the time of the Civil War the urban slum had decisively destroyed the open character of New York and other eastern cities. Long before Jacob Riis at the turn of the century dramatized to the nation how the other half lives, housing reform had become a preoccupation of the urban reformer.

The problem of housing congestion was perhaps felt most acutely in New York, but immigrants who arrived in Boston, particularly the Irish fleeing starvation during the potato famine of the 1840s, faced the same general problems of overcrowding and disease. And in some ways, the Boston immigrant was worse off than his New York counterpart. There were fewer opportunities for work in manufacturing in Boston, and the city was more culturally self-contained than New York. The Boston immigrant became aware on every side of a hostile environment; in the period before the Civil War acute ethnic and class tensions developed in the city.

Rapid urbanization did not lead to the creation of permanent stable communities within cities. Recent scholarship, particularly Peter R. Knights's study of Boston, has suggested an incredible amount of movement and rapid turnover of population going on in larger cities in the early nineteenth century. Contemporary observers were aware of this, although they probably underestimated its extent; traveler after traveler described May First, the traditional moving day in New York, as a day of fantastic congestion. Knights's figures demonstrate that 30 to 40 per cent of Boston dwellers in the 1840s changed their residence each year, and that 25 per cent of the total population passed in and out of the city each year. In any of the three decades after 1830, at least two to six times as many families passed through the city as lived there at the start of any decade. Put another way, every other year or so up to one-half of the population may have "disappeared," to be replaced by the newly born or in-migrants. This "motion" was characteristic even of day-to-day life. On one day in September 1851, a traffic count from 6:30 A.M. to 7:30 P.M. recorded over forty-one thousand people entering the city and over forty-two thousand leaving. Since the city's population was 145,000, about one-third of this total entered and one-third, an overlapping group in all likelihood, left. In short, flux and motion, rather than the permanence and stability that one might assume, seem to characterize the pattern of nineteenth-century urban life.

One of the more serious results of expanding immigration in the early nineteenth century was the continuing poverty of immigrants who remained in the cities. From the beginning a highly disproportionate share of paupers was to be found among the foreign-born. In 1835, for example, there were 4,786 native-born paupers and 5,303 foreign-born in the almshouses of New York, Philadelphia, Boston, and Baltimore. New York City in 1837 was spending $279,999 annually for the support of its poor, three-fifths of whom was foreign-born. The rising cost of living after mid-century intensified the problem of the newcomer. In 1852 more than half those requiring public assistance in eastern cities were Irish and German. By 1860 fully 86 per cent of the paupers in New York were of foreign birth. A class of pauperized immigrants crowded together in slums in huge cities seemed to many to present a fundamental challenge to traditional American values. In the period after the Civil War, this was the feature of urban life that most concerned those who attacked the evil city as the principal threat to the American nation.

The city provided no haven for the foreign immigrant; free Negroes, particularly after the 1830s, found it an even more hostile place. As Leon Litwack has demonstrated, Negroes in the northern cities before the Civil War occupied the lowest level of the social structure and were subject to pervasive discriminatory practices: "educated in segregated schools, punished in segregated prisons, nursed in segregated hospitals, and buried in segregated cemeteries." But Negroes had an affinity for urban life, as Frederick Douglas the Negro leader observed in an 1853 letter to Harriet Beecher Stowe: "It is almost impossible to get colored men to go on the land. From some cause or other . . . colored people will congregate in large towns and cities; and they will endure any amount of hardship and privation rather than go into the country."

This urban legacy extended far back into the Colonial period. Originally Negro slaves were brought to cities, and until the eighteenth century, when large-scale slave labor was introduced into southern agriculture, they were concentrated in the Atlantic ports. The important early notables of the race—Crispus Attucks, the hero of the Boston Massacre; Benjamin Bannaker, the Washington planner; and Prince Hall, who founded the first Negro Masonic Lodge, for example—lived in cities and were identified with urban pursuits.

With the rapid urbanization of the nineteenth century, the percentage of Negro population in northern cities declined. Negro communities were relatively small, constituting about 1 to 3 per cent of the population in northern cities in 1860. In New York, for example, Negroes in 1790 constituted 10 per cent of the population; this percentage had fallen to 1.5 by 1860. Between 1840 and 1860 the total Negro population in New York declined from over sixteen thousand to about twelve and a-half thousand. By this latter date, Philadelphia had the largest Negro community, over twenty-two thousand, constituting 4 per cent of the city's population. At the same census, nine other northern cities had Negro communities of at least a thousand.

In the 1830s, Negroes in northern cities operated a number of small businesses and worked as barbers, brickmakers, cooks, stevedores, and servants. By the 1850s, however, the arrival of immigrants had forced them into almost exclusively menial occupations. Competition between ethnic groups and Negroes was a source of much of the violence and disorder that plagued the early nineteenth century. As Eric Lampard has observed, there is a measure of irony in the fact that the intellectual center of America, Boston— the home of William Lloyd Garrison's abolitionist journal the *Liberator* and of the great anti-slavery leaders, William Ellery Channing and Wendell Phillips —should early force the city's Negroes to the bottom of urban society. In 1846, Jesse Chickering, an early statistician and student of Boston's population, noted reasons for the slow growth of the city's Negro population and dispassionately observed: "A prejudice has existed in the community, and still exists against them on account of their color, and on account of their being the descendants of slaves. They cannot obtain employment on equal terms with the whites, and wherever they go a sneer is passed upon them, as if this sportive inhumanity were an act of merit. . . . Thus, though their legal rights are the same as those of whites, their condition is one of degradation and dependence. . . ."

Rapid urbanization and the instability that existed in vast areas of many cities led to disorder and a breakdown in fundamental municipal services. From the early Colonial period, American cities had experienced the ordinary amount of lawlessness and immorality associated with organized communities anywhere. But until the nineteenth century, they had largely been spared the criminal districts and criminal gangs characteristic of European cities. By the 1840s, however, leaders in New York and elsewhere were concerned about the appearance of both phenomena. Particularly noted were the gangs of youthful criminals, who made war on each other and terrorized neighborhoods. Philadelphia had its Buffaloes, Blood Tubs, Rugs, and Copper Heads; Baltimore its Stringers; New York its Bowery Boys, Plug-Uglies, Highbinders, Swipers, and Dead Rabbits. The Crawfish Boys of Cincinnati indicated that western cities could not claim exemption from the problem. By 1849 juvenile crime had become so serious that New York's chief of police devoted his entire report for that year to the subject. In preaching a sermon on this report, Thomas L. Harris reflected the general point of view. "Of the young children in the denser part of our city," he lamented, "one in ten is doomed to a life of inevitable vice, misery and degradation, doomed to be ground to powder in the vortex of infamy and shame." Saving the children of the city became a major aim of such urban reformers as Charles Loring Brace, who organized the Children's Aid Society in 1853 and devoted the better part of his life to an essentially futile effort to move the less fortunate children of the city to foster homes in the West.

As to be expected, many people blamed the immigrant for the rising crime rate in the cities. John Pintard in 1828 wrote to his daughter that "as long as we are overwhelmed with Irish emigrants, so long will the evil abound." Although the immigrant in poorer areas of cities was often arrested for inconsequential crimes that might be ignored elsewhere, there is little doubt that a life of desperation and the ready availability of alcohol contributed to a high rate of serious crime among immigrants, particularly among the Irish. In New York in 1859, for example, only 23 per cent of the people arrested were native Americans and 55 per cent were born in Ireland. Most of the persons committed to the city prison in New York City during the nine-year period from 1850 to 1858 were immigrants, and seven-eighths of the total were recorded as "intemperate." In 1860, when just over half of the population of the city was foreign-born, about 80 per cent of the 58,067 convicted of crime during the year ending July 1 were born in Europe.

The rising crime rate and particularly the fear of outbreaks of disorder and violence forced eastern cities to adopt more formal systems of police. Until mid-century, even larger cities used the type of law enforcement that had existed since colonial days—a combination of day policemen and night watchmen, hired part-time, often from the ranks of the unemployed, with little provided in the way of central organization, training, or discipline in service. The system was generally inadequate. When Josiah Quincy became mayor of Boston in 1823, he extolled the law-abiding character of the city of 45,000. But as in other eastern cities, there was little concern with enforcing liquor-licensing or laws relating to crimes like drunkenness and assault. Night watches refused to enter some of the more dangerous neighborhoods of the city. Fire companies looted and battled other companies for spoils. During a week of disorder in the summer of 1825, Quincy had to take charge of a posse to restore order, although his ordinary course of action, during other disturbances of his Administration, was simply to allow mob action to run its course. In several cities the wearing of uniforms was successfully resisted for years by policemen, who argued that the uniform was a badge of European servitude. Because they were not identifiable, policemen often fled serious disturbances.

Change in this informal system came first in New York City. A law enacted in May of 1844 abolished the night watchman and other duplicating law enforcement officials. Substituted for this was a single body of police of 800 men. The politically controlled new force provided little significant reform until it was modified in 1853 by the establishment of a board of police commissioners. Over bitter opposition the commissioners required the wearing of a uniform consisting of a blue swallow-tailed coat with large buttons, gray pantaloons, and a blue cap labeled with the officer's number. Philadelphia established a central system of police in 1850, although uniforms were not required until 1860. Boston abolished its dual system of watch and police in 1854 and organized a department of 250 full-time officers. A Baltimore force was organized in 1857 with 350 uniformed policemen. With the creation of the metropolitan police district of New York in 1857, state influence began to be extended over large city police forces through state police boards.

Similarly in the provision of such other municipal services as water, fire protection, and streets, cities moved from casual, semi-private systems inherited from an era when municipalities were villages to formal programs that were entirely a part of government. In fire protection, for example, the resistance of volunteer Cincinnati firemen to the introduction of steam fire-engines led to the organization in 1853 of one of the first paid municipal fire-fighting forces in the United States. Chicago and other western cities followed the example almost immediately, and within a few years Boston, New York, and Philadelphia had adopted the method.

Philadelphia was the pioneer in the establishment of a municipal water system. The publicly owned Centre Square Water Works, designed by the brilliant architect and engineer Benjamin Latrobe and completed in 1801, was long a source of civic pride. But the supply of water it provided was often undependable until the completion of the Fairmount Water Works in 1822. The shoddy private system of the Manhattan Company furnished water to New York from 1799 until 1835, when an ambitious public system was begun which brought water by a closed aqueduct from the Croton Reservoir forty miles to the north. Completed in 1842 at a cost of twelve million dollars, the system had to be radically enlarged in 1858 because of the great growth in the population of the city. Most cities underwent a similar pattern of development: wells and springs to privately owned systems to public ones. By 1861 there were eighty private and sixty-eight public systems in operation throughout the country.

Fear of epidemic disease and the realization that something could be done to combat it was perhaps the most important influence modifying the extreme individualism of early nineteenth-century American cities. Also important, however, in producing changed attitudes toward centralized authority, an urban bureaucracy, and the professional civil servant was fear of the mob brought on by frequent civil disorders and rioting. Citizens of early nineteenth-century cities, for example, greatly admired the colorful and often heroic private fire companies, but the struggles among them eventually got so far out of hand that municipal control of professional fire fighters gradually became an established principle. Similarly, civil disturbances directly led to the expansion of police services. By the latter part of the nineteenth century, urban communities had generally abandoned the notion that city dwellers were responsible under all but extreme circumstances for protecting their own life, safety, and property.

Concern with public safety resulted particularly from a crisis of law and order during the period 1840–1860, which one authority asserts "may have been the era of the greatest urban violence that America has ever experienced." Much of this disorder stemmed from forces that had no specific relationship to cities and their growth. National depressions, the rise of abolitionism, and the emergence of catholicism were not of course an outgrowth of urbanization. Still, rioting on these matters did occur in urban locales; much of the disorder in cities stemmed from ethnic and racial tensions and frictions that were a part of urban life. Any accounting of the total number of serious disturbances in cities in this period would produce a voluminous study. The great Protestant Crusade, to use Ray Allen Billington's term, led to riots "in every American city" in the 1840s and 1850s. Initially, these were anti-Catholic and anti-Irish disturbances. In the latter part of the period, they became more broadly nativist, particularly in such southern cities as New Orleans and Louisville where, in the latter, at least twenty-one were killed and several hundred wounded in an especially bloody disturbance in 1855. Between 1832 and 1849 Philadelphia had five anti-Negro riots; Cincinnati had such disturbances in 1829, 1841, and 1862. In general, these were initiated by whites against Negroes and involved attacks on Negro residential areas of the cities.

As is often the case when considering aspects and dimensions of urban life in America, New York faced this problem of civil disorder in particularly aggravated form. The diarists and commentators on nineteenth-century New York life were frequently alarmed by the degree of disorder prevailing in the city, and Joel Tyler Headley's contemporary 1873 account of the "great riots" in the city between 1712 and 1873 is a chronicle that leaves an impression of continual violence. Moreover, New York was the site of the most serious civil disorder in our history, the Draft Riots of 1863 which, through the work of Adrian Cook, is one of the few riots in American history to receive scrupulous and objective investigation.

The availability of Cook's splendid case study is fortunate, for the historiography of urban violence at this point is deficient and permits only the most tentative and uncertain conclusions. For a long time and for a variety of reasons, American historians tended to ignore the presence of violence in our past. When they turned to the subject in the 1960s, contemporary concerns led to superficial interpretations that emphasized only class and race conflict as the explanation of serious domestic disorder. As Cook demonstrates in a survey of sixteen major disturbances in New York other than the Draft Riots, no simple explanation of historical urban violence is possible. In the period from 1834 to 1874, there was some serious disturbance every summer weekend, and many of these erupted into full-scale riots: hungry people rioted because of food shortages, Irish Catholics fought Irish Protestants, Negroes attacked whites and, more frequently whites attacked Negroes, anti-abolitionists attacked abolitionists, stevedores fought for higher wages, one gang of drunks fought another gang of drunks. In 1853, in a strange example of crowd psychology, 3,000 people attacked a surgeon's apothecary shop when the rumor spread that there were human bones in the cellar. The Draft Riots of 1863, which lasted for three days in July, started with an attack on the office of the local provost marshal of the Army by a young, largely Irish crowd opposed to the conscription laws. The police force, which was badly disorganized because of the opposition to the reorganization of 1857, was unable to quell the disturbance, and the riot turned into an attack on the Negro areas of the cities. Finally on the fourth day, Federal troops on their way back from the Battle of Gettysburg were able to restore order to the city.

These are the bare bones of the matter, but, as Cook demonstrates, dramatic events of this magnitude create an almost immediate mythology. Initial estimates of the dead ranged from over 1,100 to nearly 1,500, and these figures were later enlarged and accepted by subsequent historians. A recent urban history, for example, offers an estimate of 2,000 killed and 8,000 wounded, which, as the author observes, would be equivalent to the military losses of the battles of Bull Run or Shiloh. Through the most scrupulous examination of sources, Cook demonstrates that actually from 105 to 119 people were killed in the riot, the variation depending on what incidental deaths are included. Thirty-five soldiers and thirty-two policemen were seriously injured; thirty-eight soldiers and seventy-three policemen were slightly wounded. The figure of 128 civilian wounded might not include a few slightly wounded. Moreover, the size of the rioting mobs was drastically smaller than the contemporary estimates of thousands; probably no more than three hundred street fighters were involved in any one incident during the disturbance, and most of the roving bands numbered only twenty to fifty people. The author also demonstrates that most people involved in the riot were not motivated by the ideological or political issues emphasized by historians. "The Draft Riots were fundamentally an insurrection of anarchy," he writes, "an outburst against any kind of governmental control by the people near the bottom of society. The temporary powerlessness of the authorities released a flood of violence and resentment that was usually kept well repressed. As the hours went by, the riot itself created a devil-may-care mood of euphoria that led to more rioting. A wild melange of motives drove the mob on." Some of the rioters were generally opposed to the war and to the draft. Some took advantage of the disorder to settle old grudges. Many drunks joined in. Some took part simply to loot: "I took said property because every one else took it," one rioter testified. As other historians have pointed out, deep-rooted hatred of Negroes did influence many rioters, particularly in the form of a kind of sexual vigilantism which manifested itself in attacks on Negroes married to whites, against houses of prostitution catering to Negroes, and finally against houses of prostitution in general. Despite the prevalence of this sentiment, it is impossible however to find unity of purpose or concerted leadership in this dramatic example of mob action in America.

Exaggerations aside, the Draft Riots of 1863 did constitute a serious insurrection that intensified fears of revolution supported by the "dangerous classes" of the cities. In his *Democracy in America* of 1839, Alexis de Tocqueville, with his peculiar gift for getting under the surface of American society, had seen the growth of Negro and immigrant population in cities and the subsequent domestic disorder "as a real danger which threatens the future security of the democratic republics of the New World"; and he predicted that they would "perish from this circumstance, unless the Government succeeds in creating an armed force, which, while it remains under the control of the majority of the nation, will be independent of the town population, and able to repress its excesses." The Draft Riots of 1863 seemed to indicate the reality of this fear, but thereafter neither revolution nor the serious threat of it occurred in the cities. It is true that there were battles in cities well into the latter part of the century, but these were mainly struggles between workers and management, fought near places of employment. There are a number of explanations for the decline in urban violence. In the first place, it is doubtful, despite the fears expressed at the time, that any disturbance had really been informed by a deep-seated revolutionary purpose that might have sustained further such efforts. Second, the general state of disorder that had frequently led to riots of various kinds gradually tended to disappear, primarily as a result of the stability induced by the emergence of the boss-machine system and the slow establishment of professional police and other municipal services. Third, for all the everyday chaos and mobility in cities, an older sense of community had never disappeared, and this manifested itself in an enlarged sense of responsibility for the provision of community services and the support of various social, cultural, and recreational enterprises in the cities. The establishment of effective municipal government in the late nineteenth century was further evidence of a persistent cohesiveness. The next significant challenge to this essential urban unity would come many years later with the rise of the large Negro urban communities of the twentieth century. And then, once again, there would be violence in the cities.

CHAPTER

# 5

# The Urban Milieu: Culture, 1800–1865

THE NINETEENTH-CENTURY urban environment was often conceived as a series of problems and of efforts to resolve them. But at the same time it could be viewed as the locale in which American culture was taking root and maturing. The city was the home of the theater, the museum, and the art gallery, a fact recognized by early nineteenth-century city leaders. In all sections of the country, including the "agrarian" South and the "frontier" West, urbanism was partly defined as a process of furnishing cultural amenities. When spokesmen of western and southern cities attempted to describe the good city, they did not declare cultural independence from Europe or the East. On the contrary, they considered their cities progressing to the extent that they could furnish the kind of theater, art, and high society to be found elsewhere in the world. Henry McMurtrie, who wrote one of the first important books on a western city, described frontier Louisville in 1819 as a city proud of its cultural refinement. "There is a circle, small 'tis true," he wrote, "but within whose magic abounds every pleasure that wealth, regulated by taste, can produce, or urbanity bestow. There, the 'red-heel' of Versailles may imagine himself in the emporium of fashion, and whilst leading beauty through the mazes of the dance, forget that he is in the wilds of America." A generation later on another frontier, Robert T. Van Horn argued that the booming "young metropolis" of Kansas City could not become a real city until it had a permanent theater and other cultural institutions.

In all parts of the country, patronage of the arts was looked upon as a responsibility of the urban upper classes. During the latter part of the eighteenth century, for example, it was the support of the rich and fashionable that overcame the opposition of intellectuals and clergy to the theater as an immoral institution. The presentation of musical performances, particularly opera, which by the 1850s had become a regular feature of the social season in New York, Boston, Philadelphia, New Orleans, and Chicago, was also supported as part of an effort to consolidate the position of the upper classes in the cities. As early as 1807, John Lambert in writing of New York noted the association between rapid economic expansion, the accumulation of wealth, and an interest in art, music, and learning. This enthusiasm had tended to remedy the "deficiency of the polite and liberal accomplishments among both sexes in the United States." "The riches that have flowed into the city, for the last twenty years," he continued, "have brought with them a taste for the refinements of a polished society; and though the inhabitants cannot yet boast of having reached the standard of European perfection, they are not wanting in the solid and rational parts of education; nor in many of those accomplishments which ornament and embellish private life."

The years from 1820 to 1850 have often been portrayed as a period of growing equality in America, as the era of Jacksonian Democracy, when aristocratic pretensions were broken down and when in the name of egalitarianism, anti-intellectual and anti-artistic values became embedded in American culture. Whether or not this was true of society as a whole is debatable. It was not true in large American cities. In places such as New York, Boston, and Philadelphia, where elite groups and class structures have been studied systematically, there was increasing concentration of wealth in the hands of the few; large fortunes were accumulated; powerful families maintained their positions through intermarriage; the extremes of wealth and poverty became greater than before; and built on the patronage of wealth, an aristocratic culture flourished.

As Edward Pessen has demonstrated, substantial fortunes of $100,000 were commonplace in New York in the ante-bellum years. This was a time when $1.50 a day would provide a room and four meals at the Astor House, which had one of the finest restaurants in the city, and $3,000 a year could provide a Philadelphia diarist "a comfortable house—servants, a good table—wine—a horse—books—'country quarters'—a plentiful wardrobe—the ability to exercise hospitality," and another $1,000, he said, would have enabled him to live as a truly rich man. The popularity of social clubs of restricted membership—both small, informal groups gathered to promote literary and artistic matters or for convivial association, and also large social clubs with formal constitutions and formal membership requirements—demonstrated a concern with legitimatizing upper-class status. Despite their ostensible educational aims, many of these clubs were primarily places where people of standing could get together for food, drink, and good company, as was the case with the Hone Club of New York, founded in 1838 and named after the great diarist of the city. At its meetings Hone indicated serious matters were dealt with quickly to be followed by a "quantity of unrestrained gaiety, unalloyed wit, irrepressible noise, and unsurpassable wine." Another observer commented that the club's "festivals were of the highest order of gustatory enjoyment—the appetite could ask no more—and a Devonshire Duke might have been astounded at the amplitude of entertainment." The larger clubs with formal cultural and community objectives also seemed often to have had primarily gregarious purposes. Pessen cites the example of the Philadelphia Club, which thirteen years after its founding set up a small library at the same time one of its members entertained his fellows by drinking a glass of wine while he stood on his head.

Social clubs and similar organizations provided means by which men of business could attempt to live in aristocratic style in a society which provided no formal recognition of aristocratic standing. But the group activities of the wealthy urban elites also involved a recognition of the responsibilities of a man of wealth; business in America was recognized as a calling with stature; the man of business was expected to accept special responsibilities to promote social and cultural enterprises in society. Nowhere was this sense of obligation stronger than in Boston where an elite group from early in the nineteenth century performed in accord with the higher standards of the Puritan ethic. Martin Green, in an original study of a much-studied place, argues that during the "flowering of New England" a vivid faith in the possibility of achieving a good community in accord with early ideals still existed in Boston. The affluent leaders of the city affirmed this belief and acted accordingly in their lives. Green agrees with the view of Edward Everett Hale, who later wrote of this period: "There was plenty of money and the rich men of Boston really meant that there should be a model and ideal city."

The Boston leaders were not concerned with establishing a culture based on equality. They believed instead in providing the means whereby a culture of quality would be available to the whole community. The founders of the Athenaeum, a library founded in 1807 and one of the first of these important cultural enterprises, endorsed the idea that, because men of wealth were not called upon in the United States to support national cultural enterprises through taxation, they were obligated to direct their efforts toward their city. Because fortunes in Boston were not on the magnitude of those accumulating in New York, the library was built on a large number of donations from within the business community. The enterprise was quickly successful; by 1819 the Athenaeum was only one of three libraries in the United States—the others were Harvard University Library and the City Library of Philadelphia— with over 10,000 books. Another similar enterprise in disseminating learning in the community was the Lowell Institute, founded in 1836. The Institute sponsored well-attended lectures on science, religion, and literature. Eight to ten thousand applications for tickets to a course were received. Before its second season, Benjamin Silliman's course in chemistry was so well regarded that a crowd, lined up for tickets, crushed in the windows of the place where they were being distributed—one of the more unusual incidents of nineteenth-century urban disorder. The idea of lectures spread, and a number of organizations sponsored them. In the 1837–1838 season, there were twenty-six courses in Boston with at least eight lectures, and the total attendance was about 13,000—in a city of 80,000. The standards of the lectures, particularly at the Institute, were high, and the fees paid to lecturers were larger than the salaries paid to any professor in the country. The national Chautauqua movement of the latter part of the nineteenth century represented an extension, and to an extent a debasement, of this Boston effort to bring culture and knowledge to the whole community.

The influx of Irish immigrants into Boston in the 1840s presented a serious challenge to the city's leaders. The almost immediate appearance of poverty, slums, and epidemics denied their theoretical conception of the good society. Moreover, the Irish formed a distinct community of their own, opposed to the elite's emphasis on education, secular reform, and particularly on English literature, which embodied values and traditions the Irish hated. Despite deterioration of the ideal of the harmonious, cultivated city, the institutions that had been founded for this purpose were maintained and expanded throughout the nineteenth century. But no uniform set of cultural standards prevailed in Boston or in other large cities; instead, as successive groups of immigrants arrived, several distinct cultural patterns took root and often flourished.

The leaders of early nineteenth-century Boston placed great emphasis on literature as an instrument for building the good community. Despite the belief that writers faced lack of support and encountered outright hostility in nineteenth-century America, in reality their patronage in the cities—notably in Boston and New York—enabled many writers to live off their writings and some to live very well. There was of course no typical income for a writer, but in one year Irving made $23,500 from writing; Cooper averaged $6,500 a year during the 1830s; and Longfellow got $3,000 for a single poem. The establishment of publishing houses in cities and an increase in the number and circulation of magazines, which generally were paying contributors by the 1840s, led to the founding of urban literary circles and to the eventual emergence of a national literature.

During the period in which Boston became a center of literature, New York succeeded Philadelphia as the center of American art. Again the patronage of the mercantile classes was vital to this development, although in much larger and more diverse New York there was not the close association between culture and community that prevailed in Boston. As Neil Harris has pointed out in his study of the artist in ante-bellum America, the professional and mercantile classes of New York "fought fiercely over their art collections" in the same spirit that they completed in the world of business. Businessmen in many cities got interested in art; New York had more of them, and this accounted in large part for New York's attraction for the painter. The popularity of gift books utilizing engravings, which brought wealth to engravers like Joseph A. Adams, who was paid $60,000 for the design for one work, stimulated an interest in paintings upon which engravings could be based. Many artists in New York became part of a brilliant circle that included such luminaries as the writers Cooper, Bryant, and Irving, the painters Thomas Cole and Asher B. Durand, the sculptor Horatio Greenough, and the dramatist William Dunlap. Although literature was still considered more consequential than painting, the Hudson River School of painters found a wide audience for their work. Their theme was nature; only a group of lesser artists who migrated to the United States from Europe portrayed the urban landscape to any extent. But stylized and elevated natural scenes, which viewed the country as both majestic and tranquil, had considerable appeal to people caught up in the hustle and bustle of the city. Painters, like the writers of the period, often fulminated against the monotony and oppressiveness of the city: Henry Inman, for example, "panted to live in the country, where I can be surrounded with something pleasanter to look upon than the everlasting brick walls of a city." Yet the realization of their art was dependent on the institutions of the city, and their lives were largely rooted there.

Theater was another institution of the city dependent in its beginnings on the patronage of wealth. In its early years it was expensive, and frankly maintained for the rich. Tocqueville, the most notable foreign visitor to Jacksonian America, observed that playhouses and plays had increased prodigiously but that very few Americans actually attended the theater. "People who spend every day in the week in making money," he wrote, "and Sunday in going to church, have nothing to invite the Muse of Comedy." There was, however, particularly in eastern cities a variety of popular entertainments patronized by all classes. In the early nineteenth century, for example, New Yorkers went to see Niblo's Columbian Gardens, which contained exotic plants, large transplanted trees, and colorful fountains; heard concerts or watched fireworks displays at Vauxhall Gardens; or visited several waxwork museums that featured biblical, historical, and patriotic exhibits. In a later period, curiosities of one kind and another—animal exhibits, experiments in mesmerism and lectures on phrenology, mechanical toys such as the automaton chess player and automaton Turk—drew substantial audiences in the cities.

More serious performers in the arts were also considered to some extent as curiosities, and as the "star" system developed, theater and music tended to become more popular among the middle and lower classes. Celebrities from Europe, some of them brought to America by the famous showman and promoter, P. T. Barnum, enjoyed financial success on their tours of the cities. The most famous of these, Jenny Lind—"the Swedish nightingale," "the angel of the stage"—earned $1,000 a performance at each of 150 highly successful appearances throughout the country in 1849–1850. Earlier, the dancer Fanny Elssler, "the divine Fanny," who came to the United States in 1840, received $6,390 for eleven nights in Philadelphia and by the time she reached New Orleans on her tour, was asking $1,000 a night. William Macready and Charles Kean, who played at New York's New Park Street Theater in 1830, Fanny Kemble the most popular actress of her day, and the Swedish violinist Ole Bull were other European performers who won the favor of American urban audiences. American actors like Edwin Booth and Edwin Forrest also established star reputations.

Conflict among supporters of rival actors was common, and one such conflict—indicating the diverse causes of urban violence—led to the Astor Place Riot of 1849, one of the more serious urban riots in nineteenth-century America. A quarrel between the American Forrest and the Englishman Macready, both tragedians and Shakespeareans, had been building for some time.

Forrest had become convinced in 1845 that Macready was deliberately undermining his career, and while he was abroad organized a group that hissed Macready in Edinburgh. Forrest, in a bitter mood because of the adultery of his wife with a fellow actor, kept up the quarrel when Macready toured the United States in 1848–1849. Macready was heckled in Philadelphia; his performance of Macbeth in New York had to be ended part way through when the audience bombarded the actors with rotten eggs, shoes, chairs, and other objects. Macready booked passage for home, but a group of New York leaders, including Melville and Irving, petitioned him to stay, and he agreed to another performance. After anti-English handbills had been circulated in the days prior to and throughout the day it was scheduled, an enormous crowd gathered outside the Astor Place theater. Despite the presence of militia and 325 policemen, things got out of hand. The crowd surged forward, a warning volley failed to turn it back, and troops were ordered to fire directly into the mob. The rioters were dispersed, and a protest meeting the next day was quickly broken up, ending the incident. Thirty-one people were killed and over a hundred wounded in the conflict inspired mainly by the anti-English sentiments prevailing among New York's Irish and other largely lower-class groups. In the years before the Astor Place Riot, anglophobia had resulted in numerous minor incidents of attack on actors suspected of or expressing anti-American sentiments.

In the early part of the century, interest in the theater was a dimension of urban experience not confined to any one section of the country. The popular Irish actor, Tyrone Power, who recorded his travel impressions in the years from 1833 to 1835, wrote of his enthusiastic audiences in Baltimore, Savannah, and New Orleans. Macready played a successful four weeks of Shakespeare in New Orleans shortly before the Astor Place Riot. Ellen Tree, Fanny Kemble, Jenny Lind, Fanny Elssler, and other European performers included the cities of the South and West on their American tours. In addition to these well-known performers, traveling companies and amateur theatrical groups enjoyed greater or lesser successes in larger communities in all parts of the country.

As part of a growing interest in theater in the early nineteenth century, playhouses became established urban landmarks. Because a theater cost $30,000 or more to build, it was only in the larger cities that adequate facilities could be supplied. A boom in building in the 1820s saw the erection of the Bowery, the Chatham, the Lafayette, and the New Park Street in New York; the Tremont in Boston, probably not the only American theater with a connecting brothel; and the New Chestnut Street and Arch Street in Philadelphia. New York's Park Theater, located opposite City Hall, had seats for 2,500; after its remodeling in 1834 it became a favorite of the social elite. In the 1830s the Broadway, with seats for 4,000, also opened, marking the beginning of the most famous theater district in the country. In this same period, civic leaders in such hinterland cities as St. Louis, Buffalo, and Mobile expressed considerable pride in the local playhouses. Cincinnati as early as 1820 had a theater seating 800.

That this theater did not always represent the "refinement" emphasized by western promoters was indicated by a poster from 1830, requesting patrons "not to crack nuts while the curtain was up" and "to avoid throwing shells and apple cores into the pit." Frances Trollope, the acerbic British visitor who lived for some time in Cincinnati, repeatedly complained that she was distracted by excessive spitting and the whiskey and onion smells that wafted about many theater patrons. Because of the relatively high upkeep and taxes, as well as the large fees paid to star performers, theaters closed frequently or their ownership changed hands, but from this time on they were to be an established feature of the urban scene.

By the 1850s civic pride demanded that cities not only support theaters but also art galleries, opera houses, and museums. Boston acquired a new music hall early in the decade. Philadelphia citizens subscribed to a new $220,000 opera house; Chicago obtained a structure that combined an opera house, art gallery, and studio building. Increasingly, as part of the fruition of an urban outlook, city leaders argued that the worth of a city could be measured by how well it provided such cultural institutions. Discussing the future of New Orleans, a local writer in 1846 reflected a typical viewpoint of the era when he argued that there could be no significant "moral advance" in New Orleans unless the city supported the necessary educational and cultural agencies. Without a university, a historical society, public libraries, public lectures, and a lyceum, he argued, New Orleans could never become a truly great city.

The flourishing movement for tax-supported city libraries in the 1850s supplied a good example of this rising urban spirit. Private literary clubs and learned societies had maintained semi-public reading rooms and atheneums since the Colonial period, but not until the 1820s was there organized effort to use taxes to establish free libraries open to all city inhabitants. It was several years before these efforts bore fruit. The Boston Public Library, which had been authorized in 1845, opened in 1854, and within a decade and a half had 100,000 volumes. The Astor Library in New York, made possible by a large bequest from John Jacob Astor, opened the same year, and the Peabody Library in Baltimore was established in 1857. Western cities as remote as Leavenworth, Kansas also shared in the enthusiasm. During the decade of the fifties, the number of public libraries in the country increased eightfold to over 1,000 and their volumes multiplied fivefold, reaching a total of nearly eight million. Reflective of another aspect of the transfer of eastern cultural institutions to the West, the Chicago Historical Society was organized in 1856. It soon had a collection of 11,000 books and began accumulating maps and manuscripts. Its holdings were proudly displayed to foreign travelers as an indication of an advancing American scholarship. The growth of a reading public established the bookstore as an urban institution. The Old Corner Bookshop of James T. Fields and William D. Ticknor in Boston was a famous gathering place for writers and intellectuals during the period of the New

England literary renaissance. By the 1850s, Chicago had three prospering book-stores, one of which advertised itself as the largest in the Midwest.

Many of these bookstores were also publishing ventures. James T. Fields, for example, made The Old Corner Bookshop into one of the most important publishing firms in America. Fields, born in 1817 in New Hampshire, went to work for The Old Corner when he was fourteen. Despite his lack of family connections, money, and education, he moved upward into the highest Boston cultural circles and became a nationally-known intellectual figure. He began the systematic publishing of British writers and published such notable Ameri-can authors as Whittier, Hawthorne, and Longfellow. Fields involved himself closely, both intellectually and socially, with this major group of New England writers; for example, he coerced and drove an often despondent and lethargic Hawthorne into becoming a first-rank American novelist. In the sense of the definition of a cultural center as a place where writers and readers interact through a publisher, "it was Fields," writes Martin Green, "more than anyone else who made Boston a cultural center." When Dickens toured America in 1867, Fields was his chief host, managing his reading in Boston and organizing his social activities. Dickens made over a million dollars on this tour, reflecting in part at least the growing support of arts and letters in the cities.

In spite of the view expressed by many writers that American culture ought to reflect democratic ideals, the cultural agencies of the city—the bookstore, the theater, the music hall, the fine restaurant—could for the most part be enjoyed only by the few. Nevertheless, these were basic to the meaning of the city. The urban impressions of a traveler to the city are shaped by these agencies, and it is through the accounts of scores of travelers that we gain insight into one part of the nineteenth-century urban experience. The city has always been a place where one could go to be entertained, to be educated, or to acquire something vaguely thought of as sophistication or polish. The latter was the case with Harriet and Maria Trumbull, young (seventeen and fifteen respectively), aristocratic daughters of the governor of Connecticut, whose letters recording their six-month "season in New York" in 1801 bring alive a distinctive aspect of upper-class urban life. From start to finish their days in the "great bustling city" were incredibly busy: sessions with their instructors in dancing, music, and drawing; a continual round of formal visits, mostly made on foot; buying clothes; visits to the theater (although these received little emphasis in their accounts to their somewhat disapproving mother); church; playing cards; being entertained. They express weariness at the pace of life and at the end the less exuberant Harriet records that they would be "heartily glad to get out of this great *hen coop* of the city" and back home. But there is always in their letters a spirit of tireless enthusiasm for aspects of the urban scene that they were experiencing, although these are sometimes couched in accents of fashionable boredom, as in Maria's account of January 8th:

Tuesday was the great day among the gay folks, in the morning I went to Mr. Sebors
—and after I returned did a thing which I never did before—and I was almost going
to say never intend to again, it was to have my hair dressed by a *hair dresser,* and
after he had done and I had paid him a *dollar*—it did not look half as well as it does
when I only curl it a little myself—I positively felt ashamed. I looked so like a witch
—and then it was so extravagant. . . . at length came the long expected evening—
and all in our best bibs and tuckers we set off for the Anacreontic concert—it was in
the city tavern, in a *monstrous* room—and there were upwards of six hundred people
all most elegantly and splendidly dressed and they to be sure did make a *fine show*
—we had every thing almost that was good to eat fruit nuts, and most elegant cake,
however I did not enjoy myself very much.

There is much that seems frivolous in the experience of upper- and middle-
class youth in the city. We often conceive of cities only as dark, somber places
where horrendous social problems well up and as sites where man abuses
man. A person of responsibility and sensibility, it is held, ought to address
himself to these matters. But frivolity and gaiety have also been a continuing
dimension of the urban scene and reflect the appealing diversity always to be
found in the city.

To the urban leader and spokesman of the nineteenth-century city, it was
often the presence of urban cultural amenities that made life worthwhile. The
career of George Templeton Strong supplies a case in point. Strong won a
measure of national attention for his work on the Sanitary Commission, the
relief agency of the Civil War, but in general he preferred to avoid public life,
and is by all odds most notable for his massive diary covering the years from
1835 to 1875, one of the great diaries in the history of western letters.
Although Strong was concerned with many other matters than the city in
which he lived, his diary supplies a vivid picture of life in New York and an
intelligent, cultivated man's reaction to it in a period during which New York
grew into one of the foremost cities of the world.

Strong was representative of an early nineteenth-century group of New
York merchants, bankers, lawyers, and men of affairs, who could make their
way in the world of business but still had time for the leisure of systematic
reading, literary discussion, and occasional writing. Many of this group, for
example, gathered together in the select circle of Lewis Gaylord Clark, publisher of the *Knickerbocker* magazine; Clark's "Table," in existence through
the 1840s and 1850s, constituted one of the notable elites in the history of
American cities.

Like most members of the upper classes who wrote about nineteenth-
century cities, Strong had little sympathy for the democratic forces in American
life. He found the social structure of New York natural and proper; he disliked
the horde of immigrants pouring into the city and often held them responsible
for the congestion and disease that had taken root in the districts they
inhabited. He preferred to stay away from the poorer sections of the city.

Such a ride uptown! [he wrote on June 19, 1852.] Such scalding dashes of sunshine coming in on both sides of the choky, hot railroad car, and drawing stale, sickly odors from sweaty Irishmen in their shirt sleeves; German Jew shop-boys in white coats, pink faces, and waistcoats that looked like virulent prickly heat; fat old women, with dirty-nosed babies; one sporting man with black whiskers, miraculously crisp and curly, and a shirt collar insultingly stiff, who contributed a reminiscence of tobacco smoke—the spiritual body of ten thousand bad cigars. Then the feast of fat things that came reeking under one's nose at each special puddle of festering filth that Center Street provided in its reeking, fermenting, putrefying, pestilential gutter! I thought I should have died of the stink, rage, and headache before I got to Twenty-first Street.

Yet for all his revulsion from the immigrant and the slum, Strong did have compassion for the city's poor. One of the more moving passages in his diary consists of an extended reflection in 1851 on how the abuses of the English industrial city, "the thousands and tens of thousands that are perishing hopelessly in profligacy, drunkenness, and starvation in the cellars and workshops . . . ," the men, women, and children who lay "rotting and alive, body and soul at once, in those awful catacombs of disease and crime . . . ," were being replicated in New York. Immigrant women in the city were leading lives "barren of hope and enjoyment"; children were brutalized "almost beyond redemption by premature vice." And while all this was happening, scholars were "laboriously writing dissertations for the Historical Society on the First Settlement of the Township of Squankum" and clergymen were "compiling treatises on Ancient Egypt." Strong implied that their labors might better be devoted to the problems at hand. To help "one dirty vagabond child" out of the "pestilential sink," he concluded, "would be rather more of an achievement than the writing of another *Iliad.*"

In spite of such occasional sentiments, Strong never became directly involved in the various organizations that sprang up near mid-century to do something about the lot of the poor. Yet he did spend much of his life trying to improve the quality of urban experience. As a trustee of Columbia College, he dedicated time and energy to making an inadequate college into a great university. He worked assiduously in a number of programs for cultural improvement, expanding the work of the New York Historical Society, or heading the city's Philharmonic Commission, for example. Strong's father had acquired a horse and rode regularly through the city with the avowed ambition of becoming better acquainted with it than any other man. The younger Strong had the same kind of commitment to an urban way of life. He found many things to complain about in New York: he was continually exercised by the city's atmosphere filled with malarial and "morphic influences"; by the "tadpoles and animalculae" in the local water; by the heat, dirt, and noise of Wall Street; by mud the consistency of molasses; and by the "tepid mucilage of fog," which represented the "gaseous form of mud and civic filthiness."

On occasion, Strong, like many urban intellectuals of the period including those of the *Knickerbocker* circle, might even denounce cities in general, as "sinks of vice, corruption and misery—enlightened on the surface by the false glare of unhealthy exhalations." Yet, he was never happy for long away from the metropolis. "Got back to town this morning 'for good,' " he wrote typically in 1840, after a sojourn on Long Island, "and right glad am I to see this city of abominations again for the last three weeks or so have been as heavy and dull as the *Statutes at Large* or Rollin's *Ancient History.*" A book collector, a student of music, a patron of the arts, Strong obviously loved the cultivated life of an urbane, intellectual aristocrat in America's largest city. Although he lived in the era of rural America, Strong was as much the New Yorker as the most sophisticated mid-twentieth-century representative of that cultural type.

Strong's outlook was shaped by the cultural advantages of the urban milieu; the cultural institutions of the city absorbed much of his energies. But his was not the only kind of commitment to a nineteenth-century pattern of urban life. Representative leaders of western cities of the nineteenth century often cared little about the culture of the city; instead they became fascinated with the process of growth itself—with technology and demography, with the material city as a symbol of American progress. Jesup W. Scott of Toledo was the best-known spokesman of this outlook, but there were many lesser western urban leaders who reflected this view. A good example is provided by Robert Thompson Van Horn, journalist, politician, and a local hero of the western railroad center of Kansas City, Missouri. Like Scott, Van Horn believed that the multiplication of western cities and their rapid growth was one of the most dynamic aspects of the American experience. His life calling was in reality that of a professional urban promoter, a not uncommon craft in the nineteenth-century American West.

Born in Pennsylvania in 1824, Van Horn as a young man taught school, studied law, learned printing, and drifted west to Pomeroy, Ohio where he acquired a newspaper. Here he began arguing the typical view of the region that the nation's wealth and population and its future great cities were to be concentrated in the Mississippi Valley. After several unsuccessful ventures, in 1855 he took over the operation of a struggling newspaper in the town of Kansas, then a small frontier trading entrepôt on the western edge of settlement. Van Horn devoted his efforts to making the village a magnificent western city. He became an expert on railroads and turned his newspaper into a textbook on how to promote them. He took the lead in getting charters for railroad corporations, organizing a chamber of commerce to promote them, defeating the efforts of rival towns with their own railroad plans, and mobilizing his community behind bond issues and other inducements to corporate leaders. Unlike many promoters in the aspiring hamlets of the West, Van Horn saw his hopes realized as Kansas City in the years immediately after the Civil War quickly developed into an important railroad, livestock, and meat-packing center. He lived to be ninety-one, served for years as spokesman of the city's origins, and saw his chosen community mature into the interior metropolis he had early predicted it would become.

To an urban spokesman like Van Horn, cutting streets through imposing hills, spanning a river with a magnificent bridge, installing the machinery for a meat-packing plant, or turning prairie land into a thriving city addition were the vital aspects of the nineteenth century. But he was also able to savor the good life of a man of power in a growing city. He clearly loved the lavish meals, the meetings over bourbon, the holiday parties that were a part of community leadership. Strong's diary records the diversions of an urban intellectual in a center of culture; Van Horn's editorials supply an enthusiastic account of the recreations of a frontier outpost being transformed into a bustling metropolis—of summer circuses, touring Shakespearean companies, visits with travelers to the West, lyceum speakers, Swedish bell-ringers, and winter ice-skating parties. Robert T. Van Horn's Kansas City was not George Templeton Strong's New York, but both men identified with an urban milieu. Early and mid-nineteenth-century cities—large and small; in the East, the West, or the South—provided arenas where the able and energetic could realize their talents, enlarge their experience, and gain power.

But even for the man of talent and wealth, the mores of American society could impose limits on participation in the enterprises of the city. William Johnson, a free Negro of ante-bellum Natchez, in one of the remarkable diaries of the nineteenth century records an urban experience similar in many respects to that of Strong and Van Horn but in many respects critically different. Despite being a Negro in a slave-holding southern city, Johnson became a member of an urban elite and embraced the good life with all the hearty enthusiasm of a Van Horn. He once wrote, "I am always ready for anything," and the statement seems genuinely reflective of his outlook. But there were many things he could not do in the city. His race confined him to the colored balcony of the Natchez theater. He could only participate casually in the sport he loved—horse racing—for his horses could not be entered in official races. His diary reflects little concern about these matters, but as the years go by one can detect diminishment of happy-go-lucky spirits and the growth of sentiments of bitterness toward white leaders in the community. Being shot to death as a result of a fight over property lines was not such an unusual way to die in a place and time of considerable personal violence. But the fact that his assassin—a rumored mulatto—escaped conviction when he proved he was white, thereby ruling out testimony by Negro witnesses, supplied an ironic comment on the position of the Negro in America as urban leader, aristocrat, or man of power.

Still, Johnson's life does indicate the wide range of possibility in the American city. Born in 1809, he was freed in 1820 and grew up in Natchez with his mother who had been freed earlier. Apprenticed as a barber, a common occupation for Negroes, he went into the barber business for himself when he completed his training, branched out into bathhouses, acquired slaves, got into real estate, moneylending, and farming. Natchez in 1820 was a commercial center of 2,000 in a region beginning to undergo rapid agricultural development. It boomed during the 1830s before the Panic of 1837 and presented the kind of entrepreneurial possibilities characteristic of the western frontier community, which it resembled much more than folklore's traditional sleepy southern town surrounded by plantations and stately mansions. Johnson was a jack-of-all-trades businessman, making toys, selling wallpaper, hiring out his slaves for street maintenance, draying, and renting buggies, to name a few of his sometime enterprises. Throughout his business career he earned at least $2,500 annually, even in severe depression years. At the time of his death in 1851, he owned $6,000 worth of slaves and other property valued at over $17,000; his total estate was conservatively estimated at $25,000, a considerable fortune at the time. He had long been close to many leaders in the city including the Harvard-educated planter, Colonel Adam L. Bingaman, and knew many people of state and regional prominence.

Johnson began keeping his diary in October 1835, after he got married, and made entries nearly every day until his death. Before his marriage, his carefully kept accounts, indicating his lifetime passion for record-keeping, reveal his life as a man-about-town—a meticulous dresser who carried an expensive gold watch, a gambler, a consorter with prostitutes, a theater-goer, and a traveler to large cities. Although he became a settled family man who fathered ten children, his diary focusses on work, play, and the community, not the home. Johnson was largely self-educated, and his diary shows it. It is often crudely written; his style is colloquial, and the entries often consist of unrelated bits of information. Johnson's writing shows neither the plain-style precision of a Van Horn nor the studied elegance of a Strong. American intellectuals have tended to romanticize the Negro primitive, but putting that aside, there is still a good deal of vitality in Johnson's diary. He had an immense curiosity, and he had a passion for putting down on paper that in which he was interested. He records everything going on in the city—news and gossip, accounts of holiday celebrations, parades, sporting events, circuses, theater, railroads and steamboats, comings and goings, disease and fire.

Johnson in many respects cultivated an aristocratic style of life. He furnished his house expensively and took pride in lavish gifts to his friends. He regularly bought wines, fine liquors, and good cigars. Although he subscribed to a number of magazines and newspapers, purchased books, and set aside time for regular reading, he was not an intellectual. His time was mainly spent with people, and he enjoyed good living. He records many meals enjoyed with his constant associate Robert McCary, also a barber, who had inherited considerable money. One such occurred in 1836:

Mc and myself had a tolerable good Dinner—We had as follows—Mc had 2 Bottles of Medoc Claret, 1 Bottle of Champagne wine, Buiscuit Egg Bread, P. pork, 1 Broiled

Chicken & Beef Stake, I had a piece of good Bacon, wheat Bread, Oysters in Flitters, one Large Bottle of Anneset, one Dozen Orenges, 1 small Bottle of Muscat wine.

Next to hunting, perhaps his greatest interest was in horse racing; his diary is a catalogue of racing results and information. His early love of gambling continued throughout his life; his diary records continual bets—on horses, cockfights, and shooting matches; on when a cow would give birth, on how fast a horse could walk, and on who could shuck the most corn.

Johnson's Natchez in some regards resembles Strong's New York and more particularly Van Horn's Kansas City. There is a spirit of civic pride in cultural activities. Although Johnson pretty much stopped going to the theater after a disturbance in the colored gallery during a minstrel show in 1836, he regularly records, for example, the appearances in the city of such celebrities as Ole Bull and Jenny Lind. There is a celebration of patriotism, when notables visit on the Fourth of July. There is a tendency to associate city growth with progress. There is concern with the disasters of plague and fire. But one important difference emerges: Johnson writes continually of personal violence, a subject that seldom intrudes into the accounts of Strong and Van Horn. Johnson himself was a sometimes violent man. He frequently whipped his young slaves and apprentices; in 1836 after his mother, who seems to have been psychologically disturbed, had been brawling in the streets Johnson recorded that when she "Commenced as usual to quarrle with Everything and Every body, I, knowing, perfectly well what it Grew Out of, I thought I would take the quickest way to stop it, and I accordingly took a whip and gave her a few Cuts." Johnson frequently writes with an exuberant and frightening enthusiasm of assorted fist fights, shootings, knifings, canings, and gougings. He records over a hundred such incidents. One particular "Bloody work" which involved a fatal shooting, fist fights, a pistol whipping, and a knifing evoked his connoisseur's opinion that "It was one of the gamest fights that we have ever had in Our City before." But it is this kind of down-to-earth quality that makes Johnson's diary an important record of life in a nineteenth-century city; newspapers and other sources generally tended to ignore subjects that detracted from a city's favorable image. There are few entries in Johnson's diary that stand well alone. But perhaps a day at the races with his friend on February 20, 1836, best records the life this intriguing urbanite lived:

The Race to day between Red Mariah & Cassandra was won fairly by R. Mariah. But after the judges once gave it in favor of R. Mariah they afterwards turned and made it a Dead Heat—Old Dr Branch & A Stranger & Mr John P. Smith were the judges    Mr Ja. Perry was perfectly wronged in the race and he told them so—abused Mr Lee Clabourn for all sorts of D——— rascals & Dm thieves, rouges and Every thing else that he Could lay his tounge to—He shoved Mr Os Clabourne Back 3 times and struck him Once—They were all armed and it was thought that they would fight but neither of the Clabournes would strike—Old Mc won $10 from Love on his ½ mile Race with the other Butcher    I lost on Cassandra $5 with Burton & I Lost $5 on a

Brown Horse that Ran I mile with Mr Mardice, and I lost $10 with a Butcher on Lancasters Roan horse—I gave old Bob Larence $2. Expenses and charges against me this week is $52.

Although cities in all sections of the country would change greatly in the years after Johnson's death, many of the qualities and experiences of urban life, the everyday tensions, fancies, and diversions that his diary reflects, would endure.

CHAPTER

# 6

# The Completion of the Urban Network, 1860–1910

ETWEEN 1860 and 1910 the modern American city emerged. From 1820 on, technological and economic transformations had contributed to a high rate of urbanization in the United States. The continuance of this urban trend in the years after 1860 led to an ever increasing concentration of Americans in cities of all sizes and engendered the view on the part of many social critics that the "rise of the city" was a fundamental problem facing American society. During this fifty-year period in which the total population of the United States increased from 31,443,321 to 91,972,266, the number of people living in incorporated municipalities of 2,500 or more increased from 6,216,518 to 44,639,989—a percentage change in urban population from 19.8 to 45.7 of the total. Urbanization did not proceed at an even pace during the fifty years. Movement to the city naturally accelerated in times of prosperity and fell off in times of depression when economic opportunities in the city diminished, as was illustrated in the percentage changes in urban population during each census decade:

| | |
|---|---|
| 1860–70 | 59.3 |
| 1870–80 | 42.7 |
| 1880–90 | 56.7 |
| 1890–1900 | 36.4 |
| 1900–10 | 39.3 |

But throughout the period the urban trend was unmistakable; the United States was clearly becoming a nation of cities and city dwellers.

Most public attention during the period focused on the growth of the very large cities. Writing in 1899, the economist Edmund J. James noted the increase in the number of American cities over 200,000 population and asserted that the latter nineteenth century was "not only the age of cities but the age of great cities." The burgeoning metropolises of the East seemed, in particular, to represent to many a fundamental threat to American civilization. Here were the sites of the ghetto and the slum; here the abuses of Old Europe seemed to be growing in the New World. When Josiah Strong in his best-selling book, *Our Country* (1885), argued that the city had become a "serious menace to our civilization," he was referring primarily to the large cities of the East where he found the flourishing of inequality, socialism, political corruption, and Roman Catholicism. Other commentators on American society considered the cities of the East emblematic of the country's dynamic material progress. Scores of foreign travelers, for example, repeated the observation that in New York could be observed the essence of all the vital forces sustaining the rapidly expanding nation; it was, as one of them put it, "the magnum opus of modern material civilization."

Despite the contemporary preoccupation with the large city of the eastern seaboard, it should be emphasized that cities of all sizes, in all sections of the country, were growing rapidly. Again, the details of the federal census revealed the pattern. During the period from 1860 to 1910, while the number of cities of over 100,000 increased from nine to fifty, the number of urban places of ten to twenty-five thousand increased from fifty-eight to 369. The period traditionally marks the rise of the great American city; it also marks the emergence of a national urban network—a complex, interrelated system of national and regional metropolises, specialized manufacturing cities, and hundreds of smaller subordinate cities of varying size and function. The rapid development of new regions of the country after 1860 created great opportunities in building new cities, but by 1890 this possibility was no longer open because the urban network had been substantially completed. With the exception of an occasional city such as Miami, Florida, which sprang up after a railroad was built along the east coast of Florida in 1896, or Tulsa, Oklahoma, located at the site of an oil discovery, most of the American cities destined to achieve even moderate size had been founded by 1890. Less than a fifth of the municipalities incorporated after 1890 had obtained even the minimum urban size requirement of 2,500 by 1910. Opportunities in the exploitation of urban growth, a fundamental force in nineteenth-century American economic development, now lay in taking advantage of possibilities in established urban centers, not in creating new cities in new regions. New urban communities that became important in the twentieth century developed largely as satellites or suburbs of older nineteenth-century cities.

During the period from 1860 to 1910, the important pre-Civil War cities for the most part maintained their position. New York, of course, became one of the great cities of the world. With its five separate boroughs brought under one government in 1898, its population by 1910 approached five million. Still the leading commercial center of the nation, it had also developed important manufactures and was the center of many of the complex financial functions that were part of a national metropolitan economy. "New York," wrote Williard Glazier in his adulatory but perceptive 1884 survey of American cities, "is one of the most wonderful products of our wonderful western civilization. It is itself a world in epitome. Thoroughly cosmopolitan in its character, almost every nationality is represented within its boundaries, and almost every tongue spoken. It is the great monetary, scientific, artistic and intellectual centre of the western world." Philadelphia, though it dropped from second to third in the rank of American cities, trebled its population during the fifty years, reaching a total of over one and a half-million in 1910. Baltimore, Philadelphia's great ante-bellum trade rival, grew more slowly, falling from third place in 1860 to seventh in 1910. Boston dropped one notch from fourth to fifth. Of the major pre-Civil War cities only New Orleans showed a drastic decline in rank. Reflecting the deterioration of interior river commerce, the coming of the railroads, and the east-west pattern of trade and population movement, the city fell from fifth rank in 1860 to fifteenth in 1910.

Large midwestern cities recorded important gains. St. Louis, Cleveland, and Detroit all grew rapidly to rank fourth, sixth, and ninth respectively in 1910. And the Midwest supplied the most dramatic example of individual city growth in the period—the rise of Chicago. In 1860 Chicago ranked eighth among American cities, with a population of 109,620. It had boomed during the fifties, and local leaders in the next decade took advantage of the city's ten trunk railroads that had earlier been won to build thriving meat-packing, milling, and iron industries. They also continued their struggle with St. Louis for control of the trade of the West. During the Civil War the blockade of the lower Mississippi River and the diversion of trade northward damaged the interests of St. Louis; but its quick recovery renewed the hopes of its leaders. Chicago, however, through its magnificent railroad system continued to advance even more rapidly. Despite the disastrous fire of October 1871, which leveled two-thirds of the city and left 100,000 people homeless, Chicago had eclipsed its rival in population by 1880. By that date, 15,000 miles of railroads connected Chicago with regions of the Northwest and upper Mississippi —an area that grew more rapidly than territories naturally tributary to St. Louis. In addition, St. Louis leaders for too long assumed that the city's magnificent river connections would assure its continued supremacy and consistently demonstrated less willingness to take risks and to pursue bold policies to expand the city than did their counterparts in Chicago. As a result of its victory over its mid-continental rival and its continued development, Chicago passed the million mark in population in 1890, to become the country's second largest city. In 1910 its population was 2,185,283.

As Manchester, England had done fifty years earlier and Los Angeles was to do later, Chicago during the late nineteenth century served as the world's "shock city." Constantly visited by foreign travelers, constantly written about, Chicago with its dynamic but often brutal environment seemed to provide a portent of a new and frightening kind of urban future. To Rudyard Kipling in the nineties, Chicago, unlike San Francisco or Salt Lake City, was "a real city," the first American city he had encountered. But it was a place of barbarism, boasting, and violence. "Having seen it," Kipling wrote, "I urgently desire never to see it again." But the British reformer and editor, William T. Stead, author of *If Christ Came to Chicago,* and the leader of a crusade for civic betterment in the city, argued in the same period that Chicago had the "opportunity at her feet" to become the ideal city of the world. "She is not laden down by any *damnosa hereditas* of the blunders and crimes of her past; her citizens are full of a boundless elan, and full of faith in the destiny of their city. . . . It seems to me nowhere on the whole of the earth's surface, for one of my ideas and aspirations, could I have been more profitably employed than I was in Chicago in the winter of 1893–94."

Although Chicago supplied the most noted example of the effects of American urbanization in the late nineteenth century, numerous smaller cities demonstrated spectacular growth rates. During the decade of the 1880s, a period of prosperity following the long depression after 1873, 101 cities of 8,000 population and above doubled their size. Among the cities of the Midwest, where urbanization centered during the decade, Omaha grew from 30,500 to 140,000; Kansas City, Missouri from 60,000 to over 132,000; Wichita from 5,000 to 23,000; Duluth from 3,300 to 33,100; and Minneapolis from 47,000 to 164,000. Elsewhere, Birmingham, the new industrial city of the South, jumped from 3,000 in 1880 to over 26,000 ten years later; a southwestern city, El Paso, increased its population thirteen fold. Among the cities of the Far West, Spokane, Washington grew from a settlement of 350 to a city of 20,000; Tacoma jumped in population from 1,100 to 36,000; and Denver, already a good-sized city of 35,000 in 1880, more than tripled its population by 1890.

Numerous specialized technological and economic developments contributed to the possibilities of individual cities. Some grew through invention—Dayton, Ohio provided the site of the operations of the National Cash Register Company; Schenectady, New York in 1886 became the home of General Electric. Others grew through specialized manufactures: Holyoke, Massachusetts in paper, Corning, New York in glass, and Hershey, Pennsylvania in candy. Minneapolis in milling, Milwaukee in beer, and Memphis in cottonseed oil were examples of cities that profited from the processing of regional agricultural products. Manufacturing was fundamental to the rapid over-all urbanization of the period. During the years from 1860 to 1910, the rate of increase in manufacturing production (975 per cent) was the most significant index of economic growth—substantially greater in magnitude than the growth rates of national population, urban population, or population in larger cities. A large share of the increased urban population of the post-Civil War era was concentrated in cities that became the most important manufacturing metropolises. The eleven largest industrial cities of 1966 contained nearly 41 per cent of the total urban population by 1910. But with the exception of Los Angeles, all these cities were already established commercial centers in 1860. Manufacturing in and of itself was seldom responsible for the creation of large cities that became part of the urban network.

Similarly, the colorful mining booms of the late nineteenth century in gold, silver, copper, coal, and oil created a number of small urban communities, but many of these, in the West particularly, failed even to survive once the local mineral resources ran out. Only an occasional mining city—Butte, Montana near copper deposits, and Wilkes-Barre and Scranton in the anthracite region of Pennsylvania—achieved major-city status. More often than not in the long run, an older city benefitted from new mineral sources, as Pittsburgh did from coal and Cleveland from petroleum.

In large measure, the location and initial growth of important cities that sprang up in this era of the completion of the American urban network was tied to the building of a national system of transportation. In the early part of the nineteenth century, the outcome of struggles for transportation had drastically affected the rank and importance of the cities of the East. After 1850 this conflict was transferred to the West. The rivalry among city promoters and real estate speculators to win railroads for their communities in newly developed regions supplied one of the most dramatic chapters in the history of American urbanization. Earlier rivalries had been limited by nature—by the location of rivers and lakes. But railroads were not bound by topography, by the paths of river commerce, or by natural trade patterns. Railroads could be built anywhere, creating cities where they chose. Because the building of railroads was dependent to a considerable extent on subsidies from local communities, railroad leaders were willing to bargain with competing towns to obtain the best possible deal in stock subscriptions, bond issues, and rights of way. It was sometimes possible, therefore, for towns with few natural advantages to triumph over better situated rivals for the prize of regional dominance. The "boosterism" associated with the Midwest and areas further west is largely a legacy of the late nineteenth-century era of urban rivalry. Numerous cities in the West owe their importance to the fact that groups of energetic local promoters with substantial investments in local real estate were able, through superior organization of their communities, superior advertising, or often simply through good luck, to persuade railroads to build to their particular locations.

From early in the railroad era, railroad officials were well aware of the possibilities of profit in urban growth in the West. The platting of town sites and the sale of town lots became an established aspect of the process of building railroads into new regions. The techniques of town development and the system of bargaining with competing communities were perfected by the Illinois Central Railroad, chartered in 1851 to build southward from Chicago through the heart of the state. The company used the threat of building new towns or running its tracks through neighboring places in order to force local officials in established communities to offer concessions of rights of way, railroad-station site donations, or stock purchases. Centralia, Kankakee, Champaign, and La Salle were established as competing towns by the Illinois Central when agreements could not be effected with Central City, Bourbonnais, Urbana, and Peru. Creation of new towns was often advantageous, for it permitted a larger share of the profits from increased land values to go directly to railroad owners. The company's charter prohibited the railroad from laying out towns on its lines, but Illinois Central leaders circumvented this restriction by creating a land company called "The Associates" for the specific purpose of managing town-site speculations. The company's concern with town promoting contributed to considerable urbanization along the line of the Illinois Central. In 1850, there were only ten towns in the immediate vicinity of the railroad's route; ten years later there were forty-seven; in 1870, eighty-one. The combined population of these urban places, excluding Chicago, rose from 12,000 in 1850, to 70,000 in 1860, and to 172,000 by 1870. Profits from the Illinois Central's town promotions were large. The development at Kankakee, for example, cost "The Associates" some $18,000 to May 1855. By the end of that year the group had collected nearly $50,000 through lot sales, and the value of the property remaining was estimated at more than $100,000. After ten years of large dividends, the Kankakee business was sold for $50,000.

In advancing their town projects, the Illinois Central leaders frequently had to head off the plans of rival town-promoters. The contest for the location of the University of Illinois provides a case in point. After the passage of the Morrill Act of 1862, which provided federal lands for the support of higher education, several communities competed for the prize of the state university. The Illinois Central supported Champaign, where a number of town lots remained unsold, and offered $50,000 in freight transportation as part of the city's bid of $285,000 to the state. The bids of the three other leading contenders were higher: Lincoln offered $385,000; Bloomington, $470,000, which included $50,000 from the competing Chicago and Alton Railroad; and Jacksonville, $491,000. But, owing to the bribery of legislators and political bosses, Champaign's bid was finally accepted in 1867. The Illinois Central's investment again reaped large dividends. Real estate boomed, and by 1870 Champaign had become the most populous community south of Chicago on the branch line of the railroad.

As railroads built westward, other lines engaged successfully in town development, though their gains were not as spectacular as those of the Illinois Central. The Chicago, Burlington, and Quincy also used the device of the independent association to lay out numerous town sites in Iowa. These were widely advertised as places with magnificent futures. Charles Perkins, the land agent of the Burlington, commented more frankly to his wife in referring to the towns of Batavia, Whitfield, and Agency City in 1864: "*Towns* they are on paper, meadows or timber land with here and there a house, in reality." Two years later, near Ottumwa, Perkins supplied insight into the methods of town development by railroads. "I shall have two or three more towns to name very soon. . . . They should be short and easily pronounced. Frederic, I think is a very good name. It is now literally a cornfield, so I cannot have it surveyed, but yesterday a man came to arrange to put a hotel here. This is a great country for hotels."

The rise of Kansas City, Missouri as a western railroad center and regional metropolis supplies one of the best examples of the relationship of real estate, local promotion, and railroad planning to the growth of individual cities in this era of booming development of new regions.

The community began its existence as an insignificant frontier trading depot. During the 1830s and 40s, as trade moved up the Missouri River from St. Louis, a complex of small trading communities sprang up along the western edge of Missouri to serve a vast western empire. For its first fifteen years, the town of Kansas, founded in 1838, was little more than a collection of warehouses and general stores near the juncture of the Kansas and Missouri Rivers. The settlement functioned as an entrepôt of the river-caravan trade—a convenient location where goods could be easily transferred from steamboat to wagon for shipment to far-flung points of a distant hinterland. With the expansion of the Santa Fe trade in the 1850s, and particularly with the migration of settlers into Kansas after the opening of the territory in 1854, the town began to grow, and a group of local property holders, who were joined by investors from the East with an interest in promising western town sites, set out to build a regional city by obtaining railroads. Despite a well-organized local program, by the time of the Civil War, Kansas City, as it was now called to distinguish it from the territory, was not yet connected to the railroads being built across Missouri, nor had a frantic effort to build a local railroad succeeded. The town had grown to a four- and a half-thousand, and it had eclipsed the cluster of communities in the immediate vicinity—Parkville, Weston, Westport, and Independence. But St. Joseph, some forty miles to the north, already had railroad connections through the Hannibal and St. Joseph line, completed in 1859. Another river town, Leavenworth, Kansas, a few miles north, had begun to boom and was nearly twice as large as Kansas City.

The outbreak of the Civil War nearly destroyed Kansas City. Guerrilla fighting broke out in the region. The town's population declined by a half; it acquired a reputation as a center of secessionist sentiment, and many of its pro-southern business leaders were driven from the community; the overland wagon trade, which had earlier centered there, went to Leavenworth, near a military fort and the center of Union military operations in the region. Most observers who toured the region at the end of the war predicted that Leavenworth would be the next great city of the West. Albert Richardson, the well-known western traveler, found Leavenworth in 1866 to be more like a "great city than any point between St. Louis and San Francisco." Five newspapers, gaslights, well-built brick buildings, all gave it the "air of a metropolis."

But Leavenworth's promising hopes were never to be realized. As railroad building revived in the western regions during the closing period of the war, a few property holders in Kansas City, who had held on during the days of adversity, revived their local railroad program. Using stocks in their paper railroad companies, a congressional land grant to one of their companies, local bond issues, and blocks of potentially valuable real estate, the Kansas City leaders were able to persuade officials of the Hannibal and St. Joseph to connect with a transcontinental branch being built in Kansas—the Union Pacific, Eastern Division (later the Kansas Pacific)—by way of Kansas City rather than by way of Leavenworth. The Hannibal and St. Joseph's construction of a railroad bridge at Kansas City—the first across the Missouri River—assured the city's rapid development. By 1870 the federal census gave its population as 32,260. Within another decade, Kansas City had developed its important meat-packing facilities, and its population in 1880 stood at 55,785. Leavenworth, to a lesser extent St. Joseph, Wyandotte (which Horace Greeley in 1859 had thought the likely site for the next great western city), and numerous other Kansas and Missouri towns, whose claims to future urban greatness had once seemed plausible, had been eclipsed by the rise of Kansas City.

The growth of Kansas City owed much to the location of a federally-supported transcontinental branch in Kansas. It was through the Kansas Pacific Railroad that Kansas City became established as a cattle market and meat-packing center. Many important western cities owe their existence directly to the western railways provided by the Pacific Railway Acts of 1862 and 1864. Cheyenne, Wyoming, for example, began as a railroad construction camp casually chosen in the summer of 1867. By fall there was a hastily constructed town of 4,000 people who had got there ahead of the rails. When the trains arrived in November, another 4,000 people came in. Railroad construction moved on the next spring, but Cheyenne was already large enough to be named as territorial capital. The development of the Wyoming cattle industry and gold discoveries in the Black Hills provided a base for its continued growth. Reno, Nevada, founded as mining-provision center, became a station on the Central Pacific Railroad in 1868. M. C. Lake, a rancher, offered the company eighty acres of land as a town site provided he could retain the alternate lots. The offer was accepted, the town was laid out, 200 lots were sold on the first day of public auction, and the community was a fact. Other small isolated western trading or mining sites—El Paso, Albuquerque, Santa Fe—boomed with the coming of the railroads.

Cities of the West frequently grew almost accidentally as the result of the location of railroads. However, the early history of Denver, like that of Kansas City, indicates that community enterprise was also important in the establishment of the principal cities in the western segment of the American urban network. Well before the coming of the railroads, the gold discoveries in Colorado in 1858 had led to the creation of numerous mining communities, particularly along Cherry Creek. The possibilities in city development attracted an ambitious promoter, General William Larimer, who had lost a fortune in Pittsburgh in the early fifties and had sought to recoup through speculative town-building activities in La Platte and Omaha, Nebraska, and in Leavenworth, Kansas. Arriving at Cherry Creek to found a town, Larimer learned that a rival group had already staked a claim. Undeterred, he merely set up his own town called Denver City on the opposite bank of the stream. Promoters of the original town of Auraria and those of Denver engaged in vigorous rivalry, but in 1860, after an exchange of real estate among Larimer and other leaders, the two towns merged as Denver. Larimer, who had asserted in 1859, "I am Denver," became the "Donating Agent" for the community. He was responsible for providing lots for those who would build there and took charge of setting up the necessary urban institutions for an aspiring city— hotels, newspapers, general stores, sawmills, and a cemetery. Nourished by the mining boom, Denver began to establish itself as a regional metropolis.

Local leaders of course recognized that railroads were essential to the city's continued growth, and with the construction of the Union Pacific westward after the Civil War they campaigned for a route to cut through the mountains west of the city. When Union Pacific engineers decided to build through passes to the north in Wyoming, Denver promoters recognized a vital threat to their interests. The city had not grown much since 1860 and without a place on the line it was likely to languish. Accordingly, in 1869 local leaders organized a local company which successfully built a 106 mile line north to Cheyenne. In June 1870 the first train pulled into Denver, and in August the Kansas Pacific reached Denver, providing an alternate eastern connection. But Denver leaders did not rest on these successes. Despite the ridicule of many eastern investors, in 1871 they began the construction of a narrow-gauge trunk line to the south, the Denver and Rio Grande. The railroad tapped new mineral areas and proved enormously profitable to its owners and to the city. Denver leaders consistently demonstrated promotional zeal and skill. For example, the location of a United States mint at Denver, which provided official recognition of the city's regional status, owed much to local organizational activity. Partly as a result of this kind of effort, by 1890, though its population was still under 107,000, Denver had established its economic influence over a vast area of the West.

To the southwest in Texas, an urban frontier represented by the older settlement of San Antonio and the new towns of Austin, Houston, and Galveston, flourished after Texas independence in 1836. As on other frontiers, there was widespread speculation in urban sites and frenzied town promotion. "Towns and villages have been raised by magic," wrote an early English visitor to the Republic. "Perhaps there is not in the records of history any instance of a Nation rising so *rapidly* as the Republic of Texas has done." As Kenneth W. Wheeler has demonstrated, differences in the character of the communities and varying promotional responses influenced the outcome of rivalries among the larger urban centers. Austin, the capital, concentrated on government, and its leaders did not energetically promote railroads. San Antonio continued to look to its long-standing Mexican trade and was only slowly drawn into a broader regional economy. Galveston had a magnificent harbor that enabled it to become an ante-bellum metropolis, but like Norfolk earlier, it failed to exploit its great natural advantages. Galveston's elite concentrated on cultural enterprises, looked to Europe, and divided on local economic programs. Houston's leadership, on the other hand, energetically promoted a local railroad program, maintained community harmony and, like its counterparts in Kansas City, Chicago, and Denver, managed to identify the interests of the business community with the broad task of city promotion and building. Railroads enabled Houston to become the hub of the Texas Gulf Coast, and the city succeeded Galveston as the regional metropolis.

In addition to contributing to the location and growth of western cities, the transcontinental railroads fed grandiose schemes of countless visionaries of an urban West. Wildly speculative urban land booms were a vital aspect of the history of the growth of the region. During the early years of debate over the route for a railroad to the Pacific, spokesmen for a federally-supported project, Thomas Hart Benton and William Gilpin, had continually advanced a dream of a great chain of magnificent cities that would spring up along the line, and as railroad-building actually got underway in the 1860s, promoters attempted to realize the design. One of the more ambitious efforts was that of George Francis Train, an investor in the Union Pacific, who had been one of the organizers of the scandal-ridden Credit Mobilier established to construct the railroad. Train owned 600 acres of land in Omaha, and decided to apply the "separate-company" device, employed so successfully in the Credit Mobilier, to urban promotion. His Credit Foncier was set up specifically to build and develop cities along the line of the Union Pacific. "One of my plans," he recorded in his autobiography, "was the creation of a chain of great towns across the continent, connecting Boston with San Francisco by a magnificent highway of cities." His proposals were advanced with the usual extravagant appeals to the optimism stimulated by the country's rapid development. "Would you make money easy?" asked a Credit Foncier prospectus about Columbus, Nebraska. "Find then the site of a city and buy the farm it is to be built on! How many regret the non-purchase of that lot in New York; that block in Buffalo; that acre in Chicago; that quarter section in Omaha. Once these city properties could be bought for a song. Astor and Girard made their fortunes that way. The Credit Foncier by owning the principal towns along the Pacific line to California, enriches its shareholders while distributing its profits by selling alternate lots at a nominal price to the public."

Train realized only limited gains from his exuberant promotions. Omaha did not grow as fast as he had anticipated, nor did the towns that the company founded along the railroad automatically sprout into great cities. Train shifted his operations to Denver, and later to Tacoma, which he proclaimed the future great city of the world. To advertise its claim he made a sixty-seven-day trip around the world from the city, breaking the record of the celebrated Nellie Bly set the year before in 1890. But this effort was also largely a failure. Train broke down and was legally adjudged insane. He died penniless in 1903—one of the last of a succession of nineteenth-century prophets of a West of magnificent cities whose visions were but partly realized.

The recurrent town booms in southern California in the late nineteenth century provide one of the best examples of the general influence of the urban enthusiasm that motivated promoters like Train. As elsewhere in the West, these booms were closely tied to railroad-building. In the late 1860s, local promoters in Los Angeles, then a city of less than 6,000, were encouraged by rumors of a possible transcontinental railroad connection. In order to advance this possibility, they organized a local railroad called the Los Angeles and San Pedro to build a twenty-one mile line to a harbor site on the ocean. When the Southern Pacific planned a connection southward from San Francisco, local officials passed over control of their company, paid a cash subsidy of over $600,000, and offered numerous other concessions to ensure that the line would build by way of the city rather than choose a route behind the mountains to the east. The Southern Pacific completed its line to the city in 1876. By 1881 it had connected with the Texas and Pacific east of El Paso, which gave Los Angeles access to New Orleans as well as San Francisco.

Owing to the effects of the depression of the seventies, Los Angeles did not boom as local promoters had hoped until a rival line, the Atchison, Topeka, and Santa Fe, obtained its own tracks into the city in 1887. A rate war between the Southern Pacific and the Santa Fe lowered passenger fares to the Mississippi River to five dollars, and for a day or two one could go from Kansas City to Los Angeles for a dollar. In order to build up passenger traffic, both railroads sponsored excursion tours and engaged in lavish advertising of the virtues of southern California. The crowds of tourist and settlers who came to the region were joined by professional town promoters—the veterans of booms in Minneapolis, Kansas City, and Chicago—who came west to lay out new towns and new subdivisions in older sites. In an atmosphere of brass bands and circus exhibitions, new cities were platted throughout Los Angeles County. Within three months, thirteen town sites were laid out along thirteen miles of the Santa Fe and nearly as many along the Southern Pacific. On one day in 1887 real estate sales in Los Angeles reached nearly three times the amount of the subsidy paid to the Southern Pacific in 1872; total real estate sales for the year ranked the city third behind Chicago and New York. From January 1, 1887 to July 1, 1889, speculators laid out sixty new towns in southern California with estimated space enough for two million people, but at the end of the boom the sites had an aggregate population of less than 3,000.

Many of these promotions were the work of outrageously unscrupulous speculators, those intent upon "shearing a drove of innocent lambs from the East." Sidney Homberg sold about 4,000 lots in Border City and Manchester to easterners unfamiliar with Homberg's site on the edge of the Mojave Desert. Border City, a historian noted, "was most easily accessible by means of a balloon, and was as secure from hostile invasion as the homes of the cliff-dwellers. Its principal resource was a view of the Mojave Desert." The collapse of the boom in 1888 destroyed the paper cities; abandoned, uncompleted buildings were the principal souvenirs of the boom. At least sixty-two of the more than a hundred towns platted in Los Angeles County between 1884 and 1888 passed out of existence. At the end of the boom, the town of

Carlton had 4,060 lots, Nadeau 4,470, Manchester 2,304, but none of the places had a single resident. Chicago Park had 2,289 lots and one resident, and Sunset had 2,014 lots and a watchman.

Despite the destruction of an estimated $14,000,000 in property values in a single year, Los Angeles still had its advantages of climate, space, and energetic promoters. Led by Harrison Gray Otis, the publisher of the *Los Angeles Times,* city leaders organized the Los Angeles Chamber of Commerce, launched a program of encouraging manufacturers, established an inter-urban railway system, and advertised the natural advantages of southern California throughout the country. Moreover, a number of the boom towns in the area —Glendale, Monrovia, Burbank, and Azuza, among others—became permanent communities. Although the population of Los Angeles fell a third in the two years after the collapse of the boom, it resumed its steady growth thereafter. During the 1890s Los Angeles was second in size only to San Francisco among the cities west of the Rockies, and its rate of growth during the decade was exceeded only by Seattle.

As new cities were founded and grew in the West, the region's first metropolis, San Francisco, maintained its leadership until well into the twentieth century. The site of the city had been "conquered" by United States troops during the Mexican War in 1846. During the gold rushes of the late forties and early fifties, the settlement, which officially changed its name from Yerba Buena in January 1847, became the focal point of economic development throughout the Far West. Recognizing the commercial possibilities of a city located at one of the few west coast sites with a suitable natural port, speculators from the early 1850s had invested in San Francisco real estate, and the city experienced one of the early real estate booms. Lots that had sold for $1,500 each in 1850 had risen to $8,000 to $27,000 each three years later.

In its early years San Francisco faced the rivalry of other local settlements along San Francisco Bay, particularly Benicia, a town speculation organized by San Franciscians Robert Semple, Thomas Larkin, and others. As with all such promotions, Benicia began with high hopes. A San Francisco merchant recorded in his dairy in 1848 that "This little town is quite deserted! Larkin has been shaking his wise head and lamenting over the departing glories of San Francisco; and Dr. Semple is all smiles, and, in his enthusiasm over the promised success of her rival, almost dislocates the fingers of every hand he shakes." By 1850, Benicia, with about a thousand people, was building manufacturing facilities, had become local headquarters of the United States Army, and had been designated the depot for the Pacific Mail Steamship Company. Through lobbying in Washington, Benicia interests attempted to gain the site of the United States Mint and port-of-entry status. But San Francisco leaders got to work in the Capital and defeated both of the latter efforts. Thereafter, San Francisco quickly outdistanced Benicia in population. The other important California cities founded during the Gold Rush were interior cities such as Sacramento and Stockton, dependent on the Golden Gate transportation break. Because of the complementary character of the interior valley cities and the bay port, there was little of the urban imperialism in the region characteristic of other urban frontiers.

Until the coming of the railroads, virtually all trade to the Far West interior went through San Francisco or Portland, also located at a natural port. Railroads limited but did not destroy San Francisco's influence over a vast hinterland. The power of local capital assured that habitual commercial patterns would persist even after rival cities sprang up along the routes of railroads. "San Francisco dwarfs the other cities," Lord Bryce wrote in the late eighties, "and is a commercial and intellectual centre, and source of influence for the surrounding regions, more powerful over them than is any Eastern city over its neighborhood. It is a New York which has got no Boston on one side of it, and no shrewd and orderly rural population on the other to keep it in order." By 1880 it had become the country's ninth ranked city and was by far the largest city west of Chicago.

Limited in its growth by its location on a narrow peninsula, San Francisco early developed a group of suburban communities closely tied to the city. Oakland across the Bay, for example, became the center of railroad and industrial development in the area, and in 1880 was actually the second largest city of the Far West. This complex of communities in the Bay region was largely the work of real estate speculators, and for each successful town promotion, such as Oakland and Alameda, a failure could probably be cited. As the center of this urbanized region, San Francisco early established its reputation as an American showpiece, where the visitor could experience a varied urban environment that ranged from the dives of the Barbary Coast to the exotic castles of Nob Hill, and where local citizens prided themselves on their diligent practice of the graces of a sophisticated, cosmopolitan society. San Francisco was "the city" of the west, recognized as such in this period even by residents of rival Los Angeles.

The coming of railroads to the Pacific Northwest limited San Francisco's influence in that distant part of its vast hinterland by creating new regional cities. The development of the Pacific Northwest also contributed another important chapter to the history of nineteenth-century urban rivalry—the struggle between Tacoma and Seattle for regional supremacy. Seattle, located on Puget Sound at the best natural port north of San Francisco, had gotten its start in the 1850s as a sawmill town in a magnificent timber region. Although the community had only 182 inhabitants in 1860, early in the next decade local residents, through a donation of a site and buildings, persuaded the territorial legislature to make Seattle the site of the university. Despite the continually stated faith of local residents in the community's magnificent resources and its future, by 1870 the town had grown to only 11,000. Again, as in other western cities, local leaders recognized that railroads were necessary to end Seattle's isolation. They hoped and assumed that the Northern Pacific would choose the town as its western terminus, and in order to further this possibility offered the railroad the usual concessions—land, choice water-front wharfage, and a quarter million dollars in cash and bonds.

However, their hopes were not immediately realized. In 1873 the Northern Pacific announced that Tacoma, a tiny settlement at Commencement Bay twenty-four miles south of Seattle, had been chosen as the railroad's terminus. The decision was largely the result of an effort to realize speculative real estate profits from development of a virtually new rather than an established town site. At the other end of the line, Jay Cooke, the financial backer of the Northern Pacific, had followed a similar policy in choosing Duluth as a terminus rather than the older neighboring town of Superior, where a group of outside investors had already obtained the choicest urban sites. The Northern Pacific leaders organized a subsidiary company, the Tacoma Land Company, which acquired 3,000 acres of land in the town and 13,000 acres nearby. Frederick Law Olmsted, the distinguished landscape architect and the father of American city planning, prepared a detailed curvilinear street plan for the city that took advantage of the site's topography. But the plan was derisively rejected as totally impractical for quick real estate profits. A contemporary observed that it was "the most fantastic plan of a town that was ever seen. There wasn't a straight line, a right angle or a corner lot. The blocks were shaped like melons, pears, and sweet potatoes. One block, shaped like a banana, was 3,000 feet in length and had 250 plots. It was a pretty fair park plan but condemned itself for a town."

Officers of the company quickly adopted a more conventional gridiron plan. Pamphleteers began advertising Tacoma as the future great city of the world; like so many western cities it was portrayed as the successor of Babylon, Tyre, Rome, and London. "No one can doubt," stated one brochure, "that the sum total of Tacoma's resources, domestic and foreign, together with the entire aspect of her own and the world's present environments, are vastly superior to those of Chicago in 1852, and that it is only a question of TIME when a greater city than Chicago or New York will flourish on the more salubrious shores of Puget Sound." The Tacoma Land Company offered its lots for sale and built a magnificent hotel. The boom was on. Rudyard Kipling, who visited Tacoma in 1889, described the effects of a decade of mushrooming development.

Tacoma was literally staggering under a boom of the boomiest. . . . The rude boarded pavements of the main streets rumbled under the heels of furious men all actively engaged in hunting drinks and eligible corner lots. They sought the drinks first. The street itself alternated five-story business blocks of the later and more abominable forms of architecture with broad shanties. Overhead the drunken tele-graph, telephone, and electric-light wires tangled on the tottering posts whose butts were half-whittled through by the knife of the loafer. . . . We passed down ungraded streets that ended abruptly in a fifteen-foot drop and a nest of brambles; along pavements that beginning in pine-plank ended in the living tree; by hotels with Turkish mosque trinketry on their shameless tops, and the pine stumps at their very doors; by a female seminary, tall, gaunt and red, which a native of the town bade us marvel at, and we marvelled; by houses built in imitation of the ones on Nob Hill, San Francisco—after the Dutch fashion; by other houses plenteously befouled with jigsaw work, and others flaring with the castlemented, battlemented bosh of the wooden Gothic school.

Despite a series of booms in the eighties which produced a population increase from 1,100 to over 36,000 for the decade, Tacoma's magnificent aspirations were never realized. Again, as elsewhere, the community organization of a rival, and the ability of that rival substantially to affect the pattern of railroad connections, altered urban ambitions and calculations. After the failure to obtain the Northern Pacific terminus, Seattle residents, in the typical fashion of western urban promoters, organized a local railroad company to build a line southeastward across the Cascade Mountains to tap the productive agricultural region around Walla Walla. After the line reached Newcastle, a site of coal fields twelve miles inland, Henry Villard, who had become president of the Northern Pacific following the collapse of Jay Cooke's financial empire, purchased the coal fields and the railroad. Villard promised to extend the Northern Pacific from Tacoma to Seattle, but the company's financial difficulties forced cancellation of the plan. Seattle interests next launched a local project, the Seattle, Lake Shore, and Eastern Railroad, to connect with the Canadian Pacific. When the project received the support of eastern financial interests, the threat of competition forced the Northern Pacific to buy the local company and to connect Seattle to the Northern Pacific system. After a twenty-year struggle, Seattle had its tie to a transcontinental railroad. Two years later, in 1893, the Great Northern Railway of James G. Hill located its main terminal at Seattle, providing the city with alternative connections to the east.

During the nineties, Tacoma languished while Seattle nearly doubled its population and established a stable, three-to-one ratio in size over its rival. The victory of the community over the Northern Pacific and Tacoma became symbolic in local legend of the "Seattle Spirit," just as Kansas City's victory over Leavenworth thirty years earlier provided the central episode in the growth of the "Kansas City Spirit." In subsequent years, Seattle became noted for its support of community enterprises including extensive public-works projects, sponsorship of an international exposition, and vigorous promotion of itself as the jumping-off point for Alaskan gold. Tacoma, on the other hand, though it continued to grow, followed the course of most losers in the great nineteenth-century urban rivalries and emphasized its fine homes, genteel living, and preservation of historical traditions.

Portland, Oregon, the third of the major cities of the Pacific Northwest to emerge with the completion of the urban network, got its start during a period of town promotion along the Willamette and Columbia rivers in the 1840s. In many ways, this boom resembled those that took place along the rivers of the Midwest, the Maumee in Ohio, for example, in the period before the Panic of 1837. "Nearly every man in Oregon has a city of his own," an observer reported in 1850, "and it is impossible to tell what point on the Columbia will take the preference." Missionaries founded Oregon City; a group of Missourians, settled at Linnton; Wisconsin settlers established Milwaukie. Spokesmen for these and other communities supplied free lots, advertised their sites, and predicted that their hamlet would become a great western metropolis. But the New Englanders who founded Portland had the advantage of good port facilities and considerable capital. They successfully established the city as the commercial center of the region, though the entire area was in a sense still tributary to San Francisco. Portland's conservative railroad policy, based on the assumption that any lines built into the region would have to reach her, permitted Tacoma and Seattle to rise to positions of regional urban prominence. Although Portland eventually obtained transcontinental connections and steadily grew as an important western city, it acquired the reputation of a city fundamentally conservative in outlook. "The Columbia River has made the spirit of Portland," wrote a member of an old Portland family. "Portland people were toll takers at the gate. In time, they became conservative, took fewer chances and relied upon the geographic position of their tollgate. . . . Maybe too much sitting at the tollgate."

The growth of the Pacific Northwest cities illustrates the importance of urbanization in the development of new regions and points up the continuance into the latter part of the nineteenth century of the urban frontier fundamental to the growth of the Trans-Appalachian regions of the country. During the decade of the eighties, as Portland grew from 17,500 to 46,385, Oregon's urban population rose from 14.8 to 26.8 per cent of the total; statistically Portland gained one in five of Oregon's new population, and two in five went to the most urbanized counties. Similarly, during the decade three urban counties in Washington received half of the new population, and Seattle, Tacoma, and Spokane got one of every three new arrivals.

The cities of the West were founded as commercial enterprises; railroads and real estate were fundamental in their development. The Mormon settlement of Salt Lake City, which became an important regional city, was untypical in its founding, since initially its leaders were driven by a goal of achieving isolated self-sufficiency for a community of saints. But Salt Lake City was soon subject to the same forces that influenced other western cities. From the beginning, the settlement had performed urban functions, including complex religious activities, for a hinterland of nearby farmers. In spite of Brigham Young's resolution to avoid commerce with the Gentile world, Salt Lake City early developed trade ties to St. Louis and became a stopping point for overland travelers to the West. "Salt Lake is the city of the future," Albert Richardson recorded of his visit there in 1865, "the natural metropolis of all Utah and portions of Nevada, Idaho, Montana, and Colorado. It contains nearly twenty thousand people, and bids fair to continue the largest city between St. Louis and San Francisco. The overland telegraph connects it with the Atlantic and the Pacific, mail coaches ply daily to Nebraska and Kansas on the east, California on the west, Montana on the north, Idaho and Columbia river on the northwest, and the Pak Ranager silver region four hundred miles to the southwest. . . . Some of the trading-houses do an immense business. A single merchant has sold more than a million dollars worth of goods per annum." At this time, Mormon community leaders were actively involved in an effort to influence both the Central Pacific and the Union Pacific to choose a route that ran through Salt Lake City. When both railroads decided to build by a more northern route, church leaders, through a series of land transactions and inducements offered to U.P. and C.P. officials, insured that the Mormon settlement of Ogden rather than the "Hell on Wheels" railroad camp at Corinne— twenty-five miles northwest of Ogden—would be the terminal point of the two transcontinental lines. Outside professional speculators had chosen Corinne as the most logical place for the regional city, and at one time the town supported nineteen saloons and an Opera House. Within ten years, Corinne had become a ghost town.

After this victory, Mormon leaders next sponsored the building of a thirty-seven mile railroad between Salt Lake City and Ogden. The completion of this line made certain that Salt Lake City rather than Ogden would continue to be the regional city. As the flow of traffic stimulated the economic development of the region, the isolation of the Mormon religious community broke down further, and by the eighties Salt Lake City increasingly resembled other western cities. The president of the Salt Lake Chamber of Commerce argued in 1888 that an increase in the price of real estate was enabling the city to become more like its western neighbors. In so doing, he sounded a dominant theme in nineteenth-century urban ideology: "The present extraordinary prosperity and development of Denver, Los Angeles, Omaha, and Kansas City had their origin in real estate speculation. The one almost necessarily succeeds the other, as prices of land can be sustained in times of speculative excitement only by the building up of manufacturing and mercantile industries, to which the speculator himself is often driven for self-protection."

The importance of urban entrepreneurship—of organized civic enterprise that enabled one community to triumph over another and win railroads, manufactures, or the other necessities of urban growth—is clearly evident in the histories of the major cities in the American urban network. Its importance is sometimes more evident, and more precisely delineated, in the histories of lesser places that did not achieve metropolitan status but which proved successful urban enterprises. The example of Wichita, Kansas supplies a case in point. Wichita was a late-founded Kansas town; in 1868 urban speculators chose a town site at a convenient spot on the Chisholm Trail, the route of cattle drives from Texas to railheads in Kansas. The promoters advertised that the new center would shorten the cattlemen's trip to market, but this contention was meaningless since the nearest railroad was still some eighty miles to the north. Wichita had no unusual geographical advantages, and the older Kansas towns on the route of the Kansas Pacific seemed much more promising as potential urban centers. But, as elsewhere, community enterprise altered these considerations. Wichita leaders, through a bond issue of $200,000, persuaded the Atchison, Topeka, and Santa Fe Railroad being constructed southwestward to build a branch toward the town. Even more important, they encouraged Joseph G. McCoy, the leader in the Kansas cattle-marketing industry, to transfer his operations to Wichita from Abilene, where local opposition to the sometimes violent cattlemen had developed. The first train reached Wichita in May 1872; by the end of the year a total of 3,530 carloads of cattle had been shipped from the city. Wichita had become a booming cow town, while Abilene began its slide toward relative insignificance.

With the decline of the open-range drives and the end of the colorful era of the cattle kingdom, Wichita leaders faced a period of adversity, but they energetically converted the economy of the city into activities suitable to its location in a rapidly developing wheat-raising area—flour milling, lumber yards, brickmaking, stove and farm machinery manufacturers. They also launched a vigorous advertising campaign lauding the virtues of the "Peerless Princess of the Plains." A pamphlet of 1888 announced an inflated claim of 40,000 population and labeled Wichita, "the largest city in Kansas, a city of fine Educational Institutions, Magnificent Business Blocks, Elegant Residences and Extensive Manufacturers, with more Railroads, more Wholesale Trade, More Manufacturing, More Enterprise than any city in the Southwest."

The success of this promotional campaign set off a real estate boom in Wichita, and during the decade of the eighties the city recorded a population growth from 5,000 to 24,000. Again demonstrating an exceptional degree of community spirit, Wichita leaders initiated a program that provided the city with adequate municipal services and a range of cultural and educational institutions. Local boosters could now proclaim the city "the new Athens" of the West. After the region recovered from the depression of the nineties, the expansion of wheat raising stimulated banking and the manufacture of farm machinery in Wichita. During the 1900–1910 decade the city doubled its population to 52,000. The success of local leaders in building Wichita into a large regional marketing and manufacturing center permitted the city to take advantage of new opportunities that presented themselves in the twentieth century. Oil and airplanes enabled the city to become an important industrial center and the largest city in Kansas. Wichita lacked substantial natural advantages; yet at each stage of its development local leaders had been willing to support the community projects necessary to growth. In the completion of the urban network, the quality of urban entrepreneurship often dictated whether the enterprise of city-building succeeded or failed.

The history of American cities largely emphasizes the successful urban enterprises and fails to examine the failures and partial failures of community organization that doomed a number of promising places to oblivion or to second rank. Superior, Wisconsin once attracted national attention as the potential site for a great metropolis of the interior, but the failure of outside investors to agree on necessary promotional policies led to its becoming the lesser community of a middle size urban complex. Galena, Illinois once seemed one of the more promising cities of Illinois, but lead supplies in the region began to run out, and local leaders were unable to obtain a railroad connection. Galveston was a magic name in the writings of early western urban promoters but was seldom referred to again after it lost its position to Houston. Scores of small lumber, mining, transportation and manufacturing cities throughout the Middle and Far West did not diversify their economies at the proper time or were unable to profit from opportunities exploited by more unified or more energetic rival communities.

Other communities with grandiose initial aspirations did not become great metropolises but did achieve limited success through fortunate economic and promotional decisions made at the right time. The twin towns of Neenah and Menasha, located in the Lower Fox River Valley of east-central Wisconsin near Green Bay, developed a large-scale flour-milling industry in the 1870s based on excellent water-power facilities and had what seemed legitimate opportunity to become an urban site of national significance. When the center of milling moved westward to Minneapolis, the promotional dream ended. But local factory owners quickly moved into a new line—paper production—and as a result Neenah-Menasha became the relatively small nucleus of an important urbanized manufacturing region extending from Oshkosh to Green Bay.

During this period of the completion of the urban network, urban growth in the South in important respects resembles that of the undeveloped regions of the West. In both cases, Eastern and European capital financed ventures in town-building, the pattern of railroads determined the location of important new cities, and frenzied real estate booms were typical.

In the period before the Civil War, the South had its important cities and a pattern of urban life similar to that in cities elsewhere, yet the region had clearly lagged behind the Northeast in the extent of urbanization. In 1860 only fourteen of the country's ninety-three cities above 10,000 (15.1 per cent) were located in the South, and the percentage of urban population in the region (in places above 2,500) was only 7.2 compared to 19.8 for the country as a whole. Probably the twenty-year period of war and reconstruction did not significantly retard urbanization, but neither did it, of course, stimulate it. Opportunities of profit from urban enterprise arose primarily with the rapid economic development of the New South after 1880. Older communities, the river towns for example, developed a more diversified economic base. Recalling his days as a pilot on the Mississippi in 1883, Mark Twain observed: "I was not expecting to live to see Natchez and these other river towns become manufacturing strongholds and railway centres." Newer interior cities

—Atlanta and Nashville, and later Louisville, Memphis, and Dallas—boomed as a network of railroads was built in the region. Atlanta, in particular, was the site chosen by Northeastern investors in urban enterprise.

As part of this growth, the South experienced the customary real estate booms so common in the West. Birmingham, a new industrial city in Alabama founded in 1871, had a particularly spectacular boom in the late eighties. "Why, men would come in at four o'clock in the morning and begin making trades before breakfast," an early resident recalled. "Property changed hands four and five times a day. . . . Men went crazy two hours after getting here. A brand-new sensation was born every day." During this period, a dozen paper towns were launched within a seventy-five mile radius of Chattanooga. "The great bulk of both capital for the project and people who buy the lots, come from the East and North, some of the money from England," commented a Chattanooga newspaper. The projected town of Cardiff, Tennessee announced an auction of town lots for April 22, 1890, for which "Ten Solid Vestibuled Special Trains Will be Run from New England Alone, beside Specials from All Over the South and West." The fate of this project was indicated by the fact that Cardiff never achieved sufficient size to rate a census listing. General Fitzhugh Lee, nephew of the more famous general, led the Rockbridge Company organized to boom Glasgow, Virginia. Lee announced the sales of "Lots number 35 and 37 in Block 153 on Rockridge Road to Her Grace Lilly the Duchess of Marlborough" and two others "to George Spencer Churchill, Duke of Marlborough." The company sold large amounts of stock and began the construction of a magnificent hotel. But with the collapse of the boom the company failed, and the hotel which was never opened stood for years as a decayed ruin.

Despite the urban booming and the sometimes spectacular growth of individual cities, the South, in sharp contrast to regions of the West, remained in this period primarily a rural region with a rather consistent level of urbanization at any census period corresponding to that for the nation as a whole about fifty years earlier. In 1900, for example, urban population in the South was 15.2 per cent of the total while the national figure in 1850 had been 15.3. In 1920 the percentage for the South was 25.4; the national figure in 1870 had been 25.7. This supports the general conclusion that urbanization in the South paralleled closely the national process, with a fifty-year time lag. However, it should be noted that a disproportionate share of the increased urban population was located in the border regions of Maryland, Delaware, and the District of Columbia. After 1920 the rate of urbanization (that is the percentage change in urban population from one census to the next) became greater for the South than for the nation as a whole, and the time lag by 1950 was down to forty years.

Several scholars have argued that southern cities differed from those elsewhere because of a distinctive population with distinctive values. Growth came from the migration of poor, little educated, rural migrants from the immediate region, people influenced, it has been asserted, by traditions of "bucolic individualism," allegiance to a romantic agrarian myth, and a southern "world view" which encouraged violence by conceiving the individual as a hapless victim of blind, hostile forces in the universe. Southern rural culture patterns may have given a different cast to life in some southern cities —and of course it must be remembered that there was wide variation in the character of cities from one part of the South to another. But at the same time southern cities were affected by the general transforming trends associated with American urbanization—urban technology, suburbanization, commercial foundations of growth, business leadership, and energetic promotion. In the late nineteenth and early twentieth centuries, southern cities led the nation in the utilization of old methods of promotion and in the institution of new approaches to the problems of community development. In the period from 1850 to 1910, the South occupied a special position in the national culture and economy, and this was influenced by its lower level of urbanization. Yet, despite its much-emphasized agrarian tradition, the region was shaped by the forces that led to the growth of cities throughout the nation.

The importance of city promotion and city-building in the growth of the American economy in the nineteenth century has been insufficiently appreciated and little assessed. In a very significant respect, as Richard C. Wade has clearly demonstrated for the period before 1830, the town promoter was the true "frontiersman" in the development of new regions of the country. The speculative city he founded in the wilderness was often the cause not the result of growth and settlement. Moreover, historians have tended to ignore the cultural drama that was a part of the violent competition for success in the enterprise of city-building; town rivalry was one of the great games of nineteenth century America. "Tell them we are building a great city," a promoter of the small frontier settlement of Kansas City had typically proclaimed in the fifties. By 1910, however, this kind of urban rallying cry, once heard through the land at every promising spot on road and river, could no longer reflect the creating of magnificent cities in the wilderness through hope, enthusiasm, and energy. The urban network had been substantially completed, and something vital had passed from American life.

CHAPTER

# 7

# Transformation and Complexity: A Changing Population, 1860-1910

CREATION of new cities in undeveloped regions, rivalries among communities competing for urban supremacy, prophetic visions of America's urban future, and frenzied booms in town sites and urban land contributed fundamentally to the cultural drama of nineteenth-century America. But the rapid urbanization of the United States after 1860 involved much more than the establishment of individual cities and their organization in a complex inter-urban network. It also involved profound changes in the nature of the city itself and in the pattern of life in organized communities both urban and rural. By 1910 American culture can be said, in a number of senses, to have become urbanized, and this marked a significant change in the character of American society. During the fifty years from 1860 to 1910, American cities absorbed nearly a seven-fold increase in population, much of it in the larger cities; this striking demographic development was a concomitant of radical institutional and technological changes that altered the social and physical environment and the way people were conditioned by that environment.

The accretion of urban population alone does not necessarily cause changes in the fundamental patterns of society. In fact, the growth of population and its spatial regrouping may in some circumstances be considered an element in social change independent of—but of course influenced by—levels of technology and industrialization. Tokyo, for example, grew to a city of a million in the middle of the nineteenth century but remained in organization a kind of extended town that functioned much as it had for centuries past; a similar point could be made about many of the large cities of Africa. But urbanization in a narrow demographic sense, when coupled as it was in America with an advanced level of technology and dynamic capitalistic institutions, provided a vital force in the transformation of society. In the nineteenth-century cities of the Western world, specialization, variety, complexity, and regularity were substituted for the simplicities and lack of differentiation in earlier communities. Such fundamental human institutions as the household, the family, and the church underwent significant modification in the new environment. Observers, conditioned by the outlooks of the past, often found the city the site of social disorganization. But this disorganization was sometimes in reality only a complicated pattern of accommodation to the conditions of a new environment. As Oscar Handlin has observed, no earlier human experience had imposed the demands of the late nineteenth-century western city. Even the concept of time had to be altered. "The complex interrelationships of life in the modern city," Handlin writes, "called for unprecedented precision. The arrival of all those integers who worked together, from whatever part of the city they inhabited, had to be coordinated to the movement. There was no natural span for such labor; arbitrary beginnings and ends had to be set, made uniform and adhered to. The dictatorship of the clock and the schedule became absolute." By 1910 in urbanizing America, this new social order of the city was already being imposed on the country, and in large measure defined the character of a national culture.

The great increase in the population of American cities, which underlay these fundamental changes, was the result of population movement—of migration into cities from abroad and from the American countryside. Although the relationship between migration, birth and death rates, and urban growth cannot be examined historically with any precision, it seems reasonably certain that not until well into the twentieth century did city dwellers in America reproduce at replacement levels. Examination of this circumstance, however, is complicated by the fact that *migrants* to a city during a given period (the decennial federal census period constituting the ordinarily available span of measurement) did reproduce at a rate above replacement levels; therefore for a chosen period urban population would show a statistical natural increase. Special data available for the census period 1900–1910 suggests the characteristic demographic pattern in this era of rapid urbanization. Of 11,826,000 *new* city dwellers in 1910 some 41 per cent were immigrants from abroad, 29.8 per cent were native rural-to-urban migrants, 21.6 per cent represented natural increase, and the remaining 7.6 per cent were the result of incorporation of new territories into existing cities. Virtually all demographic evidence indicates that the growth of cities in the period 1860 to 1910 was sustained by high birth rates on the farm, including the rural areas of Europe, and among people newly arrived in the city. Periods of high immigration, in fact, relate closely to population trends in rural Europe. Baby booms of 1825 and 1840–1845 in Western Europe had stimulated the influx of immigrants before the Civil War. A population boom in southern and eastern Europe from 1860–1865 led to an immigration peak in 1880–1884; another increase in 1880–1890 produced another peak period after 1902.

Although the mass migration of the polyglot peoples of Europe to America has rightly been viewed as one of the notable themes of the national experience, in examining urbanization demographically it is convenient to consider foreign migration as one aspect of a general movement of people from the farm to the city. Most European immigrants who came to the United States were rural dwellers, and when they arrived, they settled in the cities. The use of machinery in farming, the introduction of techniques of scientific agriculture, and the opening of new fertile areas of production in Argentina, Australia, and the American West improved the efficiency of agriculture and drove surplus workers from the soil. In the United States, the productivity of farm labor increased strikingly so that by the 1890s a much smaller work force than that of the 1830s could bring in even larger crops of many of the main agricultural products. For example, through the use of modern machines, the work of one man in a wheat field in 1896 could be more than eighteen times as effective as it had been in 1830. To the economic forces pushing people from the farms were added the pulls exerted by commercial and industrial demands for ever larger labor forces in the cities. As a result of the population movement encouraged by these developments, about eleven million of the forty-two million city dwellers of 1910 had come from American farm homes after 1880; it also seems fairly certain that at least one-third of the total urban population of 1910 were American natives of rural origin. Migration to and from the United States, and the internal movement of immigrants, left a net total of over nine and a half-million foreign-born in American cities in 1910. The large numbers of people pouring into cities after 1860 forced striking changes in their function and organization. Both the European peasant and the American migrant from the farm faced the problem of adjusting to a new and rapidly changing environment, in which they were themselves a vital element in the process of change.

As early as the 1850s, spokesmen of the values of the country, such as Amory D. Mayo, had lamented the increasing movement of young people from the farm to the city and had noted the fundamental social change this movement was producing. By the 1860s the rural exodus was the subject of increasing attention. The *New York Times,* for example, complained in 1863 that the Civil War had accelerated rather than retarded urbanization: throughout the nation "the tide of population" was pouring toward the city "with undiminished impetuosity." Later in the decade, Horace Greeley emphasized the same theme: "We cannot all live in cities," he wrote, "yet nearly all seem determined to do so. . . . 'Hot and cold water,' baker's bread, gas, the theatre, and the streetcars . . . indicate the tendency of modern taste. Away behind these is the country. 'God made it.' The 'town' may have its allurements. Long valleys with independence and health whispering among the oaks and pines speak of a more vigorous race." Arthur M. Schlesinger, in his seminal study of the growth of urban America, has vividly described the "lure of the city" during the 1880s, a decade of prosperity and rapid urbanization. Although in this decade—as in every decade until the 1950s— non-urban population for the country as a whole increased absolutely, certain states and areas did show marked reductions. This selective depopulation intensified the alarm of the defenders of rural America against the wicked city. As a result of internal migration during the decade, 40 per cent of the nation's 25,746 townships showed a decline in population. Portions of rural New England were particularly hard hit as nearly 60 per cent of the townships (932 of 1502) registered a drop. State studies recorded a wide-scale abandonment of farms—3,300 in Maine, 1,500 in Massachusetts, 1,300 in New Hampshire, and, 1,000 in Vermont. In the rapidly urbanizing Midwest, there were similar pockets of rural decay. Portions of central Missouri, eastern Iowa, northern and western Illinois, and central and southeastern Indiana were drastically depopulated, largely as a result of the movement of farmers to towns and cities. There were 7,500 fewer farmers in Michigan in 1890 than there had been ten years before, although the total population of the state grew by half a million. In Ohio, 755 of 1,316 townships and in Illinois, 800 of 1,424 decreased in population during the decade, though both states, like all midwestern states during the period, grew in total population.

The predominant urban trend of the period was not the result of individuals migrating directly from the isolated farm to the huge metropolis. More frequently, people moved from rural areas to a local hamlet, then to a town or regional city, and then perhaps to Chicago, New York, or another metropolis. Young men and women often moved from the small towns in which they had been born to the larger city. "The reasons that impelled a person to leave the farm to go to a crossroads village," Schlesinger writes, "were likely to cause the ambitious or maladjusted villager to remove to a larger place, or might in time spur the transplanted farmer lad himself to try his fortunes in a broader sphere. The results were seen in the records of city growth. The pyramid of urban population enlarged at every point from base to peak, and the countryside found itself encroached upon by hamlet, town and city."

Hamlin Garland has vividly recorded the effects of this movement on individuals in describing the migrations of members of his family back and forth from farm to village to city. His work captures the feeling of rootlessness that resulted from the constant mobility so characteristic of American society in this era of migration. Late in his life, for example, Garland could sum up numerous advantages of big city life in New York, where he had settled with his family after a futile attempt to recapture the stability of the village environment in West Salem, Wisconsin. Yet, at the same time, he reflected disillusionment over something fundamental that had been lost: "No! I am not *entirely* content. Deep down in my consciousness is a feeling of guilt, a sense of disloyalty to my ancestors, which renders me uneasy. It may be that this is only a survival of the mental habit of my boyhood, a tribute to my father and his self-reliant generation." Although Garland and other writers expressed nostalgia about the land and a simpler past that probably mirrored a general cultural anxiety toward the complex new urban environment, Americans in the years 1860 to 1910 moved toward the place of opportunity and challenge—the city.

A part of this movement that had great consequences for cities and for American society in the twentieth century was the beginning of the migration of Negroes from the rural South to cities of the South and to cities of the Midwest and Northeast. Before 1910, this migration did not involve great numbers of people; it was a rather selective movement of the young and unmarried, of the first generation born in freedom. During the period, white rural dwellers moved to the cities in greater proportion and of course in vastly greater numbers. Unlike much white migration, Negro migration usually consisted of moves directly from the farm to cities, along clearly defined routes determined to a considerable extent by the most inexpensive lines of transportation. Immediately after the Civil War, there was considerable movement into the cities of the South, and the proportion of Negroes in the population of such cities as Atlanta, Memphis, Nashville, and Norfolk rose substantially from 1860 to 1870. But these proportions tended to remain constant thereafter as more southern rural Negroes migrated to the Northeast and Midwest. The approximately 68,000 Negroes who left the South between 1870 and 1880 increased steadily decade by decade, reaching 194,-000 from 1900 to 1910. Largely as the result of employment opportunities created by the First World War, the numbers then began to increase dramatically. The vast majority of the Negro migrants settled in cities; in 1890 about three-fifths of the Negro population outside the South was urban, and this figure had moved close to four-fifths by 1910. By 1900 there were seventy-two cities in the United States with a Negro population of more than 5,000. Although outside the South the percentages were small, sizeable Negro communities had developed in several large cities. New York's Negro population in 1910 stood at about 92,000 (1.9 per cent of the total); Philadelphia's 84,500 (5.5 percent); Chicago's 44,000 (2 per cent). Among more southerly cities the comparable figures were Washington 94,500 (28.5 per cent); Baltimore 85,000 (15.2 per cent), and St. Louis 44,000 (6.4 per cent).

By 1910 the solid Negro cores of the mid-twentieth century had not yet formed, but a pattern had been shaped. In Chicago, for example, considerable organized resistance to the movement of Negroes into many white neighborhoods developed in the first decade of the century. By 1910 there were still eight or nine Negro neighborhoods in Chicago and none was over 60 per cent Negro, but increasingly there was evidence of concentration of Negroes in two clearly-defined areas on the south and west sides of the city. In New York, after a collapse of a real estate boom in Harlem in 1904–1905, Negroes began to concentrate in that district. A survey in 1917 indicated that nearly 49,000 Negroes already lived in a twenty-three block area of Harlem; the entire Negro population in Manhattan was about 60,500 in 1910. By this date, "Niggertowns," "Smoketowns," "Black Bottoms,"

"Buzzard Rows," and "Coon Alleys," to cite a few of the more derogatory names, had become recognized areas of cities in both the North and the South. "There is growing up in the cities of America a distinct Negro world," George Edmund Haynes, a New York Negro leader, wrote in 1913. These neighborhoods, he concluded, were "isolated from many of the impulses of the common life and little understood by the white world."

More immediate in its effects than the limited migration of Negroes and more dramatic in its effects than the "urban drift" of white native population was the large-scale settlement of European migrants in the cities of America. In general, this, like Negro migration, was a movement of people directly to the city—and predominantly to the larger city. But until well into the twentieth century foreign immigration occurred on a vastly greater scale. The report of the famous Dillingham Commission, which reflected a bias in favor of immigration restriction and hence drew too sharp a line between the effects of the "old" and the "new" immigration, found that in 1910 78.6 per cent of the more recent "new" immigrants from southern and eastern Europe lived in urban communities compared to 68.3 per cent of the old immigrants from northern and central Europe. Over-all, about 72 per cent of the foreign-born were classified as urban residents, compared to about 46 per cent of the nation as a whole. Certain immigrant groups had a particularly high proportion of urban dwellers. Over five-sixths of the natives of Ireland and Russia lived in cities. The proportion was above seven-tenths for those born in England, Scotland, Austria, Greece and China; two-thirds for Germans; and three-fifths for Swedes. Only two nationalities—Montenegrins and Norwegians—had a lower percentage of city dwellers than did the population as a whole. In addition to their concentration in cities in general, immigrants also tended to live in larger cities, so that the percentage of foreign-born increased directly with categories of city size in the 1910 census. The influx of immigrants to the cities, particularly during the decade of the 1880s when over five million arrived in the United States, produced some striking statistics for individual cities. In 1890, New York (including the still legally separate municipality of Brooklyn) contained more foreign-born residents than any city in the world. The city had half as many Italians as Naples, as many Germans as Hamburg, twice as many Irish as Dublin, and two and a-half times the number of Jews in Warsaw. In 1893, Chicago contained the third largest Bohemian community in the world; by the time of World War I, Chicago ranked only behind Warsaw and Lodz as a city of Poles. Notable also was the fact that four out of five people living in greater New York in 1890 had either been born abroad or were of foreign parentage.

As a result of this influx, the residential areas of many larger cities began after 1860 to form a mosaic of immigrant neighborhoods and ethnic ghettos. Nationality groups tended to live in distinct areas of the city; when new-comers from another country or region began to arrive in a neighborhood, the older ethnic group moved elsewhere. New York's Lower East Side, for example, underwent an ethnic transformation in the years after the Civil War. The Irish and Germans, who had earlier lived in the district, went northward up Manhattan Island or to Brooklyn; Italians moved into the old Irish neighborhoods and Jews from Russia and Poland occupied the German districts. In Chicago during this era, Poles and Bohemians migrated into areas that had earlier been German, Scandinavian, and Irish in character. Contemporaries, particularly in commenting on New York, frequently used the metaphor of the multicolored quilt to describe the complexity of population patterns in the late nineteenth-century city. Jacob Riis, for example, in his famous *How the Other Half Lives* employed the technique:

A map of the city, colored to designate nationalities, would show more stripes than on the skin of a zebra, and more colors than any rainbow. The city on such a map would fall into great halves, green for the Irish prevailing in the West Side tenement districts, and blue for the Germans on the East Side. But intermingled with these ground colors would be an odd variety of tints that would give the whole the appearance of an extraordinary crazy-quilt. From down in the Sixth Ward, upon the site of the old Collect Pond . . . the red of the Italian would be seen forcing its way northward along the line of Mulberry Street to the quarter of the French purple on Bleecker Street and South Fifth Avenue, to lose itself and reappear, after a lapse of miles, in the 'Little Italy' of Harlem, east of Second Avenue. Dashes of red, sharply defined, would be seen strung through the Annexed District, northward to the city line. On the West Side the red would be seen overrunning the old Africa of Thompson Street, pushing the black of the negro rapidly uptown, against querulous but unavailing protests, occupying his home, his church, his trade and all, with merciless impartiality.

Behind this kind of contemporary description and analysis was an assumption of ethnic "clannishness"; in general the new immigrant was regarded as more clannish than the old. Loyalty to the old country was associated with a reluctance of the immigrant to give allegiance to his adopted land—an unwillingness to become "Americanized." But in reality, the intense immigrant group loyalties that gave cohesiveness to the ethnic communities were often provincial rather than national. New York, for example, did not contain a "Little Italy" but rather a number of distinct groups of Italians— Neapolitans and Calabrians in the Mulberry Bend district; a group of Genoese on Baxter Street; north Italians in the Eighth and Fifteenth Wards west of Broadway; and a small colony of Tyrolese Italians on Sixty-Ninth Street, near the Hudson River. In Chicago there were seventeen distinct Italian communities, each one identified with a district of the old country. In the same city two groups of Roumanians kept themselves completely separate from each other. Jews also clustered on the basis of the districts in which they had lived in Europe.

Still, for the most part, with the exception of the trade union, immigrant life was organized along lines of nationality, giving support to the argument that the "new immigration" represented a threat to established American culture. In the late nineteenth century, it was the presence of the urban colonies of immigrants from eastern and southern Europe in the larger metropolises, made up of people predominately Roman Catholic and Jewish in religion and differing in manner and appearance from older Americans, that stimulated renewed attack on the "evil" city. In this critique, "urbanism" was equated with ethnicity, only one characteristic—and in some respects a minor characteristic—of emerging urban life in America. Many interior cities, Kansas City and Indianapolis, for example, and most of the rapidly growing cities of the South, did not experience the influence of the immi-grant colonies, and certainly urbanization involved a much broader process of social change than the mere acculturation of immigrants. Yet the immi-grant did become a stock figure in statements of urban ideology. Those who attempted to formulate a cultural defense of the city and to advance a kind of counter-myth of the good city became imprisoned in the old view and tried too narrowly to define *urbanism* as a function of cultural and ethnic diversity. In short, much of the argument about the city in American life down to the present day has had only limited application to the whole of the American urban experience. "New York is not America," asserted Ford Maddox Ford; by the same token, the city where ethnic diversity flourished does not necessarily represent historical urban America.

Even in New York, where ethnic communities so prominently shaped the life of the city, the implications that are part of the popular concept of the "ethnic ghetto" are misleading. The term *ghetto* of course initially referred to the areas in European cities where Jews were officially confined, following a policy set in Venice in the sixteenth century. It was applied in the United States to the Jewish area on the Lower East Side of New York City toward the turn of the century and came generally in the rhetoric of twentieth-century progressives attacking the social problems of the city to represent any slum occupied by large numbers of immigrants. But a program of social control fundamental to the European ghetto (and in some respects to later Negro residential areas because segregation there was partly embodied in public policy) was not the cause for the formation and growth of American ethnic neighborhoods. As David Ward has shown in a careful study of urban immigrants, the location of places of work determined where people lived during the era of the pedestrian city that prevailed until the latter part of the nineteenth century. Neighborhoods formed around central business districts, where the greatest opportunities for employment existed. Improved trans-portation permitted middle-class groups to move some distance away; this vacated additional housing for continually arriving immigrants. The process was not one of an influx of people building up a permanent neighborhood but rather one of a great deal of movement of people in and out of any given area over a short period of time. Nationality groups concentrated in areas with their countrymen, but there was no large section of any city, including New York, occupied exclusively by one ethnic group. Moreover, ethnic communities overlapped one another.

At the turn of the century reformers in their attacks on the slum tended to portray the immigrant areas of cities as places of disease, high death rates, and social disorganization. Again this view was oversimplified and partly wrong. In New York the death rate in areas of the city occupied by Russian Jews was often the lowest in the city, reflecting their knowledge of living in cities and a built-up resistance to urban diseases, particularly tuberculosis. On the other hand, the death rate among Italians in adjoining neighborhoods was among the highest in the city, reflecting perhaps the fact that they came from a warmer climate and from the country. Nor was the assumed correlation between crowding and disease and early death accurate. In cities such as Philadelphia, where single-family dwellings were standard, and in Chicago and St. Louis, where there were large proportions of two- and three-family dwellings, the late nineteenth-century death rates were higher than in some of the most densely settled parts of New York. A variety of factors relating to local sanitary practices, the circumstances of sewage disposal, and the character of the water supply affected health more directly than congestion. Similarly, in examining social dimensions of the slum problem, many reformers had little insight into patterns of life among different nationalities, sometimes interpreting folkways that reflected stability as slum-induced deviations from the normal. Residential concentration also had advantages not really recognized at the time, for example, the capacity of groups to gain considerable political power.

Examination of population movement and mobility in cities in the nineteenth century (which became a productive area of scholarship in the 1960s) has done much to discredit the conception of the "ghetto" as a neighborhood of permanence—permanent at least over a period of a few years. Studies of Boston, Poughkeepsie, Atlanta, Los Angeles, and a number of other diverse places has revealed a striking fact: a remarkably rapid turnover of population in all neighborhoods, with a figure usually standing well above 50 per cent in any ten-year period. Howard P. Chudacoff in a case study of Omaha has convincingly demonstrated this point. Omaha was a representative late nineteenth-century city. In 1880 it was rapidly growing and had moved from its commercial foundations to a base of considerable manufacturing. One-third of its population was then foreign-born, and there was a steady influx of immigrants into the city thereafter. It had in its population a range of "old" and "new" immigrant groups—Czechs, Germans, Swedes, Irish, Danes, Russian Jews, and Italians. But none of these concentrated in a single neighborhood. Substantial numbers of Czechs lived near two of their churches, many Russian Jews near a synagogue. But there were always many more of these groups living elsewhere, away from the identifiable neighborhoods. As public transportation was built in the late nineteenth century, all immigrant groups dispersed in the three directions away from the Missouri River, in pretty much the same pattern. The ethnic neighborhood was a kind of optical illusion. A native church, a group of shops whose proprietors had names of obvious nationality and catered to the needs of an ethnic group, and nationality clubs visually identified an area as Jewish, Bohemian, or Italian. But a large number of people living in the neighborhood were not of that nationality and the facilities in the area were often utilized by people who came from some distance away and from all over the city.

This pattern of rapid turnover of population and dispersion has suggested to some historians that there was present in the nineteenth century a substantial *failed urban proletariat,* a floating population drifting from place to place in search of work. Stephan Thernstrom has advanced the hypothesis that this impermanence made it difficult to organize lower-class groups, thus accounting for the absence of a radical, anti-capitalistic tradition in the American labor movement. It is clear, however, that much of the moving about within cities was the result of, or the accompaniment of, an individual's improving his economic circumstances. Population studies reveal considerable opportunity and considerable upward mobility for all groups in cities save one—Negroes. This was not movement from rags to riches, from ditch-digger to bank president, as celebrated in the myth of the self-made man. But a large proportion of the people in cities did move from unskilled jobs to semi-skilled ones and from blue-collar to white-collar jobs.

In the most detailed of these numerous mobility studies, Thernstrom has found that between 1880 and 1968 in Boston, approximately one-fourth of all the men who first entered the labor market as manual laborers ended their careers in middle-class white-collar occupations, and only one in six "skidded" in the other direction. Movement from unskilled to semi-skilled jobs or from lower white-collar to higher white-collar jobs was of course much greater. The pattern of movement common in Boston was remarkably consistent from one part of the country to the other and in cities of different sizes. Ethnic groups participated in this process of upward mobility, although the extent varied from one ethnic group to another and from place to place. In Boston, native-born Americans moved up the occupational ladder in substantially greater proportion than the foreign-born, but in Atlanta, San Antonio, and South Bend immigrants did as well as natives. A study of occupational patterns in 1900 demonstrates that the children of English and Irish immigrants proportionally had better jobs than the native population, chiefly because their parents had settled in cities where there were greater opportunities for education and thereby movement to jobs of higher status. Negro migrants, however, did not share in this largesse of the city. Studies of Boston, San Antonio, and Atlanta have demonstrated exceedingly limited possibilities for even slight job improvement among Negroes. In Atlanta, to cite one example, during the decade 1870–1880, although 50 per cent of the native-born whites and 33 per cent of the immigrants were moving to better jobs, 90 per cent of the Negroes remained in the unskilled groups in which they had started. This circumstance of the American city, with all its enormous consequences, would continue down through the twentieth century, at least until very recent times.

The late nineteenth-century movement of migrants into the cities and the presence of people of different languages and cultures led to extensive and complex modification of social institutions. Immigrants were overwhelmingly peasants, but the village, which provided the primary means of organizing life in the homeland, could not be transplanted to the city nor could it really be transplanted anywhere in America. Hence, as in so many areas of urban life, there was a series of makeshift responses. Some of these responses have been well studied. The working of the boss-machine system, which represented in part an accommodation of American political structures to the immigrant, are reasonably clear. But the effects of immigration and urbanization on such basic social institutions as the family and the school, although it is clear the effects were profound, are much less clearly understood. Many of these responses, of course, did not involve change in the structures of existing society but came from within the immigrant groups themselves. The foreign-language newspaper quickly established itself as a device to assist immigrants to get along in the United States, as well as to foster group solidarity. Irish and German groups had started newspapers in the 1830s, Scandinavians in the 1850s, and every group coming thereafter did the same. By 1890 the German press included nearly 800 publications. Although many of these were in small communities, big-city dailies were published in New York, St. Louis, Cincinnati, and Milwaukee. In 1890 there were ten Jewish newspapers, some of them published in German; by 1910 as their number doubled, they were predominately in Yiddish. Abraham Cahan's famous *Daily Journal of New York* in Yiddish was perhaps the foreign-language newspaper with the greatest circulation. Newspapers reflected the diversity within nationality groups: Chicago Czechs, for example, had four newspapers, each representing a distinct persuasion within the community—Catholic, Freethinker, business, and socialist.

Many of the nationality organizations were designed primarily to provide economic assistance, but they often acquired broader social functions. Immigrant banks frequently appeared in the urban colonies to supply the needs of newly arrived settlers. The bank received money for safekeeping and took care of sending funds abroad to relatives, but it also served as a kind of information bureau and clearinghouse where the immigrant could obtain information and business services. The mutual aid or fraternal benefit society, which had its origins in the traditional death and burial associations common in European countries, was found among most immigrant groups. Uncertainty of employment in American cities accentuated the need for mutual insurance, but many of the organizations performed other functions, often supporting schools and cultural events. These societies went far beyond their scope **in** the old country, where their functions were limited and where they were supported primarily by the middle classes. At first organized on a local basis, the mutual aid societies eventually were federated along nationality lines, in such organizations as the Order of Sons of Italy (1905), the Polish National Alliance (1880), and the Pan Hellenic Union (1907). A variety of philanthropic associations took root in the immigrant communities, many of them designed directly to help those who had just arrived in the United States. To cite just one example, the New York Hebrew Free Loan Society, organized in 1892, made interest-free loans of from $10 to $200 to immigrants eager to set up independent businesses. The society's funds had grown to over $100,000 within little more than a decade, as grateful borrowers who had succeeded contributed to its capital. The activities of these various philanthropic agencies sometimes revealed divisions within ethnic groups, particularly between early- and late-comers. In Detroit, for example, the German Jews who administered Jewish charities showed little sympathy for the culture, ideals, or Orthodox religious practices of the Russian Jews who began to arrive in the 1880s, and their antagonism evoked reciprocal hostility. As a consequence, by the time of World War I, German and Russian Jews constituted two distinct communities in the city.

In addition to the agencies primarily providing economic assistance, numerous social organizations shaped the immigrant's accommodation to his new circumstances of life—patriotic societies, physical-culture associations, and the Greek and Turkish coffee houses, for example. To groups not opposed to the use of alcohol, the tavern operated by someone from the homeland provided a center of social life, a point not understood by many reformers who associated the saloon with waste of time and money, poor work habits, and an increase in poverty and crime. For the workingman, Charles Loring Brace observed, "the liquor-shop is his picture-gallery, club, reading room, and social salon, at once. His glass is the magic transmuter of care to cheerfulness, of penury to plenty, and a low, ignorant, worried life, to an existence for the moment buoyant, contended and hopeful."

There was a fundamental limitation in the efforts of all these immigrant clubs, societies, and charities, a limitation that applied also to the various activities of "social settlements" and to programs of public assistance. These agencies could deal with problems of economic and social adjustment to an extent, but they could not really address themselves to the serious psychological aspects of the move to America. As the classic account of the Polish peasant in America argued, the environment of the big city destroyed the way the peasant organized his whole individual and social life: "An individual who, like the peasant, has been brought up as a member of a permanent and coherent primary-group and accustomed to rely for all regulations of conduct upon habit and the immediate suggestions and reactions of his social milieu, . . . lacks the necessary preparation to construct for himself a new lifeorganization with such elements as abstract individualistic morality, religious

mysticism, and the legal and economic system which he finds in America."
As a result the immigrant more than others faced something more serious
than extreme poverty or dependency—a danger of acute personal maladjust-
ment that could lead to crime or insanity. In fact, some of the responses to
urban life by organized groups had characteristics that could be termed
pathological—as in the case of the movement of Italian rural immigrants into
organized crime. After 1890 the "Black Hand," a term that came from within
the Italian community in an attempt to disassociate Italian-Americans from
the Mafia of Sicily, profitably engaged in systematic extortion in Sicilian and
southern Italian neighborhoods, primarily in Chicago. Their enterprise was
maintained through a policy of murder, bombing, and terror. With the cur-
tailment of Italian immigration and better law enforcement, the Black Hand
era came to an end in the 1920s, and Italians took advantage of prohibition
to organize crime along business lines and almost give respectability to certain
illegal activities. As Daniel Bell observed in an influential essay, crime provided a "queer ladder of social mobility" for men of talent who sought
prestige and power but whose nationality and acquired attitudes toward formal education curtailed their entrance into the traditional professions.

Urban leaders had long recognized the possibility of social pathology in
the city. Although it was accepted that crime and pauperism were primarily
the result of individual failure, these conditions were still recognized to have
social dimensions. But there was one institution that could provide the means
to enable the immigrant—or anyone else—to make a satisfactory adjustment
to American society. That was the school. The programs of those concerned
with the problems of the city had education as a key demand. In the writings
of educational theorists like Henry Barnard, the mid-nineteenth-century fol-
lower of Horace Mann and the first United States Commissioner of Education,
there was the consistent theme that the school could train children to live in
a society of cities and factories. With the great migrations to the city after
the Civil War, businessmen, politicians, and reformers directed concerted
attention toward the school as an instrument of acculturation or "Americanization," a term that acquired its pejorative connotation only in the twentieth
century. The successful movement for compulsory school-attendance laws
came from the cities; six states had them by 1871, twenty-six by 1890, and by
the turn of the century they were general except in the South. The effort to
centralize authority in city school systems and to organize them along the
lines of the corporation and the factory—in accord with a general late nineteenth-century concern with ordering institutions—represented a program on
the part of substantial interests in cities to make schools more efficient institutions for training good workers and good citizens. William T. Harris, the
idealist philosopher and educator who served as superintendent of schools
in St. Louis from 1867 to 1880, and later as United States Commissioner of
Education, effectively articulated the social theory underlying the view that
the school could be accommodated to the demands of the city. Although

Harris endorsed a number of pedagogical reforms, he was essentially a conservative who emphasized the necessity of inculcating a set of traditional values that would provide the discipline necessary to face the complexities of urban life. An ordered curriculum, increasing in difficulty each year and centered around "tool subjects," would enable the elementary-school graduate to move on to mastering the increasingly complex knowledge of business and technology. The school should teach a respect for authority, and "habits of punctuality, silence, and industry"; these qualities and others such as perseverance, earnestness, and truthfulness were essential to getting along well in the city. Harris argued that the machine, the city, and the factory were benefits that could bring a better life for all; the problems they created could be solved through training and educating the individual. The way to deal with the slums, the rendezvous of the "moral weaklings of society," was not through charity, which undermined self-respect, but through education, which would provide an individual with a sense of thrift and decency. He argued that it was "to the educational systems of large cities, and to them alone, that we look for the invention of more powerful and more effective means to break the chain of heredity between the adult criminal and the criminal offspring, so as to eradicate the slum in the future."

Educational critics of the 1960s and 1970s, with their allegiance to a neoromantic, radical educational philosophy, have seen in the authoritarianism of the school in the late nineteenth and early twentieth century an earlier reflection of a continuing policy of "cruelty to the young" and a harsh destruction of diverse cultural traditions in the cause of ultra-patriotic nationalism. Some historians have interpreted the public-school movement of the late nineteenth century as an organized effort on the part of business interests to order and control society in the interests of wealth and the perpetuation of capitalism. There is evidence from here and there to sustain this view; businessmen were concerned with controlling school boards and influencing school policies and curricula. Still the implication of elitist or plutocratic conspiracy that informs so much of this writing breaks down in one fundamental regard. Immigrants were not coerced or forced into educational establishments against their will. In general, immigrant parents and organized immigrant groups advocated and promoted schools; education was viewed as a practical way of getting ahead. Timothy Smith, in a study of new immigrants arriving after 1880, finds them to be enthusiastic proponents of education. They organized parochial schools partly to preserve cultural traditions of the homeland but also to ensure that their children learned English and acquired skills necessary to make money. They were also concerned with qualifying immigrants for the "duties of citizenship." Father Paul Tymkevich, a pastor of a Ruthenian Greek Catholic church in Yonkers at the turn of the century, supported education for this purpose as part of his concern with urban problems. He argued that the customs of his people did not equip them for life in the city. "The first step in civilization is to acquire habits," he stated, "and where can they acquire them? On the streets? In the saloon?" The proper place of course was in the school. The night-school movement with its emphasis on practical education and manual training began in many places not through the support of business executives and politicians but through the efforts of immigrant associations. "Quite as much as any coercion from compulsory education acts," Smith writes, "or any pressure from professional Americanizers, the immigrant's own hopes for his children account for the immense success of the public school system, particularly at the secondary level, in drawing the mass of working-class children into its embrace." The immigrant's assessment of the importance of education was correct. Regardless of whether or not the school was authoritarian or destructive of cultural values, it did provide—as studies of immigrant mobility so clearly indicate—training and education of a kind that enabled many immigrant children to improve their lot in the city.

An institution as important as the school in shaping the accommodation of migrants to the city was the church, but its responses were so much a part of the organized community effort to cope with the problems of urbanization that its role should be examined in that regard at a later point. Our understanding of the relationship of urbanization to other institutions in this period is limited. Views of the immigrant family, for example, are contradictory. It is generally held that the necessity of a mother's going to work undermined the authority of the family and particularly the authority of the father by diminishing his role as provider. Yet local studies of immigrant families, of southern Italians in Buffalo for instance, do not reveal significant modification in the character or stability of the patriarchal family pattern. Studies of Negro families in the city also seem to show the existence of much more stability than had previously thought to be the case.

Changes in the patterns of recreation were another obvious result of immigration and the growth of cities. Gymnasiums, which became common in cities after 1880, were a European importation, stemming from the interest in German Turner exercises and later in Swedish calisthenics. The public-playground movement of the 1880s was supported as an effort to bring healthy exercise to children in the crowded parts of cities. The rise of professional spectator sports, beginning with baseball, was made possible by large urban markets. It can be argued that sports provided a necessary outlet for the tensions and frictions of the city—relief from crowds, from the struggle for survival, and from encounters with people of sharply varying backgrounds. In the late 1880s and early 1890s there was a great enthusiasm for sports of speed and violence such as cycling, football, and prize fighting. The sports mania, according to John Higham, was part of a *fin de siècle* effort "to break out of the frustrations, the routine, and the sheer dullness of an urban-industrial culture."

Although our understanding of institutional change and the city is limited, it is clear that the process was remarkably effective. Despite all the problems of the city that developed in the late nineteenth century and the growth of the view that the city had caused a crisis in American society, the cities did "assimilate" or "accommodate" enormous numbers of immigrants and remained reasonably civil places. The rioting and lawlessness that had been so much a part of the urban scene in the early nineteenth century largely disappeared. In fact, the positive achievement of cities in providing fundamental services and amenities has even led some critics (although there is occasionally more nostalgia than history in their view) to see the late nineteenth century as the golden age of the American city.

CHAPTER

# 8

## Transformation and Complexity: An Urban Technology

EXPANDED population, and the character of this population, produced significant institutional change within American cities and provided a fundamental force altering the character of urban life. But migration to the city took place within a framework of technological change, which encouraged the movement of population at the same time it provided the means that made possible the accommodation of vast numbers of new urban dwellers. Moreover, it was technological change, not change in the way social institutions functioned, that brought about improvement in the physical quality of urban life and alleviated many of the problems that had appeared in the early nineteenth-century city. Because of the great demands created by cities in all their complexity, they had continually stimulated creative invention. Beginning in 1805, Frederic Tudor, the "Ice King" of Boston, spent a small fortune and a good many years working out the technology of preserving ice in hot climates; his manager Nathaniel Jarvis White invented several machines necessary to harvest large quantities of ice. By the late 1830s Tudor had built up a successful world-wide ice business. The impetus for this effort came from cities where the demand for ice to preserve food increased greatly with their rapid growth in the early nineteenth century. By the 1840s ice was generally available in all northern cities, and women's magazines were declaring the refrigerator or ice box, as it was soon to be called, an appliance that no household could do without. Similarly, in the twentieth century the numerous steps necessary to develop air-conditioning for various purposes came in response to the demands of the city. Its perfection for home use was in large measure the result of efforts to promote and build up cities in hot climates, particularly in Florida during the 1930s.

In the latter part of the nineteenth century, as Edward Kirkland has indicated, the actual physical building of cities supplied a fundamental generative factor in the growth of the economy of the late nineteenth century. City-building, in this period, substituted for the construction of a transportation network that had stimulated the creation of capital goods in an earlier era. To build cities on a new scale, and to order the movement within cities of vast numbers of new residents, required a variety of new techniques and inventions. Fundamentally, of course, buildings in which people could live and work had to be provided. In fact, private expenditure for construction was the single most important contribution cities made to the economy in the late nineteenth century; the dollar value of building permits (in terms of 1913 dollars) reached a peak in 1880 that was not again approached until 1925.

In cities where it was possible to spread outward conveniently, the wide-scale adoption of an innovation in building of the 1830s—the balloon frame —made possible the construction of individual houses and smaller buildings with the speed and economy necessary for the quick and orderly development of new cities and of new neighborhoods in established cities. This style of construction was used by a Chicago carpenter-architect, Augustine Deodat Taylor, in the construction of a church in 1833. Although there is evidence it was tried before, he is often credited with inventing the technique, which involved using thin pieces of sawed lumber nailed together as a frame for a building instead of relying on heavy timbers with mortised and tenoned joints for support, as had earlier been the case. The balloon frame, which was at first a derisive term implying excessive lightness and hence flimsiness, elimi-nated the need for a highly skilled carpenter and an army of assistants to lift the supporting timbers into place when a building was erected. "If it had not been for the knowledge of balloon frames," Solon Robinson, an Indiana agri-cultural spokesman, told a New York audience in 1855, "Chicago and San Francisco could never have arisen, as they did, from little villages to great cities in a single year. It is not only city buildings, which are supported by one another, that may be thus erected, but those upon the open prairie where the wind has a sweep from Mackinaw to the Mississippi, for there they are built, and stand as firm as any of the old frames of New England, with posts and beams sixteen inches square." The balloon frame, coupled with abundant timber resources and the development of efficient woodworking machinery, greatly enlarged the possibility of rapid city growth in America. It was par-ticularly suitable for the quickly built promotional cities of the west.

Opportunities for concentrated commercial and industrial activity in cities with growing and mobile populations also spurred innovations in non-resi-dential building. As early as the 1840s, large cast-iron warehouses, some of which reached the height of eight stories, had been constructed in eastern cities to accommodate the demands of large-scale merchandising. A pioneer in the development of a functional type of commercial and industrial building suitable for the modern city was James Bogardus (1800–1874), an ingenious inventor who began his career as a watchmaker and devised such items as an engraving machine which produced the first English postage stamps, a pencil with lead always sharp, and a deep-sea sounding machine. Turning his talents to architecture and engineering, Bogardus, in building a five-story factory in New York in 1848, put into practice a system of construction that substituted cast-iron columns for load-bearing masonry walls as supports for floors. This lessened the need for thick, space-consuming masonry in erecting large build-ings. Bogardus's system made practical the construction of just the kind of building demanded for business and industry in the large city—one that was externally compact with space secured through additional height and with its floors virtually unobstructed to house huge machines or large stores of merchandise. Bogardus and others carried his method of using cast-iron columns a step further to construct entire buildings of cast-iron. In the years 1850 to 1880 cast-iron business buildings became common in larger American cities; Bogardus built numerous warehouses, department stores, and office buildings in every section of the country and, using prefabricated techniques that he had developed, even exported a building to Santiago, Cuba.

Bogardus argued in the 1850s that cast-iron buildings could be erected to great heights and submitted a design for an exhibition building at the New York World's Fair of 1853 that envisaged construction of a circular amphitheater with sixty-foot-high walls and a 300-foot tower rising from the center. Although such buildings might be built, in order for them to be practical for business purposes it was necessary to devise ways of transporting people efficiently to their higher stories. The idea of the elevator was an old one, and for some years various systems, often using horse power, had been utilized for hoisting merchandise to the tops of warehouses. Bogardus suggested a steam-powered hoist to carry passengers to an observation platform atop the tower of his proposed exhibition building, which was never constructed.

The "invention" of the elevator in reality consisted of a series of refinements on a well-established principle. In the year Bogardus submitted his design—1853—Elisha G. Otis perfected a safety device to protect passengers from injury should the cable controlling a hoisting platform break while in operation; the first Otis elevator was installed in a New York store in 1857. Another system—designed by a Boston inventor and called a "Vertical Screw Railway"—was used in a New York hotel in 1859. With the introduction of hydraulic power and gearing techniques, the elevator became more efficient by the 1870s and with its adaptation to electric power in the 1880s came into general use in cities. Through considerable evolution, a device had been developed to take advantage of the economies in intensive use of urban space. And a new urban experience was possible for visitors to the big city:

In the tall buildings are the most modern and rapid elevators [wrote Julian Ralph in his account of a tour of Chicago in the early 1890s] machines that fly through the towers like glass balls from a trap at a shooting contest. The slow-going stranger, who is conscious of having been "kneaded" among the streets, like a lump of dough among a million bakers, feels himself loaded into one of those frail-looking baskets of steel netting, and the next instant the elevator-boy touches the trigger, and up goes the whole load as a feather is caught up by a gale. The descent is more simple. Something lets go, and you fall from ten to twenty stories as it happens. There is sometimes a jolt, which makes the passenger seem to feel his stomach pass into his shoes, but, as a rule, the mechanism and management both work marvellously towards ease and gentleness. These elevators are too slow for Chicago, and the managers of certain tall buildings now arrange them so that some run "express" to the seventh story without stopping, while what may be called accommodation cars halt at the lower floors, pursuing a course that may be likened to the emptying of the chambers of a revolver in the hands of a person who is "quick on the trigger."

Other inventions were necessary before large buildings could be satisfactorily used for offices or apartments. Central heating was essential. Hot-air systems had been used in American hotels before mid-century, but the more efficient system of using steam or hot water circulated through pipes came into use in the 1870s. The radiator, which is critical to the method (the term is an Americanism dating from this period), was perfected by William Baldwin in 1874.

In Chicago, in the late nineteenth century, the techniques for pushing buildings ever higher were worked out. Here in the 1880s the modern skyscraper succeeded the cast-iron "cloud scraper." The need to rebuild Chicago after the 1871 fire, rapid growth, and rising land values encouraged experimentation in construction. The city moved toward tall buildings. In 1884 William Le Baron Jenney, in erecting the ten-story Mutual Savings Bank Building, used a steel skeleton as a frame without supporting walls for the upper portion of the building. Whether Jenney was forced to employ the technique as a result of a bricklayers' strike or whether, as legend has it, he was inspired to the experiment as a result of laying a book on Mrs. Jenney's wire birdcage is a question for architectural history. Nor is the claim of the Minneapolis architect, Leroy S. Buffington, to having invented the steel frame before Jenney worthy of extended examination. As with any fundamental change in building methods, the steel frame was the result of an evolution of technological means, not of a sudden dramatic discovery. (Even a method as innovative as Taylor's balloon frame was dependent for its success on the mass production of nails.) Cast-iron columns and the iron skeleton developed by a French builder, Jules Saulnier, in 1871, were precursors of the American engineering triumph.

The new system of construction, fully utilized in Jenney's Leiter Building constructed in Chicago in 1889, has been vividly characterized by Lewis Mumford as "the iron cage and the curtain wall." "This," Mumford writes, "translated into colossal paleotechnic forms the vernacular frame and clapboard construction of the old American farmhouse. The outer wall became a mere boundary of the interior space . . .; instead of the building's being a shell, it became essentially a skeleton—a skeleton with internal organs for equalizing the temperature and for circulation, with a tough external skin." The steel frame greatly simplified difficult construction problems and proved an enormously efficient form for taking advantage of valuable urban land sites. Huge supporting walls that absorbed lower-level space were no longer necessary in tall buildings. Skyscrapers also used large quantities of plate glass, perfected in this period, and Daniel Burnham's Reliance Building of 1894 and others were sometimes described as towers of glass. Innovations such as hollow tile for fireproofing and methods of speeding up construction, such as the use of salt in brick mortar during freezing weather, meant that skyscrapers could be quickly and efficiently erected. In the hands of Louis Sullivan and other members of the famous Chicago school of architecture, the new form could produce an architectural triumph such as the Guaranty Building (later the Prudential Building) constructed by Sullivan in 1895 in Buffalo, New York. But the skyscraper from the beginning contributed to greatly intensified land speculation and increasing traffic congestion, and, because human needs were subordinated to pecuniary considerations, to a frequent lack of daylight and adequate working space within buildings.

The skyscrapers were part of a new pattern of urban life based on specialization and the concentration of economic activity that necessitated great mobility on the part of city dwellers. The possibility of this mobility and the opportunities it created in the heart of cities resulted from another series of technological developments involved in the evolution of an urban system of transportation. In this sector of urban activity, there has been a consistent technological lag—or what might be more properly termed a socio-technological lag—in that certain theoretical possibilities in urban transportation required changes in customary living patterns too drastic to be accepted. Consequently the movement of large numbers of people back and forth through the space of the city has never been efficient. Moreover, improvements in transportation—including even the ingenious system of railway electrification adopted by cities at the turn of the century—were in some ways self-defeating, because they stimulated further differentiation and specialization and, accordingly, further congestion. It is historically true, as well as true of our own time, that all new means of urban transportation were almost immediately utilized beyond their maximum effective capacity. As early as the 1850s travelers to New York were noting the frequency with which the "whole traffic of the city" came to a "dead-lock"; the "diurnal stampede" from office buildings to streetcars "loaded and incrusted with double burdens in which men clung to one another like caterpillars" was a standard part of the day in late nineteenth-century Chicago. In spite of the long-standing existence of the urban traffic problem, changes in urban transportation were fundamental in creating the spatial expansion and the specialization characteristic of the modern city.

Although American cities grew rapidly in population in the early nineteenth century, they were still, until about 1850, reasonably compact; a man might walk through all the neighborhoods of even the larger places in a day. Expanded population was absorbed through a more concentrated use of residential space near the sites of work; this caused a considerable increase in population density and a high degree of congestion in eastern seaboard cities. In the late 1820s, the introduction of the horse-drawn omnibus, carrying twelve to twenty passengers back and forth to areas outside of cities, had led to some differentiation in urban land use and the creation of distinct "downtown" districts to which people came from some distance to work or to shop. The steam railroad—almost from the beginning of its use in the United States —played a part in this development. In the 1840s eastern lines began hauling regular commuters from the large cities to neighboring towns. The Boston and West Newton Railroad, for example, reported in 1857 that during the year it had carried one-half million passengers between Boston and stations no father than ten miles away. But large trains could not conveniently be utilized within the limits of cities themselves, and charters of railroads, though generous in extending rights of way privileges through cities, generally forbade the use of steam locomotives on city thoroughfares. The horse-drawn railway provided the first real answer to the problem of large-scale movement of people within cities. The "horse-car" was invented in 1832 by James Stephenson, a New York carriage maker, but it was not until a rail that could be laid flush with a city street was devised in the late forties and early fifties that this system could be practically applied. In building horse-cars, Stephenson also perfected a number of necessary improvements in brakes and springs which were later used on motorized streetcars. The horse railway came into general use by the 1850s. By 1858, for example, the five principal street railways of New York City were carrying nearly 35,000,000 passengers a year. The Metropolitan Railroad Corporation of Boston, operator of the longest horse-drawn railroad in that city, transported nearly 6,500,000 people in 1860. Although Philadelphia had been slow to adopt the system, by 1860 the city had 148 miles of street railway—the greatest of any city. The street railways existed in combination with a variety of other forms of horse-drawn transportation; the resulting congestion was sometimes fantastic. In 1866 in New York there were seven omnibus lines with 300 cars on regular routes; sixteen horse-railway lines using 800 cars and nearly 8,000 horses; 1,400 hackney coaches; and a few odd hansom cabs. Traffic was frequently so dense that it was often easier to proceed on foot. "You cannot ride," wrote Mark Twain in 1867, "unless you are willing to go in a packed omnibus that labors, and plunges, and struggles along at the rate of three miles in four hours and a half, always getting left behind by fast walkers, and always apparently hopelessly tangled up with vehicles that are trying to get to some place or other and can't. Or if you can stomach it, you can ride in a horse-car and stand-up for three-quarters of an hour, in the midst of a file of men that extends from front to rear (seats all crammed, of course,)—or you can take one of the platforms, if you please, but they are so crowded you will have to hang on by your eye-lashes and your toenails." The horse-car railway was dirty, slow, and not suitable for long distances. But the rail system was more efficient than any other form of urban transportation that used animal power. Accordingly, the horse-cars continued to spread. By 1880 they had appeared in most cities of over 50,000; in that year there were about 19,000 streetcars in operation over 3,000 miles of track.

In the larger cities by the 1860s, inventors and engineers were seeking ways to take advantage for urban transport of the only other source of power available—steam. In 1864, Hugh B. Willson, who had studied the London underground opened the year before, organized a company with capital of $5,000,000 to build a New York City subway in which a railroad could be operated, but the bill for the franchise was defeated in the state legislature through the efforts of street-transit interests. The other obvious possibility was to elevate railroads above the street. No great technological problems were involved in laying tracks on pillars, but there was the danger, particularly acute in view of the frequency of train accidents, of trains jumping the tracks and hurtling to the pavement below. Despite this fear and despite the opposition of horse-car interests and property owners along the railroads, an elevated line was begun in New York in 1867 and finally completed in 1870. An elevated railroad was expensive to build, and hence suitable only for larger cities. It was also noisy and dirty; passing trains caused vibration for some distance and locomotives often scattered oil and hot ashes on pedestrians below. But, because of the intense traffic problem of New York, the elevated proved successful. In 1878, a second line—the Sixth Avenue Elevated—was added to the original, which initially ran from the foot of the island up Ninth Avenue to Thirtieth Street and had later been extended as far as Fifty-ninth Street. Three years later, the New York "L's" were hauling 175,000 passengers a day. New lines were built and extended across the Harlem River into the northern suburbs. The system spread to other cities. Kansas City and Brooklyn built elevated lines in the 1880s, and Chicago constructed its system early in the next decade. But by this time, it had become clear that in larger cities such as New York and Chicago the capacity of elevated railroads was too limited. Trains were being run as close together as safety permitted. To employ faster or longer trains would require larger locomotives and expensive reconstruction of the elevated structures. It was virtually impossible to build new lines; by the 1890s municipal leaders were unwilling to extend additional franchises because of popular opposition to further extension of a noisy and dirty system of transportation.

In the meantime, another innovation in urban transportation, the cable car, came into use in American cities. Developed by a Scotch immigrant named Andrew Smith Hallidie, the cable car utilized an endless cable attached to a stationary steam engine as motive power. A grappling device suspended below the car passed through a slot running down the center of the railway where it was attached to the cable. The cable-car system, which essentially involved a kind of towing operation, was particularly suitable for cities with sharp street grades such as San Francisco, where it was first employed. It also offered the advantage of speed—a ten-mile-per-hour average speed was easily attainable compared to a maximum average speed of about six miles per hour for horse railways. Under ordinary circumstances, the cable car was about twice as fast as the horse railway. Primarily because of this advantage, it was adopted in a number of cities including Chicago, New York, and Philadelphia. By the middle of the 1890s, eastern cities had 157 miles of cable lines in operation, the Middle West 252, and the Far West 217. But the cable-car system soon proved to have a number of serious disadvantages—its installation costs were high; there was no possibility of making up time or of varying service at busy hours on a line because all cars had to travel at the same rate of speed; and dangerous mechanical breakdowns were frequent. As a consequence, cable cars were never in use in more than fifteen of the larger cities, and in these only in the downtown areas.

The major technological breakthrough in urban transportation was provided by the application of electric power. The development of the trolley and the electrified railroad constitutes one of the important chapters in the history of American technology and indicates how profoundly the requirements of the city affected the patterns of American science and invention. The challenge of the problem of urban transportation and the profits to be realized from successful innovations stimulated extraordinary effort on the part of individual inventors and manufacturing firms. As early as the late 1830s inventors had started experimenting with vehicles run by electric motors. But it was not until the development of the dynamo in the 1870s that the possibility could be practically considered; until that time the only source of current available was the battery, and power from this source was over twenty times as expensive as that furnished by a steam engine. Nearly a decade of effort went into the solution of the major problems of electric traction; the problems defeated even the inventive mind of Thomas A. Edison.

A satisfactory system, which utilized the results of the experimentation of the preceeding years, was finally devised by Frank Julian Sprague, an Annapolis graduate and a practical engineer, who had worked for Edison and then had gone into business for himself, organizing the Sprague Electric Railway and Motor Company in 1884. In 1887 Sprague accepted a contract to build an electrified street railway in Richmond, Virginia and the twelve-mile line over which forty cars were operated was completed the next year. There had been several earlier electrified lines, but these were experimental or operated only over short distances. Sprague's system used current from a central power source passed to the trains through an overhead wire, a technique first tried experimentally in 1884 in Kansas City by John C. Henry, a former telegraph operator. It embodied a score or more of highly technical features that became standard in street railway operation. But to construct the system had required almost superhuman effort; it eventually cost twice as much as Sprague was paid on his contract. Ten years later, he calmly reflected on the difficulties: "When the Richmond contract was signed, we had only a blueprint of a machine and some rough experimental apparatus. The hundred and one details that were essential to success were as yet undetermined. Fortunately for the future of electric railways, the difficulties ahead could not be foreseen or the contract would not have been signed." But his system was an immediate success, and he made up his financial losses many times over through the sale of equipment. By 1890 fifty-one cities had installed trolley systems; five years later 850 were in operation with lines totalling 10,000 miles. The suitability of the new system of urban transportation was demonstrated most clearly by the rapidity with which it replaced horse-car lines. In 1890, 69.7 per cent of the total trackage in cities was operated by horses; by 1902 this figure had declined to 1.1 per cent, while electric power was used on 97 per cent of the mileage.

Sprague made a second major technological contribution to urban transportation when he designed a complex multiple-unit system of control that provided the means by which elevated steam railroads could be efficiently electrified. This innovation encouraged the building of another means of urban transportation, the subway, because one of the principal objections to underground railroads had been the accumulation of gas, smoke, and dirt resulting from the operation of steam locomotives in confined tunnels. But with electrification this problem could be eliminated. Between 1895 and 1897 Boston constructed an underground line a mile and a half long at a cost of four and a quarter-million dollars. New York followed with an even more ambitious tunnel system opened in 1904, which ran from City Hall on the south to 145th Street on the north.

These new systems of transportation were efficient but they were also exceedingly dangerous. Accidents were frequent and often spectacular, particularly where electric lines were involved. A reporter for the popular magazine, *McClure's,* noted in 1907 that in New York, "in 27 days there had been 5,500 accidents on the street railways of New York City; 42 people were killed outright, 10 skulls were fractured, 10 limbs amputated, 44 limbs broken, while 83 other passengers were seriously injured. In proportion to the traffic, the New York street railways killed eight times as many people as those in Liverpool." But the demand for transportation in large cities was so great that communities were willing to pay this kind of price.

During the years in which systems of transportation were being established within cities, engineers also worked out the principles and techniques to build the bridges that would link parts of the expanding cities separated by rivers and harbors. Much of the necessary technology was developed during the construction of railroad bridges across the major interior rivers: Octave Chanute, who bridged the Missouri at Kansas City in 1869, and James B. Eads, whose famous bridge across the Mississippi at St. Louis was completed in 1874, produced the significant innovations through which piers could be put down in deep, swift-flowing water. Eads, a self-made man who had become rich raising cargoes from the Mississippi, was the first builder to use substantial amounts of steel in bridge construction. After several failures, the Carnegie works were able to turn out the chrome steel tubes in the strength required. Both he and Chanute, who was later to become a pioneer of aviation, worked out the techniques of using underwater caissons. These two railroad bridges, and those across the Missouri linking Council Bluffs to Omaha, and at Cincinnati across the Ohio, were utilized for ordinary traffic in expanding urban areas. The first large bridge financed by municipal funds was constructed across the Schuylkill at Philadelphia in 1863; for many years this cast-iron structure remained the most distinctive of the American bridges. But it was eclipsed by the famous Brooklyn Bridge, which realized an old dream of American inventors and engineers and which became a cultural symbol of national growth, progress, and power. "You see great ships passing beneath it," wrote the French traveler, Paul Bourget, "and this indisputable evidence of its height confuses the mind. But walk over it, feel the quivering of the monstrous trellis of iron and steel interwoven for a length of sixteen hundred feet at a height of one hundred and thirty-five feet above the water; see the trains that pass over it in both directions, and the steam boats passing beneath your very body, while carriages come and go, and foot passengers hasten along, an eager crowd, and you will feel that the engineer is the great artist of our epoch, and you will own that these people have a right to plume themselves on their audacity, on the *go-ahead* which has never flinched."

Brooklyn Bridge was a magnificent engineering achievement that required thirteen years to complete. Its designer, John A. Roebling, died from a tetanus infection, the result of having his foot crushed in an accident while he was surveying, before construction had even begun. His son, Washington A. Roebling, carried on the project despite a serious attack of the bends that left him crippled and in pain for the rest of his life. He was forced to direct construction from his bedroom nearby, and his wife served as messenger, as he used binoculars or a telescope to oversee operations. He had to contend constantly with meddling politicians and dishonest contractors. But despite difficulties and accidents that took twenty lives, the project was completed and the bridge was formally opened on May 24, 1883 with a great celebration attended by President Chester Arthur, his cabinet, and a number of governors. It was the longest suspension bridge in the world—over a mile long with a passageway wide enough for two railroad lines, two double carriage lanes, and a footpath. Immediately, Brooklyn Bridge began to assume its place in American myth and legend. Other cities also built major bridges during the period. Pittsburgh bridged the Allegheny River, Rochester the Genessee Gorge, Boston the Charles River, and St. Paul and Minneapolis the Mississippi. By the later part of the century, the suspension principle of the Brooklyn Bridge was frequently employed—in the Williamsburg Bridge over the East River in New York; in the Grand Avenue Bridge in St. Louis over railroad yards; and in the bridge across the bay at Galveston, Texas. By 1909, this era of bridge-building had produced 365 bridges over 500 feet in length, greatly facilitating the possibilities of movement in the growing urban regions.

The system of urban transportation developed in this period permitted American cities to spread out and maintain their functional identities rather than to fragment into a number of distinct urban units. For example, had the electrified railway not succeeded the horse-car when it did, it is possible that an independent metropolis would have developed to the north of New York, because by the 1880s travel time for those who poured into lower Manhattan each day had about reached its limit. Population densities had also reached a near maximum point in some sections of the larger cities, but the innovations in transportation permitted enough movement to outlying residential areas to relieve the most intense pressure. At the close of the century—a time when the suburbanization movement was viewed with a great deal of enthusiasm— an observer accurately described past and future patterns: "When a pair of legs was the only vehicle of locomotion which the ordinary man could afford, large cities were unavoidably compressed into very small quarters. The horse-car and the bus added a mile or two to this area, but did not dispense with the necessity of severely economizing space. The trolley has stretched it out several miles further, while future improvements in the machinery of transit may well make any spot within fifty miles of the center of an important city available as a place of residence for its wage earners. The extent to which the urban population may be distributed will be restricted only by the means of transit."

From the beginning of the growth of towns and cities in the United States, the possibility of combining the benefits of the country with the advantages of the city—the "happy union of urbanity and rusticity"—had been a part of the American conception of community. The village of Brooklyn early in the nineteenth century provided a place where New Yorkers could escape the city; a Brooklyn real estate man in 1823, advertising lots on Brooklyn Heights, encouraged this possibility in very modern terms: "Situated directly opposite the s-w part of the city, and being the nearest country retreat, and easiest of access from the centre of business that now remains unoccupied; the distance not exceeding an average fifteen to twenty-five minutes walk, including the passage of the river; the ground elevated and perfectly healthy at all seasons; views of water and landscape both extensive and beautiful; as a place of residence all the advantages of the country with most of the conveniences of the city. . . . Gentlemen whose business or profession require their daily attendance in the city, cannot better, or with less expense, secure the health and comfort of their families, than by uniting in such an association." A Cincinnati handbook in 1851 utilized considerable space in describing the advantages of suburban life in areas "unsurpassed for healthfulness, removed from the smoke and dust of the city, enjoying pure air and wholesome water." By the 1870s, Chicago promoters could claim the existence of nearly one hundred suburbs, with an aggregate population of 50,000, located along the railroads running from the city and offering the charms of "pure air, peaceful-ness, quietude, and natural scenery."

Although the rural ideal was always influential in American life, only the very wealthy were able to maintain homes away from the heart of cities until the coming of the horse-car lines in the late 1850s, and even then only a few people lived any substantial distance from the sites of work. In a meticulous and unique case study of three towns near Boston—Roxbury, West Roxbury, and Dorchester—that became late nineteenth-century "streetcar suburbs," Sam B. Warner, Jr. has described the pattern of the outward movement of people in relation to changing systems of transportation. Boston, he points out, was still a walking city in 1850, with dense settlement extending outward only within a two-mile radius of city hall; a small minority of the rich maintained country cottages and estates some distance away. Horse railroads pushed settlement outward only about another half-mile by 1873, and about another mile and a half by 1887, extending the edge of dense settlement to about four miles from city hall. In the late 1880s and early 1890s, electrification pushed the area of convenient transportation six miles outward. It was in this latter period that the three communities became genuine suburbs; virtually all the new buildings constructed were individual residences. As a result of the suburban growth of the three towns, and in other directions as well, by 1900 the character of Greater Boston had been transformed. Great expanses of land had become urban. The three communities composed only the southern segment of metropolitan Boston, but their combined area of twenty-five and a quarter square miles was about more than double that of the original city in 1850.

Moreover, the population growth had been striking. In 1870, after about fifteen years of the horse-car lines, the population of the three towns combined was 60,000. In 1900, the figure was 227,000—a growth rate comparable in order of magnitude to that of San Francisco. If the three communities had been counted together as a single city, it would have ranked above Minneapolis, Louisville, and Jersey City in population, and just below Newark and Washington. During the thirty years after 1870, more than 22,500 new houses were constructed in the three towns, providing living space for 167,000 suburbanites.

By examining 28,000 building permits and a variety of other records, Warner has been able to determine just what groups actually moved to these new suburban areas. The Boston experience was probably reasonably typical of other large American cities during the period. Predominantly, the suburbanites were from the upper half—perhaps the upper 40 per cent—of Boston society in wealth. The suburbs were rather rigidly segregated into three economic classes—the wealthy 5 per cent, the central middle class of 15 per cent, and the lower middle class of 20 to 30 per cent. The varying incomes and the different transportation needs of the three groups were reflected in large areas of similarly priced residences. In a number of respects the Boston suburbs were drab and monotonous. Architecture was undistinguished; each house looked much like the one next to it—not because of municipal zoning measures or building codes, which were virtually nonexistent at the time, but because of the natural tendency of an individual to build approximately what his neighbor had built. There was little civic vitality, little diversity of life. But in spite of this, the Boston suburbs were a source of great contemporary pride. Buildings were new, and the area was bright, clean, and healthy. In commenting on the character of the Boston suburbs, Warner has perceptively indicated the often neglected and, in our day frequently maligned, positive side of the suburban experience in American life:

To be sure, the costs of new construction were such as to exclude at least half the families of Boston; but the suburban half, the middle class, was the dominant class in the society. To middle class families the suburbs gave a safe, sanitary environment, new houses in styles somewhat in keeping with their conception of family life, and temporary neighborhoods of people with similar outlook. In an atmosphere of rapid change, the income-graded neighborhoods rendered two important services to their residents. Evenness of wealth meant neighbors who would reinforce an individual family's effort to pass on its values to its children. The surrounding evenness of wealth also gave adults a sense of a community of shared experience, and thereby gave some measure of relief from the uncertainties inherent in a world of competitive capitalism.

In addition to benefitting their own residents, in one important way the suburbs served the half of Boston's population which could not afford them. The apparent openness of the new residential quarters, their ethnic variety, their extensive growth, and their wide range of prices from fairly inexpensive rental suites to expensive single-family houses—these visible characteristics of the new suburbs gave aspiring low-income families the certainty that should they earn enough money they too could possess the comforts and symbols of success. Even for those excluded from them, the suburbs offered a physical demonstration that the rewards of competitive capitalism might be within the reach of all.

During the latter part of the nineteenth century, particularly after the advent of the streetcar, most larger American cities reflected Boston's experience and began to develop extensive residential suburbs. In Milwaukee, to use an interior city as an example, considerable outward spread began to occur by the middle 1880s. Older communities, such as the village of Humboldt, were swept into the expanding city. Other communities were able to maintain their identity as part of the metropolis. The hamlet at Oak Creek, founded in 1835, was subjected to development by the South Milwaukee Company; the Milwaukee Street Railway Company reached the community in 1896, and in the same year South Milwaukee was incorporated as a city. To the west, by the middle 1880s the village of Hart's Mill had become the thriving suburb of Wauwatosa, "the city of homes," with "no factories to speak of," "no smoke to contend with in any form," "an ideal place in which to rear a family having the best possible schools." To the north, exclusive residential communities were being developed in the 1890s at Shorewood and Whitefish Bay. Industrial suburbs such as West Allis and Cudahy were also growing rapidly. As a result of the suburban trend, the population of the city itself was spread out over a much wider area by 1900. In 1880, around 34 per cent of the city's population lived within one mile of the business center at the corner of Third Street and Wisconsin Avenue; by 1900 the percentage had dropped to less than 17. In 1880 only 17.4 per cent of the population of Milwaukee lived more than three miles from the business district; by 1900 the figure had risen to nearly 31 per cent.

A southern city, Norfolk, was also transformed by the streetcar in this period. Inspired by the example of neighboring Richmond, where Sprague had introduced his system, local horse-car companies began under public pressure to electrify their roads. The first trolley line went into operation on October 17, 1894 and within a decade the system reached a ring of suburbs —Sewells Point, Ocean View, Willoughby Spit, South Norfolk, Berkley, Portsmouth, and Pinner's Point. A real estate company purchased a tract of farmland and within a short time converted it into the suburb of Ghent, one of the city's most exclusive residential areas. By 1893 only about twenty houses had been erected or were in the process of being erected in the area; within a decade the former piece of farmland had been completely built up. Other outlying areas around the city experienced similar development; as a consequence, the area of Norfolk was soon three times as large as it had been before the coming of the streetcar.

The effect of this movement of people to the suburbs on the growth of cities themselves is difficult to evaluate, because it introduces the problematic consideration of what might have happened had efficient devices of urban transportation not been developed when they were. Late nineteenth-century observers had high hopes that suburbanization would provide the means of relieving congestion in cities. Adna F. Weber, the most systematic and the most able nineteenth-century student of demography, concluded his monumental 1899 study of city growth with an optimistic forecast: "The 'rise of the suburbs' it is, which furnishes the solid basis of hope that the 'evils of city life, so far as they result from overcrowding, may be in large part removed. If concentration of population seems destined to continue, it will be a modified concentration, which offers the advantages of both city and country life." Carroll D. Wright, United States Commissioner of Labor in the early nineties, found some evidence, on the basis of governmental examination of the slums, that congestion was lessening, and Weber, after careful study of New York population statistics for the early nineties, concluded that, with the exception of the wards of the city occupied by the most recently arrived immigrants, the congested districts of New York were losing population. It is clear that suburbanization enabled rapidly growing cities to mitigate the worst aspects of high concentration of population. Moreover, the development may have prevented eastern cities from reaching a kind of "saturation point" in growth. On the other hand, as Warner's careful study of Boston indicates, movement to the suburbs was possible only for a limited part of the urban population. The suburban pattern of life was not in accord with the notions of community brought over by many immigrant groups, but whatever their sentiments might be, well over half the people in cities, and the great bulk of the immigrants, were unable to move to the suburbs for economic reasons. The poorer districts of many cities continued to show an increase in density of population even after the general introduction of streetcars. The notorious Tenth Ward of New York, which increased in population density from 432 an acre in 1880 to 747 an acre in 1898, was quite possibly the most crowded district in the world by the turn of the century. One block, not the most crowded, had a population of 2,781, and in a large section of the ward the concentration was at the rate of over 1,700 to the acre. Over-all, the population density of New York in the early nineties was at the reasonable figure of 58.7, but this was misleading because the density below the Harlem River, the urbanized part of the city where the vast majority of New Yorkers lived, was up to 143.2 per acre in 1894—a figure substantially above that for such compactly built European cities as Paris (126.9 residents per acre) and Berlin (100.8 residents per acre). Other American cities did not experience this problem to anywhere near the degree of New York; nonetheless congestion elsewhere was considerable. In 1890, for example, one-fourth of the wards in seven of the ten largest cities had high densities of more than one hundred people per acre.

The accommodation of larger numbers of people within cities required new methods of housing and stimulated innovations in building. Annual returns of from 10 to 12 per cent were common on rental property, and an annual return as high as 40 per cent was possible. Most city dwellers rented their living quarters in the nineteenth century—in 1890 the percentage in cities above 100,000 was over 77. A number of cities exceeded this percentage: New York, 93.67 (with Greater New York about 85); Brooklyn, 81.44; Jersey City, 81.20; and Boston, 81.57 were the highest. Rochester (56.02) and Milwaukee (57.87) had the lowest percentage of renters of the larger American cities. The importance of urban land rents—which Henry George among others found the key to the economic problem of American society—encouraged property owners to make the maximum use of valuable urban land sites. Because the few building regulations in effect before 1900 were seldom stringent, experimentation in housing consisted largely of finding methods of using the available space to its limits.

Urban building styles throughout the country varied according to the topography of the individual city, the kind of urban transportation system, the timing of its building, and local custom. In Philadelphia and Baltimore, where the tradition of home ownership was relatively strong, row houses were common, and mile after mile of these extended toward the suburbs. Boston and Newark utilized the four-story "three-decker," which acquired its name from the three wooden galleries or "decks," built one above the other, initially at the front and in later years at the rear of the building. Three-deckers were particularly appropriate along horse-car lines, where the lower floor of a building was often converted to business use. Chicago and St. Louis constructed two- and three-deckers in almost solid rows, greatly increasing the population density of the two cities toward the close of the century.

New York builders and landowners, facing the enormous demand for housing caused by the arrival of immigrants in great numbers and operating under the circumstances of the city's unusual topography, evolved the most ingenious—and by the standards of our day the most inhumane—methods of crowding people together on a limited amount of space. In the 1850s and 1860s the older converted structures, which had first accommodated the new arrivals, were torn down and rebuilt as tenements. (Initially, the word "tenement" was used to apply to any multiple family rental building, and New York law defined the tenement house as a unit occupied by more than three families. Later the word was generally applied to any residential building in a slum.) One of the first large tenements, built in 1850, was hailed by civic leaders as a "praiseworthy enterprise and well worthy of imitation." The *Evening Post* commented favorably on the project: "It is built with the design of supplying the laboring people with cheap lodgings, and will have many advantages over the cellars and other miserable abodes, which too many are forced to inhabit. The depth of the building is two hundred and forty feet, with a front of thirty-five feet. Each tenement consisting of two rooms and a hall, is nearly eighteen feet in width, and about twenty feet in length giving twenty-four residents to each floor." Within a few years, flimsily constructed, three- and four-story "railroad" tenements, with closetlike rooms and dark interior bedrooms, had sprung up throughout the lower part of the city. One of the larger of the new barracks-like structures was located at Number 36 Cherry Street and was called Gotham Court. The building was five stories high, thirty-four feet wide, and ran back from the street 234 feet between two alleys. Twelve doors opened onto the wider of the two alleys, and each door provided entry for the ten families living in each section of the building—two families to a floor in identical two-room apartments, with a main room about 15 by 9½ and a bedroom about 15 by 8½. The structure housed around 500 people, without provision for plumbing or heat. Ten years later a row of privies had been placed in the basement, but by then more than 800 people had crowded into the structure. An 1865 report of the Council of Hygiene, one of the early New York housing-reform groups, argued that Gotham Court represented "about an average specimen of tenant-houses in the lower part of the city in respect to salubrity" and asserted that there were many more "in far worse condition." The council counted 15,511 tenements in 1864, housing approximately 500,000 of New York's 800,000 people. The council also found 15,000 people still residing in basements and cellars.

In these circumstances, it is not surprising that the infamous dumb-bell tenement, which came into use in the late 1870s, was greeted by housing reformers as a major improvement. The dumb-bell, an American contribution to world building styles, was encouraged by the Tenement House Law of 1879 enacted by the New York legislature, which required a window in the bedrooms of newly built tenements. The structure acquired its name from

the indentation at its middle which, combined with indentation of the tenement built up against it on the adjoining lot, formed an airshaft usually
about five feet wide. The air-shaft provided a small measure of light and
ventilation for interior rooms, and gave the plan of an individual tenement
the appearance of a dumb-bell. The dumb-bell tenement was a very efficient
structure, designed specifically to take advantage of the standard-sized 25
by 100 New York lot. It was usually built to five or six stories, and contained
fourteen rooms to a floor—seven on each side running from the front to the
rear of the lot. One family occupied the four rooms to the front, another
the three to the rear, thus providing space for four families to a floor. With
ten tenements on a block, quite ordinary blocks of dumb-bells contained as
many as 4,000 people. By the time significant legislation regulating housing
was passed in 1901, the dumb-bell had spread over New York "like a scab."
This kind of housing, occupied chiefly by immigrants, lay at the heart of one
of the chief concerns of late nineteenth-century urban reformers—the slum
problem. By 1900 the number of tenements in Manhattan had increased to
42,700, and they housed 1,585,000 people, an average of 33.58 people per
building. Although no American city was comparable to New York in regard
to congestion, slum areas had spread in numerous cities—Cleveland, Boston,
Cincinnati, and Chicago, for example. In spite of the establishment of fairly
stringent building codes in the early part of the twentieth century, slums
would continue to grow until at least the time of the New Deal when a
number of housing reforms, including slum clearance, may have checked
their further enlargement.

In the late nineteenth century, the mansions of the rich stood in unusually
sharp contrast to the dwellings of the poor, a reflection of the manifest
extremes of wealth and poverty that characterize the period. Architects and
builders might employ what was new in the technology of construction,
but their designs for castles and palaces were carefully contrived to hide
any use of new materials or innovations in technique. Aesthetically, it was
this characteristic of late nineteenth-century private and public architecture
that led to the modernist revolt of Louis Sullivan, Frank Lloyd Wright, and
others, with their emphasis on using materials naturally, accommodating
architecture to the machine, relating form to function, and building in a
way to reflect democratic values. Social critics saw in the private mansions
of the age, when contrasted with the squalor of the slums, an arrogant,
heartless, and ostentatious display of power and greed. The style of these
buildings came from the past. "It is truly ironical," James Marston Fitch
writes, "that neither these capitalists nor their architects could conceive of,
much less create, any new iconography of power. All they could do was
to borrow those of the discredited past—the feudal barony, the Roman
Empire, the Egyptian theocracy." Potter Palmer, a Chicago merchant and real
estate speculator, erected a massive Gothic castle on Lake Shore Drive, and
William Henry Vanderbilt spent three million dollars on a house in New

York City, built like a Renaissance palace. Few critics have endorsed the favorable view of a contemporary who compiled a brochure about the latter mansion. The house, he wrote, "may stand as a representative of the new impulse now felt in American life. Like a more perfect Pompeii, the work will be the vision and image of a typical American residence, seized at the moment when the nation begins to have a taste of its own." On Nob Hill, the Big Four, who built the Central Pacific Railroad, turned out vaguely Second French Empire structures. A local artist and aesthete called one of these "a delirium of the wood carver" and observed of them generally: "They cost a great deal of money and whatever harsh criticism may fall upon them, they cannot be robbed of that prestige." And that of course was mainly the point. The entrepreneurs of the era demanded that their buildings reflect their power and also their conservative view of society. But the ecclecticism that this led to—an ecclecticism that could produce an ingenious design for a building, never actually constructed, with a different historical style on every story—could also encourage flexibility. In addition to the grotesques, the period also produced the much admired, relatively plain-style New England buildings of Henry Hobson Richardson, who died at the age of forty-four in 1888, before his work was fully realized but whose emphasis on natural materials is thought to anticipate Wright. The period produced the majesty of the Brooklyn Bridge and a bridge nearly as impressive, the Eads Bridge of St. Louis. And perhaps most significantly, many of the buildings of the great Sullivan himself date from the late 1880s.

New ways of building within cities in the late nineteenth century, no matter how unsatisfactory the social results might be, and improved transportation, which enabled some people to move outward, permitted cities to keep expanding their population and enlarging their land area. But in order for these late nineteenth-century agglomerations to continue to function as cities, something else was vital—improved communication. The telegraph had earlier provided the kind of information system that enabled cities to become tied together in national and international networks. But it could not be the means for relaying large amounts of complex information back and forth within cities. Free urban mail delivery was established in New York in 1863 and gradually extended to other cities, but again this system was not efficient enough to unify the large city. "You can send a letter to Boston, or Albany, or Chicago," a New York writer commented in 1869, "with a tolerable certainty of its reaching its destination. But if you mail a missive from your office in Pine or William Street to your friend in Gramercy Park, or Lexington Avenue . . . the chances of its every being heard from are slight. The time usually occupied *in transitu* between 'down' and 'uptown' is 24 hours to 24 days." The answer to the urban communication problem was supplied, of course, by the development of the telephone. First demonstrated by Alexander Graham Bell in practical form at the Philadelphia Centennial Exposition in 1876, the telephone remained a scientific toy until it was subjected to a number of improvements, and ways were devised to utilize it in a system. The carbon transmitter, the elimination of wire noises by a metallic-circuit system, the central switchboard, and the multiple switchboard were essential for the functioning of the instrument as an urban communication device. In 1880, 148 telephone companies in eighty-five cities had obtained only about 48,000 subscribers, but with consolidation of small competitors, the service spread rapidly. By 1900 nearly 800,000 phones were in use—one for every ninety-five persons in the country. The telephone made possible rapid communication throughout the sprawling urban areas and also proved a force in breaking down the isolation of the countryside.

In addition to the fundamental improvements in transportation and communication, a number of other technological developments were significant in shaping the morphology of American cities. Considerable experimentation with paving materials and techniques—including the use of brick, granite blocks, and wood—culminated in the use of efficient asphalt paving, which proved particularly suitable for the bicycle and the automobile. Invention also provided new ways of lighting the city. The electric carbon arc-lamp, utilized as part of an efficient system by Charles F. Brush in 1879, provided a method of outdoor lighting much more satisfactory than the earlier gas and kerosene lamps. The incandescent electric lamp was demonstrated by Thomas Edison in 1879—one of the best-known episodes in the history of American invention. But an even more important step in the development of electric lighting for cities was the establishment of the first central power station at Menlo Park in 1882. Complex new generators, meters, and conductors had to be devised for the experiment; its success demonstrated that electric lighting could be utilized for commercial purposes. Although an improved gas lamp developed in Europe in 1885 and patented in the United States in 1890 gave the gaslight industry renewed temporary vigor, the electric light in the long run proved the satisfactory device for illuminating the large city. The working day in business offices could now be lengthened, factories could be operated around the clock, and the nighttime recreational activities of cities could be greatly expanded.

In view of the enormous health problems that resulted from the increased density of population in cities, new methods of removing waste and new methods of ensuring a pure water supply represented one of the more significant areas of technological change. Although the general relationship between unsatisfactory sewage disposal, water contamination and many diseases (such as typhoid fever and cholera, which decimated urban dwellers) was understood by European scientists in the 1860s and supported by many American public-health leaders, these contamination theories and the subsequent germ theory were not accepted widely enough to lead to any public demand for significant changes in methods of waste disposal. People continually complained about dirty water, but the specific health dangers of dirty water were not fully appreciated until the 1890s. The few miles of sewer that had been built in New York, Boston, Chicago, and a few other places proved completely inadequate in the face of the rapid growth of the 1870s. And most cities in the 1870s still used the old methods of private vaults and cesspools. In 1877, for example, Philadelphia had 82,000 vaults and cesspools, Washington had 56,000, and Chicago, despite its sewer system, 30,000. Chicago in 1871 had engaged in a large engineering project, headed by Ellis S. Chesbrough who had studied the sewer systems of European cities, to reverse the direction of the Chicago River, into which the city's sewers emptied, so that it discharged into the Illinois River rather than Lake Michigan. But this project had little effect. "The river stinks," commented the Chicago *Times* in 1880. "The air stinks. People's clothing, permeated by the foul atmosphere stinks. . . . No other word expresses it so well as stink. A stench means something finite. Stink reaches the infinite and becomes sublime in the magnitude of odiousness." Eventually the whole water supply and sewerage system of Chicago had to be drastically re-engineered.

Ironically, much of the advance in establishing better sewerage facilities resulted from the agitations of an individual who accepted older theories of disease, as did many of his contemporaries, and questioned the scientifically valid germ theory. George E. Waring, Jr., a scientific farmer, writer, and engineer, who achieved national attention as New York's Commissioner of Street Cleaning from 1895 to 1898, launched a crusade in the 1870s against America's inadequate sewerage methods. A contemporary commented that Waring made people so aware of the dangers to health from "sewer gas" that they "feared it perhaps more than they did the Evil One."

Waring was an anti-contagionist who accepted the idea that disease was the result of filth, although he was not as dogmatic as his opponents claimed and sometimes endorsed an eclectic interpretation. In general, however, he substituted "sewer gas" for the miasma that environmentalists had utilized as a disease-causing mechanism in earlier periods. In an 1878 essay, Waring argued persuasively that not only typhoid fever but most communicable diseases were the result of filth and decay. Outbreaks of disease, he argued, could often be traced to a foul-smelling house drain or the nearness of a drainage ditch. The poison itself might be the result of "the exhalations of decomposing matters in dungheaps, pigsties, privy vaults, cellars, cess-pools, drains, and sewers; or it may be due . . . to the development of the poison deep in the ground, and its escape in an active condition in ground exhalations." To prevent disease-causing bad air, household sanitary fixtures were necessary, and whole communities would have to be systematically cleansed.

When a severe yellow-fever epidemic struck Memphis in 1878, killing nearly 5,000 people, Waring asserted that the epidemic was the result of the incredibly filthy condition of the city. As a consequence of the attention his argument received, Waring was hired to build a sewer system for Memphis in 1880. His well-advertised efforts in no way prevented yellow fever, which in its etiology is unrelated to filth, but they set off a general campaign in

American cities to build sewers. A leader among the younger group of scientists who argued against general "filth" theories like those of Waring (which were based on the conception that disease-causing materials were spontaneously generated) was Charles V. Chapin (1865–1941), a physician and health officer in Providence, Rhode Island, and an international authority on public health. Chapin, like other pioneers of modern medicine, utilized the statistical approach in medical investigation; in 1890, after analyzing six years of data that he had collected during epidemics, he asserted that there was "no causative relation between unsanitary conditions, as ordinarily understood, and scarlet fever, diptheria, and typhoid." Many public-health officers clung to contamination theories through the 1890s, but the discovery of the real cause of yellow fever through the experiments of Walter Reed, William C. Gorgas, and others in Cuba won general acceptance for the germ theory. Chapin went to Cuba in 1902 to observe the experiments and concluded that they had driven the "last nail in the coffin of the filth theory of disease."

A fundamental tenet of Chapin's, which became part of the public-health program of the twentieth century, was that each disease could be individually identified and coped with specifically. In accord with this approach, it was recognized that pure water could prevent typhoid fever; city leaders moved quickly to ensure a pure water supply through techniques of filtration and purification. As early as 1872, James P. Kirkwood of St. Louis, after studying systems in England, had built a filtration plant at Poughkeepsie, New York. It involved a successful technique of backwashing impurities, but it was slow in operation. The perfection of sand and mechanical filters and the chlorination of water—first instituted in New York in 1893—led to great improvement in urban health conditions. By 1910, over ten million city residents drank filtered water, which helped to cut the death rate at least a fifth in New York, Philadelphia, Boston, and New Orleans. Although cities were never able to solve the problem of pollution, at least the danger was recognized, so that technological means could be devised to combat it. In addition to dealing with diseases related to sewerage facilities and the water supply, twentieth-century public-health officials also began to develop programs before World War I to deal with diseases caused by air-borne bacteria, such as diptheria and tuberculosis. The latter serious, non-epidemic disease had been virtually ignored in nineteenth-century public-health measures. Chapin recognized a truth that was crucial to the whole public-health movement: The good community could sometimes be ensured only through the imposition of a large measure of governmental authority. "When a man lives by himself," he wrote in 1889, "he can do as he pleases and let others do the same, but when 125,000 people are gathered together on 10 square miles of land they must of necessity give up certain of their liberties. It is the sacrifice they make for the sake of the advantages of city life. The denser the population the more stringent and exacting must be sanitary regulations and indeed all other regulations. Americans, particularly those whose memories reach back to the time when our cities were villages, are prone to forget this."

The relationship between a technology of public health or a technology of transportation and the physical patterns of life in a city can be determined to a reasonable extent. But the influences of an urban technology on the conceptions people had of their environment, or how these changes might be reflected in the cultural institutions of the city, is much more indefinite. Such agencies as the theater, the library, the museum, although they expanded in number and to a degree began to democratize their functions, seem not to have changed significantly from the early part of the century. But the artist working within the framework of these agencies of course began to respond to the new circumstances of society. Writers, by late in the nineteenth century, had become part of a concerted intellectual effort to try to understand the meaning of the urban community in America. The painting of this period in general memorializes a rural landscape and past rural simplicities; this approach could yield the great work of Winslow Homer. But the visual arts also experienced the transformations of technology and urbanization. This can be observed in rather subtle fashion in the work of the painter who well may be America's greatest, Thomas Eakins (1844–1916).

Eakins, whose sometimes stark realism was little appreciated in his own day and whose insistence on using completely nude models in a "genteel" time lost him his academic position, was intimately involved in the life of Philadelphia throughout his career. He cannot, however, be considered an "urban" painter in the sense that he consciously directed his work to the urban landscape or the urban milieu. His paintings are formal and static; he did not try to capture the motion or vigor of the city as did so many twentieth-century painters. Eakins consciously sought a distillation of the scene he painted; his outdoor paintings as well as his portraits were often done with little attention to background. His style was of the past, resembling that of the Spanish masters he had studied, or of Rembrandt whom he admired. But for all that, he still conveys a sense of the city in a new mechanical age. In his uncompromising conviction that the painter had to paint what he saw around him, he portrayed the leisure activities of the urban middle classes, at the concert hall, boating, hunting, or attending prize fights. His studies of surgical operations, "The Gross Clinic," the explicitness of which shocked contemporaries, and especially the later "The Agnew Clinic," with its white-clad operating team, supply an appreciation of the urban technician at work. Many of his lesser portraits of prelates, scientists, and assorted men-of-power convey an impression of class and status that can only be called urban, just as the portraits of John Singer Sargent (from the same period) convey a sense of elegance that is clearly of the city. Eakins's "Between Rounds," one of his prize fighting paintings, is essentially a collective portrait, with the prize fighter as the central figure; but it is a measure of Eakins's greatness that his relatively simple and somber background captures the spirit of the city as dark, brooding presence—and in a fashion that anticipates a later master of the urban landscape, Edward Hopper.

Eakins, as students of his work have emphasized, was an enthusiastic supporter of science, mechanics, and technology. He believed that these could be used to further painting, in the same fashion that Jenney and Sullivan accepted the view that the new building technology could contribute to creative architecture. "All the sciences," Eakins wrote, "are done in a simple way; in mathematics complicated things are reduced to simple things. So it is in painting." He became a serious photographer and a serious student of photography. He utilized the camera to better study the structure of the human body, reflecting a lifetime preoccupation with anatomy; he also used the camera to study motion systematically, and some of his efforts had significance in the development of motion pictures.

Eakins's formal style supplied no basis for an avant-garde, but he has lineal ties—by way of the group of Philadelphia painters who moved to New York, sometimes misleadingly called the *Ashcan School*—to the various artists of the early twentieth century who sought to carry his view of technology several steps further. In the first decade of the century, Alfred Stieglitz started producing his magnificent urban photographs that began the process of turning the city into a kind of abstraction of towers, shiny skyscrapers and shadowy streets, and machines at work. A little later the Precisionist painter Charles Sheeler, who based much of his work directly on his own photography, sympathetically painted the city, and especially the machines of the city, in a hard-edged, ultra-realistic fashion that made the corresponding photographs seem almost impressionistic. And beginning in 1917–1918, Joseph Stella began painting a series of dynamic abstractions of the key symbol of the city of energy and the machine, Brooklyn Bridge. Unlike most painters, who seldom write, at least not well, of what they do, he made the reasons for his preoccupation explicit:

Steel and electricity had created a new world. A new drama had surged from the unmerciful violations of darkness at night, by the violent blaze of electricity and a new polyphony was ringing all around with the scintillating, highly-colored lights. The steel had leaped to hyperbolic altitudes and expanded to vast latitudes with the skyscrapers and with bridges made for the conjunction of worlds.

Technology had not only changed the way people lived in cities; it had also altered their basic sensibility toward the urban environment. No longer was the city solely a complex organism. Urban technology had provided urban man new visions of magnificent and powerful mechanical forms and of pulsating, surging force and energy.

CHAPTER

# 9

# The Web of Government

MOST students have concluded that, judged by standards of efficiency, cost, and service, American cities in the Colonial period were well governed. As late as 1830, Alexis de Tocqueville considered local self-government one of the mainstays of personal freedom and independence in America. Lord Bryce, on the other hand, Tocqueville's great successor as a foreign interpreter of this country, argued in 1889 that city government was the one conspicuous failure of the American experiment. Many Americans agreed; cosmopolitan and well-informed Andrew D. White reflected a common view in his frequently quoted remark that American cities were the worst-governed in Christendom. Appalled at the spectacle of city administration and politics, increasing numbers of concerned citizens began to cast about for means of reform. Within a generation they had substantially changed the structure and much of the practice of city government in the United States.

The deterioration which began after the Revolution and the reform movement which began to attract widespread attention in the mid-1880s can both be understood as consequences of accelerating urbanization—and rapid industrialization—occurring in a culture where government was often regarded with suspicion. In part, the problems of city government were simply the result of growth. Governmental structures that had been adequate for cities of 25,000 or fewer inhabitants were strained beyond their capacities as the great nineteenth-century urban agglomerations grew. But despite the obvious need there was no real effort to rebuild city government until the end of the century. Meanwhile, municipal administration in the United States, which had once compared well with its European counterpart, compared badly with that counterpart after a century of growth on both sides of the ocean.

In Colonial times the power to incorporate towns and cities had, of course, resided ultimately in Parliament or in the Crown. Although this power had on occasion been delegated to proprietors, and had been exercised—with or without delegation—by provincial assemblies, a central authority coordinated developments to some extent and might have coordinated them still more effectively. In the United Kingdom this was done through the great Municipal Incorporations Act passed by Parliament in 1835. Basic uniformity of administrative structure, along with an important measure of home rule, was thereby assured for British cities. By this time, diversity, along with loss of much local initiative, had begun to characterize American cities.

The power to grant municipal charters passed from the British Government into the hands of the newly independent states. No one seriously argued that this power should be given to or even shared with the federal government, either under the Articles of Confederation or under the Constitution. The states delegated no municipal authority to the federal government with the exception of the provision for a national capital. Even in the territories the supervision of new towns was a responsibility of the territorial legislatures and not of Congress. Theoretically, there might have been a question whether the executives or the legislatures of the states would assume this particular power, but in the midst of the revulsion from strong executive authority which accompanied the Revolution, the alternatives seem not even to have been discussed, and the legislatures simply assumed the chartering function without contest.

The new city charters in the first two or three decades after independence were somewhat more democratic than the earlier ones in that the last few "close corporations" were abolished in favor of popularly-elected councils. In the "close corporation" type of government, which was common in English cities during the Colonial period and considerably less common in the colonies themselves, the council members were appointed for life and in some cases could choose their own successors. This arrangement hardly accorded with republican enthusiasm; it was, typically, adjudged "impolitic and unconstitutional" by the legislature of Virginia in 1787, when it changed the charter of Norfolk to provide for election of the city council. Among the other major colonial cities, Baltimore, Philadelphia, and Charleston also experienced the end of close-corporation government with the success of the Revolution.

It was not long before the principles of separation of powers and checks and balances, so important to the founding fathers in their deliberations on the forms of national and state constitutions, also began to appear in the government of American cities. In 1796 and 1797, Philadelphia and Baltimore received new charters from their state legislatures which provided them with bicameral city councils. This practice was not universally followed, but it spread widely; Detroit's charter of 1806 (granted by the territorial legislature), Pittsburgh's in 1816, Boston's in 1822, and New York City's in 1830, all included the provision in one or another form. Where it did exist, the bicameral council contributed increasingly, as city governments became more important, to the complexity and inefficiency of those governments.

Sometimes the bicameral institution developed out of pre-existing arrangements; in Boston's case, the lower house took the place of the older town meeting, while the upper house carried on some of the functions of the selectmen. In other cases, however, it reflected deliberate imitation of federal and state models. Its provision in New York City's 1830 charter was explained, in the words of the convention which drafted it, "for the same reason which has dictated a similar division of power into two branches, each checking or controlling the other, in our general government." The same suspicion of government which had led Americans to restrict their national and state authorities with constitutional and institutional limitations reappeared at the local level, just as the fledgling cities were about to begin careers of rapid and possibly ominous growth.

A further separation of power occurred with the emergence of the mayor as an independent municipal authority. During colonial days, mayors had been appointed either by an authority representing the imperial government, or—as in the close corporations—chosen by the municipal council itself. After the Revolution, elected governors of the states (or in a few cases other state agencies) appointed the mayors, which brought the office somewhat closer to the electorate but not particularly closer to local voters. During the last years of the eighteenth century, the manner in which the mayor was selected began to change, and this led gradually to a change in his role. By 1820, in all the larger cities he was chosen by the city councils which were, of course, elected locally. In 1822 and 1824, Boston, St. Louis, and Detroit voters were given the privilege of electing their mayors at large. This practice spread· rapidly enough so that at mid-century it was universal in American cities. By itself it gave the mayors no additional formal powers, but it did make them relatively more independent of the councils. In some places, as time passed, the mayor's powers of appointment and veto were enlarged and the office became one with great potential leverage in city government.

This development was not paralleled, however, by any immediate increase in governmental efficiency. Cities appeared to be losing powers steadily as the nineteenth century wore on. The Revolution had, perhaps ironically, depressed the value of cities' "charter rights"; when the state legislatures took over the power of granting city charters, the charters themselves became mere statutes alterable at will or even repealable by the bodies that passed them. These documents lost whatever "prescriptive" or contractual status they had in the Colonial period, and the incorporated cities and towns became simply legal creatures of the state government. As urban populations swelled and demanded more services, the cities found it necessary to ask their respective state governments either to provide the services or else to enable the local governments to do so. For many years, the first alternative was generally followed and city authorities shared local power with the state capitals.

This sharing of power between local and state agencies became important during the 1830s and 1840s, just when the basic principle of home rule had been given to English cities, and also just when a national party system was developing in the United States. The effects of this development on the quality of American city administration cannot be measured in any accurate way,

but its importance can be gauged from the fact that home rule and separation of local questions from national politics were later to become two of
the chief goals of municipal reformers. Early in the nineteenth century city
government did not impress many citizens as being of any great importance;
the states, and even the counties in many places, seemed to bear more
significantly upon daily life—to the extent that government at all bore on
daily life in the United States. In 1810, New York City, with a population of
around 100,000, spent only $100,000: one dollar per capita. Voluntary asso-
ciations took care of poor relief and shared in such an important matter
as fire prevention. It would be thirty years before there was a uniformed
police force in the United States. To many Americans it was by no means
clear that theirs was to be an urban destiny. In the circumstances, what one
student has called "the petty housekeeping of such small urban communities"
held little intrinsic interest for contemporaries.

City offices were not sought for the purpose of carrying out impressive
programs of social or economic improvement. For a time after independence
they continued to be sought and largely held in the older eastern ports by
men of wealth and leisure like Mayor Philip Hone of New York, to whom the
holding of public office seemed natural and proper. In the new towns of the
interior, these offices were taken over by the entrepreneurs who were promoting the growth of the towns in order to further the interests of their
business enterprises. The semi-aristocratic type of public servant in the eastern
cities was beginning to be shouldered off the stage by the 1830s with the
rise of egalitarian sentiments, and as the interior towns found secure bases
for growth, the original entrepreneurs turned aside from public life to pursue
their now flourishing businesses. The apparent insignificance of city government, changes in the social texture of politics, and the growth of a national
system of political parties combined to subordinate local politics to the
fortune of the major parties on state and national levels. This subordination
along with the weak legal position of city charters made city government,
for a considerable time, a kind of forgotten child in the American polity.

It was during the same period that city government became more and more
complicated and consequently more and more cumbersome. State interference, the party system, traditional Jeffersonian distrust of concentrated
authority, and the lack of any central power to coordinate city development
produced complexity and diversity which cannot be described in detail; a few
examples must suggest the way in which American city government confronted the voter by the mid-1800s and for a considerable time thereafter.
As new urban needs called for new urban services—whether to be provided
by state or by local agencies—new offices were created. In many cases these
were kept independent of previously existing offices, such as the councils or
the mayors. The St. Paul, Minnesota charter of 1868 provided that in addition
to a mayor and council members, the voters must choose eight separate executive authorities. By New York City's charter of 1867, simplifying the struc-

ture which had preceded it, voters elected the mayor, the comptroller, the Board of Councillors, the Board of Aldermen, the supervisors, the corporation counsel, and the Board of Education; the governor, elected by voters throughout the state, appointed the Central Park commissioners, the Board of Health, the police commissioners, the fire commissioners, and the immigration commissioners. In 1885, New Haven citizens had to elect a bicameral city council, a sheriff, a mayor, a treasurer, a city clerk, and an auditor; chosen in various ways (some by the whole council, some by the upper house, some by the lower house, and some by the mayor with the approval of the upper house) were police and fire commissioners, health commissioners, commissioners of public works, a Board of Finance, and several other authorities. Meanwhile, the Connecticut legislature appointed city judges for New Haven, who then appointed the city attorney. At one time Philadelphia's government included thirty separate boards to supervise special functions. In the late 1860s there were in New York City four different agencies with power to tear up the streets, but there was no agency with clear responsibility for repaving them.

The impact of state legislative action on city affairs went far beyond naming a few boards or individual officials. The New York legislature, for example, passed more laws for New York City alone in the three years from 1867 to 1870 than Parliament passed for all of the cities in the United Kingdom from 1835 to 1885; in the year 1870, thirty-nine state laws were passed for the city of Brooklyn alone. Jersey City's charter was amended by state action ninety-one times between 1835 and 1875. The date for municipal elections in St. Paul was changed—by the state legislators—three times in four years during the 1860s. An example from Chicago is both dramatic and illustrative: in 1861, the Republican Party won the state elections and the governor appointed a new police board for Chicago, made up of Republicans. Two years later, the Democrats won and reduced the terms of office of the board members, thus making it possible for them to appoint half the board's members. In 1865, the Republicans were back in power at the state capital; they restored the original terms of office for the police board, provided that new members be elected by Cook County voters (rather than by Chicago voters alone, who were characteristically Democratic), and provided also that the city's fire department be controlled by the police board.

State interference in local matters might be justified, and sometimes was, on the ground that the states had a broader tax base available to them and could supply the cities with funds indispensable to the provision of needed services. This was the case in important instances, notably when states granted money to the cities and towns, as they began to do early in the nineteenth century, to aid in the building of public school systems. In such cases, the action initially reflected an actual redistribution of public revenue to the cities' advantage. But the old suspicion of the city and city life played a great part in sustaining the practice of state interference. "It goes without saying," wrote one student of city government in New England in the 1890s, "that country districts are, as a rule, more deserving of political power than are cities. If the judges were locally elected . . . the successful candidates would often be under obligations to elements in the community which are the chief source and nurse of the criminal class." Lord Bryce, although he was English, reflected much American opinion on the matter in describing the influences that made for bad and corrupt government as "far more potent and pernicious in great cities than in country districts." Referring to the immigrant population, the poor, the aloof business men, and the cultivated individuals who disdained politics, he concluded that "in great cities the forces that attack and pervert democratic government are exceptionally numerous, the defensive forces that protect it exceptionally ill-placed for resistance. Satan has turned his heaviest batteries on the weakest part of the ramparts." A prominent and respected New York attorney and public servant, William Marcy Evarts, pointing out the evil effects of state involvement in city administration, actually included among them the proposition that the low character of urban politics was infecting the presumably purer currents of state politics: "The transfer of control of municipal resources from the localities to the capital," he asserted, "had no other effect than to cause a like transfer of the methods and arts of corruption. . . . Municipal corruption, previously confined within territorial limits, thenceforth escaped all bounds, and spread to every quarter of the state."

At the same time that they became more complicated and increasingly subject to state interference, the city governments were of necessity becoming more important. They spent more money in order to satisfy growing needs. The first service to expand noticeably in the nineteenth century was public education. States played a part in this development, but as already noted their function was originally mostly one of supplying additional money to the cities. In the late thirties, the larger places began providing for city school superintendents, and by 1870 every city in the country of any size at all—with the exception of Philadelphia—had a superintendent as well as a school board, which in some cases had independent taxing and bonding powers. The degree of state supervision varied, but in most places primary responsibility was left in local hands. From a very early period in the nineteenth century, it was common practice to regard the school boards as "outside of politics"; in many places the practice of dividing board membership evenly between the parties, regardless of which party controlled the city government, became traditional. Party politics did influence such considerations as the awarding of contracts for school construction, but educational policies and selection of teachers were usually kept free from that influence. The system was flexible enough (with local variations in the manner of choosing the school boards and in their relationships with the rest of the city government) to cope as adequately with the growth of high school education after the 1870s as it had with primary schooling in the earlier years.

Other large responsibilities were presented to city administrations from the 1840s. Water service was prominent among them. New York needs dictated the building of the great Croton aqueduct beginning in 1846; the same year a large new system of waterworks was begun in Boston, and in the next decade Chicago and Baltimore followed. Until this period, water systems in American cities had been provided mostly by private enterprise, but the large improvements needed by the expanding urban centers were beyond private capacity. The increasing size of the problem and the general feeling that water was so necessary to communities that it should not be a source of private profit led to a spreading movement in the direction of municipally owned waterworks. This added to the financial problems of the cities, because large bonding operations were necessary to build or rebuild the systems. It also added to the need for administrative skill in municipalities; the waterworks as business enterprises—and very large enterprises by nineteenth-century standards—were to be run on a self-sustaining basis as well as in the interest of the community.

Another significant expansion of municipal activity in the later nineteenth century was in public health. Here again decentralization and diversity characterized American practice at about the same time that the health activities of English cities were systematized by the Public Health Act, which Parliament passed in 1875. There had been boards of health in several American cities much earlier: New York City in 1805, Philadelphia in 1818, and Chicago by the time it was four years old, in 1837. But they had no regular staffs and had done very little except during periods of yellow fever, cholera, or smallpox epidemics, when emergency sanitary or quarantine regulations were temporarily prescribed. As a result of the cholera epidemic in 1866 the idea of a more regular service began to spread. In that year the state of New York provided a Metropolitan Board of Health for the New York City-Brooklyn area. It had a permanent force of inspectors and some latitude in prescribing permanent sanitary regulations; after 1870 the board was a municipal agency. This precedent was followed closely by Chicago, where a Municipal Board of Health was set up in 1867, and in Boston in 1872. As the boards of health appeared in city after city, their responsibilities increased and they became more expensive. By the turn of the century New York City had almost four hundred health inspectors, Philadelphia and Chicago about fifty each: cities with populations of 50,000 or more were spending around $2,500,000 for their health departments, and between 1900 and 1907 this figure had risen by 600 per cent.

As concern with public health problems grew more widespread, it was associated with concern for living conditions in the growing slums of the cities. These were areas where epidemics might start; statistical correlation between disease and filthy neighborhoods was commonly stressed by those who wanted to correct at least the worst features of life in the slums. New York City led the way in housing reform, as it had in other matters. The first law specifying minimum standards for tenement construction, in 1867, followed closely upon the establishment of the Metropolitan Board of Health and reflected the same impulse. This law was ineffective, and an amendment in 1879 which required a window in each bedroom merely spurred proliferation of the dumb-bell tenements. Other suggested standards—such as some "means of egress" in case of fire—were far from adequate and even so went for the most part unenforced. Amendments to the law, in 1884, were also almost entirely ineffective; meanwhile, the tenement problem grew larger and the sudden burgeoning of interest in contagion and community health strengthened the position of reformers. Under the urging of Lawrence Veiller, a state commission was established in 1900 to study tenement conditions and recommend corrective legislation. Veiller had participated in relief activities in New York during the depression of the mid-nineties and had served two years as an inspector of building plans in the city's Buildings Department. He had devoted a great deal of time to systematic study of urban housing and probably knew more about the subject than anyone else in the United States; appropriately, he was named secretary of the investigating commission and its proposals (along with their embodiment in the law of 1901) reflected mostly Veiller's ideas. Out of the commission's investigations and recommendations, which were well publicized and excited widespread interest, came New York's Tenement Law of 1901. It prohibited future construction of dumb-bell buildings and required certain improvements in the thousands already existing; it required courtyards varying in width with the heights of buildings, provided more stringent fire protection measures, and required a separate bathroom for every family dwelling-unit. This was the first carefully drafted building code in the country, and it was also to be the first carefully enforced one. The law provided for a separate Tenement House Commission, which within two years had 166 building inspectors of its own with more than two hundred other employees. In its first twelve years of operation the commission processed nearly half a million complaints of violations. By 1920 at least forty other large cities, usually following the New York model, had acted to tighten up their building codes and to provide improved enforcement machinery. All in all, while this did not solve the social problems of poverty in urban America, it did represent a significant extension of governmental action. As Roy Lubove has commented, "Veiller left as a permanent legacy to the nation the principle of a community's right to high minimum standards of restrictive housing legislation."

Regular police and fire departments constituted part of the growing burden of local government. Modern uniformed police forces began in New York City in 1845, and the example was quickly adopted elsewhere: in Philadelphia, Boston, and Baltimore, for example, before the outbreak of the Civil War. By that time, a strong trend in the direction of state control of large city police forces had set in; the trend probably reflected the exigencies of party politics, and it abated in the 1870s as feeling against state intervention in general began to grow. In the larger cities, the police forces usually came to be supervised by special commissions appointed in a variety of ways, sometimes by state authority and sometimes locally. In 1900, cities with 30,000 or more people were paying for 28,000 uniformed policemen. Fire protection became more expensive and more effective during the same period. The older volunteer fire brigades yielded to regular paid forces during and after the 1850s, at about the same time that fire-fighting equipment, including steam engines and complicated pumping machinery, was becoming more expensive. In the case of fire protection, at least, American cities surpassed their European contemporaries; the New York City and Boston fire departments were, by 1900, regarded as the best in the world. Chicago's force had as many men as London's, along with more horses and steam engines, although Chicago was only a third as large as the English metropolis.

Beginning in 1823, the city of Boston took over control of sewage disposal. In 1849 New York did the same and within twenty years had laid almost two hundred miles of pipe for this purpose. Chicago constructed its first public sewers in 1856, and in fifteen years it had built 140 miles. Street cleaning was another municipal function which grew rapidly after the Civil War, associated (as was interest in better sewage disposal) with the public-health movement. George Waring's vigorous reforms in the New York City system resulted in the city's employing over 5,000 street sweepers and garbage collectors by 1900 to carry off 3,000,000 cartloads of refuse annually. One of Waring's innovations, which came to be widely imitated, was provision for quick snow removal; John Fairlie, a contemporary political scientist, accurately placed this new practice in the widening category of "increase in the scope of municipal action with a corresponding increase in expenditure."

Public parks came to be regarded as important to American cities partly because of their relationship to community health and partly because it was felt desirable to provide socially wholesome areas of recreation for children and for the poor. Philadelphia bought some land for a small park as early as 1812. In 1851, New York City received authority from the state legislature to acquire land that was to become Central Park; its construction began under the supervision of Frederick Law Olmsted in 1858. Slowly the idea spread to other cities: Baltimore began a 700-acre park in 1870 and in the next twenty years most American cities were looking for land that could be made into public parks. Olmsted's great success with Central Park, along with the planning necessary for Chicago's Columbian Exposition in 1893, encouraged the movement that did so much to improve the quality of life in cities. Contemporaries expressed great pride in the accomplishments of American cities at the turn of the century, and to a large extent, despite problems of continuing political corruption, this sentiment was justified. The establishment of basic municipal services during a period of rapid urbanization represented a genuine accomplishment of collective community action. There was, however, an important exception: the failure to provide and to enforce measures regarding the use of private property. Housing codes and similar regulations affecting residential property, despite their popularity and despite the importance of the principle they established, were often laxly administered in many places, particularly where neighborhoods were declining. Although restrictive housing legislation became general, in practice the strong tradition of private property in American society often meant that there was limited restriction on what an individual might choose to do with his piece of urban real estate. As a consequence, the slum problem intensified in the first decades of the twentieth century.

The establishment of new services led to a variety of new specialized agencies. Parks, for example, were ordinarily overseen by boards created for this purpose; they usually had to share their responsibilities with boards of recreation and public works. By the turn of the century residents of American cities had become used to this kind of overlapping authority. As the governments of the cities became more complicated the need in each city for some coordinating force grew more apparent. To the degree that this need was met at all, it was met by the party organizations. These organizations, though their purpose was to win and retain office and not necessarily to furnish efficient administration, were at least cohesive and provided a measure of discipline (in the sense of predictable behavior) in the ramifying and fragmented structures within which urban public affairs were conducted. In the process whereby the political party became, in E. S. Griffith's words, "the coordinating agency," jobs in the city government became patronage, and contracts or franchises for public construction became graft. In each city the men in the political organizations who could allocate the patronage and the graft most skillfully, with a view to winning elections, reached positions of power. They were called *bosses,* and although they varied greatly among themselves in characteristic techniques and in personality, still their objective function was the same everywhere: to provide the city governments with at least the minimum of regularity, without which the governments could not have functioned at all.

Expanding municipal needs, coming in the same period as deteriorating government, inevitably meant bad local services. Though there were mitigating circumstances and though the picture was not always quite so dark as it was painted, still no serious contemporary could have argued that cities in the United States were well governed in the post-Civil War period. Even in New York, the nation's metropolis, which had pioneered in so many lines of municipal activity, reliable testimony in the late 1870s described an unattractive prospect: "the wharves and piers are for the most part temporary and perishable structures; the streets are poorly paved; the sewers in great measure imperfect, insufficient, and in bad order; the public buildings shabby and inadequate; and there is little which the citizen can regard with satisfaction save the aqueduct and its appurtenances and the public park." In Philadelphia, which had been a model urban community a hundred years earlier, the situation was no better: "Public work has been done so badly," stated a bipartisan committee, "that structures have had to be renewed almost as soon as finished. Others have been in part constructed at enormous expense and then permitted to fall to decay without completion. Inefficiency, waste, badly-paved and filthy streets, unwholesome and offensive water, and slovenly and costly management have been the rule for years past throughout the city government."

Expanding needs and deteriorating government also meant expensive government, and herein lay important seeds for later reform. Municipal affairs cost the individual taxpayer more and more throughout the Western world during the nineteenth century. Although the population of Great Britain increased by 300 per cent, the burden of its local taxation increased by 700 per cent. Between 1840 and 1900 the population of France went up only 16 per cent, but local expenditures went up by 600 per cent; similar figures characterized the other European countries. The rising incidence of city expenses and city taxes was just as pronounced in the United States, and especially in the large cities; between 1850 and 1900, per capita city expenditures in New York, for example, rose from $6.53 to $27.31.

Two factors especially rendered growing per capita expenses of city government more burdensome. In the first place, the thirty years between 1867 and 1897 saw a marked deflation in the general level of prices. Accompanied as it was by two major depressions, 1873–1878 and 1893–1897, deflation meant that in spite of the national economy's growth, each individual dollar was harder to come by. Even during relatively prosperous years the appreciating value of the dollar along with anxiety about the "business cycle," as it was coming to be called, lent urgency to demands for retrenchment and reform. Deflation also meant that measuring increasing city expenditures in dollars understated the real values reflected in the increases.

In the second place, interest on indebtedness accounted for an even larger proportion of these expenditures. In the decade after the end of the Civil War, when the fifteen largest American cities saw their aggregate population rise by about 70 per cent, the debts of the same cities rose by 271 per cent. This produced a relatively inelastic item of expense—interest on the debt—and as time went on and city debts continued to rise, it placed a growing burden of current outgo on each year's budget, in addition to casting its lengthening shadow over future generations of taxpayers. St. Louis's revenues, for example, doubled between 1850 and 1858 but during the same years its bonded indebtedness trebled. Interest on the debt of Providence, Rhode Island accounted for 40 per cent of its tax revenues in 1880, and in the same year debt service was eating up an average of 50 per cent of the revenues of cities in New Jersey. At about the same time, one-third of Cleveland's income went to pay interest, and the charges on debts of cities in New York came to more than the whole cost of running the state government.

Much of the debt increase was the result of public building programs, the costs of which were often underestimated at the outset. Thus a courthouse in New York City, the cost of which had been estimated at $250,000, ultimately came to cost $14,000,000. There were special circumstances, notably the

Tweed ring, to explain this spectacular divergence, but elsewhere, procedures were similar: a city hall for San Francisco estimated at $1,500,000 actually cost $3,500,000; a market house for Houston estimated at $228,000 actually cost $470,000; and a waterworks for Peoria estimated at $310,000 actually cost $453,000. In many places, part of the debt was the result of lavish encouragement to railroads, which stemmed from local rivalries during the booster years; city and county obligations of this kind were conservatively estimated at $185,000,000 in 1870.

Inefficiency and corruption explained some part of the cities' skyrocketing obligations—how much cannot be estimated realistically. The federal census of 1880 brought the figures together in such a way as to impress and even startle many citizens: it triggered an outcry against corrupt city governments. Remarks by a writer in *Harper's New Monthly Magazine* in 1884 were representative: "The story of our political methods for the last twenty-five years is soonest told by the immense increase in our municipal indebtedness." The writer went on to lament that the "best men" in the cities did not interest themselves in public affairs, and were too occupied in "money getting." While these people were politically indifferent, undesirable types were "making their municipal budgets and confiscating their property." But this was, at best, only a partial explanation. By 1880, the expenses of local government had been rising for at least forty years: in other words, since the time when urban population growth had begun decisively to outstrip rural. It must be remembered that the expanding services of the large cities made large capital investment necessary in any case; the municipal debts represented the creation, in a very short time, of what Eric Lampard has called a new "urban infra-structure." The largest payments by American cities toward the close of the nineteenth century were, in this order, for public buildings, education, streets and bridges, police and fire protection, and interest on their public debts.

Some cities found themselves unable to pay their debts. Mobile repudiated many of its bonds outright; several other places were forced to suspend interest payments for a period; Memphis, with its problems intensified by nationwide depression and a terrible yellow fever epidemic in 1878, saw the state of Tennessee take over its financial operations in their entirety. In other places, too, states were called on to step in and remedy deplorable urban financial practices, although not so drastically as in Memphis's case. In 1872 Illinois enacted strict legislation to control the form and content of city council appropriations, especially in Chicago. Other states enacted constitutional limitations onto the debt-creating power of their cities—limitations which frequently proved ineffective because they were difficult to enforce in court.

A growing number of taxpayers felt that the burden on them, however necessary had been the objectives of expenditure, was unnecessarily high. One of the reasons for this was quickly found in the practices that had grown up in providing for street transportation and later for street lighting. These utilities were different from the water systems, which came to be typically public enterprises. Street railways and lighting systems for the most part were built and operated by private companies which carried on their work under franchises granted by city councils. A franchise was a contract in which the private company's performance was stipulated and its future financial obligations to the city were specified, usually for a given number of years, after which the contract could be renegotiated. These franchises were valuable privileges because they conferred a monopolistic or semi-monopolistic position upon the favored company. The growth of the cities insured that there would be increasing business for as long as anyone could predict.

In order to encourage entrepreneurs to build desired street railways, it was generally agreed that franchises should be attractive. Consequently, little thought was taken of the future value of the privilege to the companies and much was made of the present value of the companies to the city dwellers who needed transportation. Franchises, which were quickly, carelessly, and generously drawn up and passed by city councils, were made to last for long periods, and provided for low taxation on the companies' property. The first street railway franchises were granted in New York City in 1851 and 1852; the companies were allowed to charge a fare no higher than five cents and a vague provision was included requiring them to keep the part of the streets adjacent to their tracks in good condition, but the franchises had no terminal dates at all. Most early franchises were drawn for periods of fifty to a hundred years; Albany granted one for a thousand years, and even toward the end of the century, Buffalo granted a 999-year franchise.

The circumstances were similar in regard to franchises for lighting the cities' streets. Gas lighting had been introduced in Baltimore in 1816, and lighting became an important urban service after the early 1820s when both Boston and New York City began to use gas for this purpose. In this instance also, the service was ordinarily provided by private companies which needed power to tear up streets or, later, to string wires along them. These companies had positions which were increasingly recognized as monopolistic, and they operated under special franchise grants from city councils. When, during the 1880s, cities began using electricity for lighting, the procedures were the same. All these businesses attracted investors in the larger cities; around the turn of the century (considering only privately-owned utilities), over $300,000,000 was invested in gas works, about $250,000,000 in electric lighting plants, and over two billion dollars in street railway systems.

Utilities other than water service were for the most part privately owned in the larger cities, where they were profitable enterprises. Chicago and Detroit were unusual, with their municipally-owned electric lighting plants. Philadelphia had a municipal gas works from 1845 to 1899 but then leased it to a private company. Even the Brooklyn Bridge cable-car line, owned and operated jointly by New York City and Brooklyn between 1883 and 1889, was leased to a private company in the latter year. Opportunities for profit were not extensive in small cities and towns, and there public ownership was common.

In the earliest days of franchise-granting, there were rare cases where the potential problem was recognized, and great care was taken in the negotiations. Thus, in 1859, Mayor Swann of Baltimore successfully insisted that applicants for a street railway franchise agree to pay the city 20 per cent of gross revenue plus a license tax on each car, and also incorporated a provision that at fifteen-year intervals the city might consider buying out the company. But the general trend was different: cities welcomed the companies proposing to supply public utilities, in the same way in which the nation at large welcomed railroads, and the history of the relationship between public authority and private enterprise was similar in the two cases. Even in Baltimore a reaction against Swann's cautious policy soon led to much more generous franchises there. New York City's first elevated railroad was built with no restrictions on street occupation; whereas the company had to pay 5 per cent of gross revenue to the city, later lines were not subjected to this requirement. By the end of the 1880s most city-lighting franchises contained no restrictions on rates, and were carelessly or ambiguously worded on the matter of future renegotiation.

Toward the end of the century, public utility companies began to consolidate. Where there had once been thirty street transportation companies in Philadelphia, there was only one by 1895, and a comparable trend was evident in most other cities. Consolidation was in part the result of technological changes which necessitated high capital investment costs, and it brought with it the possibility of sizeable economies of scale. During the 1880s, a further stage in concentration took place as control of utility companies in different cities was absorbed by holding companies, each of which might own lighting or traction systems, or both, in many places. By the early 1900s, holding companies located in the East controlled the street railway companies of most American cities of over 30,000 population. One syndicate controlled companies in a hundred cities; their aggregate capitalization was around one billion dollars. This trend continued well into the twentieth century, resulting in the huge corporate pyramids of the 1920s associated with such names as Sidney Mitchell and Samuel Insull. One of the nation's best-known corporation lawyers described the Insull empire as "impossible for any man to grasp . . . so set up that you could not possibly get an accounting system which would not mislead even the officers themselves." Financial expansion of the utility companies greatly complicated the tasks of the city governments in dealing with them; when regulation was seriously attempted, long years of litigation delayed it almost everywhere.

One result of the lenient policy in granting utility franchises in American cities was that this country got extensive street lighting and transportation systems much more rapidly than European countries, where more cautious policies were followed. Another result, however, was additional strain and stress on the governing process. The utility problem grew rapidly from small beginnings along with the cities themselves. Brand Whitlock, in his autobiography *Forty Years of It,* recalled from the days of his boyhood the jingling bell of a small horse-car coming along the main street of the town he lived in. The town grew into a middle-sized city; the horse-car line became an electric street railway with vastly increased income. "I ceased to hear of the individual owner any more," Whitlock wrote; "I never saw him in his shirt-sleeves in his little office at the end of the line counting up the nickels of those new families which each meant $73.00 per annum . . . , and it must have been about the same time that I began to hear of the traction company." The line still operated on the original franchise, however, which had given it monopoly privileges and which also assured that the company would be taxed at a very low level. The company, which came to be owned far away in an eastern city, was an important force in city politics because of the franchise it possessed, the value of which had risen so sharply with city growth. Later on, as Mayor of Toledo, Whitlock found himself struggling almost continually with utility interests that wanted to escape revision of their franchises.

By the time city dwellers realized some of the effects on the finances and the politics of their communities, the problem was already sizeable. As late as 1900 only three cities—Chicago, Baltimore, and Louisville—were deriving any significant revenue from franchise taxation. Private enterprise and public authority were delicately interlocked, and powerful corporations had large stakes in the control of city governments. "My experience in fighting monopolistic corporations as Mayor of Detroit," Hazen Pingree wrote in the 1890s, ". . . have . . . convinced me that they . . . are responsible for nearly all the thieving and boodling with which cities are made to suffer from their servants. They seek almost uniformly to secure what they want by means of bribes, and in this way they corrupt our councils and commissions." A few years later Lincoln Steffens described the city council of St. Louis as totally corrupted by the utility interests, selling franchises and other legal favors to these interests on a carefully worked-out scale on which was computed what each councilman should receive for the votes he cast. The best description of the kind of negotiations Pingree and Steffens singled out for censure was probably given by Theodore Dreiser in two novels, *The Financier* and *The Titan.* Inspired by the career of Charles T. Yerkes, a Chicago traction magnate, the plot details the history of a shrewd and imaginative man (whom Dreiser names Frank Cowperwood) as he becomes wealthy on Philadelphia street railway franchises. Blocked there by misfortunes resulting in a penitentiary term, Cowperwood moves west to Chicago, which was lustily rising from the ashes of the great fire, where he consolidates gas and street railway companies —carefully paying off the important city politicians—into a fortune far surpassing his earlier success in Philadelphia.

As the problem became more obvious and the utility companies drew increasing criticism, reform efforts began to shape a more carefully guarded approach to franchises or the regulation of public utilities. In 1885 the Massachusetts legislature set up a commission to supervise gas companies; two years later it was given the same oversight of the newer electric lighting companies. The commissioners were well paid and protected at least partly by civil service rules; they were expected not to involve themselves in any other remunerative work during their terms of office. No consolidations could be made nor could stock or bonds be issued without their approval; they could disallow any franchise that a city or town proposed to grant. This early example of a strong regulatory agency was not immediately imitated; the notion of public regulation of utilities caught on slowly. A reaction against long-term franchises led to their being limited generally to twenty-five years by the 1880s. In 1889, Colorado restricted all franchises to no more than twenty years, and other states took similar action. In 1907 the state of New York provided for a Public Service Commission to oversee the utilities of its metropolis, and in the same year Wisconsin established a regulatory commission with state-wide authority. By 1920 regulatory commissions were functioning in most of the states, and the most egregious evils of earlier days had been at least partly corrected.

In the meantime, mounting evidence of the extent of corrupt practices, and concern for tax rates which were believed to be needlessly high, led more and more citizens to consider the possibility of general municipal reform. The reform current was weak at first; its beginnings may be traced to the state investigations and the taxpayers' associations of the 1870s. It gathered force, however, so that by the end of the next decade the desirability of reform became almost a cliché. Although the stages of its development were not distinct and the fate of reform efforts varied widely from city to city, certain key elements can be identified. There was a movement away from state interference in city affairs culminating in demands for municipal home rule. There was a steady tendency toward concentration of executive authority, along with efforts to simplify the organization of the governments. In some places reformers tried to divorce city elections from national and state politics. Toward the close of the nineteenth century separate local reform movements began to try to coordinate their goals and share their experiences. As the twentieth century opened, two wholly new proposals for administrative structure gained popularity: the commission plan and the city manager plan.

While the constitutional status of cities remained unchanged—they continued to be, as they are today, legal creatures of the states—state legislators in the 1870s began having second thoughts about continually passing local legislation. States adopted restrictions in this regard which usually took the form of classifying their cities according to size; general laws could then be made for the different classes. In Illinois this action, taken in 1870, helped reduce the total number of laws passed annually from about 3,000 to about two hundred. The same state followed its abandonment of special lawmaking for cities with a Municipal Corporations Act in 1872 which broadly outlined the areas in which city governments might act on their own initiative. New York City was given a charter in 1870 that abolished state appointments of the boards in charge of public health, police, Central Park, and several other local activities. At almost the same time the state constitution of Virginia was amended to include a model-city charter which communities meeting certain size requirements might adopt. The California constitution's provision, in 1879, represented the trend: "Corporations for municipal purposes shall not be created by special laws, but the legislative by general laws shall provide for the incorporation, organization, and classification in proportion to population of cities and towns. . . . Cities and towns heretofore organized or incorporated may become organized under such general laws whenever a majority of the electors voting at a general election shall so determine." The California legislature soon proceeded to authorize the more populous cities to frame their own charters subject to its acceptance of the finished products. Missouri had already provided this privilege, in its 1875 constitution, for cities with 100,000 or more inhabitants; at the time this applied only to St. Louis, but Kansas City soon joined the classification and began its charter-framing history in the late 1880s.

Home-rule privileges of this scope were still rare by the end of the nineteenth century. Only Washington and Minnesota had followed California's and Missouri's far-reaching provisions, although the inconveniences arising from detailed state legislation were gradually mitigated elsewhere. As reform sentiment spread and gathered force, home rule became one of its rallying cries and along with it were implications at least that the traditional American suspicion of government was being reconsidered. Frank Goodnow, a leader in municipal reform movements during the late nineteenth and early twentieth centuries, observed in 1897 that "the fact that a city is an organization for the satisfaction of local needs makes it necessary that its action be determined by local considerations. To this end it must have large local powers." At about the same time, one of Goodnow's fellow reformers asserted that "the most cursory survey of municipal problems will show that they must be such as favor, rather than impede, positive action." Home rule was also promoted as being in the interest of greater democracy; it would, as one writer put it in 1911, make "the people themselves directly responsible for municipal government." At the same time it would remedy the condition in which the "best people" were largely indifferent to local politics. If city administrations were given adequate powers to deal with the problems facing them, reformers urged, "men of ability and patriotism will come to the aid of the city."

The keynotes were clearly efficiency and economy, and swelling demands for these encouraged another development during the same years that saw the promotion of home rule: stronger executive power emerged as a considerable force in the government of cities. This can be traced back to the days when mayors were first popularly elected, but even after that innovation the office typically remained weak for another generation. The tendency toward strengthening the mayor's hand probably reflected growing distrust of the councils, especially in financial matters. It was frequently accompanied by other moves in the direction of budget reform, such as provision for a comptroller more or less independent of other authority whose approval was necessary before any money could be paid out of the treasury. By the end of the century, city councils in many places had lost all power to appropriate money outside of budgets that were submitted by mayors, comptrollers, or other specially designated agencies.

It was after 1870 that the mayor began to acquire important executive authority. His veto power was extended, first in connection with the budget and then over all actions of the council. With demands for economy and retrenchment came realization that the ramifying complications of the various administrative boards contributed to inefficiency and waste; they began to lose powers which were often given to the mayors. One significant power was greatly strengthened when Brooklyn adopted a charter in 1882 which abandoned the traditional requirement that the council approve the mayor's appointment of administrative officials. This was widely imitated; in 1885 Boston took away the council's power to confirm removals from office. The mayor's emergence as a strong municipal power in his own right tended to pose him against the council at moments of crisis or near crisis in local politics. This meant that reformers tied their hopes more and more to the mayors; it also encouraged the tendency in reform thinking to promote executive power at the expense of legislative power, and thus prepared a way for the later commission and city manager plans.

Part of the mayor's growing strength was symbolic: he represented, and might almost come to "personify," the whole city, rather than any special area within it. The special identity of the mayor, wherever it was achieved, stimulated a movement toward what came to be called nonpartisanship in city elections. While political parties provided a degree of coherence amidst the confusion of municipal administrative structures, and thus made those structures at least partly usable, the domination of local politics by the state and national machines of the major parties had tended to obscure legitimate conflict over issues which were really local. Governor Tilden's 1877 commission to study city government and to make proposals for its improvement condemned the intrusion of major party political contentions into city affairs: "There is no more just reason," the commission reported, "why the control of the public works of a great city should be in the hands of a Democrat or a Republican than there is why an adherent of one of the other of the great parties should be made the superintendent of a business corporation."

Some people suggested that local politics ought to generate local parties, unconnected with the national organizations. Something like this actually happened often enough, although on a temporary basis, when successful reform groups were established; they transcended the lines of national party division and carefully avoided use of the words "Republican" and "Democrat." But these organizations were still pitted against regular party machines, whether Democratic as in New York and Chicago or Republican as in Philadelphia, and typically they did not last very long. They did not represent efforts to build durable local parties; most reformers felt that parties by their very nature were an excrescence on the urban body politic. "Whoever heard," asked a prominent reformer in 1895, "of a Republican park or playground, a Democratic swimming bath, a Prohibitionist street cleaning department, or a Populist mortuary?"

Use of nonpartisan ballots, where no party designation was permitted to appear, became possible during and after the 1880s when states began adopting the Australian system of placing the names of all candidates on ballots printed by the government. As a device for separating city affairs from state and national politics its success has been limited, but it was nevertheless widely adopted in American cities during the early years of the twentieth century and is now used in about two-thirds of all communities with populations over 5,000. By 1921, the mayors of almost half of the two hundred largest cities in the United States had been elected as "independents."

Along with this trend came efforts toward civil-service reform. Here the federal government led the way with passage of the Pendleton Act in 1883. It set up a commission to supervise certain kinds of jobs, appointment to which came on a nonpartisan basis and only after an applicant had passed an examination. The states of New York and Massachusetts imitated this legislation the following year, and the principle of a classified civil service began very slowly to make an impact on city government. Milwaukee, Seattle, and Tacoma all adopted limited civil service provisions in the 1890s; San Francisco's charter of 1898 applied the principle to a wide range of jobs in the city government. By the 1930s it had been generally adopted in America's largest cities. Its spread reflected partly the reaction against influence of party organizations on city administration, but also—and this became more important as time passed—it reflected a growing understanding of the need for expert knowledge in the increasingly large and sophisticated tasks that the city governments were being called upon to do. By the end of the nineteenth century it was no longer true, if it ever had been, that jobs in the public service were, in Andrew Jackson's words, "so simple that men of intelligence may readily qualify themselves for their performance."

Toward the end of the 1890s another reform measure appeared on the urban agenda; in the same 1898 charter which had promoted civil service examinations so prominently, San Francisco included provisions whereby citizens might legislate directly. By petition, a proposed law which the city council seemed unwilling to pass, could be placed on the ballot at the next general election; it would then go into effect if enough voters supported it at the polls. Similarly, laws passed by the council might be directly repealed by the voters if they saw fit to do so. This was the "initiative and referendum"; in 1903, Los Angeles's charter added provision for dismissing certain public officials by popular vote: a kind of "reverse election" named the *recall*. Initiative and referendum were quite generally adopted in American city government by 1930; recall did not spread rapidly despite the enthusiasm of its proponents and is possible only in a relatively few places. None of these changes had much effect on city government, with the possible exception of the referendum which was used in some cases to invalidate franchises granted by city councils.

Along with concern for the condition of American city governments went growing interest in studying ways in which European cities were run. The impact of this kind of study cannot be determined, but it is evidence of a developing sense that city affairs required professionalism in their handling. European cities, whereas they often experienced just as rapid a growth as American cities and felt as heavily the dislocations of industrialization, had still been administered in political cultures which did not denigrate politics and government as they were denigrated in the United States. In many cases these cities also had histories that went back for centuries into the past and around which clustered traditions of local patriotism and public service. While all of this did not enable Europeans to solve their broad political and social problems any better than similar problems were solved here, it probably did make it easier for them to devise efficient administrative mechanisms. At any rate, Americans increasingly visited Europe with a view to examining different facets of city administration. Thus German public school policy attracted the interest of superintendents of education in Illinois and New Jersey, who visited that country in 1872 and 1877 respectively. Milwaukee and Boston both sent delegations to study the handling of various urban problems in several European countries during the 1880s and 1890s. In park administration, London and Paris proved especially interesting to Americans concerned with that subject. The Chicago Citizens Association, a reform organization, recommended in 1892 that English cities be studied as models of good government in general. The progressives' interest in efficient city government in Europe gradually weaned them from customary American suspicion of public authority. Albert B. Shaw, a prominent progressive editor and journalist, was favorably impressed not only with city government in Germany, but with the philosophy that lay behind it. "The practical management of German cities," he wrote in 1895, "proceeds in harmony with the German conception of the municipality as a social organism. . . . It is enough for us to understand that in Germany the community, organized centrally and officially, is a far more positive factor in the life of the family or the individual than in America. . . . There are, in the German conception of city government, no limits whatever to municipal functions. It is the business of the municipality to promote in every feasible way its own welfare and the welfare of its citizens." The notion of creative government was not immediately welcomed, however, and few of his contemporaries would have gone as far as Shaw in recommending what in the mid-twentieth century has come to be known as a "welfare state."

All the while, as municipal reform became a national movement in the last two decades of the nineteenth century, and as trial-and-error practice built up a growing fund of professional and expert knowledge about the exigencies of city government, agencies to coordinate the movement began to take shape. State municipal conventions appeared first in Iowa in 1877. Early in 1894, a group of Philadelphians invited other organizations elsewhere to send representatives to that city for what would be the first Annual Conference for Good City Government. Out of this convention came a new association in the following year, called the National Municipal League. The League prospered and soon began to issue the *National Municipal Review* in which articles and editorials discussed the administrative problems of many cities. In the last years of the century the League adopted a "model charter," incorporating what its leading experts considered the best proposals for governmental structure practicable at that time. The model charter (which was revised from time to time in future years) called for a strong mayor, an independent comptroller, a large measure of civil service, limitations on franchise-granting by the council, and considerable home rule—although there was argument on this point from those who felt that strong state administrative boards were good for city government.

The League was not a leader in municipal reform. It arose rather as a result of maturing reform movements in almost every city in the country. The provisions of its model charter had each been tried out in a variety of ways in individual cities across the land. Most significantly the League did not anticipate (and came rather gradually to support) the two most important of all structural reforms in American cities: the commission and manager plans. But the League's appearance did signal an important stage in the development of American attitudes toward city government. It certified, so to speak, that concern with urban political affairs had become nationalized, and it marked the coalescence of efforts and campaigns that had previously been isolated. "Good government" could now start building its own traditions.

Aside from negative Jeffersonian notions about the desirability of "creative government," theory never played a great role in the shaping of city government in this country. The essentially pragmatic character of reform appears clearly in the emergence of the commission and city manager plans, which stemmed neither from European models nor from doctrinaire considerations of any kind, but rather from special and local circumstances. In 1900 a hurricane and tidal wave struck Galveston, Texas with devastating force. In twenty-four hours one-sixth of the population had been drowned and one-third of the property destroyed. The regular city government proved unable to cope with the terrible emergency and the staggering tasks of reconstruction; the state legislature had to come to the rescue. It did so by appointing a commission of five well-known local businessmen to govern Galveston during the emergency period. The arrangement was extremely autocratic but it also turned out to be highly efficient. The city's affairs were divided into four categories, each with a commissioner in charge; the fifth commissioner was a coordinator and acted more or less like a mayor. So ably was the city administration conducted that the legislature provided for continuance of the new system in a city charter in 1903, according to which three of the commissioners were to be appointed by the governor and two elected locally. This, although it had solid backing in the Galveston business community, was invalidated by the state supreme court, and the legislature then changed the charter so that all the commissioners were to be elected. In this basic form, with many local variations, the "commission system" spread rapidly. One prominent and encouraging adoption was in Des Moines, Iowa where the proposal was successfully promoted as "businessman's government." By 1917 about five hundred communities had adopted the plan (the largest were Memphis and Jersey City), and then its popularity began to wane. In some places people were disappointed to find that the new system did not necessarily eliminate "politics" from city government, nor did it automatically result in increased efficiency—which depended entirely upon finding the right candidates for election to the commission.

Another reason for declining popularity of the commission plan was the appearance of a competitor in the shape of the city manager plan. In the 1890s, while reformers were stressing efficient executive administration and expert knowledge in government, the notion of a "municipal manager" had occasionally been aired, but no effort was made to institute such an office until 1908. In that year the city of Staunton, Virginia hit upon the scheme of having the mayor and council hire a man to control all of the administrative functions of the government, choosing his own assistants who would be the heads of the various departments. This was a way of achieving (or at least aiming at) the kind of simplification and efficiency that were so impressive in the Galveston example; it would also get around the requirement in Virginia's constitution that cities must have mayors and councils, a requirement duplicated in many other states. Staunton's experiment proved that the manager system was workable and in the next four years several other small cities imitated it. Then nature intervened once more in the history of American city government, when a disastrous flood hit Dayton, Ohio. There had already been considerable agitation in Dayton (and elsewhere in the country) for adoption of the city manager plan; John M. Patterson, president of the National Cash Register Company with headquarters in Dayton, became a tireless advocate. The flood convinced enough people of the need for unencumbered city administration so that the manager plan was adopted. After Dayton, cities adopted the plan in increasing numbers and by 1923, 310 had done so. In the following year Cleveland decided to try the plan, and in 1926 Kansas City, Missouri, and Cincinnati did the same. This in some respects was the high point of the plan, at least in terms of its influence in shaping the over-all character of urban government in metropolitan America. Thereafter, the rate of adoption began to slow, and defections began to occur, particularly among larger cities, Rochester, Cleveland, and Dayton among them. Still, the number of city-manager cities had increased to 637 by 1945. After World War II, the plan boomed among smaller cities, especially among those created by new growth and rapid suburbanization, as in California. Buena Vista became the one-thousandth city-manager city in December, 1950; by July, 1959, the fiftieth anniversary of the movement, the number was close to 1,500, over half of all incorporated places. By January, 1961, the total stood at 1,756. The plan was particularly popular among upper-middle class and middle-class communities, where the business methods emphasized by the plan had the greatest support. There were a number of large city-manager cities in 1960, four of them over half a million, and twelve between 250,000 and 500,000; but this was the result of the growth of cities already having the plan, not of adoptions by larger cities. Of these places, only San Antonio had adopted the plan after 1933. Despite its success, the council-manager plan did not significantly influence big-city government and politics in post-World War II America.

The commission and manager plans were rationalized in classical reform terms: they provided efficient administrative systems and they permitted democracy to function better—the voter could participate more intelligently and effectively in self-government in these relatively simple governmental frameworks. Yet some of their characteristics had other implications. Both plans were frequently compared to the organization of business corporations; much of their success was the result of the spread of the idea that city government ought to be conducted on business principles. Bryce, in the 1891 edition of *The American Commonwealth,* had observed that Americans were beginning to draw the lesson that cities "are not so much little states as large corporations." A representative reform view, expressed a few years before the Galveston experiment, had it that "government of cities is business and not politics." Patterson had argued as early as 1896 that "a city is a great business enterprise whose stockholders are the people." The affairs of the city should be "placed on a strict business basis," not run by Republicans or Democrats "but by men who are skilled in business management and social science." Municipal reform, and especially the two innovations just described, represented largely the application of business ideology to city government; most of the support for reform charters came from businessmen and from the professions. In city after city, committees composed of the most powerful and influential business leaders sponsored plans for commission and council-manager governments.

Another important controlling assumption in the movement to reform city government was that expert administrators were necessary and that the voters were not equipped to pass upon the complexities of administrative powers.

The tendency of reform was toward relatively unhampered initiative in the hands of the officials, with the voters exercising—in effect—a periodic referendum on the over-all results. As an active reformer expressed it, "the details of departmental administration can never be made the subject of intelligent determination by the mass of the electors." The effects of this assumption—the correctness of which in twentieth-century conditions need not be questioned—are at best problematic. It is worth noting that the idea of "big government" was assimilated by Americans on the local level before it was assimilated on the federal level.

Much of the history of American city government since the days of Boss Tweed is described unavoidably in terms of bosses *versus* reformers. Without analyzing the implicit value judgments, it may be noted that they can obscure important aspects of governmental development. In the first place, the relationships between bossism and the proposals of reformers have been more complex than is often assumed. Significant measures of administrative centralization and home rule came to New York City in its charters of 1867 and 1870: both of them were secured from the state legislature by Tweed himself, and after his downfall no one proposed to alter their key provisions in later charters. Memphis adopted the commission plan in 1909 and Jersey City followed in 1911; Kansas City, Missouri adopted the manager plan in 1926. Out of the first of these changes arose the machine of Edward Crump; out of the second arose the machine of Frank Hague; and out of the third arose a revivified machine in the hands of Thomas J. Pendergast. Centralization of authority and responsibility was at best a two-edged weapon.

In the second place, there has been one constant factor in the development of city government, quite independent of both bosses and reformers: with mushrooming urbanization, the size, complexity, and cost of city government have grown. In spite of taxpayers' anxieties and in spite of widespread adoption of many measures which undoubtedly increased the efficiency of city government, its cost per capita rose by 53 per cent between 1902 and 1918; this figure does not include interest on indebtedness, and American city debts more than doubled during the same years. The *City Beautiful* movement of the turn of the century placed an additional burden on municipal governments. The civic and cultural centers with museums, city halls, libraries, and other public structures that were a part of this effort were largely financed and built by local governments. Even greater expense was involved in providing the transportation facilities, subways, elevateds, and new streets necessary to move traffic in and out of the rebuilt downtown areas. When the Great Depression hit in the 1930s, many cities were driven to the point of bankruptcy as the result of financing transportation and civic construction. And all this had been done in the name of progressive reform, which supposedly meant economical government. In the autumn of 1901, a group of reformers in New York City backed Seth Low, already famous for his fine record as former Mayor of Brooklyn as well as of New York itself, against a surprise reform nominee of the Tammany organization, Edward M. Shepard, a Democrat also from Brooklyn where he had worked with Low for civil service reform. Low was elected, on a platform calling for "progressive, businesslike, and nonpartisan administration of municipal affairs, with a special view to cutting down public expenses and reducing the present excessive burden of taxation." Many of his backers were surprised when Low's first budget exceeded the estimates prepared by the out-going Tammany mayor by $600,000. An editorial in *The Outlook* magazine noted that it should have been expected: "The more alert the citizenship of a place and the greater their confidence in their city officials the larger is the work the municipality is required to perform for its members." In short, reform was likely to be at least as expensive as corruption.

Regardless of reformers or bosses, there was no way to avoid the increasing range and scale of governmental activity. As early as 1889, the device of the specialized metropolitan commission had been used to provide sewerage facilities in the area of Greater Boston; this was followed by a park commission in 1893 and a water commission in 1895. By the 1920s special commissions dealing with a variety of metropolitan problems had become relatively common. When the five boroughs of Brooklyn, Queens, Richmond, Bronx, and Manhattan were joined into Greater New York City in 1898, the second largest urban agglomeration in the world presented its needs and problems to the new officials. An even more impressive example of the growing size of government in response to acutely felt needs was in the creation of the Port of New York Authority twenty-four years later. New York City and several New Jersey communities had shared the great eastern harbor since their earliest days, but they had not done so with any noticeable harmony. Controversies over navigation, pilot, and quarantine laws, which were different in the two states, marked the relationship from the beginning; in the nineteenth century, conflict over railroad rates intensified mutual hostility and rendered interstate cooperation all but impossible. The experience of World War I brought the basic problem to a head when, by 1917, 200,000 railroad cars were backed up in the area around New York City, Hoboken, and Jersey City, waiting to be unloaded at the port facilities. The federal government took over the railroads directly when the United States entered the war, but meanwhile the state legislatures of New York and New Jersey had been persuaded to appoint commissions to propose long-term remedies for the port's problems. On their own initiative the two commissions merged into one; after three years' consideration, it recommended creation of a new interstate agency with wide powers over the area's transport and docking arrangements. Both of the legislatures approved measures embodying this recommendation, whereupon it was quickly approved by Congress under the "compact clause" of the federal constitution. The Port Authority grew rapidly because it obviously met a crying need. At the outset its operations were financed by yearly appropriations of $100,-

000 by each of the legislatures, but its supervision of income-producing facilities enabled it to develop its own bonding program. The first bond issue
was for $14,000,000 in 1926; by the early 1960s the Port Authority's outstand-
ing debt amounted to about three-quarters of a billion dollars.

The New York Port Authority has not been directly imitated elsewhere,
simply because it was designed to meet a highly specialized problem; however, it is an example of needs generated by urbanization that evoke notable
extension of public authority. The use of special commissions also represented a pragmatic response to a new circumstance faced by municipal
governments in the twentieth century: the inability to annex (i.e., to add
unincorporated land to a city) or to consolidate (i.e., to absorb another
municipal government, usually an adjacent one) the new areas of settlement
around their boundaries. Orderly acquisition of these new areas was a regular
part of nineteenth-century urban growth. Annexation, which was the common
method of adding land to cities, was generally supported. It benefited real
estate interests and provided better services to the outlying areas. Even
when the process was resisted, the courts generally upheld the right of
forced annexation. The formation of Greater New York in 1898 represented
the high point in the annexation-consolidation stage of American city growth.
As early as 1874, Brookline avoided consolidation with Boston, and increasingly, particularly in the twentieth century, annexation and consolidation plans
encountered serious and continual resistance. Bills providing for consolidations were defeated in legislatures, which had begun to reflect the rise of
suburban interests. Voters turned down referendums authorizing annexations.
Even where proposals were carefully planned, presented, and supported, they
failed. Both St. Louis, whose boundaries had been fixed since 1876, and
Pittsburgh failed to win popular endorsement of moderate expansion plans in
the 1920s despite tremendous campaigns in support of them. Several influences accounted for this new state of affairs: the rapid growth of suburban
residential communities and the movement of men of wealth and power to
them; fear of the new ethnic minorities of the late nineteenth century and,
particularly in the twentieth century, fear of Negroes, who had begun to
find their way into northern cities in great numbers; a legacy of distrust of
strong, bureaucratized government which began to prove more powerful
than an opposing tradition, i.e., that size and numbers affirmed democratic
progress; and the provision of better basic services in the suburbs.

As time went on, the failure to unify municipal governments and the use
of specialized agencies created a bewildering complexity of government in
the huge metropolises. By the 1960s, the New York metropolitan region had
1,400 separate units of government; Chicago had more than 1,000. The
lenient incorporation laws prevailing in most states had always led to a
proliferation of municipalities in growing urban areas. In Dade County, Florida,
for example, which encompasses Miami, many towns were incorporated for
the sole purpose of getting liquor licenses, because the law allowed only

two to a municipality. The bulk of these "governments" performed only limited and special functions. The Advisory Commission on Intergovernmental Relations, created by Congress in 1959, emphasized in its 1965 report that fragmentation of government was one of the chief reasons that cities could not cope with their problems. The report supplied an example of the "array of local jurisdictions" responsible for just one small place, Park Forest, a suburb of Chicago: Cook County, Will County, Cook County Forest Preserve District, village of Park Forest, Rich Township, Bloom Township, Monee Township, Suburban Tuberculosis Sanitarium District, Bloom Township Sanitary District, Non-High School District 213, Rich Township High School 227, Elementary School District 163, South Cook County Mosquito Abatement District.

Concern with this problem and the example of the successful Toronto "metro" government established in 1953 led to a movement in the 1950s to provide consolidated government over metropolitan areas. It produced some results: Dade County, Florida established a metropolitan government in 1957; Nashville, Tennessee set up a government for five counties in 1962; Indianapolis instituted its "Unigov" for Marion County, which extended the area of the city from eighty-two square miles to over 400, and made suburbanites pay city taxes. But success was limited. Even in a new area like Dade County, where there was little allegience to an array of old units of government, the plan could be narrowly passed only after it had been considerably weakened. Attempts to carry out parts of the plan there led to political controversies that resulted in the resignation of the first manager and a struggle between his successor and the elected county commissioners. Elsewhere efforts to institute metropolitan government often encountered overwhelming resistance. St. Louis, a city unusually well surrounded by large independent municipalities, sponsored a plan to establish a metropolitan district in 1955. The campaign for its approval was well financed, carefully thought out, and was not vigorously opposed. It lost by a margin of three to one in the suburbs and by two to one in the city itself.

These defeats often seemed attributable to the continued American endorsement of a Jacksonian ideal of local government which included self-government for any organized community no matter how small, distrust of the professional and the bureaucrat in government, and the exposure of acts of government to popular veto. In the 1950s political scientists argued the necessity of creating a new view of government that was more suitable to the needs of the complex twentieth-century metropolis. But during the 1960s in response in part to riots and minority demands, the old tradition powerfully reasserted itself in a movement to decentralize city government into the neighborhoods. This effort tended to eclipse the metropolitan-government approach to the problems of cities. The calls for decentralization included sometimes vague proposals for little city halls, neighborhood corporations, and special local school agencies. A fashionable rationale developed that the established American city government represented a kind of imperialist structure controlled by a mercantile oligarchy who ran the city in its own interests. Although some experts on government argued that power to the neighborhoods for some purposes was not incompatible with centralized direction of metropolitan growth, it was difficult to comprehend how the complex circumstances of the huge metropolis could be managed through decisions made within a federation of self-serving principalities, to continue the kind of pseudo-historical metaphor introduced into radical polemics of the seventies. The history of American municipal government suggested that its positive achievements (in fields such as health, sanitation, transportation, and perhaps even police) had been achieved through centralization of authority and the development of bureaucratic, specialized professional agencies. In any event, by the early 1970s the neighborhood-government movement had produced little in the way of new techniques and forms, and its impact on the direction of city development seemed to be slight.

CHAPTER

# 10

# Bosses and Reformers

THE APPEARANCE of "the boss" as a key figure in the American political system was closely related to the cumbersome machinery of city government, physical expansion of the cities, immigration (which made them into cultural and ethnic patchwork quilts), and commercial and industrial growth which crowned the efforts of successful city promoters. Inefficient administrative structures encouraged the flow of power into the hands of men who could get things done by cutting corners or even, if necessary, by ignoring the laws. City growth provided an increasing number of tasks that had to be fulfilled. The presence of varying and often mutually hostile linguistic, religious, and racial groups within the urban population complicated the problems of social communication and furnished representative government with a new kind of constituency, one not generally anticipated when the country was founded. The success of urban promotions directed the attention of most businessmen to the management of their private enterprises and away from community problems. Into this gap between the need for government and a growing shortage of volunteers to provide it, strode the professional city politician. People whose exigencies he understood and responded to sustained him at the polls, and when he succeeded in building a reliable voting organization, he was called a boss. The boss, along with his equally typical opponent, the reformer, dominated the urban political scene in the United States for almost three generations.

The boss was stereotyped by the early 1870s, most effectively by the cartoons of Thomas Nast in *Harper's Weekly* during the struggle to oust William Marcy Tweed from the government of New York City. Tweed, himself, clearly understood the power of this new political device. "I don't care a straw for your newspaper articles," he said, "my constituents don't know how to read, but they can't help seeing them damned pictures." Other cartoonists elsewhere in the country took up similar themes and soon a recognizable, predictable character was sketched out. The "boss," in this stereotype, was sometimes snarling, sometimes jovial. He often smoked cigars and wore a derby hat. His face almost always had Irish features. He was usually portrayed with his hand in the public till, surrounded by ill-washed, grinning, and rough-looking cronies.

Like all durable stereotypes, this one has some connection with reality, but it smothers individual differences and ignores context: only one element is singled out and stressed, at the expense of complexity and understanding. Bossism was not a simple phenomenon, but rather a pervasive form of political behavior. Moreover, it did not emerge full-blown on the urban scene in the late nineteenth century but had many antecedents in past municipal politics. In the early part of the eighteenth century, David Lloyd organized a coalition of lower-class, ethnic, and religious interests in Philadelphia that contended successfully against the Quaker leadership of the city. He represented a kind of personal politics that would later be called bossism. In the 1720s, Elisha Cooke, Jr. helped to organize the Boston Caucus, which functioned much like later machines, using land deals, tax manipulations, and free liquor to gain and maintain power. Bossism grew quite naturally in the nineteenth-century urban environment on many levels—from the precinct to the whole city—and with many variations. It can best be understood when urban communities are regarded as partly organic (rather than as mere collections of individuals), so that at stages in their growth they develop needs; these needs can be met, in turn, only by use of the social materials and resources available at these particular stages. The different fortunes and the contributions of bosses and reformers alike can be assessed in relation to these needs and resources.

New York City offers an example in Boss Tweed, who bequeathed to his city the best publicized political machine in the United States and whose career excited international comment. The city's politics had never been regarded as pure. One editor asked in 1753 "how often have the votes of the people been purchased . . . without the least endeavor to conceal the bribery?" In 1768, a letter in a newspaper described a tavern where "every freeholder or freeman, who was willing to part with his vote, might there meet with a purchaser." It was proposed in 1780—unsuccessfully—to introduce the secret ballot in New York elections, "to prevent men of property, power, and tyrannical dispositions [from] . . . intimidating the electors from a free disposition of their votes."

By the time Tweed reached voting age, in the early 1840s, the Tammany organization was already a considerable power in the city. It traced its origin to a Jeffersonian political club started in the 1790s as the Society of St. Tammany. (The name "Tammany" was probably that of a Delaware Indian chief.) Many such clubs appeared in the United States during these years, as various groups and interests organized to oust the tightly-knit Federalist elite from power. The Tammany club continued to play a political role through the early nineteenth century, without notable success; for example, it fought against DeWitt Clinton's Erie Canal project. It also provided a social center and, like many voluntary associations, burial insurance for its members.

Under the guidance of hopeful local politicians, the Society began in the 1820s and 1830s to back proposals which were to become increasingly popular: abolition of imprisonment for debt and passage of a mechanics' lien law were two of these. During the depression from 1837 to 1842, Tammany officials prominently distributed quantities of fuel, clothing, and food in the poorer quarters of the city. As the modern national party system began to coalesce, Tammany grew into the main agency in New York City for the Democratic Party. As it became consistently (and then officially) Democratic, it also became increasingly popular; its charitable activities and its hospitality to the newly arrived Irish immigrant—along with its staunch opposition to rising anti-Catholicism—made Tammany something of a "poor man's club."

As the party connection became clearer, Tammany also acquired another source of power: patronage. The club was consulted in the choice of candidates, and candidates who won with Tammany's help consulted it about the distribution of city, state, or federal jobs. While federal patronage was not large by modern standards, the New York City custom house did supply a considerable number of opportunities. With the growth of the port, duties collected there became the government's largest single source of income by the 1820s. Between 1827 and 1843 the custom house staff grew from 164 to 503 and its payroll from $112,000 to $489,000. An investigation in 1839 revealed a well-established system of "cut," whereby Tammany got people jobs on the New York customs staff and in return the job holders gave part of their salary to the organization. The same investigation uncovered defalcations by custom officials amounting to a million and a half dollars. Wholesale ballot frauds were common; in the city election of 1844—the first in which Tweed was old enough to vote—55,000 votes were cast; the figure is about 10,000 higher than the number of residents eligible to cast them. Tweed, in other words, did not invent the boss system. The system grew naturally, as cities grew.

William Marcy Tweed came from a family of relatively prosperous craftsmen; in his youth he passed through apprenticeship as a carpenter. He was good at his trade and soon owned two shops. Big, full of energy and good will, he was popular with his neighbors and was elected captain of the volunteer fire company to which he belonged. The first time he ran for a ward office he lost, but came back again to win a seat as alderman. Running against a popular Whig, Tweed had persuaded a friend, also a Whig, to enter the race; this split the opposition enough to enable Tweed to get in by less than fifty votes.

On the board of aldermen, Tweed set about centralizing the previously individualistic enterprises of the officials, and raising the scale of these enterprises. By the Civil War decade, political corruption was organized to an impressive degree. Tweed persuaded the aldermen to contract with one man for the entire city's street cleaning, instead of doing it by district as the practice had been. The successful bidder was paid $279,000 for a year's work— and immediately "kicked back" $40,000 from his fee. Again, under Tweed's effective leadership, the city paid $100,000 for a plot of ground for a potter's field; its market value would normally have been $30,000, and the pleased seller gave some of his money from the land sale back to the group of men who had made it possible. At one time the city hall was actually sold to satisfy a claim against the city; it was later bought back for more than had been received at the first sale.

These anecdotes, revealing as they are (and there are many more about the Tweed period), constitute only part of the story. All the while, whatever his reasons may have been, Tweed was seeing that some important things were accomplished. Streets were extended in the sprawling city; franchises were granted for horse-drawn street railways; the planning of Central Park went ahead; a new county courthouse was built. Tweed got himself elected to the New York State Senate in 1868, in part for his own ends but also to make possible welfare programs for the poor and more public support of Catholic schools in New York City. Twice during Tweed's public career, New York City's governmental structure was overhauled in the interests of some much-needed efficiency. Tweed favored both charter revisions necessary to bring this about; of the second (in 1870) he even said it had cost him $600,-000 to get it passed.

It is clear, of course, that the boss could line his own pockets from building and street-paving contracts, and franchises, and that centralization of authority through charter revision was likely to strengthen him. Still, the process of urbanization called for these things, and the New York example suggests that in the circumstances corruption was the agency by which they were provided. After his downfall, Tweed remarked that "The fact is New York politics were always dishonest—long before my time. There never was a time when you couldn't buy the Board of Aldermen. A politician in coming forward takes these things as they are. This population is too hopelessly split up into races and factions to govern it under universal suffrage, except by the bribery of patronage or corruption." A recent scholar, Seymour Mandelbaum, has endorsed Boss Tweed's analysis, writing that "only a universal payment of benefits—a giant 'pay-off'—could pull the city together in a common effort. The only treasury big enough to support coordination was the public till."

Tweed and his friends were driven out of City Hall in the fall of 1871, after bankers and others had become seriously alarmed at New York's precarious credit standing in the international money markets. He was indicted on 204 counts, convicted on most of them, and sentenced to jail in a curious, tearful courtroom scene where judge, prosecutor, jurymen, and observers all had recourse to their handkerchiefs. After a dramatic attempt to escape in disguise to Europe, the "boss" was put in prison where he died after a few years. The end of the Tweed ring and the subsequent history of the Tammany organization need not occupy space here. That bossism as illustrated by the Tweed experience was expensive is beyond dispute. New York City's bonded debt rose during the two-and-a-half-year period up to September 1871 by around forty million dollars. The total increase covers the refunding of inconvenient short-term bonds into long-term bonds and the conversion of revenue bonds (issued to finance an operation or facility, the income from which is supposed to retire these bonds) into part of the city's general debt; this made the debt more expensive to carry while the principal amount was increasing rapidly. Moreover, the account books were in an almost undecipherable condition when the reform party came into office. This meant that time had to be spent bringing order into the complicated columns of figures. It also meant that for some time the New York authorities actually did not know how much the municipality owed or to whom; uncertainty about the city's current financial position made accurate budgeting impossible. How much was lost through inflated payments to suppliers and contractors will never be known. Still, the costs of the system could be reasonably assessed only if the likely costs of an alternative system could be computed, and one of the questions at issue is whether there were any real alternatives for the community.

The Tammany organization's long life, along with the almost universal experience of other American cities, suggests that the system was strongly rooted in the conditions of urban growth. A reform coalition drove Tweed and his associates out, but the Tammany-led Democrats were back, victorious, at the next election and held power most of the time thereafter in New York. The organization's features—and over the following two generations, its character—changed; the most flagrant practices from the Tweed period were abolished. But long after the twentieth century began, observers still described the boss system flourishing on its diet of personal influence, patronage, and special favors.

Philadelphia's machine government, during the same period, was in many ways similar to that of New York. The Philadelphia machine, however, was Republican and immigration did not play as large a part in its growth as it did elsewhere: Philadelphia was the most "American" of all the big cities. Moreover, Philadelphia also counted a larger property-owning group than any of the other metropolitan centers in the last third of the nineteenth century. Whereas most city bosses were Democrats, with ethnic and class factors important to them, the system still could flourish in either party; immigration alone does not explain its emergence.

In 1835, a private company began supplying Philadelphia with gas. Six years later the city bought out the company and proceeded to run the gas works as a municipal enterprise. A special board of trustees was set up to superintend the operation. This was done to keep the important utility "out of politics"; ironically, a powerful political machine soon developed in the Gas Trust itself. The trust had the power to contract for construction and repairs and could issue its own bonds, which meant that it could distribute favors and profits to many contractors. It also hired and fired the 2,000 people employed by the gas works, which gave it the largest block of patronage in the city.

Shortly after the Civil War, James McManes began to emerge as the dominant influence in the Gas Trust. Skillful distribution of contracts and jobs gave him and his associates power over most of the city's other activities as well as the gas works. They bought into Philadelphia's largest street transportation company, and this gave them another block of jobs to hand out. Soon Mc-Manes had almost absolute control over the Republican Party in Philadelphia, with great influence at the state capital and in Washington as well.

The Gas Trust met and deliberated in secret; McManes kept all payroll and personnel records to himself. City elections were regularly won by the machine. City employees were just as regularly assessed part of their salaries in order to help finance the machine; policemen, for example, had to pay anywhere from ten to twenty-five dollars a year, depending upon how large a campaign effort seemed necessary. Several city government posts provided their holders with sizeable incomes from fees—the Collector of Delinquent Taxes made $200,000 one year—and a share of these incomes was also turned back to the machine.

The system proved expensive in Philadelphia, as it proved in New York; between 1860 and 1880 the city debt increased from $20,000,000 to $70,-000,000. This was a powerful influence in the formation of an anti-McManes reform coalition at the beginning of the eighties. A group of the city's best-known businessmen, calling themselves the Committee of One Hundred, of whom almost all were Republicans, cooperated with the local Democratic Party in 1881 to oust the McManes-controlled administration. There followed a wave of legal prosecutions, a thorough paring of the voting rolls which had been heavily padded, and a series of measures to introduce order and accountability into the city's finances. McManes was not indicted, and simply retired to private life. Nevertheless, reform's triumph was short-lived. Within a few years the Committee of One Hundred disbanded, and Philadelphia's affairs again passed into the hands of professional machine politicians. Around the turn of the century, Lincoln Steffens claimed that of all the boss-governed cities in the country, Philadelphia was "the most corrupt and the most contented."

Chicago provides still another example of bossism with variations of its own. Throughout the nineteenth century and well into the twentieth, no single machine controlled Chicago's public life. This may have been partly the result of the extremely rapid growth of the place, from next to nothing in 1830 to over a million in 1890. It may owe something to the sprawling geography of the city, from its business heart near the lake in three directions—north, south, and west—to where, as Theodore Dreiser described it in *Sister Carrie*, "narrow board walks extended out, passing here a house and there a store, at far intervals, eventually ending on the open prairie." For whatever reasons, no leader appeared who was able to control enough of the unstable and heterogeneous elements in Chicago's population to dominate the city.

Instead, there were always several machines, sometimes contending, sometimes cooperating, giving the city's politics an inconsistency that made it possible for reform organizations to score more frequent victories than they did in most other cities. Steffens noted that "Minneapolis has cleaned up, Pittsburgh has tried to, New York fights every other election, Chicago fights all the time." There were many bosses in both major parties. Some, like the Carter Harrisons (father and son), Charles Deneen, and William Lorimer, had public appeal and ran their factions from the strongholds of elective office, as mayors or governors or senators. Others, like Roger Sullivan, preferred to move behind the scenes, placing men politically indebted to them in the public offices. Each had particular sources of support: Deneen was popular in the middle-class residential south side, another faction generally won the northern wards, Sullivan was powerfully entrenched with the utility companies, and the Harrisons made great appeal to the Irish Catholics, as William Hale Thompson did to the Negroes. "Classes, races, religions, regions," Charles Merriam wrote, "are the background against which the play is built."

In spite of the absence of a central figure controlling the others, Chicago's procedures were like those that prevailed elsewhere. Jobholders in the city government were assessed a percentage of their salaries for the benefit of those to whom the jobs were owed. Boodling—largely the authorizing of franchises in return for money payments to the aldermen—was on a remarkably decentralized basis. At one time, one of the aldermen worked out a scheme for negotiating franchises block by block! During four administrations in the 1890s, there is good evidence that at least fifty-seven of the sixty-eight men who sat as aldermen accepted bribes for their votes.

The universality of bossism is indicated perhaps most forcefully by the experience of the nation's capital in the 1870s. Washington, D. C. was never an industrial city, and its form of government has been unlike that of other American cities. Early in 1871, Congress provided it with a government modeled partly on procedures in the territories. The President appointed a governor and an upper legislative chamber, as well as a board of public works with wide powers to build and to assess costs against the taxpayers. The lower chamber of the council was elected by the city's voting residents; the District was given a non-voting seat on the congressional committee which was responsible for its affairs. One effect of the provisions of the 1871 act was to reduce sharply the power of recently enfranchised Washington Negroes. In a popularly elected city government these people might have played a part corresponding to that of poor immigrants in sustaining bossism in many other cities. As things were, the government of the District of Columbia was not necessarily designed to be responsible to the local popular will.

There was much building to be done. The capital had never presented a finished appearance and the Civil War years had pushed thoughts of completion into the background. Now, however, progress was in the air. Congress authorized a great new structure to house the State, War, and Navy Departments. Private real estate business quickened as the new form of government went into effect. The role of the Board of Public Works was clearly going to be important.

Very soon the personality of Alexander Shepherd, one of its five members, impressed itself indelibly on the rest of the board. The other board members did what Shepherd told them. He had been born and raised in Washington, and after the Civil War had come into prominence as a highly speculative developer of residential property. Shepherd wanted to move fast in the building of a modern metropolis; he designed and promoted a system of improvements for the city. The political environment for his operations was surprisingly like that in New York, Philadelphia, and Chicago: jobs in the city government constituted patronage for a political machine. But in this case, the machine was the national Republican Party under the leadership of President Grant. Shepherd was a friend of Grant's, and this explained his appointment to the board. Later, Grant named him Governor of the District of Columbia.

His program included a new drainage system, the leveling of hills and filling in of depressions, extensive street paving, and provision that views of the Capitol from various points in the city should be impressive. The plan, in the words of historian Constance M. Green, was "calculated to create a city with unrivalled sanitary facilities and clean, well-paved, well-lighted thorough-fares."

It was also expensive, but Shepherd had his way. Over the objections of men who feared the financial consequences—with good reason—he pushed a large bond issue (which did have to be approved by local voters). It passed, helped by Shepherd's judicious distribution of jobs at the disposal of his board, by a twelve to one margin. Within a short time the District's indebtedness had risen to a level where it was surpassed by that of only seven states. References to "Boss Shepherd" began to appear in public print, and critics compared him with New York's Tweed. Still, a cleaner and more attractive city was emerging under the eyes of Shepherd and his critics alike. When his grandiose schemes, along with the panic of 1873, brought Washington to a point where only Congressional intervention could save it from outright bankruptcy, Shepherd lost his job and retired to Mexico.

His public career had resembled Tweed's in many ways: the use of public posts as patronage, graft in the awarding of construction contracts, and the role of financial accounting in bringing about his downfall all testify that bossism flourished in the nation's capital under an explicitly authoritarian government as it did in other cities more responsive to democratic pressures.

Cincinnati's experience with machine government during a somewhat later period suggests further complexities in the tasks performed by the boss in meeting the demands of the city brought about by the rapid urbanization of the late nineteenth century. The role of the machine in representing and reconciling class interests has been well documented, but as Zane Miller has shown in a pioneering study of Cincinnati politics, boss government also provided a way of reordering political life in the wake of the chaos created by rapid physical growth of the cities, and dramatically changed residential patterns brought about by suburbanization.

In the early years of the twentieth century, Boss George B. Cox of Cincinnati was frequently castigated in national journals in the customary terms of the period as "The Biggest Boss of Them All," and as Lincoln Steffens put it, the head of a system that was "one great graft," "the most perfect thing of the kind in this country." His career, his public image, his character fitted the boss pattern. He was a self-made man of the city who acquired an early and intimate knowledge of urban life. Born to British immigrant parents in 1853, he grew up in a decaying central-city area of Cincinnati; after his father's death when he was eight he worked at a succession of jobs—bootblack, newsboy, lookout for a gambling joint, salesman, bartender, grocery delivery-man. He eventually acquired a saloon, ran with a sporty set often called the *bonifaces,* who later supplied leadership in his organization, and got into politics, though not again as a candidate after his second defeat for county clerk in 1888. Cox had the easy ways of the boss, the taste for the good life, and the urge to display the tokens of success. Like so many bosses, he was driven from office when financial scandals were exposed. And like so many of them also, he worked closely with powerful special interests. When Cox was building his organization, General Andrew Hickenlooper, the Cincinnati gas magnate, recorded in his diary in 1891 that he had "concluded [an] arrangement with George B. Cox for services at $3500 a year quarterly to last for three years."

Although in several regards he represented the much-denounced boss system, Cox, like Shepherd and Tweed, made substantial positive contributions to his city and, according to Miller, demonstrated the truth in Cox's remark in 1892 that a boss was "not necessarily a public enemy." In the 1880s when Cox began to build his organization, Cincinnati was on "the brink of anarchy" —torn by crime waves, general disorder, racial and labor riots, and continual violence. Cox brought a degree of order to the city by establishing a Republican organization that represented new residential areas created by the disappearance of the "walking" city. Although a number of groups and interests were represented by his alliance, fundamentally he based his organization on these residential areas, not on class and ethnic affiliation. He united affluent suburban voters of the "Hilltops" interested in municipal reform with lower-middle-class groups who had moved into the immediate areas away from the central city, the "Zone of Emergence," against the Democratic central city, the "Circle." The organization won a series of elections, sometimes by close margins, and during the 1890s and the first decade of the twentieth century quieted the conflict and disorder that had been constant in the city, pushed through a series of municipal improvements involving fire protection, police, parks, sewers, and education, and instituted some control of public utilities and some containment of vice. "The Republican regime, in short," concludes Miller, "brought positive government to Cincinnati."

Bosses and machines did not function the same in all places, but even where they served the cause of positive government, political corruption was a part of the system, and it was the prevalence of political corruption in American cities of the nineteenth century that led to demands for change. In Milwaukee a grand jury handed down more than seventy indictments against public officeholders in the year 1903 alone. In St. Louis it was reported that one council member inquired about the possibility of suing a utility official who had offered a bribe but had not paid it. Lincoln Steffens gained his first fame as a journalist going from city to city and describing the bosses and the machines in each for readers of *McClure's Magazine*. Many lesser known writers exploited the same material; few subjects bulked larger in the newspaper and magazine press between the 1880s and World War I.

There were reformers, of course, and they could count—especially in the early twentieth century—significant victories against the bosses. Moisei Ostrogorski, in his pioneering study of American party organization published in 1902, described what he called "an outburst" of civic reform organizations beginning in the mid-eighties. He concluded that these groups had achieved lasting results: "the aspect of things has changed perceptibly for the better. . . . Municipal reform is not only before the public, but fashionable." Eight years later even Lord Bryce—whose remark that city government was "the one most conspicious failure of the United States" became one of the frequently quoted sentences on the subject—asserted that none could doubt "that things are better than they were twenty-five years ago."

Municipal reform during the late nineteenth and early twentieth centuries usually stressed efficiency and honest accounting in public administration. Its main achievements were structural changes that made those goals easier to achieve or, as many hoped, more difficult to avoid. Home rule for cities, the short ballot, nonpartisan municipal elections, regular independent audits of city accounts, and finally the commission and city manager forms of government, all revealed widespread talent for political innovation and tended to bring government within a more manageable compass. The reformers' analysis of bossism was usually cast in terms of good people *versus* bad people; they argued that undesirable types got into local administrations through the cracks and crannies in the inefficient, obsolete, and impossibly complicated structure of local government. If this was so, then a reform in structure should encourage reforms in substance.

Sometimes another reform dimension was added, when moral crusaders attacked the machines' connection with prostitution, gambling, and bootlegging. The most famous of the crusades during this period was led by a clergyman. In 1894, the Rev. Charles Parkhurst of the Madison Square Presbyterian Church toured some of the more unsavory districts on Manhattan Island and publicized what he learned about police protection of vice. His effective portrayal led to a legislative investigation and roused enough voters to unseat Tammany for two years, during which time some improvements were introduced into police administration by Commissioner Theodore Roosevelt. In the same year, the English journalist William T. Stead published *If Christ Came to Chicago,* which described the same close connections between politicians, police, and criminals in the Illinois metropolis. Seven thousand copies of Stead's book were reported sold on the day of its publication; it triggered a reform movement in Chicago, and continued to attract attention there and elsewhere to the problem with which it dealt.

The structural reforms suggested by political science and the moral ardor usually stemming from religious impulses were not in themselves enough to regenerate any American city. Triumph along these lines was typically evanescent; the reformers captured city hall, fired some policemen, prosecuted some "machine" public officials, and administered what R. Richard Wohl called "disaster relief" to the city treasury, only to be swept away at the next election by the resurgent power of the bosses. The usual associations of the moral and political reformers were upper-class, native American, and Protestant. They rarely drew any warm response from the cities' poorer masses, many of whom were, of course, immigrants and Catholics. Theodore Roosevelt represented the social philosophy of many reformers when he wrote in 1886, "Voters of the laboring class in the cities are very emotional . . . if a man is open handed and warm-hearted, they consider it as being a fair offset to his being a little shaky when it comes to applying the eighth commandment to affairs of State." A few years earlier, in the wake of Tweed's downfall, a reform-oriented commission appointed by Governor Samuel J. Tilden recommended that voting rights in municipal elections be limited to taxpaying property owners. Inclinations of this kind gave reform a "highbrow" stereotype and made it very difficult for it to find a mass base.

In a few important cases, reform leaders were able to build stable and victorious organizations for themselves—to become, as it might be said, "reform bosses." In these cases, one finds the structural and moral elements included within a somewhat larger program, linking the problems of the city to the more general environment of the American economic scene itself. One also finds the reformer making a deliberate bid for the votes of the common people, attempting to democratize reform out of its long association with upper-class values. The best known examples are Hazen Pingree of Detroit, Samuel M. Jones of Toledo, and Thomas L. Johnson of Cleveland.

In an influential study of urban politics centering on Detroit, Melvin G. Holli has suggested that these well-known mayors along with a few others represented a minority position within the municipal reform movement. More typical, he argues, were the structural reformers like James Phelan of San Francisco or Seth Low of New York, who attempted to make city government less corrupt and more efficient but who were not concerned with extending municipal democracy or with limiting the privileges of the wealthy and of the propertied interests. It was this structural approach, with its emphasis on the expert and on formal techniques of administration, that eventually came to represent urban progressivism in the twentieth century. Still, it was the mayors identified with social reform who received most attention for their programs in the period. Their efforts to make municipal government more representative of broad community interests established an important strain in a continuing urban reform tradition.

Hazen Pingree, less well known than Jones or Johnson but an equally effective reformer, was a well-to-do businessman, first elected mayor of Detroit in 1889; he was successively re-elected until 1896 when he became governor of Michigan. During his municipal administration Pingree publicized the corruption of Detroit's officials, especially by utility companies. He gained great popularity fighting for carefully restricted franchises for the street railways and gas companies, and managed to have a municipally-owned electric lighting plan built. His activities did much to popularize the whole issue of municipal ownership. "Good municipal government is an impossibility," Pingree said, "while valuable franchises are to be had and can be obtained by corrupt use of money. . . . I believe the time has come for municipal ownership of street railway lines, water, gas, electric lighting, telephone, and other necessary conveniences which by their nature are monopolies." This emphasis tended to associate the evils of city government with the larger questions inherent in the relationship between private business and public service.

Samuel Jones, called "Golden Rule" Jones, had made a small fortune manufacturing oil-drilling equipment. He became mayor of Toledo in 1897, remaining in office until he died in 1904. Like Pingree, Jones supported municipal ownership of utilities, and actually became an idealistic kind of socialist. He pushed the development of public playgrounds, free concerts in parks, and free kindergartens in schools. He established an eight-hour day and a minimum hourly wage for city employees. He got a new charter from the state which contained provisions for the initiative, referendum, and recall. Jones broke with the regular Republican organization that had first helped to elect him, and in his three subsequent campaigns he ran as an independent. "The fact of the matter is," he wrote, "there is little hope for improvement, for progress, in the direction of scientific government in our municipalities until we shall first get the people freed from the baneful superstition of partisan politics." Jones's combination of nonpartisan campaigns with a program stressing social welfare suggested that reform itself could be almost unbeatable at the polls.

In Cleveland, Thomas L. Johnson performed comparably as mayor between 1901 and 1909, when he was finally defeated in a close election. He was something of an inventor, had invested heavily and profitably in steel mills and utility franchises, and was a rich man by the time he was forty. During a train trip one day, he fell into reading a copy of Henry George's economic reform classic, *Progress and Poverty,* and was so affected by it that he began building a second career—this time as a reform politician. With great popular appeal, he served two terms as a Democratic congressman in the nineties, and then turned his attention toward the problems of Cleveland. As its mayor, he broke up the connection between the police and the brothel keepers by promising not to prosecute the madams if they would agree to remain orderly, not to pay anything to policemen, and not to steal from their customers. (A friend of Johnson's remarked that the mayor was not trying to enforce Christianity, but rather to make it possible.)

Like Pingree and Jones, he fought to limit utility franchises, and finally forced the street-railway fare down to three cents, which endeared him to many voters. He was tireless in advocating municipal ownership of utilities. "Only through municipal ownership," he stated, "can the gulf which divides the community into a small dominant class on one side and the unorganized people on the other be bridged; only through municipal ownership can the talent of the city be identified with the city; only by making men's ambitions and pecuniary interests identical with the welfare of the city can civil warfare be ended." At the same time that Johnson fought to bring utilities under public control, he promoted social welfare projects such as municipal bath houses, recreation areas, and careful inspection of meat and dairy products. To help him in the large task he had undertaken he introduced a degree of expertise into his administration, gathering about him a *brain trust* of young men who brought professional scholarship into the practical study of city government. Lincoln Steffens claimed that Johnson made Cleveland the best-governed city in the United States.

These three men resembled one another in that each used some of the arts of the demagogue—each, that is, carefully established his own image as a "friend of the people." At the same time, they attacked municipal problems that meant more to more voters than did honest accounting taken by itself. In this way, they gave municipal reform in their own cities a wider and more durable appeal than the Reverend Parkhurst or the National Municipal League or the Committee of One Hundred could supply.

In achieving power by means of broad popular appeals and then using their power to achieve reform goals that included social welfare projects, these three men did not typify municipal reform during the years in which they flourished. Jones's inclination toward socialism especially placed him outside the ranks of representative reformers. For political reform was ordinarily conceived in business terms, sponsored by successful businessmen, and designed consciously or unconsciously to serve business ends. Pingree, Jones, and Johnson were themselves successful entrepreneurs, but they left their businesses behind them when they turned to public life, and did not regard the latter as a function of the former. The business motivation behind most municipal reform in the eighties, the nineties, and much of the twentieth century reflected the social sources of the reform movements and bore significantly upon the failures and successes of the political reformers themselves.

The boss system arose partly out of universal suffrage and local, decentralized representation in an urban environment. When Tweed explained New York City's political corruption by the diversity of its population, he was largely accurate. Big cities in the explosively industrializing United States in the nineteenth century were governmental units, but socially they were increasingly fragmented as their development proceeded. They became patchworks of neighborhoods that were for most purposes separate sub-communities. Economic and social equality never characterized American cities, but disparities in wealth and status grew wider in the early stages of industrial progress. At the same time, the cities grew so large physically that communication through the ranks in their hierarchies became practically impossible. Men could no longer walk from one neighborhood to any or all of the others at will. In Tweed's day, before the telephone and before rapid transit, it might well have been easier for a man living in Brooklyn to reach another man in Chicago by letter than to reach an administrator in New York's City Hall.

Supposing the physical barriers to communication had been overcome—as they were overcome by invention and innovation—there remained cultural barriers. Cosmopolitan, comfortable George Templeton Strong and the recently arrived Polish laborer might have had much of interest to say to one another, but how could they have said it? Not only would the languages of the two be different; so would almost all of their basic assumptions about society, wealth, poverty, religion, community and family life, and about what the city was good for. It is most likely, indeed, that neither would have felt impelled to seek out conversation with the other. Yet they were both New Yorkers.

By the mid-nineteenth century the forms and styles of life in New York were various and were becoming more so. On the map, they were distributed into residential districts marked out by class and ethnic lines: rich, middle class, poor, Irish, German, Negro, Jewish, and so on. When Jacob Riis wrote *How the Other Half Lives,* he was able in many cases to mark out the boundaries of the districts by specific blocks and street numbers. In social and cultural life these groups kept largely to themselves. In politics, the system of voting by precincts and wards gave each group a chance to be represented and to have its imperative needs recognized and discussed near the centers of public power.

At the same time, the system reinforced the physical fragmentation of the cities. From a cost-accounting standpoint it was not an efficient system; there was always the possibility of financial disaster, as in the cases of Tweed, McManes, and Shepherd. Moreover, the wealthy groups found that the system made it difficult and sometimes quite impossible for them to assert any control over city affairs. Whether their motives were rooted in public spirit or in anxiety about tax rates, more and more of them grew restive under the restraints and burdens of bossism. Among the better-off businessmen

were to be found most of the leaders of the spreading political reform movements in and after the 1880s.

This is especially noticeable in movements for the commission and city
manager plans. These structural changes proposed to introduce the efficiency
of the private corporation into the processes of city government. Clinton R.
Woodruff's description of the commission plan was representative; it was, he
wrote in 1911, "an application to city administration of that type of business
organization which has been so common and so successful in the field of
commerce and industry." Chambers of commerce almost always led in local
efforts to make these changes. Analyzing the organizations that supported
charter reform in Pittsburgh in the early 1900s, Samuel P. Hays has found
that of the names of 745 members, almost two-thirds were in social registers
and other directories which together included only 2 per cent of the families
in the city. In the forefront of the movement were representatives of the
biggest banks and industrial corporations in Pittsburgh.

While the reformers of city politics had to appeal for votes at the polls,
and defined their objectives as serving the public interest in general, their
assumptions about social class and political eligibility were often far from
democratic. One spokesman at the National Municipal League's 1907 convention urged that it stood to reason "that a man paying $5,000 taxes in a
town is more interested in the well-being and development of his town than
the man who pays no taxes. . . . Shall we be truly democratic and give
the property owner a fair show or shall we develop a tyranny of ignorance
which shall crush him?" In 1911, a reform publication contended that "employment as an ordinary laborer and in the lowest class of mill work would
naturally lead to the conclusion that such men did not have sufficient education or business training to act as school directors." And in city after city
the reformers found most of their voting support in the wealthier wards and
very little of it in the poor wards. William Rockhill Nelson's pro-reform
*Kansas City Star* was happy to observe, after a victory at the polls, that "it
was in the wards where people live the year 'round and own their own houses
that the . . . pluralities were the greatest." Nelson, as well as others like him
elsewhere in the country, usually claimed that the reform proposals were
particularly in the interest of the "middle class" but he was himself a wealthy
man, as were most of his associates.

The Chicago reform movement which followed W. T. Stead's revelations
is illustrative. In addition to a graft-ridden police force, Chicago was plagued
with widespread unemployment during the winter of 1893–1894. Stead was
able to bring together some of the city's leading businessmen and labor
union representatives to discuss community problems. Out of these meetings
emerged the Chicago Civic Federation. Well financed and carefully organized
down to the level of wards and precincts, the federation proposed to deal
with unemployment relief and labor relations, conditions in the public school
system, the problem of gambling, securing honest vote-counting in city

elections, street cleaning, and what it called civic beauty. Over a three-month period in 1894, the federation provided thousands of dollars in work-relief. Applicants were given jobs cleaning streets; they were paid in certificates that they could exchange for necessaries at specified places. Soon the federation was hiring detectives to investigate fraudulent voting; this led to many indictments and convictions. Detailed investigation of Chicago's street railways followed. The federation opposed municipal ownership; it preferred to advocate refinancing of the companies in the interests of cheaper and more efficient service, and its recommendations did produce some improvements. In 1900, an organization called the National Civic Federation came into being, modeled upon the Chicago organization and dedicated to a coordinated attack upon the same types of problems.

But in spite of its impressive record of achievement, the Chicago Civic Federation never had mass support; it never became a peoples' organization. Time after time it sought an overhauling of the city's charter along with the taxing system, only to suffer defeat at the polls. The labor union leaders who had at first participated in the federation's activities soon dropped out and left it an organization largely of Chicago's business elite. The Civic Federation's leadership came for the most part from the directorates of the biggest banks and industrial corporations, the Board of Trade, the real estate business, and the insurance companies. The leaders were public-spirited but also conservative in their social philosophies; unlikely to establish warm and lasting relationships with the city's depressed classes, they represented what Daniel Levine has called "the right wing of the reform movement."

The emphasis on business efficiency, and the feeling among well-off businessmen that bossism denied them adequate representation in city government, help explain one of the most frequent features of municipal reform campaigns: attacks of one kind or another upon the ward and precinct system. Larger electoral units, the reformers felt, would make it more difficult for the bosses to keep their power, which rested on an informal and highly personal kind of politics. If the unit of representation was enlarged so as to include diverse ethnic and economic interests, no one could successfully barter votes in return for simple privileges keyed to the desires of any one group. Wherever the commission or manager plans went into effect, the size of the municipal legislature was drastically reduced and the members represented larger constituencies than had been the case before reform.

In short, while their programs varied considerably and while there is danger in oversimplifying their motives and objectives, it is clear that most of the reformers took a "stake in society" approach to city politics. They believed that ownership of property subject to taxation, experience in business, and educational preparation gave special qualifications for representation and public office. This understandable attitude lent an upper-class connotation to most of their campaigns, which was for many years a serious obstacle to their success. In the early years of the twentieth century they began, however, to score increasing victories, with the result that the characteristic structure of American city government was markedly different by 1930 than it had been in 1870.

But the successful reformers, and periods when they controlled city governments, were exceptional, temporarily interrupting the over-all domination of bosses and machines. The urban environment of nineteenth and much of twentieth-century America was apparently more stimulating for bossism than for reform. There were several reasons for this, one of which was the general character of the American party struggle. Although many people identified political corruption as an urban phenomenon, it was not; boss rule in the cities was one form which it might take. C. Vann Woodward has described the patterns of corruption and favoritism by which the rural southern states were governed in the post-Reconstruction period. William Allen White recalled in his *Autobiography* how widespread was the understanding, before the turn of the century, that one transcontinental railroad "owned" the legislature of Nebraska and another "owned" that of Kansas. The American writer Winston Churchill wrote a novel about the almost unbeatable machine that dominated New Hampshire in the 1870s and 1880s. Adams County, Ohio, without a sizable town in or near it, was the scene of astonishing corruption in the early 1900s. A Republican boss controlled the political life of rural North Dakota for over twenty years. The big-city bosses represented an urban phase of American politics.

The bosses' power was partly a result of their professionalism; they made the study of politics and political organization a full-time job, which very few other Americans could do or cared to do. George Washington Plunkitt, who made a fortune in real estate during his lifetime as a Tammany official, described the need for professionalism in plain words: "Politics is as much a regular business as the grocery or dry goods or the drug business. You've got to be trained up to it or you're sure to fail. Suppose a man who knew nothing about the grocery trade suddenly went into the business and tried to conduct it according to his own ideas. Wouldn't he make a mess of it? . . . It's just the same with a reformer. He hasn't been brought up in the difficult business of politics and he makes a mess of it every time." And Plunkitt described his own apprenticeship for his interlocutor: beginning at the age of twelve, he progressed up the organization's ladder by making himself useful during every waking hour.

Moisei Ostrogorski repeated a comment made by many observers when he wrote that Americans dedicated themselves to private pursuits: "The desperate race for wealth has absorbed the citizen, and has not left him time to attend to the public welfare; it even encouraged his want of public spirit and converted it almost into a virtue." Businessmen had their own affairs to tend, with little time left over for the demands of politics. The Philadelphia Committee of One Hundred, disbanding after three years, found that it could not keep workers in the field on a purely voluntary basis; "its members became tired of the thankless task of spending time and money in what must be a continuous, unending battle." In New York, Tilden's commission, which studied proposals to improve city government, noted that most citizens did not expect to be asked to give much of their time to politics. Governments were "contrivances" to protect people earning honest livings: "when these contrivances . . . become themselves the occasion of incessant watchfulness and enormous expense they fail in their essential purposes." Noting the rapidly expanding commercial and industrial life around him in 1871, E. L. Godkin thought it hardly possible "for men to pay any fruitful attention to politics without neglecting their private affairs."

It is not quite accurate to say simply that the businessman's loss of interest in politics contributed to the rise of bossism. It should be noted as well that most people in the changing economy of nineteenth-century America had plenty to occupy their attention in their concern with getting a living, or getting ahead. How much time was left over for the ordinary citizen—the clerk, the wage earner—in which he could consider community policies? There were hundreds of candidates for local and state office; there were highly technical questions about rates of interest, legal and constitutional intricacies, durations of franchises, advantages and disadvantages of various taxes—matters which demanded concentrated study before an informed opinion about them could be offered. It is not strange that only a few people could give much time to city politics. William Allen White was probably too generous when he estimated in 1910 that "in any precinct of two hundred voters . . . not over fifty people in either party paid serious attention to politics." In the circumstances, bosses and their henchmen performed services that few other Americans ordinarily cared to perform.

In the complicated and badly designed formal structures of the city governments, with mayors and councils (sometimes bicameral) supposed to check and balance each other, with independent and partly independent commissions existing beside them, and with lines of legal authority and responsibility hopelessly confused, there was not only opportunity but also need for effective control—which almost had to be informal. This control was provided by the bosses and their machines. At whatever the price, streets did get paved, lighting, heat, telephone and transportation services were provided, and fire and police forces grew. This was done in spite of sets of explicit and legal rules which were such that they themselves tended to prevent publicity and to make any open, systematic attack on these urban problems impossible. Blake McKelvey points out that sometimes the ablest municipal servants "were so eager to press ahead with street paving, sewer construction, and the like that they quickly learned to play politics with jobs and contracts." It was one way, and possibly the most direct available way, to get things done.

A study of Kansas City during the early years of the Pendergast machine shows James Pendergast, older brother of the better-known Tom, supporting bond issues for school and other construction purposes, park and boulevard legislation, and important improvements in the garbage disposal service—the desirability of which was clearly recognized by many of the local anti-Pendergast forces. During the machine's later growth it identified itself even more firmly with the most impressive building programs the city had ever known. Frank Hague in Jersey City, Huey Long in New Orleans, and many other comparable figures could be cited. Building projects, especially, might strengthen the machine's sources of power, but this does not affect the proposition that the bosses and the machines supplied an element of vital organization in communities where this might have been difficult to achieve in any other way.

That the bosses found ways to exert authority on their fragmented (and legally, almost disorganized) communities was generally evidence of their superior executive abilities. Bryce, whose sympathies were always with the reformers, had to concede certain virtues to Philadelphia's Boss McManes: "personal capacity, courage, resolution, foresight, the judicious preference of the substance of power to its display." A comparative study of twenty city bosses who flourished during the early twentieth century found one characteristic common to all of them: each had abilities that would have brought success in any regular line of business enterprise. "Have you ever thought what would become of the country," asked Plunkitt, "if the bosses were put out of business, and their places were taken by a lot of coat-tail orators and college graduates? It would mean chaos."

The business talents of bosses were also demonstrated in a social context: many of them were immigrants, or sons of immigrant parents, and found through politics secure places for themselves when other doors were not as widely open. Neighborhoods populated by immigrant groups quickly became the most frequently noted sources for the voting strength of the machines, and many observers concluded that there was an organic connection between bossism and immigration. The connection was usually felt to lie in the immigrant's ignorance of the representative institutions and accepted civic practices of his new country. This explanation would not have accounted for the native-born businessmen who were busily financing many of the boss's operations even while the immigrants were voting for him, but it runs through most contemporary comment on the American urban scene.

The connection between bossism and immigration was certainly a close one, but it was more complicated than most accounts have suggested. In the first place, most of the immigrants were poor. They were poor at a time when government was not generally regarded as a social welfare agency. There were no public works programs, free school lunches, food stamps, or social security payments. No progressive income tax modified the market's distribution of wealth. Charitable and other philanthropic enterprises were carried on by private individuals and voluntary associations, and their scale of operation was by no means adequate to ameliorate significantly the lives of the millions of immigrants who added their number to the native urban poor. Much depends upon the definition of *poor;* the word's quantitative and qualitative meanings changed with the uncertain course of the national economy between prosperity and depression. After carefully discounting a multitude of statistical studies, however, Harold U. Faulkner concluded that around the turn of the century "fully eighty percent of the people lived on the margin of existence while the wealth of the nation was owned by the remaining twenty percent." Poverty was a rural as well as an urban phenomenon, but in the cities it concentrated more visibly in growing slums; a large percentage of the inhabitants of these slums were foreign-born or were the children of foreign-born parents.

A man with some influence in the city hall could do much for these people; if he did, his influence could be expected to grow along with their gratitude expressed in votes. In case a poor man found himself in jail, he needed help with the law. In bad times, he needed someone to keep the heat and light in his home from being turned off. He needed assistance in locating jobs for himself and for his children. These services were provided by the bosses. The charitable activity of Tammany representatives during the depression of 1837 was an early example. Boss Tweed's generosity to the needy was better known to them, at least, than his under-cover operations in the city treasury. In the winter of 1870–1871, he gave a thousand dollars to each of the aldermen to use for charity in their districts, and spent $50,000 himself in his own ward. In Kansas City, James Pendergast built up a reputation (and an increasingly powerful machine) by his distributions of jobs and charity where they were most appreciated. In later years the free Christmas and Thanksgiving dinners given by his younger brother, Thomas J. Pendergast, were well-known in the riverfront wards.

The presence in cities of large numbers of immigrant families lent a special dimension to bossism. The foreign-born worker, and in most cases his children, had to contend not only with poverty but also with language difficulties and with attitudes of hostility or contempt on the part of the native-born population. In the 1840s and 1850s, the Irish were described in the newspapers of eastern cities in the same terms that were later to be applied to Negroes. When Italians and Slavic immigrants arrived in this country, they found the same experience waiting for them. Anti-Catholic and anti-immigrant impulses found nation-wide expression in the "Know Nothing" party before the Civil War, in the American Protective Association during the nineties, and more recently in the revival of the Ku Klux Klan in the 1920s.

Most city bosses fought these nativist movements, thereby offering a political and social haven to the immigrants. As part of the developing relationship between bosses and immigrants, the political machine became an avenue of advance—and, quite possibly, of "Americanization"—for many citizens with foreign names. The machine offered more than labor jobs in public or utility construction. For the brighter and more ambitious young men, there were clerical and other white-collar positions in the machine itself; such positions represented for many the first step toward middle-class-respectability. There was opportunism in all of this, for both the boss and the immigrant, but there was more to it than the buying and selling of votes. As Oscar Handlin observes, the boss—himself often exemplifying the success story of an immigrant boy—represented deeply felt, if intangible, values for members of his constituency: "Often the feelings of group loyalty focused upon him. He was a member of many associations, made friends on every block. In the columns of every newspaper his name reflected glory on the whole community and he in turn shared its sense of solidarity." Bosses played large roles in the acculturation process which mass immigration rendered necessary in the United States.

The boss also responded to a limited extent to the racial tensions that became a part of the urban scene in the nineteenth century. Boss Cox in Cincinnati quieted unrest by suppressing violence at the polls, thus permitting Negroes to vote, and thereby drew Negro groups into his coalition. In the same period during the 1890s, James Pendergast, the founder of Kansas City's much-publicized machine, protected Negroes from harsh treatment by police and courts and extended patronage control to Negro politicians in his organization. Pendergast's was the first machine of many that followed to woo Negro voters systematically. Bosses of the period hardly stood for or promoted racial equality, but they did more for Negroes than most of their contemporaries.

It has recently been argued that bossism is disappearing from the American scene. Mass immigration has ended and the third and fourth generations in what were immigrant families have been absorbed into the general American society; they no longer feel special needs because of the spelling of their names. In the wage-earning population, flourishing labor unions now provide the social life and the needed sense of solidarity formerly offered by the machine. The economic policies of the federal government are likely to maintain a widely diffused prosperity, lessening the number of those whose needs stem simply from their poverty. For the rest, government—and especially the federal government—is now assumed to be a social welfare agency; people in need of help can get it from officially sanctioned sources and do not have to turn to the extra-legal money and influence of the boss. There is substance in this argument, and it is certain that the character of city politics has changed in the direction sought by the reformers.

Immigration, however, was important in sustaining bossism predominantly because it presented problems of cultural assimilation. Cultural assimilation is still a problem in American cities and will remain one for some time; it is most visible in the matter of race relations, but exists elsewhere as well. Moreover, some commentators have noted that as government becomes more complex (at the same time that it has more things to offer) there develops a need for people who can explain which door to knock on and which form to fill out. It is not impossible that a new variety of bossism will take shape, to mediate between the citizen in need and the confusing bureaucratic tangle that surrounds him.

In any event, it should be clear that bossism, typifying American urban politics for most of the nineteenth and much of the twentieth centuries, is no simple phenomenon. Any complete estimate of its effects—political, financial, cultural—is, of course, impossible. Bosses capitalized on the in-group feelings of many immigrants as well as upon the needs and the frustrations of the poor. This may have exacerbated these feelings, and prolonged their life. On the other hand, the availability of help and the possibility of advance that the machine offered may well have mitigated ethnic and class conflicts. Even as it marshalled its voters at the polls, the machine did more than buy their votes; it brought them into the body politic, where they probably represented less of a threat to established institutions than they would have represented outside of it.

The effects of bossism upon those who were appalled or shocked by its manifestations is an equally complicated matter. The well-known padding of registration rolls, the falsifying of election returns, the connections between most bosses and certain kinds of crime, the fraudulent franchise grants—these things undoubtedly reinforced the conviction of many Americans that politics was necessarily a dirty game, beneath the concern of respectable people. It might be argued, though, that bossism evoked reform, and also forced it toward more realistic and more penetrating analyses of community life. Part of the great strength of the bosses lay in the fact that they knew their communities as few other men did. They knew what happened in the alleys and the byways as well as at city hall, and they put their knowledge to practical use. The political reformers began by regarding the city primarily as a problem of constitutional structure, or as an arena in which good and bad principles came into contention. As the boss continued to dramatize the problematic and threatening aspects of American urbanization, more and more of the reformers came to see a need for broader understanding of the city's life styles. They set about examining the consequences of urban growth. When this happened, the city began to be naturalized in American thought. No longer purely an object of vituperation or celebration, the American city became an object of study.

CHAPTER

# 11

# The Urban Community Examined

T HE PACE and the momentum of American urbanization, with its manifold and changing problems, bewildered many observers. Even while city growth was opening opportunities for success and advancement, it made difficult the maintenance of any sense of continuity with the past. Henry Blake Fuller's 1894 novel about Chicago, *With the Procession,* describes not only the emergence of ostentatious luxury and elaborate social rituals in the western metropolis, but also a feeling on the part of several older citizens—who were living in wealth and comfort—that Chicago had grown beyond their understandings. In the novel, a wealthy merchant, who came to the city before the Civil War, becomes involved in a misdemeanor case in a municipal court, which he discovers to be dominated by corrupt politicians. Urged to drop the case, he refuses. "I want to see for myself," he says, in anger and frustration, "how things really are. I want to learn what conditions we are living under. I want to understand the things that are really going on about us." A bit later on in the novel, the man's son, a young lawyer, tells him what he will discover: "You'll find a hell-broth: thieves, gamblers, prostitutes, pawnbrokers, saloonkeepers, aldermen, heelers, justices, bailiffs, policemen—and all concocted for us within a short quarter of a century."

In 1888, Dr. Theodore S. Case of Kansas City, Missouri, who had arrived there thirty years earlier when the place had been a raw but optimistic little river town, edited a thick volume of local history. In the introduction he confessed that the steady obliteration of old and familiar landmarks, consequent upon successful city promotion, was confusing to the older settlers; their imaginations could not embrace the progressive alteration of their environment. The newer arrivals had no time for systematic consideration of the city's development: "even the present," Case wrote, "is more than they can keep up with." Another Kansas Citian, surveyor and speculator John C. McCoy, who had come to the spot even before there was any permanent settlement, reflected in the 1870s upon the swift growth of an industrial community of 30,000 people; he concluded that no human will or purpose could have accomplished such a result. It had been dictated by geography; "sheer necessity alone," said McCoy, "caused the upbuilding of the city today." The implication was that cosmic destiny had driven a modern city beneath the feet of startled, if pleased, enterpreneurs.

McCoy's recourse to overriding determinism, in order to explain phenomena which seemed otherwise to defy rationalization, was by no means
peculiar to him; many comparable examples can be found in the local and
state histories and volumes of urban reminiscences which appeared in great
numbers in the closing decades of the nineteenth century. "New Haven,"
wrote one of its historians in 1888, "has entered on a new career of civilization as varied as science and as wide as mankind, and . . . its old-time quaint-
ness, simplicity, and homogeneity will be seen no more forever." Whether
inspired by nostalgia or progressive optimism, local history flourished in the
post-Civil War epoch as it never had before. The National Centennial Fair
at Philadelphia in 1876 stimulated its production; a committee which met
during the fair devised a standard format for writers and distributed it widely
over the country. Individual authors sometimes turned out histories of several
places; one indefatigable clergyman named Charles Tuttle published twenty-
eight of these during the period 1873–1876. J. Thomas Scharf, a Baltimore
journalist, turned out a history of that city in 1874, one of St. Louis in 1883,
and one of Philadelphia in 1884. Every large city found several chroniclers,
amateur or professional, who in the aggregate produced a significant, if not
often inspiring, body of writing during the period when Americans were endeavoring to come to terms with their urban surroundings.

Although they vary widely in quality, these histories do not typically offer
sophisticated case studies in urbanization. They stress picturesque features of
the local scene: a visit by the President of the United States, portrayal of a
colorful Civil War hero, and interviews with the oldest inhabitant. They generally suppress issues that have divided or embarrassed the particular cities,
in favor of optimistic accounts of growth. They include many figures and
tables showing the rise in real estate valuation, bank clearings, and commercial transactions. Chambers of commerce sometimes sponsored books of this
kind. They were sometimes put together by writers who proposed to sell them
by mentioning as many local names as possible; "biographical" appendices
running to twice or three times the length of the chronicles themselves were
common. Whatever the underlying motives, its great volume, especially between 1870 and 1910, suggests that local history met some needs. It helped
to satisfy, however partially, an intense and widespread curiosity about the
rise of the city.

Curiosity was stimulated not only by rapid growth, but also by some of its
menacing consequences. Violence in a dozen eastern cities accompanying
the railroad strikes in the summer of 1877, the shock of the Haymarket bomb
in Chicago nine years later, the pitched battle between strikers and a small
army hired by their employers at Homestead, Pennsylvania in 1892, and the
destruction and carnage in Chicago stemming from the Pullman strike of
1894, all seemed to indicate that urban society was vulnerable, that American
city dwellers were living on the rim of a social volcano. Charles Loring Brace,
a clergyman who dedicated his life to rescuing destitute children from the vice

and filth of the streets of New York, described *The Dangerous Classes of New York* in a book with that title which appeared in 1872. Homeless, near the edge of starvation, and disease-ridden, thousands of the city's inhabitants, according to Brace, had no stake in preserving community peace. "Let but Law lift its hand from them for a season," he warned his readers, "or let the civilizing influences of American life fail to reach them, and if the opportunity offered, we should see an explosion from this class which might leave this city in ashes and blood." Increasingly, and in many ways, Americans turned to the examination of their cities, often in the hope that in knowledge they would find power to order the urban environment.

Their studies confirmed much that was shocking and threatening. Some people believed that the problems of urban community life defied solution and that civilization as they had known it was on the road to collapse. Lincoln Steffens exemplified this view. In the years after the appearance of his exposé of corrupt city government, *The Shame of the Cities,* he decided that corruption was a permanent and essential feature of American public life. Since it could not be got rid of, it should be used: Steffens toyed with the notion of achieving good ends by persuading bosses to support them. But nothing came of this, and Steffens finally concluded that the problems of modern life could be met only by a revolutionary dictatorship. Most concerned people were not this pessimistic; appalling conditions revealed by their examinations of urban phenomena ordinarily impelled them to work out ameliorative programs. Community self-study was closely related to reform, and the broadening goals of reform interacted with the broadening scope of the studies that were made.

While Steffens' pessimism was not representative, there was a great deal of anxiety about the consequences of city growth. Henry George, in his widely read *Progress and Poverty* (1879), the book which deeply affected Cleveland's Tom Johnson, noted that "the type of modern growth is the great city. Here are to be found the greatest wealth and the deepest poverty. And it is here that popular government has most clearly broken down." He then epitomized the bosses as the ruling class of the cities; these men "stand to the government of these cities as the Praetorian Guards did to that of declining Rome." Sharing presentiments of Gothic horrors with many other writers of his time, George predicted that unless steps were quickly taken "the sword will again be mightier than the pen, and in carnivals of destruction brute force and wild frenzy will alternate with the lethargy of a declining civilization." Edward Bellamy, author of the popular Utopian novel *Looking Backward* (1889), also felt that society was moving toward cataclysm. The hero of *Looking Backward,* a scion of the late nineteenth-century Boston aristocracy, recalls for his host in the twenty-first century, "we felt that society was dragging its anchor, and in danger of going adrift. Whither it would drift nobody could say, but all feared the rocks. All I can say is, the prospect was such when I went into that sleep that I should not have been surprised had I looked down from your house-top today on a heap of charred and moss-grown ruins instead of this glorious city." Josiah Strong, a crusading Congregationalist minister whose book, *Our Country: Its Possible Future and its Present Crisis,* was a best seller after it appeared in 1885, wrote that "the city has become a serious menace to our civilization." Urbanization, in his view, threatened to inundate American institutions with poverty, immigration, Catholicism, and socialism.

George and Bellamy were both confident, however, that urban society would reform itself in time, and even Strong felt that the Anglo-Saxon genius he so admired would meet the challenge successfully. With the triumph of Christian reform, Strong believed, would come the new city, "the symbol of *heaven*—heaven on earth—the Kingdom fully come." Bellamy's future metropolis on this site of Boston was described as "a great city. Miles of broad streets, shaded by trees and lined with fine buildings, and for the most part not in continuous blocks but set in larger or smaller inclosures, stretched in every direction. Every quarter contained large open squares filled with trees, among which statues glistened and fountains flashed in the late afternoon sun. Public buildings of a colossal size and an architectural grandeur unparalleled in my day raised their stately piles on every side." The narrator soon learns that the amenities of social and individual life in this city are fully worthy of its physical perfection. And it should be noted that Bellamy believed his own prediction; in his words, it was "a forecast, in accordance with the principles of evolution, of the next stage in the industrial and social development of humanity, especially in this country." Bellamy's visionary optimism went beyond that of most reformers; still, intuitions of the good community coexisted in their minds with feelings of disgust and revulsion from the contemporary scene. These sentiments formed the content of many constructive studies of urban life.

That the "good community" seldom resembled existing cities—which certainly impressed their investigators as largely undesirable habitats—has led some students to characterize the urban reformers as basically anti-urban. Traditional agrarian rhetoric often crept into their utterances, and some reform campaigns did posit escape from the streets of the city as essential; but, from the 1880s on, the reformers' program was mainly not to abandon the urban environment but to reshape it. The city as the central fact of American social life was accepted; the argument was no longer over whether or not city development should be encouraged, but over what directions it should be given.

This important change in attitudes toward the city took place gradually. The careers of William Augustus Muhlenberg (1796–1877) and Charles Loring Brace (1826–1890) illustrate its early stages. Rector of New York City's Church of the Holy Communion and deeply committed to the cause of social betterment, Muhlenberg was not instinctively anti-urban. During a trip to England as a young man, he could not repress a sense of boredom in the quiet cathedral town of Ely. "On the whole," he noted in his journal, "I believe I should thrive better, body and soul, amid the rattle and clatter of Sixth Avenue and Twelfth Street!" Back in New York, Muhlenberg threw himself into an effort to provide fresh-air vacations for poor children, especially after the 1849 cholera epidemic. As he analyzed the city's spreading slum problem, particularly with respect to its bearing on children raised in slums, he became convinced that it was self-perpetuating; the bad conditions made bad upbringing inevitable for most of the children of the poor: "The noxious physical and moral [influences] are ever acting and reacting with cumulative force." The slum had outgrown men's power to reform it; the evils of overcrowding were "too gigantic for any grasp of reform at all conceivable." Political apathy and the rapacity of slum landlords put legislative action out of the question; benevolent agencies worked with commendable zeal, "but anything like the elevation of a whole locality is beyond their hopes. They cannot remove causes. . . ." Muhlenberg came to believe that the only effective help for children who would otherwise grow up in the slums lay in transporting families to what he called "a Christian industrial community" in which the environment would be planned to encourage spiritual growth. In the later 1860s, with money from wealthy Episcopalian acquaintances, he bought a 500-acre farm on Long Island Sound where he planned such a community for families from the "deserving and industrious poor." It was to include four or five hundred people—tailors, shoemakers, and seamstresses, for example—along with a print shop, a church, and a school. Muhlenberg's project, which he conceived as one of social reconstruction, was never realized, partly because its financial backers regarded its economic communitarianism as a threat to American individualism. Muhlenberg, moreover, in his declining years did not make much of an effort to see it through. The farm on which he had hoped to build a Christian industrial community became first a home for crippled children and ultimately a home for the aged.

During the same years, Brace had promoted a scheme of juvenile reform which was at the outset more anti-urban, and which attracted more attention, than Muhlenberg's scheme. Brace, in whose New England background socially conscious religious ardor was a prominent feature, traveled to England and continental Europe after his college education at Yale and Union Theological Seminary. The reform of juvenile delinquency had attracted much attention in other countries, and Brace was especially interested in German and British organizations which tried to separate children from deleterious urban environments. Back in America, he settled in New York where, in 1853, he and several other ministers founded the agency which was later to adopt the name of Children's Aid Society; he served as its secretary for almost forty years. The organization's main program was to adopt slum children and resettle them in farm or small-town homes in the countryside. They should have the benefit, in Brace's words, of "pure country air, instead of the gases of sewers; trees and fields in place of narrow alleys." The idea was not new, even in this country; Joseph Tuckerman had tried it out on a small scale in Boston. But under Brace's direction the program swelled until about 90,000 children had been "sent west" in forty years (upstate New York was actually where many of the children were placed). While it could claim some noteworthy successes, Brace's program drew increasing criticism. Some children failed to adjust quickly to their new surroundings; in these instances Brace was often taxed with exporting New York's problems and thereby "polluting" the country districts. Many Catholics saw his activities as directed primarily against their church. In the 1870s and after, social workers (whose numbers were growing rapidly) argued that attempts to resettle the children simply drew constructive attention away from conditions in the city. Brace continued all his life to defend resettlement, but his own energies went more and more into institutional church work in New York City. Forced, as R. Richard Wohl has observed, to retreat from his original emphasis, "he increasingly geared his activities to the assumption that underprivileged city children would remain permanently in the city."

By the 1870s, a movement which came to be called "the social gospel" was already discernible within the older Protestant church groups in America; Muhlenberg and Brace were among its progenitors. The association of religion with social reform was neither new nor peculiarly American—nor had it ever been especially limited to protestantism. But between the 1860s and World War II, many Protestant congregations tried to confront some of the consequences of urbanization. The United States had been largely Protestant while it had also been largely rural, and the anti-urban themes of early American culture had influenced the social philosophy of the Protestant churches. American catholicism and Judaism had grown in America as the cities grew; accordingly, these faiths did not experience as sharply the necessity of intellectual adjustment to the urban environment.

Intellectual adjustment was forced upon Protestant ministers when it began to appear to them that their churches were losing all communication with the rapidly expanding urban population. Washington Gladden, a Congregationalist minister in Columbus, Ohio, compared his heavily white-collar congregation with the population at large, and discovered that though about a quarter of the country's population was made up of wage earners, not more than one-tenth of his membership came from working class districts. At approximately the same time, a Pittsburgh minister took an informal census which showed that businessmen along with salaried and professional workers who made up 10 per cent of the local population constituted almost two-thirds of the membership of the city's Protestant churches. In the older eastern cities especially, these churches had included members who, as their early business ventures prospered, became wealthier and moved away from the center of town, while waves of immigrants filled the houses they left behind. On Manhattan Island, the area below Fourteenth Street gained 250,000 people between 1868 and 1888; during the same years it lost seventeen Protestant churches.

It is not surprising, in the circumstances, that some ministers—like Gladden, Brace, Walter Rauschenbusch, and others—sought ways to stem the urban erosion of their clienteles. As early as 1865, delegates from several churches, meeting in Cleveland, formed an evanescent American Christian Commission to study their mutual problem. Churches in the cities, the commission's first report declared, were hampered by "want of knowledge of [the cities'] moral condition; lack of organization of the wealth, piety and labor which exist there; need of experimental knowledge of the best agencies . . .; and want of trained, tried, permanent laborers in the various spheres of city labor." While it lasted, the commission conducted surveys of poorer areas in thirty-five cities, and on the basis of the resulting data recommended intensive home missionary work; it also set up a committee to study what had been done in European cities. In the following decades Episcopalians, Methodists, Unitarians, Presbyterians, and Congregationalists attacked the slum problem. The "institutional church," with its lodging houses, reading rooms, adult education classes and recreation centers, became a fixture on the urban scene. These projects were often expensive, and wealthy parishioners were asked to contribute heavily. This necessitated a certain amount of educational work by socially-conscious ministers; Muhlenberg and Brace tirelessly assembled data to convince rich acquaintances of the value of their schemes. Spectacular success occasionally crowned their efforts; William E. Dodge, a New York City magnate, contributed $140,000 for an institutional church in the Bowery, and the Chicago Methodist Society raised a million dollars in fifteen years and St. George's Episcopal Church in New York raised two million for the same purpose.

Separate churches found it advisable to cooperate, however their doctrines might diverge. Many well-known social-gospel ministers and laymen, including Gladden and Richard T. Ely, helped organize the American Congress of Liberal Religious Societies at the Chicago World's Fair in 1894. Doctrinal controversies retreated to the background as they heard Albion W. Small, the University of Chicago sociologist, argue that all "forms of religion . . . have a common tendency, varying in degree, but essentially social." Interdenominational cooperation for social ends was the main influence in producing the Federal Council of Churches of Christ in America in 1905.

The relevance to American urban history of this widely-studied movement lies mainly in two of its characteristics. First, the social-gospel ministers conducted studies, including house-to-house surveys of their neighborhoods, and publicized the results as widely as they could. These surveys played a part in enlightening contemporaries about some of the social characteristics of urban America. Secondly, the exigencies of urban reform led many Protestants further from the old belief that success and failure were the social rewards respectively for individual virtue and vice. Environmentalism began to infiltrate social philosophy at least as early as Tuckerman's reform activities in Boston. Brace had asserted in 1852 that "Material Reform and Spiritual Reform . . . must go on and mutually help one another." A leader of the institutional-church movement in New York City conceded in 1893 that poverty lay "very close to the problem of sin." A social-gospel minister in Buffalo asserted that, if one cared to save the people, who languished "in squalor, poverty, and degradation," he must "exchange their tenements for homes. And to do that," he added, "you must put your finger on legislation. . . . If you wish to prevent the perpetuation of slum life you may as well understand that it will not be done altogether by direct evangelization." The social-gospel clergymen were approaching the Salvation Army's inspiring slogan, that drowning men needed ropes, not tracts.

Others, in addition to worried ministers, sought to acquaint themselves with their burgeoning urban surroundings, and found acquaintance difficult to gain. "Who shall fathom the vast and deep mystery of a city?" asked novelist Charles K. Lush in *The Autocrats* (1901), a story with a Milwaukee locale. "The city," Lush went on, "is the Dark Continent of this century, into the depths of which have gone many explorers, each returning with but a fragment of knowledge; none with the whole truth." At another point in the novel he notes that "a city is made up of circles, or groups, great and small, divisions and sub-divisions, the members of which have apparently little in common, whose mode of life is dissimilar, and who really know as little of each other as do Hottentots and Esquimaux." In the early 1890s, *Scribner's Magazine* ran a series of articles entitled "The Poor in Great Cities"; "what we need to know," the editor commented, "is what is doing, here and elsewhere . . . and especially, what are the facts with which our own efforts are to deal, and how facts elsewhere compare with them." No source of information could reveal how many people in the United States were on relief. When one of the first systematic analyses of poverty appeared in 1904, its author listed as examples of questions still unanswerable: "how many people in this country are in poverty? Is the number yearly growing larger? Are there each year more and more of the unskilled classes, pursuing hopelessly the elusive phantom of self support and independence?"

The quest for data produced results. Between 1890 and World War I, a "factual generation"—as Robert Bremner has accurately characterized it—greatly extended the area of available and verifiable knowledge about the conditions of urban living in America. Within a period of about fifteen years books, articles, and government reports (federal and state) poured from the printing presses to enlighten concerned citizens. Since reform sentiments generated these studies, most of the investigating was directed toward the poor and toward the slum. Even so, Ward McAllister's *Society as I Found It,* along with Henry B. Fuller's novels, *With the Procession* and *The Cliff Dwellers,* all of which were published between 1890 and 1894 (and perhaps Thorstein Veblen's *The Theory of the Leisure Class,* which appeared in 1899), enlightened many readers about the behavior of the higher ranks in social life.

The settlement house movement was a logical development of the increasing concern with immigration and poverty that marked the decades after the middle of the nineteenth century. Charity-organization societies, institutional churches, and agencies especially interested in living conditions of city children had begun to publicize some of the most painful accompaniments of large-scale urbanization. In the late 1880s, idealistic young people in several of the nation's largest cities began to establish residences in slum districts; these houses, which were called settlements, became centers radiating a wide variety of reform impulses—most of them designed to stimulate community spirit among the poor. A London settlement started in 1884, called Toynbee Hall, caught the attention of traveling Americans; they brought the idea back to this country to adapt it to conditions in New York, Boston, Chicago, and other places. Thus Stanton Coit opened Neighborhood Guild in a noisome New York City tenement house in 1886; it immediately began a program of social and educational events, later changing its name to University Settlement.

Three years later, Jane Addams and Ellen Gates Starr opened what would soon become the best-known settlement in America, Hull House. After a trip to Europe, which included visits to Toynbee Hall, they returned to Chicago excited by the possibilities that city offered for reform. They acquired an old mansion on South Halsted Street, in the middle of an immigrant neighborhood. Contributing their own money, and raising more from contributions by rich Chicago matrons, the two young women began with a kindergarten for the small children in the neighborhood. They added clubs for the older children, a day nursery to help working mothers, and an employment bureau. A series of adult education courses and lectures by visiting speakers soon developed into one of Hull House's most popular features.

The early settlements were widely imitated; by 1895 there were at least fifty of them in the country and the number continued to grow. Their significance has had many facets; particularly important was their role in clarifying the picture of the city, in adding to the systematic data which was available to Americans seeking to understand the urban milieu around the turn of the century. People who participated in settlement work became tireless agitators —partly in their need to raise money from the better-off sections of the cities —carrying their descriptions of life among the poor to other quarters of the community. In 1895, a New York publisher brought out *Hull House Maps and Papers: A Presentation of Nationalities and Wages in a Congested District of Chicago,* a series of essays and carefully prepared data gathered by the Chicago group. Men and women active in the settlements often became public officials, as state and local governments added social welfare agencies to their functions. Florence Kelly and Julia Lathrop, again from Hull House, served respectively as chief factory inspector and on the board of charities of the State of Illinois. The programs of the successful settlements served, in fact, as pilot projects which local governments took over once the need had been sufficiently publicized. As Ray Ginger has observed of Hull House, "if an enterprise proved its worth, the next step was to convince the city to enter the field.

The playground, the public bath, the kindergarten—such projects instituted by Hull House were year by year taken over by the city." This testified to the effectiveness not only of the specific reform enterprises but also of the educational campaigns carried on by the settlement workers.

As the settlement houses were appearing in city after city, and at the same time that discussion of the germ theory of contagion stimulated interest in public health, Jacob Riis published *How the Other Half Lives;* a detailed description of New York City's immigrant neighborhoods, it quickly became popular and was influential in the growing movement for housing legislation. It was, so to speak, a book whose time had come in 1890; its popularity reflected increased interest in the city which was in turn encouraged by studies of depopulated rural counties in many parts of the United States, anxiety over the social effects of immigration culminating in movements to restrict it, and widening consciousness that "the frontier"—in the sense of free land in the West—was gone. Riis had grown to early manhood in a small, closely-knit Danish town where he had become a carpenter. Emigrating to the United States in 1870, he held a succession of jobs, coming finally to journalism. Thirteen years as police reporter on two New York dailies sharpened his prose style and gave him a great amount of poignant and colorful data, which his own background as an immigrant enabled him to use sympathetically. After *How the Other Half Lives* catapulted him into prominence, especially in reform circles, he promoted the idea of reconstructing decayed neighborhoods by developing recreational and adult educational activities in the public schools. His success was limited by the fact that neighborhood reconstruction came to be mostly in the hands of the settlements, and also by the steady turning of reformers' attention toward housing codes as a weapon against the slum.

Congress itself authorized an investigation in 1892, "relative to what is known as the slums of cities." The language suggests a tentative approach to a new and still only dimly-perceived phenomenon, and the investigators found it difficult to define slums. These, "according to the dictionaries, are dirty back streets, especially such streets as are inhabited by a squalid and criminal population; they are low and dangerous neighborhoods." To avoid ambiguity, the investigators decided to confine their attention to the very worst areas, "concerning which there can be no difference of opinion as to whether or not they are slum districts." Led by Carroll D. Wright, Federal Commissioner of Labor and one of the early systematizers of social statistics, the team carried out what could only be regarded as a preliminary study. Coverage of the slums in the nation's sixteen cities with populations over 200,000 had been projected, but the $20,000 Congress appropriated sufficed only for a survey of four cities that were considered as representing different types. New York, Philadelphia, and Baltimore were all seaports; New York was regarded as primarily commercial, Philadelphia as more heavily influenced by manufacturing, and Baltimore as "the most typical southern business city in the Union." For the fourth, "Chicago, as a great inland city with all its varied interests of transportation, manufacturing, and general commerce, and the varied nationality of its population, was naturally selected." The neighborhoods to be studied were chosen after consultation with local authorities; their aggregate population of 83,000, Wright insisted, did not comprise the whole slum population of the four cities, but only that part of it over whose slum characteristics no one could possibly disagree.

There were few surprises in the report. Curiously, its careful house-to-house survey found no greater incidence of disease in the slums than in the cities at large; Wright suggested this might be because of the surveys having been conducted in the healthiest part of the year, late spring, when "people were living with open windows and thus not subjected to the foul air which might be found in the winter." The slum was better equipped with saloons than the rest of the city; arrests for crime were more frequent there; illiteracy was higher. Foreign birth or parentage was much more common in the slum than elsewhere; the report included the interesting information that the foreign-born constituted between 44 per cent and 62 per cent of the voting population of these districts. Working hours, wage rates, and living expenses were touched on rather lightly. The most significant feature of the report was neither in its contents nor in any direct consequences attendant upon its publication —in fact, there seems to have been none. It did represent, however, an important stage in the identification and the emergence into community thought and discourse of an urban problem. More graphic and exciting data could be found in Riis's book and in other privately sponsored examinations of the urban scene which were beginning to appear in rapid order.

The campaign for improved housing legislation, which matured in New York City in the 1890s and then spread to other cities, provided additional impetus to the process of community self-study. Lawrence Veiller's work on the various public and private tenement house commissions during the decade was especially significant. Veiller's most striking contribution to the urban education of his contemporaries was made in 1900, when he and his associates were nearing the successful conclusion of their effort to get the New York legislature to adopt a practical tenement housing code. Working, as he later recalled, six hours a day for months (in addition to many other responsibilities), Veiller constructed a three-dimensional exhibit to clarify the tenement house problem. He made a model of an actual tenement block out of cardboard and papier-mâché, around which he assembled hundreds of photographs, charts, and tables which detailed the characteristics of slum housing. There were many correlations of disease and crime with tenement housing; Veiller added comparative data from other cities both American and foreign. Ten thousand visitors saw the exhibit in February and March, 1900; it was then sent on a tour to other cities and proved to be an attraction at the Paris World's Fair in that year. Most of the data that had gone into the exhibit appeared three years later in *The Tenement House Problem*, a two-volume report of the state tenement commission prepared by Veiller and Robert W. DeForest. Veiller's work, of course, was crowned with success in the passing of the 1901 New York Tenement Law, and this added to the importance of his close and systematic study of life in the slums. It seemed to prove, in Robert Bremner's phrase, that "the path to reform lay through research."

The research itself became more systematic. In 1905 a Charities Publication Committee, including both Riis and Jane Addams, was formed and began quickly to plan comprehensive surveys of urban social problems. The magazine *Charities and the Commons* served as the committee's organ; in 1905 and 1906, two special issues—one on "The Negro in the Cities of the North" and the other, entitled "Next Door to Congress," on Washington, D. C.— attracted much attention. The committee then launched an investigation of Pittsburgh, Pennsylvania on such a large scale as to dwarf anything that had come prior to it. Money was contributed by the Russell Sage Foundation (then headed by Veiller's one-time associate, Robert W. DeForest), a staff of trained social workers headed by Paul U. Kellogg was assembled, and two years of field work got under way. The condensed results began to appear in print in 1908, but full publication of the Pittsburgh Survey took five years (1909–1914) and six large volumes.

The Pittsburgh Survey defined its subject as a complex of pressing social problems; the satisfactions of life in the steel city were not analyzed or described. This definition simply emphasized the close relationship between the development of social studies and urban reform. The underlying inspiration of the Survey, and much of the research that preceded and followed it, was to attack social waste and social dangers armed with knowledge about their causes. What the Pittsburgh study added to its predecessors was its scope: no single "problem" monopolized its pages but rather many problems were seen as interrelated. Crime, prostitution, city politics, housing, the labor of women and children, wages and hours, the family as an institution—all of these were given exhaustive treatment.

The survey idea spread rapidly, and maintained its close connection with reform-minded groups. The Sage Foundation sponsored surveys in six other cities from Atlanta, Georgia to Topeka, Kansas. Other communities organized their own self-study programs; *Charities and the Commons* changed its name to *Survey*.

Although they were concerned with politics, administration, and especially finance, the appearance and rapid spread of the municipal reference bureaus deserves mention as part of the deepening current of community self-examination. The first one was established in New York in 1906; by the 1920s most of the big cities had them. They carried different names, and bore different relationships to the governments of the cities; some even had tax support. Most were organized by business groups in the interests of efficient and economical city government; the major functions of these agencies were to study local financial operations in great detail and to publicize the results of their studies. Their typical concerns were therefore quite different than those of the social investigations, but still the objectives were often cast in broad terms. The language of the Bureau of Municipal Research in San Francisco suggested that the concept of efficiency, which it sought to promote, was a wide one, including "development of a constructive programme for the city that shall be based upon adequate knowledge and consideration of community needs. . . ." In their investigations of local government economy, the bureaus frequently studied public education and recreation programs, as well as the operation of city housing commissions and health departments, which brought them into areas where their concerns were shared by the social workers.

All the while, books and articles about the ills of urban society were published in ever-growing numbers. The year 1899 alone saw W. E. B. Du Bois's *The Philadelphia Negro;* Robert Woods's description of poor neighborhoods in Boston, *The City Wilderness;* and Algie M. Simons's description of the stockyards area in Chicago, *Packingtown*. These were followed by Robert Hunter's *Tenement Conditions in Chicago,* in 1901, and his classic study including all of the larger cities, *Poverty,* in 1904. Roy Lubove cites no fewer than nine published investigations of the standards of living of workers between 1904 and 1911.

At about the same time, city governments began to establish municipal welfare departments. Kansas City, Missouri was the first to do so, in 1910, and the operation of its department demonstrated the connections between social gospel, community self-study, and urban reform. In the background of its establishment had been an investigation into unemployment in the city during the winter of 1909. The report of the investigation related unemployment to other social problems, and recommended the new governmental agency to plan not only for the unemployed but also for the sick and for those in the city's correctional institutions. The emphasis was to be preventive: "we believe," the authors of the report said, "that poverty, disease, and crime should not be accepted as a matter of course, but should be recognized as results of conditions . . . subject to control." The Welfare Department's first superintendent was Leroy Halbert, a young graduate of Chicago Theological Seminary who had served as assistant pastor to Charles Sheldon, author of the famous social-gospel tract, *In His Steps*. Halbert exemplified his generation's passion for the facts of urban living when he proposed a local survey which, had it ever been carried out, would have gone well beyond the Pittsburgh Survey. "The only way to really measure the city's problem," Halbert wrote, "is to establish in the city a thorough system of sociological record keeping. . . . Every family is as worthy of record as every lot is, and every individual should be as carefully accounted for as every dollar is." Study of "the entire population" was not practicable at the time, but Halbert instituted a research bureau in the department which did make a complete card catalog of one depressed area in Kansas City, calling attention to "the immediate need of socializing efforts" there and in similar neighborhoods.

The explicit motives of urban reformers embraced practical as well as humanitarian considerations. Reform, it was argued, was necessary to the good order or even the preservation of the community; at the very least, its accomplishment would save money and trouble. As early as 1857, a special committee of the state legislature investigating New York City's housing reported that "had the evils which now appall us, been prevented . . . by wise and simple laws, the city . . . would now exhibit more gratifying bills of health, more general comfort and prosperity, and less, far less expenditure for the support of pauperism and crime." After the Civil War, reformers recalled the 1863 draft riots which had cost many lives and almost paralyzed the metropolis for several days; the mobs which participated in them "were gathered in the overcrowded and neglected quarters of the city." The urban slum was a sore on the body social from which infection, in the forms of disease and crime, could spread into the quarters of the middle- and upper-class districts. Alfred T. White, who tried to develop model low-cost housing as a private enterprise in the later nineteenth century, described the tenement areas in 1879 as "nurseries of the epidemics which spread with certain destructiveness into the fairest homes . . . hiding-places of the local banditti . . . cradles of the insane who fill the asylums and of the paupers who throng the almhouses; in fact [the tenements] produce these noxious and unhappy elements of society as surely as the harvest follows the sowing."

Warnings such as these seemed to imply a corollary proposition that a changed environment would result in more desirable individual character. Those who called for the abolition of the slum moved steadily toward a consistent environmentalist theory of personality development. Henry George, though not specifically an urban reformer, expressed the emerging view in his *Progress and Poverty:* "How little does heredity count," he wrote, "as compared with conditions. . . . Change Lady Vere de Vere in her cradle with an infant of the slums, and will the blood of a hundred earls give you a refined and cultured woman?" In the first half of the nineteenth century, most urbanites regarded slums, along with poverty and failure in general, as evidence of personal shortcomings and vices; drink was the favorite explanation offered. But by the end of the century the more common view was coming to be that slums and poverty were active causes while personal shortcomings and vices were results. Two generations of concern for the effects of city living, especially on children, had been the main influence in bringing about the change. Jacob Riis spoke for many people when he maintained in 1893 that "as we mould the children of the toiling masses in our cities, so we shape the destiny of the State. . . ."

By the 1880s and 1890s, reformers almost without exception assumed that the large city was permanently on the social scene. They aimed at mitigating the harsh impact of urbanization on those who had fewest advantages in the struggle for existence and improvement, but they did not doubt that the city was and would continue to be the locale of their major endeavors. In his introduction to the final report of the Country Life Commission in 1909, President Theodore Roosevelt expressed the dawning notion that however farming might be encouraged, "city life is advancing more rapidly, because of the greater attention which is being given by citizens of the towns to their own betterment." Harvard economist Thomas Nixon Carver wrote in 1910 that although "the cry 'back to the farm' may possibly check the migration from country to city, it will not be able to stop it completely. We must expect, as far in the future as anyone is able to see, that the stream of migrating youths will continue to set cityward."

This recognition, accompanied by the development of environmentalist interpretations of personality and behavior, encouraged the growth of the notion that society is organic: that communities constituted living, unified organisms of which each individual was a member, in the sense that fingers are members of the physiological body. Individual fates and lives were vitally interlaced, so that the unfolding of each bore directly on all the others. By the first decade of the twentieth century, most of those who studied city life were concluding that its very nature, compelling—as one of them wrote in 1910,—"manifold cooperations," was forcing the individual to "conform his acts in an ever increasing degree to the will and welfare of the community in which he lives." A contemporary writer stressed that "the life of the individual must be brought into organic and vital touch with the life of the community. The citizen must think of the city as far more than a protector of life and property." Efforts to rebuild neighborhood life, such as those backed by Riis and the settlement workers, were thought of as promoting healthy social organisms. Jane Addams noted that the people at Hull House were forced "to regard the entire life of their city as organic . . . and to protest against its over-differentiation." One of the best-known urban reformers, Frederick C. Howe, who had worked with Mayor Tom Johnson in Cleveland, stated simply in 1915 that "the city has destroyed individualism."

Theories of organic society and their possible application to the problems of city life deeply influenced the development of urban studies in American universities, which were just beginning, toward the close of the nineteenth century, to develop social science graduate programs on the German seminar model. Beginning in the 1880s and 1890s, the city came increasingly under scholarly examination. As early as 1883, Herbert Baxter Adams had begun encouraging his doctoral candidates at Johns Hopkins to produce historical studies of American cities and towns; these generally focused on political institutions and administrative structure. In 1899 at Columbia University, Adna F. Weber published the first comprehensive statistical analysis of European and American urbanization. By that time a sociology department had been initiated at the new University of Chicago, and almost immediately concentrated its attention on urban problems.

The University of Chicago sociologists were well acquainted with Jane Addams, Graham Taylor, and other settlement workers; scholars and reformers mingled inside and outside of the classroom. In fact, the early history of scholarly urban study cannot be understood apart from its close relationship with reform. Sociologist Nels Anderson observed retrospectively in 1929 that "we cannot separate the beginnings of urban sociology from the perennial battle to wipe out the slum." To many teachers and students, it appeared that the close study of urban society was primarily an effort to give a rational and systematic basis to philanthropy.

Under the direction of Albion W. Small, William I. Thomas, Charles R. Henderson, and Charles Zueblin, graduate students in the Chicago department began to use the city about them as a laboratory for social science. The first serious attempt to elaborate a theory of urban life came out of the "Chicago school" in 1915, when Robert Park published his essay, "The City: Suggestions for the Investigation of Human Behavior in the City Environment." Park had begun his adult life as a newspaperman in Minneapolis. His inclination, however, like Lincoln Steffens's, was to generalize upon his observations; he went to the University of Michigan, to Harvard, and then to Europe, trying to work out a satisfactory philosophy of journalism. Returning to the United States, Park joined the already flourishing sociology department at Chicago and began to analyze urban neighborhoods as "natural areas" of communication. The key fact about urban society was precisely that it was complex; its shape resulted from the dynamic equilibrium and tension among the many different groups, or sub-communities, of which it was made. People congregated in neighborhoods (which Park sometimes called "moral areas") as they were impelled together by similarities in culture, language, economic status, and temperament. Thus the city should be studied as a developing organism whose parts were neighborhoods; on this premise Park and his associates began a long series of investigations into Chicago's characteristics and problems. Books with titles such as Louis Wirth's *The Ghetto* (1928), Frederick Thrasher's *The Gang* (1927), and Harvey Zorbaugh's *The Gold Coast and the Slum* (1929), indicate their lines of investigation and also reveal a close parallel in subject matter with the earlier writings of Veiller and the authors of the Pittsburgh Survey.

In 1923 a Social Science Research Committee was established at the University of Chicago to coordinate research activities. In quest of an organizing framework for research, which would enable various scholarly projects to reinforce one another, committee members concluded that the city at their doorstep was, as Charles Merriam wrote, "an ideal scene [for] cooperative investigation. . . . It becomes increasingly important to understand as nearly as possible the inner nature of cities and find the key to the understanding of their problems." A new dimension was added to concerted urban study when the committee decided to sponsor a detailed history of Chicago. Bessie L. Pierce was invited to the university in 1929, and commenced work upon the history with the help of a research staff and financial backing from the university and from foundations. Scholars had interested themselves in the history of cities on earlier occasions, but the initiation of the history of Chicago project marked urban history's coming-of-age as a recognized field for research.

Meanwhile another landmark in the sociological examination of American cities was in preparation, as Robert and Helen Lynd moved into Muncie, Indiana with a team of helpers, to live there and gather data for two years. The Lynds were trained in sociology at Columbia University; Robert Lynd also had a degree from Union Theological Seminary, which suggests latter-day echoes of the social-gospel movement. Their object was to describe the effects of industrialization on the social structure and institutions of an urban community. Muncie was chosen partly because its modest size and almost entirely native-born population seemed to render it a manageable subject for a small group of scholars; after 1929, when the Lynds published *Middletown,* the Indiana city found itself attracting more intellectual attention than it ever had. *Middletown's* conclusions were neither startling nor wide-ranging; a community culture, largely bourgeois in its leading features, embraced both the business and working classes, but people on different rungs of the social ladder responded to the culture with varying degrees of warmth. Muncie was a business-dominated city, and the Lynds found interesting indications that the elements of business culture "filtered down," as they put it, "through various intermediate levels," to sustain a sense of community across class lines. Nevertheless, the main lesson they drew from their studies of Muncie was that of "the extent and complexity of the task confronting social science."

Even as it became more sophisticated and more scientific, urban study did not completely lose its connection with urban reform. In his foreword to *Middletown,* the noted anthropologist Clark Wissler asserted that the book "should enlighten the conscientious citizen and serve as a suggestion as to what information is needed by those who attempt to direct the affairs of an American town." Earlier, Robert Park had written that the basic problem of urban society was "the problem of achieving in the freedom of the city a social order and a social control equivalent to that which grew up naturally in the family, the clan, and the tribe." The examination of community life was posited, for scholars as well as others, on the assumption that knowledge is power. Understanding the city would lead to improving it.

The growth of urban studies in the early part of the twentieth century reflected the acceptance of the view by at least the time of World War I that the city had come to dominate the economic, social, and cultural life of Americans. Their novelists, short story writers, and poets may have helped them reach this conclusion, and in any event fully shared it. As an environment for life and conflict, the city had been naturalized in American letters by the turn of the century. William Dean Howells, with his Ohio small-town boyhood, could still regard the metropolis as something of a curiosity, but his two greatest novels, *The Rise of Silas Lapham* (1885) and *A Hazard of New Fortunes* (1895), unfold their plots in Boston and New York, respectively, with no suggestion that these cities are in any way unusual settings, or that they threatened moral destruction to individuals any more than other settings might do. All of Henry James's major writings have big city locales: Venice, London, Paris, and again New York and Boston in the United States. The characters in these stories reflect conflicting social values, along with representative human vices and virtues, and there is in both Howells and James much implicit protest against social or cultural conditions which they deplored. Still, their criticisms are directed largely against capitalism or materialism, and not against the city itself.

One of the themes inherent in American urbanization that attracted late nineteenth and twentieth-century writers was the enthusiasm of town promoters. Mark Twain satirized it in *The Gilded Age* (1871), recording the lugubrious collapse of the plans of Colonel Beriah Sellars, who had described a future metropolis on the banks of a Missouri creek-bed in terms which Jesup Scott or Robert Van Horn would have found familiar. But the later chapters in *Life on the Mississippi* (1883), with their approving descriptions of the urban progress along the river from St. Paul to New Orleans, show that Twain wrote sympathetically of Sellars, and regarded the unfortunate booster as naive and caught up in the machinations of others rather than as a man who was basically reprehensible. A short passage catching the spirit of the promoter in Stephen Crane's story, "The Blue Hotel," has been less noted. A Swedish immigrant arrives in a rough and tough Nebraska town in the 1870s; he has heard blood-curdling stories about the cowboys and villains of the American West, and fears for his life. When he tells the owner of the hotel (one of the town's leading citizens) that he expects to be killed, the owner replies: "Why, man, we're goin' to have a line of ilictric street-cars in this town next spring. . . . And there's a new railroad goin' to be built down from Broken Arm to here. Not to mintion the four churches and the smashin' big brick schoolhouse. Then there's the big factory, too. Why, in two years Romper'll be a met-tro-*pol*-is." The booster-promoter does not appear frequently enough in works of fiction to be called a stock figure, but authors did find him useful. Finally, in Sinclair Lewis's *Babbitt* (1924), he became a hero. George F. Babbitt is a real estate developer in the city of Zenith, who becomes confused by the social and cultural diversity of his city; after a series of misadventures (two of which were later cited by W. lloyd Warner for the accuracy of Lewis's sociological insight) culminating in a love affair with an artistically bohemian woman, Babbitt comes to understand that his proper place in the scheme of things is found in his office and his home. In order to write *Babbitt*, Lewis toured midwestern cities, staying for weeks at a time in Indianapolis, Kansas City, and other places, to get material with which to construct his synthetic

Zenith; he subscribed to several real estate journals in order to familiarize himself with the business; with the help of his wife, he even constructed a three-dimensional model of Zenith, naming the streets and buildings, and carefully following his characters on it as he caused them to walk or drive through the fictional city. *Babbitt* became a best-seller in the 1920s, and although it was at first widely misunderstood, it ranks near the top of any list of serious urban fiction in America.

Another theme that authors elaborated upon was the lure of the city: the magnetic power urban centers exerted on people of imagination and ambition. Willa Cather described the lure with intense pathos in her story, "A Wagner Matinee," which appeared in 1903. A young Boston resident learns that his old aunt, who has spent most of her adult life on a Nebraska farm which he had long ago left, is to visit him. He remembers that in his boyhood this aunt had taught him something of literature and music, and hopes that an afternoon at the opera will please her. She listens to the music entranced, and memories of her earlier hopes of being a musician come flooding back into her mind. When the concert is over, the two remain in their seats until everyone else has left; the aunt finally "burst into tears and sobbed pleadingly. 'I don't want to go, Clark, I don't want to go!' I understood. For her, just outside the door of the concert hall, lay the black pond with the cattle-tracked bluffs; the tall, unpainted house, with weather-curled boards, naked as a tower; the crook-backed ash seedlings where the dish-cloths hung to dry; the gaunt, moulting turkeys picking up refuse about the kitchen door."

The city's lure was often sentimentalized, even by first-rate writers. Theodore Dreiser exploited it in *Sister Carrie* (1900) in lachrymose terms: "The city has its cunning wiles, no less than the infinitely smaller and more human tempter. There are large forces which allure with all the soulfulness of expression possible in the most cultured human. The gleam of a thousand lights is often as effective as the persuasive light in a wooing and fascinating eye. . . . Unrecognised for what they are, their beauty, like music, too often relaxes, then weakens, then perverts the simpler human perceptions." But for Carrie, the net result of her migration to Chicago and later New York is a life of fame and wealth as an actress. Southerners felt the same urban attractions, even though many of them denied it. George Washington Cable and Walter Hines Page found it impossible to live in southern or rural environments in the later nineteenth and early twentieth centuries and sought the northeastern cities. A generation later Thomas Wolfe gave poetic expression to the drawing power which Boston and New York exercised on a young North Carolinian: "the city would always be the same when he came back. He would rush through the immense and glorious stations, murmurous with their million destinies and the everlasting sound of time, that was caught up forever in their roof—he would rush out into the street, and instantly it would be the same as it had always been, and yet forever strange and new."

Authors described the overwhelming poverty and filth of the slums much as Riis and Veiller had done; indeed, the coinciding of the work of those writers with several works by Crane and Dreiser testifies once more to the insatiable curiosity that American urban development had aroused by the twentieth century. Crane's *Maggie: A Girl of the Streets* was not widely read in this country until thirty years after it was written; when it appeared, in the 1890s, it was still too realistic for most editorial taste in the United States. Briefly, Crane tells the story of a girl brought up in one of New York City's tenement districts; she is "ruined" by a faithless lover, becomes a prostitute, and ultimately jumps in the river. As an episode in *How the Other Half Lives,* Crane's story would have fit perfectly. He describes a tenement house in memorable words:

A careening building, a dozen gruesome doorways [giving] up loads of babies to the street and the gutter. A wind of early autumn raised yellow dust from cobbles and swirled it against a hundred windows. Long streamers of garments fluttered from fire-escapes. In all unhandy places there were buckets, brooms, rags, and bottles. In the street infants played or fought with other infants or sat stupidly in the way of vehicles. Formidable women, with uncombed hair and disordered dress, gossiped while leaning on railings, or screamed in frantic quarrels. Withered persons, in curious postures of submission to something sat smoking pipes in obscure corners. A thousand odours of cooking food came forth to the street. The building quivered and creaked from the weight of humanity stamping about in its bowels.

In another story, probably written about the same time, called "The Men in the Storm," Crane describes a crowd of men waiting outside a charitable establishment where they can have a bed for the night and something to eat next morning for five cents. A blizzard descends upon the city, and the men crowd and fight to get in when the doors open:

The tossing crowd on the sidewalk grew smaller and smaller. The snow beat with merciless persistence upon the bowed heads of those who waited. The wind drove it up from the pavements in frantic forms of winding white, and it seethed in circles about the huddled forms passing in one by one, three by three, out of the storm.

Dreiser described almost exactly the same kind of institution in *Sister Carrie,* as George Hurstwood steadily descends the social ladder in New York until he reaches the bottom on Blackwell's Island—where he is buried with other paupers.

This kind of literature was often regarded as unacceptable. Both *Maggie* and *Sister Carrie* were suppressed for some time by publishers, whereas Riis, Veiller, and the Pittsburgh Survey authors were read widely and taken to heart. Why the novelists and the housing reformers had such contrasting receptions, when their material and often their language was so similar, is difficult to explain. But it must be remembered that Dreiser and Crane did not offer their descriptions of the seamy side of urban civilization wrapped about in the mantle of reform. It may be that artistic portrayal of observed truth was felt to have less justification than portrayal of the same truth when offered as a spur for social improvement.

However they used the urban environment, the writers sought the values that it embodied. The city represented power; Frank Norris, in *The Pit* (1902), described Chicago as

the Great Gray City, brooking no rival, [imposing] its dominion upon a reach of country larger than many a kingdom of the Old World. For thousands of miles beyond its confines was its influence felt. Out, far out, far away in the snow and shadow of northern Wisconsin forests, axes and saws bit the bark of century-old trees, stimulated by this city's driving energy. Just as far to the southward pick and drill leaped to the assault of veins of anthracite, moved by her central power. Her force turned the wheels of harvester and seeder a thousand miles distant in Iowa and Kansas. Her force spun the screws of . . . innumerable squadrons of lake steamers crowding the Sault Sainte Marie. For her and because of her all the Central States, all the Great Northwest, roared with traffic and industry; sawmills screamed; factories . . . clashed and flamed; cog gripped cog; beltings clasped the drums of mammoth wheels; and converters of forges belched into the clouded air their tempest breath of molten steel.

Dreiser, looking backward to earlier days, wrote in 1931, "I loved Chicago. It was so strong, so rough, so shabby, and yet so vital and determined. It seemed . . . like a young giant afraid of nothing, and that it was that appealed to me."

In addition to representing power, the city also represented freedom. Even writers who later on described the large cities as corrupting influences and compared them invidiously with the small towns of their youth had left those small towns in order to find literary careers in the urban centers. For Dreiser's Frank Cowperwood, in *The Titan* (1914), Chicago represented escape from ruin; after his jail term in his native Philadelphia, Cowperwood had to find a new field in which to rebuild his life. Chicago, "a seething city in the making," offered the necessary opportunity: "Why it fairly sang! The world was young here. Life was doing something new." For Hart Crane, a young poet with consuming ambition to compose the great American epic, New York City, with its great symbol, Brooklyn Bridge, stood for nothing less than the spiritual integrity of modern man. In his "Proem: To Brooklyn Bridge" (1930), Crane invoked the spirit of the Roeblings' masterpiece; he found myth-sustaining intimations of divinity in the vaulting curves of the bridge rising above the swarming city. The quest for positive and creative values implicit in urban life could hardly be carried further. By the time of the Great Depression, Americans had examined their cities closely and had accepted their urban destiny for better or worse. The city was to be the theater for their cultural, political, and social dramas; the city's priorities would shape their thoughts and their actions.

CHAPTER

# 12

# The Growth of a Planning Tradition

THE LATE nineteenth-century effort of writers and scholars to comprehend the American city had a counterpart in the attempt of a group of architects and landscape designers, some of whom began calling themselves planners, to order the physical growth of the city. Out of this attempt came organizations, experts, and a formal planning movement shortly after the turn of the century. The movement built on views of the environment and the community present in American society since colonial times. But the establishment of a craft or science of planning and its institutionalization provided further recognition of the importance of the city in American life and marked the beginning of another significant effort to naturalize the city in American society.

Notions of the desirability of consciously shaping the urban environment had always been present in American thought. The Puritan doctrine of "soul liberty" in the "city on a hill," William Penn's careful planning for Philadelphia, and James Oglethorpe's commodious design for Savannah reflected the view that the good society can be achieved in a properly laid out city. The plan for Washington had explicitly recognized that a capital city should embody the aspirations and expectations of a nation. But this conception, though never completely forgotten, was often lost sight of in the growing cities of the nineteenth century. The city was seen primarily as an agency of capitalistic expansion, a place where a man could make money by doing as he pleased with his piece of property.

The general acceptance of the gridiron design in laying out cities facilitated this conception of private rights by making property transactions simple and convenient. The example of colonial Philadelphia had popularized the gridiron; and New York's adoption of the design, in 1811, for the undeveloped part of Manhattan Island north to 155th Street (most of the island), furthered its wide use in the towns and cities of interior America. There was open recognition in New York's action that the design was adopted in order to advance commerce. The report of the commissioners selected to propose a plan emphasized the great advantages in the gridiron—ease of layout, ease of legal description, and ease of merchandising. John Randel, Jr., the commissioners' surveyor, explained that the main virtue of the plan was in facilitating the "buying, selling, and improving of real estate." The basic question, the commissioners said, was whether the city should adopt a rectangular street plan "or whether they should adopt some of those supposed improvements by circles, ovals, and stars, which certainly embellish a plan, whatever may be their effect as to convenience and utility. In considering the subject, they could not but bear in mind that a city is to be comprised principally of the habitations of men, and that straight sided and right angled houses are the most cheap to build, and the most convenient to live in. The effect of these plain and simple reflections was decisive." The gridiron plan admirably fitted the speculative needs of western promoters, since town plans could be conveniently superimposed on the lines of the rectangular land surveys provided by the land ordinances of the 1780s. And in a religious age, the gridiron even had the sanction of Holy Writ, which accounted for rectangular designs in many of the religious colonies of the nineteenth century. The New Jerusalem of the Book of Revelation, the Heavenly City, "lieth foursquare, and the length is as large as the breadth. . . ."

In examining the effects of the gridiron, the New York plan commissioners clearly indicated the tendency in nineteenth-century city-building expediently to disregard the future of life in a city when present business interests were at stake. Their rationale supplied a significant statement of nineteenth-century urban ideology: "It may, to many, be a matter of surprise, that so few vacant spaces have been left, and those so small, for the benefit of fresh air, and consequent preservation of health. Certainly if the City of New York were destined to stand on the side of a small stream, such as the Seine or the Thames, a great number of ample places might be needful: but those large arms of the sea which embrace Manhattan Island, render its situation, in regard to health and pleasure, as well as to the convenience of commerce, peculiarly felicitous; when, therefore, from the same causes, the price of land is so uncommonly great, it seemed proper to admit the principles of economy to a greater influence than might, under circumstances of a different kind, have consisted with the dictates of prudence and the sense of duty."

The gridiron plan, despite its utility, was not universally adopted. John Reps, in his monumental study of early town and city design, has found at least two dozen plans modeled in part on the one for Washington, including those of Buffalo, Indianapolis, and Detroit. He has also shown that within the framework of the gridiron there was considerable experimentation. However, even where diagonals were employed the property between was usually plotted in the customary squares. Imaginative designs, such as the ingenious hexagonal plan employed in downtown Detroit, were seldom extended beyond the initial limits of the city. And where efforts were made in gridiron plotting to retain natural park areas in the city, commercial interests were usually able to get municipal governments to open them quickly to private development.

The initial revolt against the "tyranny of the gridiron" was aesthetic and grew out of the romantic movement of the early nineteenth century, with its emphasis on nature, particularly nature cultivated, experienced, and absorbed, as instructive and elevating. Nature artists and nature poets and writers, with their message that nature had lessons to teach, began to win a wide audience by the 1840s. As early as 1830 an anonymous writer on the state of architecture in the United States attacked the mechanical character of the gridiron city and the leveled terrain that it necessitated: "We turn from street to street," he wrote, "but the same dead level is before us. We look to the right and left, but the same prospect opens on either side; our feelings become stagnant and we can consent to live there only by consenting to become as dull as it. Such is a level city." Like so many nineteenth-century writers on environment, this critic was also concerned about the contamination of a city lacking natural ventilation, but his primary emphasis was on the destructive effects on personality of a city that did not retain natural features in its design.

Influential in incorporating mid-nineteenth-century romantic conceptions of nature into architecture and design was Andrew Jackson Downing, a pioneer in the park and boulevard movement which marks a significant stage in the history of American city planning. Born in 1815, Downing, after slight formal education, became the proprietor of a nursery in the Hudson River town of Newburgh where he lived the rest of his life. In the 1840s he began turning out treatises, manuals, and essays on such subjects as landscaping, gardening, and building country homes and country cottages. Although he had no formal knowledge of engineering or architecture, he became a consultant to owners of country estates and traveled about advising landowners on building methods, landscaping, and related matters. He also published an influential journal *The Horticulturist,* and a few years before his death set up a landscaping firm. In 1852, while on his way to Washington where his firm had been working on the landscaping of the mall, he died in a fire on a Hudson River steamer. Downing's writings are not characterized by much style or profundity. His ideas on the value of the cultivated landscape are conventional and tediously expressed. Much of his writing is technical and detailed—how-to-do-it instructions for the most part. Yet by all reports, he was an enormously popular writer in his day. The Swedish novelist, Frederika Bremner, for example, recorded during her visit to the United States in 1849–1851 that "nobody, whether he is rich or poor, builds a house or lays out a garden without consulting Downing's works; every young couple who sets up house buys them." As a result of this interest in nature and the cultivated landscape, trees and floral designs became a part of the thinking of those who influenced the shapes in which cities grew. Downing noted the vogue for large, sylvan cemeteries which were by then to be found in all the bigger cities. Many people regarded them more or less as parks, and thousands of visitors enjoyed the rural surroundings of Philadelphia's Laurel Hill, Boston's Mount Auburn, and New York City's Greenwood. Downing urged that the obvious lesson should be drawn from these cemeteries, and that the cities should establish regular public parks on similar plans. "The true policy of republics," he wrote, "is to foster the taste for great public libraries, sculpture and picture galleries, parks and gardens, which *all* may enjoy, since our institutions wisely forbid the growth of private fortunes sufficient to achieve these desirable results in any other way."

As New York's growing population crowded onto Manhattan Island in the 1840s and 1850s, the idea of a great park simply to make the city livable was more frequently discussed; and in 1853 the state legislature authorized the beginning of work upon what became Central Park. Three years later, the commission in charge of the park's development chose Frederick Law Olmsted to superintend it and in so doing established the life career of a figure who was perhaps more instrumental than anyone in reshaping for the better the way in which American cities were to grow. Olmsted has long occupied a prominent place in writings on parks and design; Lewis Mumford early termed him "one of the best minds" turned out in late nineteenth-century America. But his larger contributions to urban history were generally unrecognized until he emerged around the time of the sesquicentennial of his birth in 1972, when several studies and exhibitions of his work appeared, as a pioneer of urban ecology whose ideas had particular relevance to contemporary American society. A central concern in Olmsted's work was consistently the need to consider the city in relationship to the whole physical environment.

Born into a well-to-do merchant family of Hartford, Connecticut, Olmsted had a casual formal education; an eye disease cut short his attendance at Yale. He traveled widely, to China, to Europe, and through the American South, these latter journeys producing one of the classic travel accounts of life in the slave states. Meanwhile in the period 1846–1857, he studied engineering as an apprentice, set up a scientific farm, unsuccessfully ran a magazine, and as a friend of Downing got interested in landscape architecture and design. Later, during the Civil War he won national attention as head of the United States Sanitary Commission, the precursor of the American Red Cross.

Olmsted's design for Central Park, prepared with the collaboration of Calvert Vaux, who had been Downing's partner before his death, departed from the European tradition of the stylized park and emphasized the topography of the area. Natural features would soon be obliterated elsewhere on the island, and the planners thought it desirable to interfere with the park's "easy, undulating outlines, and picturesque, rocky scenery as little as possible. . . ." The hope was to preserve rural nature in a close relationship to the city. To further the individual's enjoyment of a natural setting, the plan made a significant contribution to design by separating the various kinds of traffic— pedestrian walks, roads for vehicles, and bridle paths. Central Park introduced into planning the first systematic use of the overpass. Olmsted pointed out that his design would be less costly than any which proposed large-scale alteration of the topography, but it is clear that he considered the aesthetic advantages most important. Explaining his ideas, he wrote in 1870 that the

object of city parks was to bring natural beauty to bear upon city life—
"the beauty of the fields, the meadow, the prairie, of the green pastures,
and the still waters." In summary he remarked that "what we want to gain
is tranquillity and rest to the mind."

There was nothing "anti-urban" in this. In the same 1870 article, Olmsted
pointed out that urbanization would continue and that it was closely related
to advancing concepts of freedom, culture, and general prosperity; the city
was not only inevitable, it was also basically a good thing—one which could
be made better, especially if people would "prepare for a continued rising
of the townward flood." In a fragment of autobiography from around 1877
entitled *Passages in the Life of an Unpractical Man,* he made the point even
more explicitly: "Our country has entered upon a stage of progress in which
its welfare is to depend on the convenience, safety, order and economy of
life in its great cities. It cannot prosper independently of them; cannot gain
in virtue, wisdom, comfort, except as they also advance." Parks, in Olmsted's
mind, were means of strengthening community feeling in urban centers: they
would preserve the health of the body social. He recalled seeing fifty thousand people at one time in Central Park. Where else, he asked, could so many
be found together, "with an evident glee in the prospect of coming together,
all classes represented . . . each individual adding by his mere presence to
the pleasure of all others . . .?" Olmsted's insistence on a rural environment
in his parks derived from his insight into its urban usefulness. "By making
nature urbane," Lewis Mumford accurately observes, "he naturalized the
city." As were so many of his contemporaries, Olmsted was concerned with
the effects of the tensions created by the city on individual personality—
by the "nervous feebleness or irritability" and the "various functional de-
rangements" of urban life. The well-designed city with ample park facilities
would alleviate the peculiar American nervousness particularly experienced
by the newcomer to the city.

The success of Central Park was quick and impressive; it commanded
emulation and within twenty years a dozen other cities had summoned Olmsted for help in designing their own marks. He urged them to create whole
systems of parks, connected by broad and tree-lined boulevards; even the
city's business and industrial areas would then be within reach of the
fresher air and the soothing colors of rural nature. Olmsted's firm was highly
successful. From 1875 on, when he and his partners began to keep records,
he laid out, according to Mumford's accounting, "37 public pleasure grounds,
12 suburban developments, the grounds of 11 public buildings and hospitals,
13 colleges, 4 large schools, 4 railroad stations, and 12 considerable private
estates." Aside from his 1870 pamphlet, Olmsted did not present systematically his ideas about parks, cities, and the environment. But certain significant themes do emerge from the various plan statements and prospectuses
he wrote. In his plan for Stanford University, for example, he emphasized
the ecological view that plants, shrubs, and trees used in landscaping should

be natural to the site and appropriate to the climate. As a planner of suburbs, he advanced the desirability of the urban village, the distinct community within the metropolis that would fuse the best of city and country. "No broad question of country life in comparison with city life is involved," he wrote, "it is confessedly a question of delicate adjustment." The well-designed suburb would be the vehicle of this delicate adjustment, blending and integrating the landscape into the cityscape. Suburbs, he asserted, are "the most attractive, the most refined and the most soundly wholesome forms of domestic life, and the best application of the arts of civilization to which mankind has yet attained."

Popular evaluation has perhaps overemphasized Olmsted's role as a reformer confronting the abuses of the chaotic, materialistic, industrial city. He was concerned with making the city more humane and livable, but like many of his contemporaries in the early planning movement, he did not address himself to the economic considerations that produced slums, decay, and poverty in the city. Although he retained his view that design had to reflect the needs of an organic social and physical environment, increasingly after 1878 he placed more emphasis on the aesthetic rather than the social side of planning, partly no doubt as a result of the fact that he was thereafter employed by wealthy, private clients. But in advancing the view that the city was here to stay, that the problems of urban society could be dealt with through thought and effort, he provided inspiration and ideology to the whole twentieth-century effort to reorder the environment of cities.

As Olmsted was building up his planning business, others studied his methods and objectives; the notion of closely juxtaposing urban and rural environments, in order to improve the former, generated a park and boulevard movement in the United States beginning in the 1870s. Like Olmsted himself, many of these new planners were often largely self-trained. One of the most important was Henry W. S. Cleveland, who collaborated with Olmsted on a boulevard plan for Chicago and designed a plan for Minneapolis. Like Olmsted, he had taken an early interest in scientific farming but was also a trained surveyor and civil engineer. He designed cemeteries, estates, and public parks in cities and towns in New England, the South, and the Midwest. In his book, *Landscape Architecture as Applied to the Wants of the West*, which appeared in 1873, Cleveland warned growing cities that they should acquire tracts of land for park systems before private real estate development made it impossible. Proposing a system of parks and boulevards for Minneapolis, he wrote in 1884: "look forward to the time when the city has a population of a million, and think what will be their wants." In Kansas City, Missouri George Kessler produced a scheme for parks and boulevards in 1893, which the city began almost at once to construct. Kessler pointed out the need for quick action while desirable land for parks was still available—"lands that, in addition to serving the purpose of local recreation grounds or parks, would permit of retaining for all future time some of the characteristic features of our natural scenery, and would protect localities that possess especially fine views."

With all its emphasis on the virtues of rural surroundings, the vision of these men was essentially urban; they prescribed a measure of ruralization as antidote for city disorders. Sylvester Baxter, who played the leading part in designing Boston's metropolitan park system, described what he called "an ideal city" in 1893: the aesthetic features of natural topography would be preserved, and open spaces would alternate with residential and business areas. Baxter was an enthusiastic disciple of Edward Bellamy, and in his writings combined Olmsted's environmental views with Bellamy's nationalist theories. "A city planned in this way," he continued, in language reminiscent of Bellamy's, "besides its frequent great parks and its water-side esplanades, would probably have its houses so arranged around pleasant garden-like open spaces . . . that every dwelling would face upon a pleasure ground of some kind." Cleveland predicted the results of adequate park and boulevard planning in immense detail, stressing that all of the city's functions would be enhanced. In order to secure "the full enjoyment of its theaters, museums, libraries, lectures, and social pleasures," he wrote, "it is essential that the means of access to them should be rendered not only easy, and free from danger or discomfort, but attractive and elegant. . . ." Inhabitants of the slum and tenement districts of cities did not entirely escape the attention of the landscape architects. Baxter was actively involved in housing reform in Boston. Cleveland indicated the advantages of a sound park system for the "education of children who are born and bred in the crowded tenement-houses which are the (so called) homes of thousands of the inhabitants of every city." Olmsted told residents of Detroit that good park planning would "divert men from unwholesome, vicious, and destructive methods and habits of seeking recreation." Kansas City's Kessler gave sharp expression to the urban intuition of the landscape architects when he wrote that a program of beautification through parks and boulevards "would not only make this a beautiful city but would give the city a special character and beauty of its own." It would "create among our people warm attachments to the city, and promote civic pride."

The park and boulevard planners of the late nineteenth century have been criticized as representing patrician reform ideals of the powerful and the elite. Parks and improvement of the landscape did not directly influence such matters as the poverty and the racial and ethnic conflict of the city. Although the importance of their improvement of the city may be arguable, improve it they did, and Mumford's sympathetic assessment, written in 1931, seems reasonable and still valid: "They renewed the city's contact with the land. They humanized and subdued the feral landscape. Above all, they made their contemporaries conscious of air, sunlight, vegetation, growth. If we still defile the possibilities of the land, it is not for lack of better example."

During the same period which saw the widening influence of the park and boulevard movement, another approach to community planning was on the way to disaster. Planned manufacturing towns in America dated back to the efforts of New England industrialists to attract laborers to their water-power mills after 1815; they were also trying to avoid the horrifying social conditions with which their observations of English factory cities had acquainted them. The best known example of their urban enterprises was, of course, Lowell, Massachusetts, but private town planning in the interest of industrialism reached its high point later in Pullman, Illinois.

George M. Pullman, the railroad car innovator, had directed the Pullman Corporation so successfully that by the mid-1890s its capitalization amounted to $36,000,000 and its assets to $62,000,000. Pullman, who single-handedly dominated the operations of his company, came from a poor family in upstate New York. Talent, determination, and no doubt some luck had made him by 1880 one of Chicago's most successful businessmen. In the words of Almont Lindsay, "he was brusque, unapproachable, and domineering"; his attitude toward organized labor was one of unyielding hostility. Nevertheless, Pullman had a considerable measure of social imagination, and he resolved to create a model industrial community in which his workers might live away from the abuses of the city. Waste caused by the dissipation of workers and their other "costly vices," he said, were the result of urban circumstances that compelled workers "to live in crowded and unhealthy tenements, in miserable streets, and subject to all the temptations and snares of a great city." His planned town, he hoped, would soften the bitter antagonism which wage earners often felt toward their employers, and would enable him to attract a stable and highly competent labor force; it would also earn 6 per cent on the money invested in it.

In 1880 he chose a spot that was still open prairie just south of Chicago, where he built facilities for the construction and maintenance of his railroad cars and the town of Pullman. There were impressive experiments in company towns in England, France, and Germany, which Pullman may have studied; they were widely publicized during the Gilded Age when urbanization seemed to be offering society an almost insoluble problem in labor-management relations. In any event, George Pullman's company bought 4,000 acres of land on Lake Calumet; an architect and a landscape engineer were retained to draw up a plan, and early in 1881 the town of Pullman was in full operation. Difficult problems of sewerage and water supply were ingeniously surmounted, streets were carefully macadamized, and terraced front yards sloped back to rows of neat, clean houses. A large Arcade Building contained a shopping center; near it were the Florence Hotel (named for Pullman's wife), the Pullman Post Office, and the Pullman Bank. A luxurious library, an even more luxurious theater (which, according to one newspaper report equalled "the most elegant theaters in the country in point of architectural beauty and artistic design"), a church, and a school provided for a complement of social and cultural institutions. The town had neither saloons nor brothels.

Pullman's population reached 12,600 just before the onset of the depression of 1893. From the start the experiment was viewed from abroad as an imaginative solution to the problems of industrial society. The *London Times* stated in 1888 that "no place in the United States has attracted more attention or has been more closely watched." An International Hygenic and Pharmaceutical Exposition, held at Prague in 1896, considered it the best town in the world from the standpoint of public health. Visiting speakers and artists offered a varied program of entertainment and adult education. Until 1889, Pullman was legally governed by the Village of Hyde Park, within whose boundary it lay. In that year Chicago annexed Hyde Park, but effective control of the model town lay always in the hands of George Pullman. He named a "town agent" to supervise the community's affairs, somewhat after the manner of a city manager. These affairs were run well; while rents averaged higher in Pullman than in nearby places, its tenants had generally better quarters and more efficient services than were available elsewhere. A writer in *Harper's New Monthly Magazine* commented in 1888 that Pullman was "The only city in existence built from the foundation on scientific and sanitary principles. . . . Its public buildings are fine, and the grouping of them about the open, flower-planted spaces is very effective. It is a handsome city with the single drawback of slight monotony in the well-built homes."

Still there were rumblings of criticism from the beginning, and Pullman was never the idyllic community its owner had projected. There were serious strikes (broken by the company) in 1882, 1884, 1886, 1888, and 1891. Workers usually had trouble paying the high rents, and could not do so in slack times. Some attentive visitors to the town reported much discontent among the residents. Richard Ely, the well-known economist and student of municipal reform, described Pullman as embodying ideas foreign to democratic America: "It is not the American ideal. It is benevolent, well-wishing feudalism, which desires the happiness of the people, but in such a way as to please the authorities." The absence of any local participation in government contributed, according to some observers, to a lack of civic pride; and over all, there seemed to hang a blanket of suspicion and hostility.

The violent Pullman strike in 1894 focused much unfavorable attention on the model town. To many, it proved that paternalism had failed to solve the problems of urban communities. In 1898, the Illinois Supreme Court ruled that the Pullman Company's charter did not authorize its community enterprise; within another decade the company had divested itself of its town property and Pullman simply became a part of Chicago. Little regret was expressed at the passing of this urban experiment; most opinion seemed to agree that its paternalism, its "feudalism," ought not to have been applied to an American community. Pullman, himself, was embittered by the failure of his experiment. At his death in 1897, in accord with his instructions, tons of steel and concrete were placed on his coffin in its grave in order to forestall any effort by labor radicals to exhume his body. Pullman was the last impressive effort to build a satisfactory industrial community on the company-town model. City planning was evolving only slowly and uncertainly in the framework of voluntary business and political action across the nation: there was much waste and much left undone. But the Pullman experience suggested strongly that authoritarian direction would produce no better results.

Meanwhile, landscape architecture and city planning were being fused into one concept by the Chicago World's Fair of 1893–1894, called the Columbian Exposition, which celebrated the four hundredth anniversary of the discovery of the New World. Such world's fairs have frequently marked the recognition of cultural trends. The Philadephia Exposition of 1876 had demonstrated the importance of technology and the machine. The Chicago World's Fair came to symbolize the rise of the city in American life. The idea of having the celebration had been discussed intermittently in the 1880s, somewhat prominently at a session of the American Historical Association's convention in 1886. Congress provided official sanction in 1890, and after considering the spirited rivalry of many cities that wanted to host the exposition, it chose Chicago. Especially in view of Chicago's resurgence from its own ashes after the fire of 1871, this choice was appropriate, and great enthusiasm gathered around the planning and construction of the fair. The most active supervisor was Daniel H. Burnham, a well-known Chicago architect with talents for organization and propaganda; "beauty," he once said, "has always paid better than any other commodity and always will." He consulted Olmsted on the choice of a site, and brought together many architects, landscape planners, engineers, and sculptors to participate in building the fair. After one joint consultation, Augustus St. Gaudens remarked to Burnham that it had been "the greatest meeting of artists since the fifteenth century."

The scope of the project meant that in order to hold the fair at all, a brand new city must be built. As the grounds were laid out, in accord with a design provided by Olmsted, and the white buildings rose on every side— even a canal was cut through the Jackson Park location to enhance the fairgrounds—water, sewerage, transportation facilities, police and fire protection, in short a whole complex of urban services, had to be provided. Burnham oversaw the labors of seven thousand workmen, seventeen of whom died from accidents which were frequent during the frenetic activity. The fair opened in May 1893; on the first day almost half a million people swarmed onto the grounds, and by the time the Columbian Exposition closed in October more than 27,000,000 admissions had been counted.

People began calling the fairgrounds "the White City," and realized quickly that it constituted an unparalleled example of building a city to a pre-established plan. The fair's success stimulated intense enthusiasm for city planning. The president of the Fair Commission anticipated this in 1893, saying that "as an educational force and inspiration, I believe the buildings, their grouping, and laying out of the grounds will in themselves do more good in a general way than the exhibits themselves." A character in Fuller's *With the Procession,* returning to Chicago in 1894, met with "the universal expectation that the spirit of the White City was but just transferred to the body of the great Black City close at hand, over which it was to hover as an enlightenment—through which it might permeate as an informing force." In later years, the reputation of the Columbian Exposition as the great generator of subsequent city planning became distorted, obscuring the significance of the park and boulevard movement that had preceded it. Nevertheless, the symbolic value of the magnificent fair can hardly be overstated; it encouraged people to think about their cities as artifacts, and to believe that with sufficient effort and imagination they could be reshaped nearer to images of civilized living.

The White City also established the monumental architectural style that was characteristic of the subsequent effort at civic improvement called the City Beautiful movement. Burnham's commission decided that the principal structures at the exhibition be in either Classical or Renaissance style, greatly provoking the wrath of the modernist Louis Sullivan, who had begun to make his case for functional architecture and whose building at the fair was the only one that deviated from the requirement. With the coming of the fair, he wrote, "Architecture died in the land of the free and the home of the brave,—in a land declaring its fervid democracy, its inventiveness, its resourcefulness, its unique daring, enterprise and progress. Thus did the views of a culture, snobbish and alien to the land, perform its work of disintegration, and thus ever works the pallid academic mind. . . ." But expressions of popular opinion were enthusiastic. "The fair! The fair!," proclaimed *Harpers'* magazine. "Never had the name such significance before. Fairest of all the World's present sights it is a city of palaces set in spaces of emerald. . . ." Critics of nineteenth-century urban design and architecture have reflected Sullivan's view that a democratic people have no need of palaces and monumental street and boulevard designs—particularly when inspired, as the White City was, by a dictator, Napoleon III, rebuilding his capital. Yet there has been a tendency in recent years to view all manifestations of the turn-of-the-century style more sympathetically. Perhaps even a democratic society requires evidence of the grandeurs of civilization and reminders that the urban present, even in a brave new world, has continuities with an urban past.

The first important application of the principles both explicit and implicit in the White City came in Washington, D. C. Once more an anniversary helped focus attention: in 1900 Washington would celebrate its centennial. Beautification of the capital city had always excited thought in some minds; in the early 1850s Downing prepared a plan for that purpose, and in the

1870s Alexander Shepherd had refurbished much of the city in the ambitious building program that ultimately ruined him. In 1900, the American Institute of Architects devoted its convention (held in Washington) to consideration of improving the city's design. The architects' interest was encouraged by Senator James McMillan of Michigan, who pushed a measure through Congress directing the District of Columbia Committee to take the matter up officially. The committee called for advice upon several men who had been active in developing the Chicago fair: Burnham and Charles McKim were among them, and Frederick Law Olmsted's son was also included. This group drew up a plan centered upon reconstructing L'Enfant's project for a great mall between the Capitol and the Potomac River; additional historical monuments were to be built, and Rock Creek Park was to be completely landscaped. McKim, Burnham, and their associates prepared an exhibit consisting of hundreds of drawings, models and photographs to clarify their ideas to President Roosevelt and other government officials. Agreement with the president of the Pennsylvania Railroad made it possible to eliminate a railway station blocking the mall, and piece by piece the plan, in its essentials at least, was carried out.

The notion of city beautification received added impetus from the improvement of Washington. Burnham popularized beautification tirelessly, carrying his contagious enthusiasm to every part of the country, and finally back to Chicago. Here, with the backing of the Commercial Club, he and an associate, Edward H. Bennett, launched the Chicago Plan of 1907, in which the expansive and carefully laid out lakefront had its origin. Describing the plan for Chicago, Burnham and Bennett revealed how the ideas of the romantic park and boulevard landscape architects had blended with the ideal of magnificence which recalled the name of L'Enfant's plan for the District of Columbia. But along with the magnificence, Burnham and Bennett wrote, recourse to nature must always be available. "Natural scenery furnishes the contrasting element to the artificiality of the city. All of us should often run away . . . into the wilds, where mind and body are restored to a normal condition, and we are enabled to take up the burden of life in our crowded streets and endless stretches of buildings with renewed vigor and hopefulness. . . . He who habitually comes in close contact with nature develops saner methods of thought than can be the case when one is habitually shut up within the walls of a city." Appropriately, they referred to Chicago's Latin motto, *Urbs in horto:* a city in a garden.

The plan for Chicago was one of the most successful efforts of the City Beautiful movement; its history demonstrates the methods, character, and some of the fundamental limitations of early city planning. The plan was conceived on a grand scale, and in order to be realized considerable rebuilding of streets and relocation of industry and business would have to be done. In addition to the extensive improvement of the lakefront, the plan advanced proposals for a new metropolitan highway system, relocation of railroad facilities, changes in street patterns to direct traffic downtown, an outlying park system, and various new civic and intellectual centers. "Make no little plans," wrote Burnham in 1912, "they have no magic to stir men's blood. Make big plans; aim high in hope and work." In order to carry out an effort of this scope it was necessary to utilize some of the old methods of early town promotion: gain the support of powerful interests in the city and organize public support for the bond issues necessary to finance public improvements. A public agency, the Chicago Plan Commission, was organized, and under the energetic leadership of Charles H. Wacker, a brewer and investor, it launched an enthusiastic publicity campaign that included, along with such usual efforts as lectures, motion pictures, and pamphlets, the ingenious device of a textbook on the plan which was made a required part of the curriculum in the public schools. A generation of schoolboys and schoolgirls thus came to identify the plan with good citizenship. Despite the cost of many of the programs, the voters approved the necessary bond issues; by 1930 the plan was largely complete. Fundamentally, the effort was successful because it promoted the city of business and trade.

The *Plan of Chicago,* a sumptuous statement and defense of the plan, is a seminal and a fascinating document in the history of planning, but it is informed by the view that planning should promote enterprise and suburbanization. Its broad design was thus in accord with the existing pattern of American metropolitan development: "The plan frankly takes into consideration the fact that the American city, and Chicago preeminently, is a center of industry and traffic. Therefore attention is given to the betterment of commercial facilities; to methods of transportation for persons and goods; to removing the obstacles which prevent or obstruct circulation; and to the increase of convenience." The problem of slums, which of course was critical to the future of the city, was barely considered—in two brief paragraphs which rather ambiguously seemed to imply that not much could be done about them in any case. The remedies suggested were short and simple: first, the "cutting of broad thoroughfares through the unwholesome district," and second, rigorous enforcement of regulations concerning cleanliness and sanitation. The rationale of the plan was not change in the basic social conditions in cities, but a classical emphasis on the city as a symbol of civilization: "The experience of other cities both ancient and modern, both abroad and at home, teaches Chicago that the way to true greatness and continued prosperity lies in making the city convenient and healthful for the ever-increasing numbers of its citizens; that civic beauty satisfies a craving of human nature so deep and so compelling that people will travel far to find and enjoy it; that the orderly arrangement of fine buildings and monuments brings fame and wealth to the city; and that the cities which truly exercise dominion rule by reason of their appeal to the higher emotions of the human mind." It is easy to argue that the psychology of the report is naïve and that the good community should be concerned with meeting more elemental needs than the craving for civic beauty. But this is a viewpoint of the present, and nothing changes more quickly than contemporary notions about human needs and the roots of human behavior. In any event, the creation of the City Beautiful in the physical sense was not an ignoble task, as some critics seem to say. Charles M. Robinson, a self-trained planner, writer, and propagandist of the City Beautiful, reflected the evangelical optimism about the city's future that was a part of the movement: "When the heavens rolled away and St. John beheld the New Jerusalem," Robinson wrote, "so a new vision of a new London, a new Washington, Chicago, or New York breaks with the morning sunshine upon the degradation, discomfort, and baseness of modern city life. There are born a new dream and a new hope."

By the time of the Chicago Plan, the City Beautiful movement had fully matured, and rebuilding cities and parts of cities in accord with its conceptions was common. Burnham designed new civic centers in Cleveland and Duluth. San Francisco and Los Angeles among other cities undertook extensive downtown rebuilding projects. Several places instituted systematic tree-planting programs along city streets. New state capitol buildings at Providence, Harrisburg, Madison, and St. Paul were an outgrowth of the movement. Olmsted did not observe the flourishing of this attempt to order the urban environment that he had done so much to inspire. His mind failed in 1896, and he was institutionalized. He died in 1903.

In the first decade of the century planning was becoming a part of governmental machinery, with planning agencies—usually with little independent power—appearing in such places as New Haven in 1907 and Chicago in 1909. Further formalization occurred with the convening of the first national conference on city planning held in Washington in 1909. The meeting reflected new strands of thought that were to become part of the twentieth-century planning tradition. Benjamin C. Marsh, secretary of the Committee on Congestion of Population in New York, who was instrumental in organizing the conference, had begun to argue the need for comprehensive housing and planning legislation that would deal not only with physical aspects of city growth but also the social problems of urban life. John C. Nolen, another prominent planner, emphasized in his keynote address at the conference that planning had to move beyond mere beautification toward a concern with the whole city environment and the most efficient utilization of the resources of the city. Earlier notions of social improvement, in accord with the environmental views of progressivism and the concept of organizing a landscape that would blend city and country, were still a part of the planning outlook, but by this time scientific planning, with its emphasis on technical regulation and the provision of standards, was becoming dominant. In a report on the Madison park system published the next year, Nolen reflected this new view. "The most important features of city planning are not the public buildings," he wrote, "not the railroad approaches, not even the parks and playgrounds. They are the location of streets, the establishment of block lines, the subdivision of property into lots, the regulation of buildings, and the housing of the people."

Nineteen-hundred-and-nine was a memorable year in the history of planning. In addition to the national conference on planning and the publication of Burnham's plan, it also witnessed the completion of the famous Pittsburgh Survey, the introduction of a new course on planning at Harvard University, and the publication of the first textbook on the subject, Benjamin Marsh's *Introduction to City Planning*. With the huge sprawling metropolises already beginning to form on the urban scene and with the great regional megalopolises not many years away, from this time on planning in all its diverse manifestations would shape the character of American urban growth.

CHAPTER

# 13

# The Emergence of Metropolis

INFORMING much of the late nineteenth-century examination of the problems and the prospects of the American city was the view that city and country represented distinct environments, opposed ways of life. This view would continue to influence the character of popular argument, especially in political debate, until at least the 1950s. But an occasional observer around the turn of the century recognized that the conception of city as one thing and country another—a conception which had such deep roots in western culture—could no longer be applied to American society. The city by this time had enormously extended its spatial area and its influence. There was often difficulty in physically distinguishing city from countryside, for the two often blended together in sprawling urban regions. The country no longer represented an independent community, because it was affected in hundreds of economic and social ways by the city. "The city has become the central feature in modern civilization and to an ever increasing extent the dominant one," wrote the municipal reformer Frederic C. Howe in 1906. "This rural civilization, whose making engaged mankind since the dawn of history, is passing away. The city has erased the landmarks of an earlier society. Man has entered on an urban age."

In a general way, Howe was describing an aspect of the phenomenon of "metropolitanism," the extension of the influence of the large city over enormous hinterland regions. A few years later, the phenomenon received more explicit demographic recognition in the statistics presented in the federal census of 1910. As early as 1880, the census bureau had provided data for the metropolitan district of New York and its suburbs. Aware of the inadequacy of the customary urban classifications (populations of 8,000, 4,000, and 2,500 had all been used), demographers now applied the statistical notion of the metropolitan district to the whole nation. Twenty-five metropolitan districts were identified, ranging in size from New York (including Newark) with its 616,927 acres of land and 6,474,568 people, to Portland, Oregon with its 43,538 acres and 215,048 residents. Through this device it was possible to indicate the unity of such urban areas as the twin cities of Minnesota, the cities on San Francisco Bay, and the two Kansas Cities along the Missouri-Kansas border. Also evident was the importance of the clusters of suburban communities around the large eastern cities of New York, Boston, and Philadelphia. Through continued growth over the next half century, these cities and their suburbs would come to constitute a kind of continuous metropolitan region, which may represent a new stage in urban organization—the megalopolis.

The growth of the metropolis constitutes a central theme of twentieth-century American urban history.* For the 1950 census, demographers devised a more sophisticated device than the metropolitan district to assess the importance of the rise of metropolitan regions. This was the Standard Metropolitan Area (renamed the Standard Metropolitan Statistical Area in 1960), which was defined as a whole county containing a central city of 50,000 or more, plus any adjacent counties that appeared to be integrated to the central city. For over-all examination of twentieth-century metropolitan growth, it is perhaps most convenient to use the principal S.M.A.'s (those with 100,000 or more population at a given census), which the census bureau has "retrojected" to past census periods. But whatever measuring scheme is employed the trends are evident.

First, there was a great increase in the number of metropolitan areas and in the total population that lived in these areas. During the period from 1900 to 1950, the total United States population increased from 76.0 million to 150.7 million, but the number of principal S.M.A.'s increased from 82 to 147 and their total population from 24.1 million to 84.3 million. This represented a percentage change in the metropolitan population from 31.9 per cent of the nation's total to 56.0 per cent.

Second, for the entire period the growth rate for the principal S.M.A.'s was substantially higher than for the country as a whole:

32.6 per cent as opposed to 21.0 per cent from 1900 to 1910,
25.2 per cent as opposed to 14.9 per cent from 1910 to 1920,
27.0 per cent as opposed to 16.1 per cent from 1920 to 1930,
 8.3 per cent as opposed to  7.2 per cent from 1930 to 1940, and
21.8 per cent as opposed to 14.5 per cent from 1940 to 1950.

For every decade in the period except 1900–1910, when it was 15.0, the growth rate for nonmetropolitan areas of the country was substantially below 10 per cent.

Third, there has been a tendency for rapid growth to take place in the outlying areas of metropolitan centers at an accelerating rate. After 1920, metropolitan "rings" grew much faster than "central cities" themselves, by the 1940–1950 decade nearly two and a half times as fast (34.8 per cent as compared with 13.7 per cent). During the first decade of the century, metropolitan rings claimed only about one-sixth of the total United States population growth (15.7 per cent); in 1940–1950 this figure had risen to nearly one half (48.6 per cent).

* The term "metropolis," as is evident from Chapter One, acquired a different meaning in the twentieth century than it had historically.

The metropolises of the twentieth century, whose growth constituted the most dramatic demographic development to be found in statistics of United States population, were much more than greatly enlarged traditional cities. Involved in the concept of the modern metropolis are complex changes in function and structure within the city and its suburban areas—decentralization of numerous activities, separation of areas of residence and work, and a high mobility over greatly extended spatial areas. Also involved are many relationships with other cities and areas outside the immediate limits of the urban region.* The sociologist R. D. McKenzie in his pioneer study of metropolitan communities in the early 1930s argued that these considerations were so striking that the huge city of the twentieth century, with its surrounding suburban towns and cities and its far-reaching economic relationships, ought to be considered as "practically a new social and economic entity." A few years earlier, N. S. B. Gras had examined the existence of a world-wide metropolitan community and the intricate relationship of world cities of various sizes within that community. "We may think of metropolitan economy as an organization of people having a large city as nucleus," Gras wrote. "Or we may put it this way, metropolitan economy is the organization of producers and consumers mutually dependent for goods and services, wherein their wants are supplied by a system of exchange concentrated in a large city which is the focus of local trade and the center through which normal economic relations with the outside are established and maintained."

"Just as villages remained when town economy prevailed," Gras continued, "so do towns remain when metropolitan economy comes into existence. Towns remain, but in economic subordination to the metropolis. They continue to play a part, but as tributaries to a larger center. A closer examination of these dependent towns would show different types performing different functions, but all subordinate."

Gras's conception of "metropolitan dominance"—the control of the huge city over vast surrounding areas—influenced much of the subsequent study of the metropolis. Yet, as Gras himself recognized, "dominance" alone supplied an insufficient explanation. Not only were outlying areas of the metropolis dependent upon the city, but the city in turn was dependent upon its hinterland. In fact, the whole series of relationships within a metropolitan area was so complex that the biological term of symbiosis was often employed to indicate their nature. The twentieth-century metropolis provided a new system of social and economic organization—a distinctive social configuration. As Leo F. Schnore observes, the metropolitan area cannot profitably be

---

* The terminology relating to the metropolis is confusing. Some writers use the term *metropolitan community* to designate the area where population is integrated on a daily basis to the locale, that is, pretty much the commuting area of a metropolis; the term *metropolitan region* can then describe the larger area of more indirect influence. Employing the latter concept, it would be possible to divide the whole nation into a number of extended *metropolitan regions*. But there is little consistency in the use of metropolitan nomenclature, and we have not attempted to be unduly precise here.

conceived of "as a simple two-part arrangement of center and ring, a large city with its adjacent territory. . . . The metropolitan community must be viewed—in organizational terms throughout—as a highly specialized mosaic of subareas tied together into a new functional unity. Moreover, it is to be viewed as a multinucleated territorial system. Within these broad areas, the large centers are marked by functional diversity, while the smaller places, many of them formerly independent cities in their own right, tend to be narrowly specialized. At the same time, however, the main centers are specialized in the coordinating functions of administration and control."

The rise of the metropolitan region is often associated with the introduction of the automobile. Up to a point this is accurate. Statistically, if all American cities are considered together, the great jump in suburban population occurred in the 1920s when the automobile became the main device of urban transportation. Nevertheless, it is clear that the process of population decentralization—a fundamental aspect of the rise of the metropolis—had begun for some cities and in some regions of the country in the latter part of the nineteenth century. Schnore, one of the few contemporary urban sociologists to undertake detailed historical analysis of urban demography, has provided an ingenious study of decentralization of population in ninety-nine metropolitan central cities that had a population of at least 100,000 at some point in their growth. His study, which takes into account annexations and the persistence through thirty-year periods of decentralizing patterns, indicates the early tendency of a number of individual cities to grow more rapidly in their peripheral areas than at their centers. New York began decentralizing as early as 1850. Nine other cities had begun to decentralize by 1900; another thirteen cities were added to the list during the first decade of the century. The process speeded up after 1920, of course, and fully sixty cities began to decentralize between 1920 and 1940. In short, suburbanization, although it greatly accelerated in the twentieth century, is a trend in American urban development that extends back at least a hundred years. In Philadelphia, to cite an extreme example, the population movement away from the center of the city was proportionally greater in the fifty years between 1860 and 1910 than in the half century between 1900 and 1950.

The basic economic institutions that enabled larger cities to develop highly specialized metropolitan functions within a network of varying sized towns and cities also had nineteenth-century origins. The techniques of modern merchandising—with their emphasis on trade over vast regions—were fully developed by the end of the century. In the 1860s, Marshall Field's in Chicago combined the features of a number of large stores in Paris and New York—a fixed price system, large display advertisements, and numerous special departments—to establish the modern department store. R. H. Macy in New York and John Wanamaker in Philadelphia pioneered the use on a large scale of newspaper advertisements for the wares in their department stores. The Great American Tea Company, which was to become the first chain store, was organized in 1864 in New York; its owners adopted a number of promotional merchandising techniques to sell tea and later other groceries: band music on Saturdays, weight-guessing contests, cashiers' cages in the form of Chinese pagodas, to list but a few. Five years later it became the Great Atlantic and Pacific Tea Company and began to establish branches throughout the country. By 1912 the company had nearly 500 stores. Frank W. Woolworth opened his five-and-ten at Lancaster, Pennsylvania in 1879, established branches at Harrisburg and Scranton, and within a decade owned stores in a number of localities. Like the A & P, Woolworth's company flourished. By 1900 his volume of business was over $5 million, and by 1910 it had reached $15 million. The marketing institution that played the most significant part in extending the influence of the metropolis to the countryside, the mail-order house, also had nineteenth-century origins. Aaron Montgomery Ward started his mail-order business in a loft in Chicago in 1872 with a capital of $2,400. In 1883 Montgomery Ward's catalogue claimed goods in stock of over one-half million dollars. The other major firm began when Richard Warner Sears, a railroad station agent, began selling watches by mail out of a small Minnesota town. In 1887 he moved to Chicago, took a watchmaker, Alvah Curtis Roebuck, as a partner, and after selling his business, then restarting it, turned to general mail-order merchandising. By 1893 when the company had acquired its firm name of Sears, Roebuck & Co., it was selling a wide variety of goods from a 196-page catalogue. Although the mail-order house had to have customer confidence to succeed, Sears, who employed advertising effectively, during his company's early years occasionally indulged in the unscrupulous merchandising hoax of the period—doll furniture advertised in the fashion of regular furniture with the word *miniature* appearing in fine print, and the one-dollar sewing machine: a needle and thread. As has frequently been observed, the mail-order house brought the customs, styles, and manners of the city to the whole of American society as time went on. Modern advertising techniques, low-cost mass insurance, centralized stock exchanges, and specialized banking were examples of other metropolitan activities that developed in the latter part of the century. Technological innovations in printing —new presses, linotype machines, improved halftones—permitted city newspapers greatly to expand their circulations. This provided another particularly important means through which the influence of the metropolis was extended. In the early work of American urban sociologists, measurement of newspaper circulation provided a convenient way of estimating the range of metropolitan influence.

Another significant aspect of metropolitanism with nineteenth-century origins was industrial suburbanization—the growth of *satellite cities,* as Graham Romeyn Taylor termed them in one of the first investigations of manufacturing communities on the outskirts of large cities. Although this aspect of decentralization has not received as much attention as the creation of the residential *dormitory* suburbs, the suburbs of employment and production have been equally important in shaping the character of the modern metropolis. In the late nineteenth century the use of electric power, which unlike steam power could be transmitted miles from its source to the most efficient site, and improvements in transportation made it possible for manufacturers to move away from central cities, and they were encouraged to do so by a number of factors: the need for vast amounts of cheap land to build factories incorporating all stages of large-scale complex production, lower taxes, and freedom from regulation in regard to smoke and noise. Early attempts to build industrial communities in America had been influenced by conceptions of social control. Through the establishment of small carefully planned rural manufacturing towns, it was hoped that America might escape the abuses of the European manufacturing city. But after the disastrous Pullman strike of 1894, which stemmed in large part from the system of paternalistic control instituted in George Pullman's planned community, American manufacturers abandoned social planning in setting up their decentralized manufacturing centers. To the extent that they had to provide housing and urban facilities for workers, they did so in the simplest and most economical manner, and as quickly as possible got out of the business of managing communities.

Gary, Indiana, the largest city ever built by an American manufacturer, illustrated the new approach. In 1905, the United States Steel Corporation, as part of an effort to expand and consolidate portions of its vast productive facilities, purchased eleven square miles of empty land in an unpopulated area of swamps and sand dunes below Lake Michigan on the Calumet River in Indiana. While new mills were being constructed at the site, the corporation, through its subsidiary Gary Land Company, constructed a system of basic utilities for a city of 200,000, platted out streets and lots on the simple, efficient gridiron design, had houses built through private contractors, and sold these to incoming workers on long-term contracts. Eugene J. Buffington, who managed the U.S. Steel Corporation at Gary and also headed the Gary Land Company, reflected the new outlook of American manufacturers when he stated that "the most successful attempts at industrial social betterment in our country are those farthest removed from the suspicion of domination or control by the employer. . . . Gary is nothing more than the product of effort along practical lines to secure right living conditions around a steel manufacturing plant." Gary, like so many new industrial developments, was hailed as an American triumph. A promoter called it the "largest enterprise of the human race in all history," and Henry Blake Fuller, the Chicago novelist, predicted in 1907 that the Gary area would soon become "the premier industrial region of the world." Gary was organized as an ordinary municipality; aside from trying to restrict the sale of alcohol, the Gary Land Company made no attempt to impose controls on workers. U.S. Steel's experiment in decentralizing manufacturing was strikingly successful. Gary was well located in relation to the railroads and the labor market in Chicago, and in a few years, a vast suburban industrial complex, "the cities of the Calumet," had developed in the region.

Occasionally in the founding of smaller twentieth-century industrial communities—such as Morgan Park, a suburb of Duluth built by U.S. Steel, or Goodyear Heights, developed by the Goodyear Rubber Company outside Akron—the utilization of techniques of planning did help provide a desirable environment for living and working. But more often than not, the industrial satellites had dismal slums right from the start. Many areas in the manufacturing complex that grew up across the Mississippi River from St. Louis (including the communities of East St. Louis, Granite City, Madison, and Venice) lacked even elemental urban services. Particularly miserable was Granite City, where 65 per cent of the 8,500 workers in a granite-processing factory lived; a large densely settled slum area known as "Hungry Hollow" remained a part of Granite City for several decades. Norwood and Oakley, outside of Cincinnati; Lackawanna built in a swamp outside of Buffalo; and South Omaha were other early twentieth-century industrial suburbs that demonstrated the deleterious effects of the absence of planning and control.

Even though U.S. Steel provided satisfactory urban services at the beginning, and later financed a number of recreational and educational projects, Gary, too, developed many of the problems of the large manufacturing city. The first construction workers at the site had lived in tents and various thrown-together shacks of tar paper, tin, and board. The area was allowed to remain for a time, and the structures became homes for many of the unskilled immigrant laborers in the mills. The company also built dormitories for unskilled workers; they were soon overcrowded, and the area where they were located deteriorated into a slum called "Hunkeyville." When the temporary camp area was finally cleared, many of the workers moved into a section south of Gary called "The Patch," where developers had thrown together ramshackle housing outside the control of Gary municipal officials or the company. When, as part of a clean-up attempt, the company forced the tenants out of the Hunkeyville housing, most of them also moved to The Patch. Although skilled workers were able to obtain adequate living quarters, this was not possible for the unskilled. The slum areas around Gary soon developed the customary problems of alcoholism, prostitution, and crime. However, primarily because of a good natural water supply, they were not struck by serious epidemics. The government of Gary early fell into the hands of real estate interests, and the portions of the city outside the company's original holdings were developed in haphazard, essentially unplanned fashion. As the years went by, Gary and the surrounding urban-industrial complex turned into one of the dreariest and dirtiest of American industrial regions. The abandonment of industrial paternalism after Pullman had clearly led to deterioration in the social conditions of American manufacturing.

The building of industrial towns and cities in the early part of the twentieth century reflected a general pattern of decentralization clearly indicated in statistics of manufacturing. A Bureau of the Census study of twelve of the thirteen largest "industrial districts" showed that from 1899 to 1904 the number of persons employed in industry in central cities increased by 14.9 per cent while in the outlying zones the number increased by 32.8 per cent. From 1904 to 1909 the increase in central cities was 22.5 per cent but in the surrounding zones it was 48.8 per cent. For the decade, the growth rate was over two times as great for the suburbs—97.7 per cent to 40.8 per cent. This trend toward industrial decentralization became even more pronounced with the general acceleration of suburbanization after 1920. In 1919 eleven central cities in the country's forty largest manufacturing counties still accounted for 85 per cent of the manufacturing workers; by 1937 this percentage had fallen to just under 60. The number of wage earners in the eleven central cities during the period declined from 2,045,789 to 1,808,692, while in the outlying areas of these cities the number increased from 365,403 to 1,218,465. In addition to the decentralization of manufacturing, many of the commercial functions of the nineteenth-century city showed a marked tendency to decentralization, again, particularly after 1920.

Cheap electric power and the telephone were important in the decentralization of economic activities. Also important was the mobility of labor permitted by the trolleys and inter-urban railroads. But the most significant development stimulating rapid suburbanization was the automobile and, to a lesser extent, the motorized truck. In the early 1890s, mechanics in the United States and in Europe had put together workable automobiles. But until the turn of the century they were built on individual order and were largely a toy of the rich, with only 8,000 vehicles registered by 1900. During the next decade, actual manufacturing began. By 1910 the number of motor vehicles had risen to 468,500, and in 1915 to 2,490,932. Then came the tremendous post-World War I expansion of the industry: motor vehicle registration jumped from 9,239,161 in 1920 to 19,940,724 in 1925, then to 26,531,999 in 1930. In spite of the depression of the 1930s, the number of motor vehicles still increased by nearly a third during the decade, reaching a total of 32,035,424 registrations in 1940; by 1950 the number had grown to 48,566,984.

In addition to the obvious effects of increasing the mobility of workers and consumers and facilitating the movement of goods and materials in cities, the general use of motor vehicles also modified the spatial pattern of the metropolis. In the late nineteenth and early twentieth century, cities spread out along the lines of trolleys and inter-urban railroads. The suburbanized parts of the metropolis resembled tentacles extending from the central city in radial fashion. Highways, particularly in older and larger cities like Chicago and New York, first tended to follow the railroad lines. The new suburbs made possible by the automobile became part of the older pattern of growth. Gradually, however, as road building greatly expanded after the passage of the Federal Highway Act of 1916, the interstices of the metropolitan area began to be filled in. Complicated lateral movements of traffic became a defining characteristic of the metropolis. The transportation systems of older cities, even after the automobile came into general use, still tended to funnel traffic into the center, greatly intensifying the problem of congestion.

Los Angeles, of course, provided the best example of a city shaped by the automobile. Its rapid growth in the twentieth century fitted into a new urban pattern characterized by low density of population, great scope of movement for all but a small minority of people who could not afford automobiles, and the absence of a single downtown section. Unlike other cities in the period, Los Angeles, whose citizens were early committed to a spread-out style of living, turned down proposals for public transportation in the early part of the century, and existing public transportation deteriorated during the depression of the 1930s. A key decision that fixed the character of future development occurred in 1939 when a plan for a freeway system was adopted. The plan provided for freeways crossing one another in a rectangular gridiron, thus ensuring a multicentered pattern of development. This contrasted with the traditional spokes-of-the-wheel transportation pattern which necessitated the flow of all traffic through one central downtown. The Los Angeles freeway plan was carried out during the following years. It allowed a good many people to experience a good many new amenities in urban living, but it also tied Los Angeles to the automobile and eventually led to serious environmental problems.

During the 1920s and early 1930s, engineers perfected and governments adopted the various devices that were part of a high-speed system of motorized transportation—grade separation of highway from city street, traffic circle, divided dual highway, and synchronized stop lights. Control of parking was necessary, and the first parking meter was installed in Oklahoma City in 1935. These techniques, along with new bridges such as the George Washington in New York and the Camden-Philadelphia, and an innovation such as the Holland Tunnel under the Hudson, permitted easier movement of automobile traffic through the huge, sprawling metropolitan region. But just as in past eras, the rush-hour, weekend, and holiday traffic jams were an all too familiar aspect of urban life.

The expanded economic opportunities created by the automobile stimulated an urban land boom that radically inflated property values in American cities. Particularly where automobile routes tended to follow older fixed forms of urban transportation, considerable expansion took place in central business districts. This expansion contributed to an optimism that caused property values to rise, and as Homer Hoyt has dryly observed, "In each successive land boom there is a speculative exaggeration of the trend of the period." In 1920, the total value of land in American cities of over 30,000 population—only about one-fifth of 1 per cent of all the land in the United States—was estimated at $25 billion; by 1926 this figure had doubled to $50 billion. During the same period the value of American farm land dropped from 55 to 37 billion dollars—a figure 33 per cent less than the value of land in cities above

30,000. Real estate on Manhattan Island was assessed at over five billion dollars in 1930; this was more than the value of the farm land in 23 states in 1925. The corner of State and Madison in the heart of Chicago's Loop was leased during the decade at a rate of $50,000 a front foot, a rate equivalent to $21,789,000 an acre. One small holding at 1 Wall Street in New York City sold for $100,000 a front foot, a rate of nearly $44,000,000 an acre.

Inflation of downtown land values and the post-World War I prosperity of many sections of the economy stimulated the great era of skyscraper-building in American cities. For the most part, the American city in 1915 was low and squat; outside of Chicago and New York, buildings of over twenty stories were rare. But ever since Jenny's initial efforts, architects had been experimenting with the new building form; the Woolworth Tower of New York, completed in 1913, established a standard style. Chicago's group of towers along the Chicago River, built in the early 1920s, differed little from the new skyscrapers that sprang up in New York. Cleveland, Pittsburgh, San Francisco, and Kansas City developed the jagged sky lines characteristic of the twentieth-century American city. By 1929, American cities had 377 skyscrapers of more than twenty stories in height, largely built without concern for the character of the surrounding urban space and without concern for the patterns of traffic created by the buildings. Even in the cities of the plains the skyscraper was as much demanded as on the tight plots of lower Manhattan Island. Many of the nation's tallest buildings were begun in 1928 and 1929 and only completed after the depression. The most famous skyscraper of all, the Empire State Building, was finished in 1930 and for many years was a white elephant in a city which, during the depression, had more than enough office space. Not until the late 1950s were the pressures of urban growth great enough to stimulate another era of skyscraper-building.

Planners criticized the skyscraper for its contribution to intense traffic congestion. Architects and students of architecture, at the time and for a generation thereafter, criticized the "Woolworth Gothic" style of the skyscraper for its lack of aesthetic distinction. But in recent years the buildings of this period are being seen as representative of an artistic movement which produced works of quality—Art Deco or the somewhat more inclusive *Style Moderne*, or simply "modernistic," as it was popularly called. The skyscraper of the period, with its emphasis on extreme horizontal and vertical effects, flat and extensive decoration, hard lustrous surfaces, and particularly the conscious use of artificial materials combined with standard building materials pays homage to the machine as beneficial force, but it embodies this tribute to the functional in elaborate decoration derived from a past romantic tradition. The combination is often successful. One of the notable buildings of the era, New York's Chrysler Building, with its extensive use of steel and cadmium and with its machine-like precision of design, supplies a fluent statement on the century of mechanical progress celebrated enthusiastically at the Chicago World's Fair of 1933. And when contrasted with the harshly functional skyscrapers of a few years later, the Chrysler Building seems symbolic of the passing of a better time.

During the 1920s and 1930s, it was through the jagged towering skylines of great cities that many observers perceived the character of the new metropolitan civilization. The German director Fritz Lang was inspired to make his classic motion picture "Metropolis," with its frightening though sometimes unintentionally amusing vision of the urban future, after a visit to Manhattan in the mid-1920s. The French historian, Bernard Fäy, who visited New York late in the decade, echoed the sentiments of many travelers to the city in finding the mass of skyscrapers an appropriate symbol of a new order:

The very thing which I admire most in New York is its adaptation to the continent. In this sense, its architecture is intellectually reasonable, logical, and beautiful. Skyscrapers are the dwellings of the supertrusts; they are Eiffel Tower cathedrals which shelter Mr. Rockefeller, the Emperor of Petroleum, or Mr. Morgan, the Czar of Gold. . . . Some say that New York crushes them—and not without reason; the individual is overwhelmed by these great buildings. This is not an architecture for men, like the Parthenon or the châteaux of the Loire and Versailles. It is an architecture for human masses. Such buildings do not shelter or isolate men as do those of Europe. They gather and shuffle them. Often more than five thousand persons are united under one roof. . . . The New York skyscrapers are the most striking manifestation of the triumph of numbers. One cannot understand or like them without first having tasted and enjoyed the thrill of counting or adding up enormous totals and of living in a gigantic, compact, and brilliant world.

As cities went upward, they also went outward. The introduction of the automobile launched a great era of suburban building. The 1920s saw the complete emergence of modern residential suburbs and this was reflected in spectacular percentage growth rates during the decade for some of the more famous of them: Beverly Hills, 2485.0, Glendale, 363.5, Inglewood, 492.8, Huntington Park, 444.9 (suburbs of Los Angeles); Cleveland Heights, 234.4, Shaker Heights, 1000.4; Garfield Heights, 511.3 (suburbs of Cleveland); Grosse Pointe Park, 724.6, Ferndale, 689.9 (suburbs of Detroit); Webster Groves, 74.0, Maplewood, 70.3, Richmond Heights, 328.3 (suburbs of St. Louis); Elmwood Park, 716.7, Oak Park, 60.5, Park Ridge, 207.9 (suburbs of Chicago). Numerous new towns and villages appeared around large cities, as demonstrated in the incorporation statistics for the decade. Of the thirty-eight new incorporations in Illinois, twenty-six were located within the metropolitan regions of Chicago or St. Louis; of the thirty-three in Michigan, twenty-two were suburbs of Detroit, and of Ohio's fifty-five incorporations, twenty-nine were near Cleveland. Cities in the 2,500–10,000 bracket showed a rapid growth rate for the period, chiefly because so many of them were located on the fringes of metropolitan areas. A substantial part of the urbanization recorded in the censuses from this time on actually reflected the growth of suburban municipalities around large cities. Between 1920 and 1970 the percentage of total population in metropolises (as measured by one accepted designation of places of 250,000 or more) increased only slightly, while the population in urban places between 2,500 and 250,000 increased from 31 per cent to over 50 per cent of the total population.

In addition to all their other effects, the urban transportation devices of the twentieth century added new dimensions to one of the oldest economic activities associated with American urbanization—town promotion. No longer could promoters create great cities in the wilderness through the winning of railroads, but they could build highly profitable suburbs on car lines and highways. Early in the century, promotion was tied to the trolley and the inter-urban railroad, and as in past eras, the activity occurred in all sections of the country. Before World War I, New Orleans interests, through the able use of trolley lines, built a number of profitable suburbs along the Mississippi River and on the north shore of Lake Pontchartrain. Similar communities sprang up around Shreveport when the Shreveport Railway Company and the Gladstone Realty Company joined their operations. Another Louisiana real estate firm, the Kent Company of Alexandria, gained control of the Alexandria Electric Railway Company and used the line to develop a suburban area. The company provided a typical inducement when it promised free streetcar rides for three years to anyone who bought a new lot in its subdivision.

In southern California, Henry E. Huntington through the use of these methods enlarged the family fortune and set off a land boom comparable to that of the 1880s. In 1901 he incorporated the Pacific Railway Company and began building a network of electrified inter-urban lines around Los Angeles that by 1913 had reached forty-two incorporated cities within a radius of thirty-five miles. In virtually all instances, Huntington's railroad-building was tied to the promotion of suburbs. One of his more spectacular successes involved his development of Redondo Beach along Santa Monica Bay. Within a few weeks after the project got underway, he was able through the sale of lots to regain what he paid for the inter-urban line leading to the area and for the land picked as the site of the suburban community. By persuading the president of the Los Angeles Metropolitan Water District to join his enterprises, he was even able to set off a boom in the waterless San Fernando Valley. As a result of Huntington's promotions, some thirteen new cities were incorporated from 1910 to 1920, all except one of them located on his lines. The Huntington Land Company, which he had formed with a capital of $100,000 in 1902, had increased its value in the meantime to $10,000,000 in 1912 and to $15,000,000 in 1917. Huntington got out of inter-urban transportation in time to avoid the crash in the business caused by the introduction of the automobile. Even during their heyday, inter-urbans often did not make a profit in hauling passengers, but when tied to real estate ventures in suburban communities, as they generally were, they could be spectacularly successful.

One of the most famous examples of this kind of suburban development was Shaker Heights outside of Cleveland. Shaker Heights attracted attention by demonstrating how new planning conceptions could be applied to real estate development. The community served as a model for hundreds of less successful experiments in suburb building. Shaker Heights was the creation of two business-tycoon brothers, Oris P. and Mantis J. Van Sweringen, who had started out as office clerks in Cleveland, had briefly owned a bicycle shop, and had become interested in real estate at the turn of the century. After success in buying a tract of land beyond the Cleveland streetcar line and then persuading the local company to extend its track to their property, the two promoters purchased 1,400 acres of country land, which had once been the site of a Shaker religious community. Their plan was to develop a rigorously controlled residential suburb containing separate sections of homes in various price categories so that cheaper houses would not depress the prices of the more expensive ones. The Van Sweringens employed many of the features of suburban residential development that were to become standard: abandonment of the traditional gridiron and the substitution of curving and semi-elliptical roads running from main automobile boulevards; the preservation of natural park areas throughout the development; and strict architectural and decorating requirements. With the opening of a rapid-transit system to the community in 1920, Shaker Heights began to boom. From 1919 to 1929, nearly three hundred new houses were built each year; the community's population jumped from 1,700 to 15,550. The price of one-hundred-foot lots rose from $20 a foot to over $200 a foot in some sections of the community; by the end of the decade the valuation of the property had climbed to $80,000,000. The Van Sweringens used their profits from real estate to engage in some of the more grandiose railroad speculations of the 1920s, and until their pyramid of holding companies collapsed in the 1930s, they occupied a high rank among American corporate leaders.

The use of the automobile greatly enlarged opportunities in suburban promotion; the new era in town booming began in spectacular fashion with the Florida land boom of the 1920s. With the building of highways, tourists from the northeastern seaboard, by driving south for only a few days, could escape winter temporarily. During the early twenties, people flocked to Florida in ever increasing numbers. Hundreds of promoters and salesmen went to work selling lots—usually on option through a "binder"—and advertising new town sites. A journalist reporting on the boom in 1925 for *Harper's* indicated that for a $2,500 binder, he could have purchased a lot priced at $60,000 and could have sold it two weeks later for $95,000, a profit of $35,000. Right then and there, he said, he succumbed to the "Florida boom bacilli" that had been turned loose on him and his family a little earlier by an old and trusted friend. Much of the boom went on in Miami, which grew from 30,000 in 1920, to 75,000 by 1925, and to over 110,000 by 1930. But, as on so many past urban frontiers opened by transportation, fabulous claims were advanced for fabulous new cities—Silver Heights, Coral Gables, Picture Bay, Montezuma Manors, Sea Cove Crest, and Biscayne Bay. The number of lots platted in Florida during the boom, according to some estimates, reached twenty million, which with

a little overcrowding would have been sufficient to house the entire population of the United States. Large profits were sometimes realized in series of
frenzied property transactions. Before the boom, a New Yorker bought a
stretch of land in West Palm Beach at a low figure and sold it for $800,000 in
1923. The tract was then turned into city lots that sold for one and a half-
million dollars; by 1925 the tract was valued at four million dollars. One Carl
Fisher bought a tract in Miami Beach for $8,000,000, paying $3,000,000 down.
Two weeks later he had sold it for $11,000,000, collecting a down payment of
$4,000,000. The boom continued through 1925; early in 1926 it began to fall
off slightly as fewer people appeared in Florida for the winter. A severe
hurricane which struck the state on September 18, 1926 turned many of the
shoddily constructed developments to ruins, ended the boom, and wiped out
virtually all the ambitious speculators. Although in the long run a good share
of the land involved in the boom was utilized as urban property, as late as
ten years afterwards the bulk of the lots were weed-grown or under water.

The Florida land boom is often considered as another bizarre episode of a
decade of excess. Yet it was part of a pattern of overdevelopment of land for
urban purposes encouraged by the use of the automobile. Portions of Los
Angeles County experienced subdivision development similar to Florida; 75
per cent of the total platted area of Burbank, California, for example, was
vacant in the early 1930s. In 1929, 175,000 of Cleveland's 375,000 lots were
empty; over 65 per cent of the lot area in Duluth, 50 per cent in Portland,
Maine, 30 per cent in El Paso remained unused a few years later. Similar
premature subdivisions occurred in the metropolitan area of New York. The
announcement of plans for the George Washington Bridge set off a boom in
Bergen County, New Jersey, characterized by many of the same features as
the Florida boom. A large section of farmland was platted and divided by
"paper" streets; lots were sold at auction, through high-pressure mail campaigns, and by newspapers as part of their subscription efforts. But little of the
area was actually developed. During the 1920s, lots sufficient for all the inhabitants of the five boroughs of New York were platted on Long Island. By
late in the decade, nearly half the lots had become county property because
of unpaid taxes. The chaotic development of subdivisions in the 1920s greatly
complicated the problems of urban leaders in trying to provide municipal
services over vast, thinly settled areas and in attempting to impose some
degree of social order on the rapidly burgeoning American metropolises.

In the twentieth century, expansion upward and outward modified the
morphology of American cities. In addition, the character of urban population
and its distribution throughout the areas of the city also changed. The decade
of 1900–1910 was the last in which foreign migration contributed substantially
to the growth of American cities. In 1907, the high year for the decade,
1,285,349 immigrants arrived in the United States. With the outbreak of war
in Europe, the number fell to 326,700 in 1915 and reached a low point of
110,618 in 1919, with European immigration constituting less than 25,000 of

this total. Immigration revived in the early 1920s, reaching 805,228 in 1921, but the legislation establishing a quota system passed in that year (and revised in 1924) reduced annual immigration to around 300,000 in the years from 1925 to 1929. During the depression of the 1930s it dropped even more drastically and not until 1946 did the annual figure again rise above 100,000.

With immigration from abroad sharply restricted, cities grew largely through internal migration until the 1940s, when the birth rate of urban dwellers began to rise substantially. One of the most significant aspects of this rural-urban migration was the acceleration of the movement of southern Negroes to the cities of the East and Midwest, and on a lesser magnitude to the cities of the South. From 1820 to 1910 the urbanization of the white population of the United States had always been at a more rapid rate than that of the Negro. But failures of the cotton crop in the South in 1915 and 1916 and the demand for industrial labor caused by the war reversed this pattern in the next decade, as the percentage of native white population classified as *urban* increased by 6 per cent and that of Negroes increased by 6.7 per cent. The trend was intensified during the next decade, with the percentage of native white population classified as urban increasing by 4.9 while that of Negroes increased by 9.7. In 1910, 89 per cent of all Negroes lived south of the Mason-Dixon line; as a result of the migrations, by 1930 20 per cent of the Negro population lived in the Northeast and Middle West, with 88 per cent of this group classified as urban. During the period the total number of Negroes in the two latter sections increased from 637,000 to more than two and one-half million, while the Negro population classified as urban in the South rose from 1,365,000 in 1900 to almost three million in 1930. This urbanization of the Negro population represented primarily a movement to the larger cities, and it continued during the years of depression. Between 1930 and 1940, for example, the Negro population of Chicago increased by more than 43,000, an increase of 18.7 per cent. During the whole period from 1900 to 1950, the percentage of Negroes outside the South increased from 10 per cent to 32 per cent and the percentage within cities rose from 17 to 48 per cent.

Urbanization of the Negro population modified the social patterns of larger cities. The older ethnic colonies had always contained a fair number of people not of the predominant group. In addition, these colonies had been relatively impermanent, with one ethnic group succeeding another in a given area. The Negro colonies in northern cities were much more homogeneous, and, as time proved, much more permanent. Wards in New York and Chicago had percentages of Negro population that approached 95 by 1930. To a large extent, cities within cities had been created. "Black Metropolis is the second largest Negro city in the world, only New York's Harlem exceeding it in size," wrote St. Clair Drake and Horace Cayton in their 1945 study of Negro life in Chicago. "It is a city within a city—a narrow tongue of land, seven miles in length and one and one-half miles in width where more than 300,000 Negroes are packed solidly. . . . Walk the streets of the Black Belt and you will find no difference in language to mark its people off from others in the city. Only the black and brown and olive and tan faces of Negro Americans seem to distinguish it from any other section of Midwest Metropolis. But beneath the surface are patterns of life and thought, attitudes and customs, which make Black Metropolis a unique and distinctive city within a city. Understand Chicago's Black Belt and you will understand the Black Belts of a dozen large American cities."

As Drake and Cayton's account so clearly indicated, the Negro ghetto intensified old urban problems and created new ones. Past migrants to the city had been able to move from slums to better jobs and better neighborhoods. But racial animosity toward Negroes had become so well institutionalized by the time of the great migration beginning during World War I that they were systematically confined to lower occupations. Moreover, residential segregation was rigorously enforced through a variety of informal and formal institutional devices and, if necessary, through violence. The black metropolises of Chicago, New York, Cleveland, and Detroit were areas where few could benefit from the economic and cultural advantages of the city but where all the long-standing urban problems of crime, poverty, and disease existed in aggravated form. Even in a newer city such as Los Angeles, characterized by mobility and a suburban pattern of life, the efforts of Negroes to move from their area of original settlement to developments along the ocean or into surrounding communities were thwarted by local governments and by organized private groups, chiefly through restrictive covenants that forbade the sale of properties to Negroes.

Negro migration to cities and the white response this evoked revived an old urban problem—the riot. In southern cities migrant Negroes were absorbed into more firmly established social structures, and the residential communities there were older and more clearly delimited; accordingly they encountered no extensive overt hostility. But Negroes in large numbers in northern cities, seeking jobs and places to live, set off a number of bloody incidents. One of the worst occurred in East St. Louis, Illinois, where several days of violence (the result of resentment that had been building up for some time over the use of Negro strikebreakers) culminated in a vicious attack on Negroes on July 2, 1917, after two policemen had been shot and killed by a retaliating Negro mob. A downtown street became a "bloody half-mile," Elliot Rudwick writes in a vivid history of the riot:

Streetcars were stopped: Negroes, without regard to age or sex, were pulled off, stoned, clubbed, and kicked. A large group of whites marched through the streets shouting that colored people should leave East St. Louis immediately and permanently; this demonstration of community support emboldened the rioters who after the noon hour began killing Negroes along Collinsville Avenue. . . . By the early afternoon when several Negroes were beaten and lay bloodied in the street, mob leaders calmly shot and killed them. After victims were placed in an ambulance 'there was cheering and hand-clapping.' . . . two or three Negro men held their hands high in a gesture of surrender, but were clubbed with gun butts. When they fell, young girls got blood on their stockings while kicking the victims, and the sight amused the rioters.

The riot climaxed that evening in the burning of two hundred Negro homes, the shooting of several people trying to flee the flames, and a grizzly lynching of an already badly wounded man. Finally during the night the state militia restored order. All told, the riot claimed the lives of at least thirty-nine Negroes and nine whites.

In 1919, a year of widespread race riots, Chicago had five days of violence that left twenty-three Negroes and fifteen whites dead. The disturbance produced one of the most startling photographs in American history of a group of whites stoning a Negro to death. Washington, D. C. and Omaha had serious riots the same year. Tulsa had one in 1921 in which twenty-six Negroes and ten whites were killed. But the Tulsa riot pretty much ended this era of racial violence. The return of a measure of prosperity and the slowdown in the pace of Negro migration from the war years led to several years of relative stability in urban race relations. Like riots in the nineteenth century, those of this period were the subject for immediate gross exaggerations of plots and conspiracies, of numbers killed and numbers participating. But some objective study at the time, and by later scholars, revealed patterns that had continuity with the past. In general, these were race riots with violence directed against Negroes by whites upset over their residential expansion and to a lesser extent their job encroachment. There was an underlying objective of "putting the Negro back in his place." Negroes retaliated against white attacks, but the retaliation was limited and did not extend into white areas of the city. There was seldom any large-scale invasion of Negro residential areas by white mobs. Much of the attack on Negroes occurred on the periphery of their neighborhoods or in downtown areas; often those riding on streetcars were attacked as they passed into a white area. As in the case of the Draft Riots of 1863, the number of actual rioters was much smaller than estimated at the time, although there were often substantial numbers of bystanders on the streets and, as also in the past, the mobs were composed primarily of teenagers and young male adults. In large part, these riots represented a traditional kind of failure of municipal authority. The existence of weak or corrupt police forces, the failure of police to take firm action, or their tacit encouragement of rioters—all of which was a part of the East St. Louis riot, for example—have always been crucial to the burgeoning of a riot from a commonplace, run-of-the-mill incident of violence. As Allen Grimshaw, a student of the history of violence in America, has suggested, "the occurrence or non-occurrence of violence depends less on the degree of social tension . . . than on the strength and attitude of police forces. . . . In every case where major rioting has occurred the social structure of the community has been characterized by weak patterns of external control." In short, these race riots, for all their horrors, were limited in scale. They were not battles in an all-out racial war, as they have sometimes been pictured to be, but represented instead a rather selective breakdown in the functioning of urban institutions.

The urban segregation of the Negro reflected a general tendency to increased economic and cultural segregation in the twentieth-century metropolis. The wealthier and more powerful members of the community steadily moved to the outer zones of the city and to the new suburban areas. A study of over 2,000 substantial Detroit families in the early 1930s demonstrated a striking deconcentration of that city's elite. In 1910 nearly 52 per cent of this group still lived within a three-mile radius of the main business center of Detroit, and only 9.7 per cent outside the municipal boundaries. By 1930 these percentages were nearly reversed, with only 7.5 per cent of the substantial families near the business district and 50 per cent in suburban areas. Numerous studies of economic zones within cities and of spatial zones away from the center made by the urban sociologists of the 1920s and 1930s demonstrated clearly the cultural advantages and the greater stability of the outer regions of metropolitan centers. Crime, the need for public welfare, and infant mortality decreased radically in the outer areas and usually in direct proportion to the distance of the area from the center of the city. In the past, many had resented the city because its extremes of wealth and poverty seemed a denial of American equalitarian beliefs. In the twentieth-century metropolis these inequalities appeared more obvious, more rigidly confined, and more permanent.

The rise of the metropolis presented a whole new set of considerations to those concerned with ordering the urban environment. But despite the complexity of the twentieth-century super-city and its tremendous influence on society, much of the debate about the city in America was still conducted in terms of the old country-city polarity. The effort to restrict foreign immigration, the crusade for religious fundamentalism, the prohibition movement, and the election of 1928 were aspects of national history influenced by the traditional defense of the values of the country and the traditional attack on the values of the city. People could still accept at face value the famous photograph of President Calvin Coolidge seated on a hay wagon with rake in hand, his clothes spotless, while in the rear his assistants stand by an automobile waiting to whisk him back to the city. Writers of popular fiction in the twenties and thirties still employed the nineteenth-century imagery of the soulless city. To find "real values" one had to flee the city. "I have had to do many things, terrible things, things no decent man should have done," says a hero of a 1925 *Cosmopolitan* short story who finds peace in the wilderness. "Thank God that's all behind me now. Out here I can be a real person again." On a higher level, twelve southerners in their notable manifesto *I'll Take My Stand,* published in 1929, defended an idyllic rural life that probably never existed. "Back to the land," a position popularized by Ralph Borsodi who established a subsistence homestead outside New York City in 1920 and preached the virtues of the Thoreauvian way of life, became an organized movement that influenced federal policy during the depression of the thirties. Its disciples offered a classical Jeffersonian defense of the agrarian ideal. "The farms have always produced our great leaders in finance, industry and states-manship," a witness testified before a House committee in the early 1930s. "The vast population must depart from the congested industrial centers and cities and once again become self-sustaining on our vast and fertile farms, pasture, and prairie lands. Herein lies the real hope for the bright destiny of America."

Despite the persistence of these old ideals, many thinkers and reformers abandoned the simple notion of country versus city and began to develop new conceptions of the social environment that emphasized the community, the neighborhood, the region. The old problems that had special urban dimen-sions—health, poverty, and the slum—had not disappeared, and housing the poor of the cities continued to be one of the principal concerns of urban reformers. But the complexity of the new metropolitan communities forced consideration of ways of reordering the whole urban environment. Proposals for new kinds of cities and for comprehensive plans that encompassed whole urban regions now became part of the discussion of the future of American cities. Writing in 1922, Lewis Mumford, who was to become one of the better known students of urban civilization, reflected the urgency of the new point of view: "Our metropolitan civilization is not a success. It is a different kind of wilderness . . . but the feral rather than the humane quality is dominant; it is still a wilderness. The cities of America must learn to remould our mechanical and financial regime; for if metropolitanism continues they are probably destined to fall by its weight."

As had so often been the case in the past, the inspiration for new ways of dealing with urban problems came from Europe. Particularly influential was the Garden City idea of Ebenezer Howard, a London court reporter and reformer. Drawing on the nineteenth-century British tradition of community planning, which had earlier influenced American experiments, Howard pro-posed a new kind of community that he hoped would combine the best features of town and country. The size of the Garden City would be limited to 30,000 people. A permanent greenbelt would surround it, and enough industry would be developed in carefully specified areas to ensure the com-munity's self-sufficiency. The land on which the city was built would be owned by the community as a whole and administered by a public authority. All leases would contain specific and detailed building requirements and areas of greenery would be preserved throughout the city. The profits of growth would go to the community rather than to the speculator, because only limited dividends could be paid to the original investors in a Garden City project. This would also ensure that there would be no temptation to modify land use or increase the planned density of the city. Howard foresaw Garden Cities being founded throughout England, providing a way of checking the continued growth of the huge, congested industrial cities. The successful establishment of the first Garden City of Letchworth, England, begun in 1903, led to a world-wide Garden City movement; interest was reinforced by the start of a second community called Welwyn in 1919. Letchworth and Welwyn were the only two cities built in accord with Howard's over-all plan, but his ideas influenced a number of American planners and architects. Although they seldom embodied the significant aspects of Howard's conception of a new kind of community, "garden villages," "garden suburbs," and "garden homes" became the fashion of the day after about 1910.

Forest Hills Gardens on Long Island, financed by the Russell Sage Foundation and designed by Frederick Law Olmsted, Jr., was completed in 1911, and the project, though it became simply a suburb for well-to-do commuters, demonstrated the possibilities in carefully planned housing developments. Many of the conceptions that were part of Garden City and other plans for new-style towns and cities were initially applied by businessmen who were not unduly concerned with creating a good community but who foresaw large real estate profits. The term *garden city* was often used to describe any planned new community that preserved a natural setting; the Van Sweringens in promoting Shaker Heights utilized the appeal of Howard's conception. Torrance, California—one of several of the small, planned suburban industrial communities developed in the early years of the century—was labeled by its founder, the industrialist Jared Sidney Torrance, as the "greatest and best of the garden cities of the world." In 1914 the limited-dividend principle, which had been a fundamental part of Howard's plan, was employed in the development of a suburban area of Boston called the "garden suburb" of Billerica. Nowhere, however, was more than a portion of Howard's plan utilized during this first period of enthusiasm; often in the 1920s, "garden city" became a description of any suburban housing project.

Utopian city proposals that required a drastically new conception of the rights of landed property—as Howard's plan did—could not be expected to make much headway in a nation committed to traditions of individual enterprise. Yet the planning and zoning movement, which flourished between World War I and the depression, reflected to a limited extent the same concern with the whole environment of metropolis that motivated Howard. In part, the vogue for planning had its origins in the City Beautiful movement, but it also drew support from the popularity of the Garden City idea. As a result of the interest in planning, the number of planning commissions and planning boards had grown from seventeen in 1914 to over 735 in 1930, and although they remained primarily advisory agencies, their powers tended to increase. Professional planners in this period began turning out comprehensive regional plans that recognized the metropolitan character of twentieth-century urban development—Russell V. Black's plan for Philadelphia or Harland Bartholomew's for the San Francisco Bay region. The most important of these was the *Regional Plan of New York and Its Environs,* which cost a million dollars to prepare, took ten years to complete, resulted in ten books, and is considered a landmark in the study of the American city. These kinds of plans often ran into substantial local and organized business opposition. Even when they were partially carried out, they tended not to change the status quo. The New York plan was largely realized over the years and provided some ordering of the New York area by encouraging a measure of decentralization, but it did not alter significantly the pattern of intense concentration of economic activity on Manhattan Island.

Closely related to the establishment of planning commissions was the passage of zoning regulations, for zoning was ordinarily a part of plans for city redevelopment and growth. The techniques of zoning had initially been applied in German cities beginning in 1900, and California cities early in the century had begun to pass nuisance-zone statutes that limited certain types of business such as saloons, dance halls, and slaughterhouses to designated sections of the city. However, the institution of modern zoning practices in the United States was largely a development of the postwar period. Before 1916, only five American cities had general zoning regulations, but New York's adoption in that year of a zoning law for the entire city popularized the approach. Between 1916 and 1920, twenty-five cities passed zoning laws, and by 1930 the number of zoned cities had risen to 981. Edward M. Bassett, a Brooklyn lawyer and politician, established the basic zoning procedure of drawing a zoning map only after extensive and systematic consultation with neighborhood landholders. Bassett also drafted a model zoning statute for the U.S. Department of Commerce in 1924. After several years of litigation, the United States Supreme Court finally upheld this type of governmental regulation in 1926. The earliest zoning ordinances in the United States were designed mainly to keep residential areas free from business and industry and only regulated land use in various districts of the city. The laws passed after 1925 in accord with the model statute tended to be more comprehensive and regulated not only land use but the height and bulk of buildings as well. A study in 1929 indicated that of the 754 municipalities with zoning, 475 had comprehensive ordinances controlling the use, height, and area of buildings. Measures requiring set-backs on the upper portions of taller buildings contributed to the uniformity of the tower skyscrapers of the 1920s, and in general led to more consistent building styles in American cities.

Although zoning and planning were advocated by urban reformers who were genuinely concerned with trying to make cities better places in which to live, the movement to some extent merely intensified certain problems of the metropolis. Building requirements often contributed to the segregation of groups within the city on the basis of wealth. Many residential suburbs, for example, were kept as enclaves of wealth through rigorous zoning requirements. Until they encountered court difficulties, early zoning measures in southern cities were rather frankly aimed at maintaining the segregation of Negroes. It has been argued that zoning requirements represented an effort by older inhabitants of cities to maintain control of the downtowns they were abandoning. In this way, they protected their investments at the same time they kept newcomers to the city confined.

Business interests often supported planning and zoning, not out of an altruistic concern to improve the quality of urban life, but rather because they recognized that these programs would make cities economically more efficient and easier places in which to do business. Powerful support for the basic New York zoning law of 1916 came from Fifth Avenue merchants, who were distressed by the encroachment of garment industry plants into their shopping district. The reports that preceded the law appealed to this kind of sentiment. "The natural result of a poor utilization of its land areas by a city is high rents for occupiers and low profits for investors," stated the New York Committee on Building Heights in 1913. "It may seem paradoxical to hold that a policy of building restriction tends to a fuller utilization of land than a policy of no restriction; but such is undoubtedly the case. The reason lies in the greater safety and security to investment secured by definite restrictions."

The relationships between planning and zoning, new conceptions of community, and business profit are clearly illustrated in the career of Jesse C. Nichols, a leading spokesman of real estate men in the 1920s and 30s, whose Country Club District of Kansas City, Missouri attracted international attention. In his real estate operations, he was concerned with making a profit but he was also genuinely concerned with establishing new patterns of business and residential location that would alleviate some of the problems of the sprawling metropolis. Nichols grew up on a farm near Olathe, Kansas, graduated from the University of Kansas, and studied economics at Harvard University, where he wrote a thesis on land development. On a visit to England during his student days, he was impressed by the parks, lawns, and gardens of the smaller English cities and later maintained that the notion for the Country Club District was conceived at that time. After leaving Harvard, he got his start in business building houses for workers in Kansas City, Kansas. With capital accumulated from this venture, in 1905 he began buying property south of Kansas City, Missouri. The residential district he established was a success from the beginning. It was eventually to cover 6,000 acres, one-tenth of the area of the city.

In the 1920s Nichols's Country Club District became one of the most extensive restricted residential developments in the country, and the techniques he employed were widely copied by real estate men elsewhere. On all property sold by the Nichols company, comprehensive deed restrictions controlled land use, minimum cost of buildings, open space, set-back lines, and sales to Negroes. The Nichols company was probably the first to employ the device of self-perpetuating deed restrictions. These were automatically continued unless a majority of the owners in an individual subdivision moved to change them at least five years before the expiration of the usual twenty-five-year term of initial subdivision deeds. Nichols also sponsored the formation of self-governing Homes Associations, which received charters from the state. These associations, which had grown to twelve in number by 1926, levied assessments on residents and provided a variety of governmental, cultural, and recreational services such as garbage and snow removal, lawn contests and flower shows, and maintenance of parks and playgrounds initially provided by the Nichols company. Students of the city, including a number of English visitors who made comparisons with the Garden City, pointed to the Homes Associations as a desirable system to promote the spirit of neighborhood in the impersonal metropolis. City planners from as far away as South America and Australia visited the Country Club District. The British planner Charles Read echoed their reactions when he commented that no man in the world had done as much as Nichols "to carry beauty and comfort into everyday life."

Nichols also won attention for his development of the first large decentralized shopping center in the United States, the Country Club Plaza Shopping Center, begun in 1922. The Frederick Law Olmsted firm in 1907 had provided a parking lot for a small shopping district located in the planned suburb of Roland Park outside of Baltimore, and this may have influenced Nichols's planning. In the early 1920s, he visited the garden cities of Welwyn and Letchworth and also toured Spain to get ideas for the project. His carefully planned and controlled shopping center successfully and pleasingly harmonized Spanish-style architecture with the natural setting of the district, although the architectural style was hardly appropriate to the city. Nichols maintained close control of the center through renting all the properties for a fixed amount plus a percentage of gross business returns. Suburban developers widely copied the design for the center, but few other planners were able to preserve the harmony and architectural integrity that Nichols insisted upon. Nor were other developers generally concerned with maintaining control of the subsequent use of their property.

Primarily because of the attention his Country Club District received, Nichols became a national leader in the real estate industry. In his speeches he consistently defended zoning and planning. Zoning, he suggested, could provide a means of ensuring "air, light, sunshine, and decent surroundings" for the laboring man as well as for the owner of the large estate; it would bring "order instead of chaos into American building." Lack of planning intensified the problem of the automobile; traffic congestion was largely the result of "stupid application of the conventional checkerboard scheme without regard to grades or traffic needs." In addition to pointing out that planning could make cities more livable, Nichols always emphasized to business audiences that planning could also be profitable. "City planning," he told the Kansas City Chamber of Commerce in 1921, "is based on love,

ambition, and profit. . . . If you are ambitious for the growth of your business, your institution or your city, if you believe in its future growth, you
plan for healthy expansion."

Nichols, like many less practical theorists of the city, was acutely sensitive
to the ugliness of the new metropolitan environment that was rapidly being
created in the 1920s. In a 1926 essay on shopping centers, he developed
this theme:

In American cities of any considerable size our new outlying business centers frequently are becoming the ugliest, most unsightly and disorderly parts of the entire
city. New traffic throats of congestion are being created that will sooner or later call
for the expenditure of gigantic sums of public funds to relieve. Buildings of every color,
size, shape, and design are being huddled and mixed together in a most unpresentable
manner. A mixture of glowing billboards, unsightly rubbish dumps, hideous rears, un-
kempt alleys, dirty loading docks, unrelated, uncongenial mixtures of shops of every
type and use, with no relation to one another; shacks and shanties mixed up with
good buildings; perfectly square, unadorned buildings of poor design, are bringing
about disorder, unsightliness, and unattractiveness that threaten to mar the beauty and
good appearance of the residential regions of American cities. . . . The abandonment
of formerly beautiful residential areas, neglected and blighted former business sections,
should arouse in everyone a determination to protect the appearance of his city as
well as the property values themselves.

Nichols was aware of the problems of metropolis and attempted to do
something about them. His innovations helped to provide a better way of
life for many city dwellers. But not everyone could benefit from the amenities
of Nichols's Country Club District. Deed restrictions kept out Negroes, a
practice not invalidated by the Supreme Court until 1948. Construction requirements assured that lower income groups would not live there. By the
1930s, the area contained a homogeneous population of upper-white-collar
and professional families. The Country Club District reflected the difficulties
in private efforts to develop new living patterns in cities. Well-planned industrial villages and luxurious residential suburbs did virtually nothing to
provide housing for the poor. And this was one of the most significant problems of the metropolis. Real estate men like Nichols frequently accepted the
need for government regulation of urban expansion through city plans and
zoning laws. But they did not, of course, advocate any significant departure
from the established practices of private ownership and private development
of land in cities. It remained for reformers outside the real estate business to
argue the necessity for more drastic approaches to the problems of the metropolis.

Much of the agitation for new policies toward cities stemmed from a very
old urban problem—inadequate housing. The new restrictive codes popularized by Veiller improved the quality of housing but did nothing to provide
homes for the poor. The shortage of housing for low-income groups became
so serious during World War I that it interfered with production, and as

an emergency measure the federal government instituted a program of public housing. Through two agencies, the United States Shipping Board's Emergency Fleet Corporation and the Department of Labor's United States Housing Corporation, the government built, sponsored, or controlled a number of housing projects for war workers. Developments like Yorkship Village (later the Fairview Section of Camden, New Jersey) and Union Park Gardens near Wilmington, Delaware provided reasonable, attractive, and well-designed housing. The projects also permitted American architects and planners —many of them imbued with Garden City concepts—to experiment with urban design, including curvilinear street systems, the row house, and balanced residential neighborhoods. Despite protest, as soon as the war ended Congress liquidated the program as quickly as possible. But the experiment could be pointed to as a precedent for government action in housing.

The acute housing shortage that followed the armistice indicated the need for new policies. Shortages of capital and inflated construction costs checked the anticipated resumption of normal building, which had helped to justify quick termination of the government programs. Building increased after 1921 and was one of the factors sustaining the mixed prosperity of the 1920s, but expansion was accompanied by a highly disproportionate rise in building costs. Rents also rose much faster than wages. Moreover, there was considerable deterioration in the older tenement districts. Well before Franklin D. Roosevelt's second inaugural address, there was recognition that one-third of the nation was ill-housed. The 1930 census indicated that more than 6,000,000 homes in cities, over 25 per cent of the total, did not meet minimum standards. Because of the seriousness of the problem, much of the early twentieth-century discussion of the future of cities had housing as its central emphasis. City planners and housing reformers generally agreed that private builders operating within a free market were simply not able to provide satisfactory low-cost housing. As a result of their agitation, there were efforts after World War I to encourage the establishment of limited-dividend and cooperative housing projects. A precedent-breaking Wisconsin law of 1919 permitted counties and cities to purchase stock in cooperative housing companies; a Milwaukee cooperative company with support from the city, erected 105 houses, at alleged savings of $1,500 a house. Other private housing cooperatives, totalling forty in number in 1925, were organized, virtually all of them in New York City. The New York State Housing Law of 1926 provided tax exemptions to limited-dividend housing projects, permitted municipalities to exempt the projects from local taxes, and set maximum rents for authorized projects. Two cooperatives and one limited-dividend company built a total of six projects in New York City under the law. But these private and public efforts to supply low-cost housing before the New Deal period were so restricted that they had no effect, virtually, on the general problem. Nevertheless, there was increasing recognition of the fact that some type of government intervention in housing had become a necessity.

A group particularly influential in establishing this point during the 1920s was the Regional Planning Association of America, an informal association of planners, architects, social theorists, and housing experts who began meeting in 1923. The organization included many of the leading students of city problems. The RPAA evolved from other groups concerned with the postwar housing crisis, and good housing for the poor remained a dominant concern of the organization until it broke up around 1933. But the group went much further and attempted to formulate ways to plan whole metropolitan regions. Their program emphasized the development of a new kind of regional city, which would preserve small towns and villages and renew metropolitan centers through a comprehensive, flexible ordering of the relationships between population, resources, and institutions.

As part of their effort to develop more reasonable and more livable urban communities, the RPAA turned to Howard's Garden City as a beginning. In 1923, Clarence Stein, an architect who had been most responsible for the formation of the group, convinced Alexander M. Bing, a New York real estate man, to support RPAA plans for building residential communities along Garden City lines. Bing sponsored the formation of a limited-dividend housing company, the City Housing Corporation; between 1924 and 1928 the corporation built the first of its two Garden City-style communities, Sunnyside, New York. Sunnyside was located on a seventy-acre tract in the borough of Queens on land purchased from the Pennsylvania Railroad. Unable to obtain modification in the existing gridiron plat for the area, Stein and Henry Wright, an expert on housing costs and site planning, nevertheless laid out an attractive development of row houses and apartments enclosing large central gardens. Contrary to the hopes of its founders, the project did not supply housing that accommodated low-income groups. Even though the dividends of the City Housing Corporation were limited to 6 per cent and certain economies in efficient site-planning were realized, Sunnyside did not provide housing that was competitive with that built by large-scale, private speculative builders.

The RPAA's most significant effort—and one of the most significant housing efforts of the early twentieth century—was carried out in New Jersey on a 1,258-acre site some seventeen miles from New York. Sunnyside had been a kind of trial run; Radburn, New Jersey was to be a real Garden City of 25,000 people. Before the project could be completed, the depression hit; Bing's corporation was thrown into receivership; and Radburn remained a town of about 1,500. But in the period between 1928 and 1931, Radburn was considered the closest approximation to a Garden City in America, and was internationally hailed as a "town for the motor age." Radburn had no unique features of building or design, but it artfully synthesized most of the proposals for planned communities in the 1920s—the 40-acre superblock, interior parks, curvilinear streets and, perhaps most significantly, a system of roads that separated the automobile from the pedestrian. Benton MacKaye's 1930 plan for the "townless highway," which anticipated most of the features of the modern turnpike, was suggested by the Radburn experiment. But Radburn was at most only a limited success. Because of high land costs, no greenbelt was provided, and the founders were never able to attract industry as they had hoped. Rather ironically, in the 1930s Radburn became a suburb of white-collar commuters instead of the self-sufficient, neighborly community that the RPAA leaders had wanted to establish. Radburn, like J. D. Nichols's Country Club District (based on an altogether different ideological position), might lessen for a few the effects of the feral wilderness that Lewis Mumford, a leader in the RPAA, conceived the twentieth-century city to be. But Radburn and all the other urban programs, policies, and plans of the early metropolitan period of American urban history had shown little promise of providing the humane metropolitan society that Mumford had hoped for.

CHAPTER

# 14

# A Federal Urban Policy

THE COMING of the Great Depression ended the expectation that private experiments could substantially modify the character of the urban environment. The depression era marked a new stage in American urban history: for the first time the policies of the national government were formally and explicitly directed toward shaping the character and quality of life in American cities. A number of federal actions and programs in the past had indirectly influenced cities. The planning and building of the national capital, for example, affected the physical design and public-building styles of many cities. The information gathering of the Bureau of the Census gave impetus to city promotion and growth. World War I housing experiments involved direct federal participation in urban development, but this of course was recognized as a temporary, emergency measure, and the program was quickly terminated at war's end. About the same time, however, the federal government instituted significant permanent policies. River and harbor improvements stimulated the economies of individual cities; Houston began to grow rapidly after Congress provided for a deep-water channel to its port in 1919. The expanded services of the Post Office Department in the 1920s shaped urban communications and particularly relationships between cities and their hinterlands. Rural free delivery, for example, enlarged mail-order merchandising and the circulation of magazines and newspapers published in cities. In addition, the Post Office Department required cities to institute a number of civic improvements such as building sidewalks, putting up street signs, and assigning house numbers before mail-carrier routes were provided.

Herbert Hoover, as Secretary of Commerce from 1921 to 1928, extended the scope of federal concern with the city through his program of "voluntary cooperation" and encouraging private associations among various economic interest groups, many of them urban centered. He established a Division of Building and Housing within the Commerce Department; the agency conducted research and furnished information to the building industry on a number of subjects related to housing, such as construction methods, financing, and the selection of sites. The division also sponsored the model zoning law for cities, and encouraged the use of standarized building materials and the adoption of uniform building codes. Whether these and similar urban programs of the 1920s and earlier provide precedents for the urban programs of the 1930s forms a part of the debaters' question over whether the New Deal was "evolution or revolution," and cannot be answered conclusively. It is clear though that in the New Deal years administration planners specifically recognized that cities had tended to be ignored in the past and that federal action should henceforth be directed toward their problems. The National Resources Committee, a New Deal agency, argued in its 1937 landmark report on "Our Cities: Their Role in the National Economy," that "widespread neglect of the cities as a major segment of national existence" had been one of the major sources of urban problems. "Indicative of this neglect," the Committee declared, "is the fact, although the United States has been a predominately urban nation for more than two decades, this report . . . is the first inquiry of national, official, and comprehensive scale into the problems of the American urban community." The report forcefully asserted that "the United States Government cannot properly remain indifferent to the common life of American citizens simply because they happen to be found in what we call 'cities.' The sanitation, the education, the housing, the working and living conditions, the economic security—in brief, the general welfare of all its citizens—are American concerns, insofar as they are within the range of Federal power and responsibility under the Constitution." From this time on, concern with the city and attempts to order the urban environment would be a persistent feature of national policy.

The general impact of the depression on the great cities is a well-chronicled subject in American history. Cities had frightening unemployment, sometimes reaching 50 per cent in large industrial centers. The relief agencies that had been efficiently organized into community chests and similar agencies in accord with the scientific philanthropy of the 1920s quickly exhausted their funds, as relief costs rose seven-fold between 1929 and 1932 and the number of unemployed increased from 1,864,000 to 15,653,000. Malnutrition, disease, and even starvation stalked the cities. The depression, in addition to these general effects, also had special urban aspects. Housing in cities had always been inadequate, and for a century housing reformers had been demanding changes. Now conditions suddenly worsened. Building nearly came to a halt in many places. Repairs were not made. Slums expanded. Between 1928 and 1933 construction of residential property fell 95 per cent; the amount spent annually on housing repairs dropped from fifty-million dollars to half a million. A study of sixteen Illinois cities showed that the amount of building based on an index of 100 for the years 1921–1929 had fallen to an average of 6.4 in 1933 and stood at 4.2 in Chicago. The prolonged crisis in building was particularly significant for, traditionally, a revival in construction was expected to stimulate the recovery from a depression. Also critical was the problem of foreclosures. In 1932, 273,000 people lost their homes; during the next year a thousand homes a day were being foreclosed. "The literally thousands of heart-breaking instances of inability of working people to attain renewal of expiring mortgages on favorable terms, and the consequent loss of their homes, have been one of the tragedies of this depression," wrote Herbert Hoover.

Much of the early legislation designed to cope with the problem of depression in the cities was of an emergency nature: provide employment and relief funds. Grants for these purposes, extended via a variety of federal agencies and programs created during the first hectic years of depression, were generally administered by local governments. Even though the federal government through Social Security and the like assumed some of the welfare functions earlier performed by the political machine, big-city machines and bosses, contrary to the popular view, may actually have been strengthened in the New Deal era, because they were able to gain control of federal relief and recovery programs on the local scene. The effort to provide relief led to the creation of an important agency for the expression of urban demands. The attempt of Frank Murphy, mayor of Detroit (a city particularly hard-hit by the depression), to gain federal assistance was instrumental in the organization of the United States Conference of Mayors in 1933. In addition to coalescing urban demands over the years, the organization eventually became a vehicle by which big-city mayors could try to become national political figures.

Early in the depression, the federal government also attempted to deal with the emergency of foreclosures. In July, 1932, at the urging of President Hoover, Congress had established twelve Federal Home Loan Banks to lend funds to building and loan associations, banks, and other mortgage agencies whose credit had been nearly exhausted. Hoover, like many policy makers in the administration of his successor Franklin D. Roosevelt, was committed to the ideal of a nation of homeowners. "To possess one's own home," Hoover told a housing conference in 1931, "is the hope and ambition of almost every individual in our country, whether he lives in hotel, apartment, or tenement. . . . Those immortal ballads, *Home, Sweet Home, My Old Kentucky Home,* and *The Little Gray Home in the West,* were not written about tenements or apartments . . . they never sing songs about a pile of rent receipts." The Home Loan Bank plan was designed to foster "the home ownership aspiration" and "to revitalize the building of homes," but the program, which was tied fundamentally to the operation of the inadequate private housing market, had only limited success. The Roosevelt administration continued this policy and supplemented it with the Home Owners Loan Corporation in June 1933, which refinanced individual mortgages of home owners at long terms and low interest and permitted needed repair costs to be added to the loans. During its period of operation, ending in June 1936, the HOLC extended over a million loans and assumed about one-sixth of all home-mortgage indebtedness in cities. Largely as a result of this policy, foreclosures by 1937 had fallen to half of what they had been in 1933.

This program assisted the relatively well-to-do middle classes—those who could afford to buy houses in the first place. The same point could be made about a more permanent New Deal program enacted in June 1934 that created the Federal Housing Authority. This agency was authorized to insure loans made by private agencies for the construction, repair, and improvement of houses. In the long run, its activities, in addition to raising standards of construction, brought about significant changes in the system of financing American residential building: the length of mortgage loans was greatly extended, down payments were drastically reduced, the second mortgage was generally eliminated, and the single monthly payment on a mortgage, covering amortization of the loan, taxes, and insurance, became common. Between 1938 and 1941 the FHA was insuring 35 per cent of all mortgages. The National Housing Act of 1934, which set up the FHA, also created the Federal Savings and Loan Insurance Corporation to insure savings up to $5,000 in building-and-loan and saving-and-loan associations. Because these companies mainly extended mortgage loans, this provision also contributed to the stabilization and expansion of housing. These new procedures and policies—particularly after World War II—extended the possibilities of home ownership to a wider group in society and added impetus to suburban growth.

Concern with the cities was also reflected in the early stages of the recovery program. The Reconstruction Finance Corporation established during the Hoover Administration had power within its broad lending authority to make loans to private limited-dividend housing corporations. Although this program had little effect, its approach was continued during the Roosevelt administration by the Housing Division established in the Public Works Administration —a basic recovery agency of the early New Deal. The National Industrial Recovery Act of June 1933, establishing the PWA, authorized the agency to provide for "low rent housing and slum clearance projects." Initially, the Housing Division, reflecting the conservative cast of many New Deal efforts, attempted to carry out these programs through private enterprise. But owing in large part to the efforts of real estate interests to unload undesirable property in cities at high prices, only seven of the five hundred applications from limited-dividend corporations were approved by the government. Forced to abandon this method, in February 1934, the Housing Division moved directly into the management of slum clearance and low-cost housing projects. This effort encountered bitter resistance from private real estate interests. A federal circuit court decision in Kentucky in 1935 found the direct condemnation of property by the federal government an unconstitutional extension of the right of eminent domain. The decision forced the Housing Division thereafter to manage its projects through state or municipal authority, foreshadowing the character of the eventual permanent federal housing policy.

The Housing Division during its four and a half years of operation did engage in a number of significant individual projects. Eleven slum blocks in Atlanta were cleared and became the site of Techwood Homes. Lakeview Terrace succeeded Cleveland's Whiskey Island tenement-house area. Brooklyn's Williamsburg Houses replaced twelve slum blocks with modern apartments for 6,000 people. But on the whole this program represented a minimum effort. The PWA built or started forty-nine projects with less than 22,000 units. Over-all, this did relatively little to alleviate the problem of housing for the poor; administration leaders did not consider the program a success. "From what I saw and heard," Harold Ickes, head of the PWA, confessed in his diary after a tour of Chicago projects, "I was very much disappointed with the progress that has been made. There isn't any doubt that something is wrong in the Housing Division, in fact, has been wrong for a long time. We are not getting results."

During the course of the New Deal, federal policy embodied, on a limited scale for the most part, virtually all the approaches to housing that had been suggested by urban planners and reformers during the preceding twenty years: the conservative policies of mortgage insurance and loans to limited-dividend housing companies, as well as relatively more radical approaches of slum clearance and garden cities. Roosevelt himself, although quite willing to cultivate an urban constituency, had little interest in the programs of housing reformers concerned with the slum and improving cities, and showed more sympathy to the decentralization schemes of those who wanted people to get back to the land. In 1913 he had suggested that farms in the suburbs ought to be provided for city dwellers so that city life could be improved and cities made places "where people will be pretty proud to hail from." It is doubtful that he ever substantially modified this outlook, which after all was compatible with one important urban reform tradition represented by Brace, Olmsted, and many of the intellectuals in the Regional Planning Association of America. Rexford G. Tugwell, a Roosevelt "brain truster" who headed the Resettlement Administration, recalled in the fifties that Roosevelt "always did, and always would think people better off in the country and would regard the cities as rather hopeless."

Accordingly, although Roosevelt eventually came to its support, the major piece of New Deal housing legislation, the National Housing Act of September 1937 (the Wagner-Steagall Act), was not really an administration measure; it was supported by reformers in Congress concerned with housing, notably Senator Robert F. Wagner of New York. If Roosevelt had supported the bill, it would actually have become law one year earlier than it did. It had died in committee on the initial try when the administration did not endorse it. The United States Housing Authority created by the act took over the PWA projects and was authorized to make sixty-year loans at low interest to local public agencies for slum clearance and housing projects. Under its "equivalent elimination" provision, the law required that one unit of public housing had to be built for each unit of housing destroyed in slum clearance. Through this law, the slums of Chicago, San Antonio, Memphis, New Orleans, and a number of other places, came under attack. Of all the New Deal measures, this one may have been of most benefit to the urban Negro. Gunnar Myrdal declared, in his monumental study of Negro life, *An American Dilemma,* that the USHA gave Negroes "a better deal than has any other major federal public welfare agency." By 1941 the agency had made contracts for 511 low-rent public housing projects, providing a total of 161,162 units. Although the administrator of the USHA optimistically proclaimed in 1939 that "for the first time in a hundred years, the slums of America ceased growing and began to shrink," it is doubtful that New Deal public housing did more than ameliorate somewhat the problem of the slum. As with many of the earlier private efforts to provide better living conditions for the urban poor, many of the New Deal projects themselves rather quickly deteriorated into slums. But the act had established the precedent for action, and a permanent policy for urban renewal along these lines was provided after World War II.

The counterpart of slum removal was planned suburban development. Tugwell indicated the relationship when he wrote early in 1935: "My idea is to go just outside centers of population, pick up cheap land, build a whole community and entice people into it. Then go back into the cities and tear down whole slums and make parks of them." The presence of this viewpoint among government planners led to the most significant of the New Deal experiments involving urban life—the *greenbelt towns.* "In world-wide influence," writes Paul K. Conkin, "they rank high among New Deal accomplishments; in the field of public works they are hardly excelled, even by the Tennessee Valley Authority, in imagination, in breaking with precedents, and in broad social objectives. They represented, and still do represent, the most daring, original, and ambitious experiments in public housing in the history of the United States." The greenbelt towns were an attempt to create the Howard-type garden city in America. But as it developed, the greenbelt program drew on the whole nineteenth-century American tradition of suburb and park planning plus, in Tugwell's view, the demographic evidence of suburban growth. The greenbelt towns were to be decentralized communities of varying size and function, located outside of metropolitan centers, designed in accord with the best theories of professional planners, sustained by preservation of a natural setting, built by the government but leased to local cooperatives made up of residents. Supporters of the greenbelt towns argued that they would not only help solve the housing problem of the city but would also help provide an answer to the problem of the urban slum. Tugwell optimistically hoped that 3,000 of the communities could be built in America. After initial study by the Resettlement Administration, which had been established in June 1935, twenty-five cities were selected for location of the towns. Roosevelt approved eight projects, but Congressional cuts in appropriations reduced the number to five. A St. Louis greenbelt town was eliminated because of opposition from a local housing commission. A New Jersey project called Greenbrook, designed by Henry Wright of Radburn as a self-sufficient industrial community and closest of all the towns to the Howard ideal, was stopped by injunction proceedings in the courts. In the end, three greenbelt towns were built: Greenbelt at Berwyn, Maryland seven miles from Washington, D. C.; Greenhills near Cincinnati; and Greendale outside Milwaukee. Limited funds hampered the establishment of the communities; none of them was as large as planned. They were continually fought by real estate interests, and after the decision involving Greenbrook, such a threat hung over them that it was clear that no more projects could be initiated. They were denounced as "communist towns" and were perhaps one of the most bitterly hated New Deal experiments. After World War II they were sold at a great loss by the government. Yet, during the late New Deal period, for those concerned with the quality of urban life they provided a vision of a better future that might lie ahead if only systematic planning could be applied to the town, the city, and the region. They were visited by 1,200,000 people during the first year of operation, and European planners consistently praised them. A government housing expert, Tracy B. Augur, conveyed the enthusiasm of those associated with the project when he remarked that the greenbelt towns signalled "the birth of an urban nation."

But providing an attractive environment for only 2,267 families can hardly be considered that significant, and perhaps the greenbelt towns only suggested what might have been. Despite the accolades of planners and intellectuals, they were never quite the idyllic communities they were portrayed to be. It was true that the towns were well designed and provided excellent housing. The initial residents, who were young, averaging about thirty years at the start, plunged into community projects with a good deal of energy and drive. But as was often the case with Utopian ventures in America, particularly those not sustained by religious zeal, the enthusiasm faded. Reaction set in against rules and regulations, the frequent meetings that proved necessary, and the excessive sociability life in the towns entailed. The towns also faced a problem that became common in all types of subsidized housing. The income limits imposed meant that they would be occupied by a restricted societal group—in this instance those with low to moderate incomes, not the very poor. The towns attracted many young people with considerable ability, and when they reached the upper-income limits, as many of them did, they were forced to move. This caused resentment in some instances; even if it did not, the requirement contributed to a feeling of impermanence in the towns. The towns did not provide a demonstration project (like the TVA in the field of electric power) of how good housing could be furnished at a reasonable cost. This had been the intention, but the projects proved expensive to construct, with unit costs ranging from about $15,400 at Greenbelt to $16,600 at Greendale. At the rental rates of 1941, it would have taken three hundred years to pay for the cost of Greenbelt, even if interest on the debt were disregarded. The greenbelt towns, as their historian Joseph L. Arnold observes, "cut so deeply against the American grain" that their quick liquidation after World War II caused no furor. The three thousand towns that Tugwell had proposed might have provided one answer to the problem of inadequate housing in America, but considering the costs involved, it was virtually inconceivable that such a plan could have won support. The American tradition of private property, so fundamental in shaping the history of American cities, had once again defeated attempts to provide a better kind of community. The same point might be extended to the whole of the New Deal program insofar as it dealt with cities, for its accomplishments in improving urban life were singularly limited. In the end, perhaps what was most important during this era was the recognition in federal policy that the city was here to stay and that it could be a positive force in American culture. "Surely in the long run," asserted the National Resources Committee, "the Nation's destiny will be profoundly affected by the cities which have two-thirds of its population and its wealth. There is liberty of development in isolation and wide spaces, but there is also freedom in the many-sided life of the city where each may find his own kind. There is democracy in the scattered few, but there is also democracy in the thick crowd with its vital impulse and its insistent demand for a just participation in the gains of our civilization."

Much of the New Deal's planning in regard to cities was based on the view that urban population in the future would be stable or would even decline. Scholars who influenced national policy argued that the falling birth rate of the 1930s combined with the increasing proportion of people in cities meant that city growth could no longer be sustained by migration from the farm. But the prediction, although it was based on a mass of statistical evidence, proved dead wrong. With the end of World War II and the continuance of a long era of general prosperity, American cities once again began another great period of growth. In these years a number of urban programs became a permanent part of federal policy. Although there was recognition that the national government had to be involved in the improvement of life in cities, the programs designed to carry out this commitment from 1945 to the early 1970s were insufficient, often worked at cross purposes, and could not, from the perspective of the mid-seventies, be considered successful.

World War II had effects on the physical environment in American cities similar to those of World War I. Housing had been inadequate beforehand; wartime reallocations produced an acute housing shortage. Accordingly, housing reformers once again won a hearing for their argument: a large-scale national program was necessary if something was to be done about the "one-third of the nation ill-housed." The proposals for postwar reconstruction that began to be formulated fairly early in the war often contained programs for public housing, slum clearance, model communities, and city and regional planning. But there was substantial opposition in the American business community to any scheme that seemed to interfere with the workings of the private real estate market. Opponents of the New Deal in the Seventy-Eighth Congress elected in 1942 were strong enough to kill the National Resources Planning Board. This agency, which had sponsored the report on

"Our Cities," conducted wartime demonstration projects through which three cities, Corpus Christi, Salt Lake City, and Tacoma, obtained federal assistance in drawing up comprehensive plans for growth and development. It had also been generally responsible for formulating urban programs in the Roosevelt Administration. Roosevelt did not resist the demise of the board. Instead, he rather shrewdly took political advantage of the circumstance to shift some of the responsibility for postwar planning to Congress itself. As a consequence of Congressional inquiry and the continuing efforts of housing reformers, there was some recognition in Congress at the end of the war that the federal government would have to assume a fairly substantial responsibility for the problems of cities.

In the immediate postwar period, President Harry S. Truman, who had succeeded Roosevelt in 1945 after the latter's death, included a demand for public housing and slum clearance in his comprehensive program of domestic reform called the Fair Deal. In part, Truman had political motives; he recognized the importance to the Democratic Party of the urban middle- and lower-class constituency that Roosevelt had forged. But Truman's biographers tend to accept that his frequently professed sympathy for the underdog and the common man was reasonably genuine, that he did believe—in spite of turnings and shiftings on the matter—in the necessity and wisdom of providing everyone an adequate place in which to live. "A decent standard of housing for all is one of the irreducible obligations of modern civilization," he declared in a message to Congress. "The people of the United States, so far ahead in wealth and production capacity, deserve to be the best housed people in the world. We must begin to meet that challenge at once."

Truman's housing bill, like all parts of his Fair Deal, encountered sharp resistance. The private-housing industry launched a concerted attack against the parts of the bill providing for public housing. Slum clearance aroused less opposition, because it was recognized that this program, as proved to be the case, could be profitable to a number of interests involved in the private real estate market. But public housing was "European socialism in its most insidious form," and "the cutting edge of the Communist front." The bill was before Congress for four years. It was only after Truman's dramatic upset victory in 1948, which expanded his political strength, that the bill finally passed, and then only by a razor-thin margin, as a key vote in the House carried by a margin of only five. In the end, of decisive importance was the support of conservative members of Congress like the influential Senator Robert A. Taft, who saw a national condition of "no room at the inn," as the housing expert Charles Abrams put it, as contrary to Christian principles. "I do not believe that public housing is socialism," Taft told Abrams, "if it is confined to the furnishing of decent housing only to that group unable to provide housing by its own means. We have long recognized the duty of the state to give relief and free medical care for those unable to pay it, and I think shelter is just as important as relief and medical care." In advancing

similar sentiments on another occasion, he concluded, "All of us acknowledge the duty of the community to take care of those who are unable to
take care of themselves." But this did not imply that Taft accepted the view
of many reformers that housing was a right of citizenship or that the federal
government should begin the systematic reconstruction of either the physical
or social environment of cities. Taft reflected a very old tradition of Christian
responsibility in the urban community. The pervasiveness of this tradition,
noble though it may be, meant that public housing and similar programs
tended to be viewed as a form of charity, a circumstance that limited the
effectiveness of any policy aimed at reordering the way of life in cities.

Still, the National Housing Act of 1949, which proved to be about the only
part of Truman's Fair Deal enacted, did provide a national commitment to the
principle of federal reconstruction of cities and public housing. A national
goal, the act stated, should be to provide as soon as it was feasible "a decent
home and a suitable living environment for every American family." Truman
recognized the importance and the implications of the act's statement of a
national housing policy. "Here, for the first time in our history," he wrote,
"is a declaration by the people of the United States, through their Congress,
that every American, regardless of his income or origin, is entitled to an
opportunity to obtain decent housing. It is one of the most significant actions
taken by the Congress in recent years."

The initial enthusiasm of housing reformers over this measure proved excessive. The national housing policy stated in the act has never been retracted,
although in the early 1970s the Nixon Administration perhaps came close to
doing so in the way it administered certain programs. But never have the
means been provided to carry out the commitment of the policy. The act
authorized the building of 810,000 units of public housing over a six-year
period, which was only a small fraction of the total housing needed, and, as
it turned out, it was actually twenty years before this figure was reached. As
in the New Deal housing measures, public housing in the 1949 act was tied to
slum clearance and rebuilding, or *urban development,* as it was now termed.
The "equivalent elimination" provision of the 1937 act was not included, and
this meant that in practice the relatively popular slum-clearance part of the
program would receive more emphasis than the furnishing of new housing.
The act also followed another procedure established during the 1930s—the
administration of programs by local housing or renewal authorities. These
were officially called local public authorities and were frequently referred to
technically as the LPA. Ordinarily, the LPA could not be the city government
itself, but it could be a part of the city government, or a separately created
agency. The LPA in charge of urban development had the power of eminent
domain. Its purchase of slum properties was financed by the federal government in large part, through grants-in-aid up to two-thirds of the amount. This
subsidy permitted the cleared land then to be sold to a private developer at
a marked-down, level-of-the market price. Even the worst slum properties, of

course, were worth much more than the cleared land; in fact, the rate of return to the owner could be high. Government, in short, was making up the difference between the value of the slum properties and the land on which they stood. Cities presumably would retrieve their one-third share through increased taxes on the redeveloped properties. The federal grant, in effect, constituted a subsidy to the private developer (in the form of a marked-down price for the land) to rebuild areas formerly occupied by slums. Public housing projects would be built by private firms, not the government itself, through contracts with the local housing authority administering the federal grant for this purpose. In short, the Housing Act of 1949, especially in its urban redevelopment aspect, was intended to operate within the structure of the private real estate market. The act also respected the principle of local control. But this approach—continued fundamentally in later revisions of the act and supplemental programs—contributed to serious problems in the program. Local administration under federal standards and controls meant complicated procedures and much red tape before any renewal or housing project could be carried through all its stages from submission to completion. More important, local administration meant that powerful local economic interests could readily influence renewal programs and policies. Accordingly, there were early significant shifts away from the original intent of the law. For example, proponents of the measure had assumed that public housing projects would be built on a substantial part of the renewed sites, but of the first fifty-four urban redevelopment projects, only three actually provided public housing for those evicted from the areas.

During the first years, in fact, the entire program of public housing, for a number of reasons, hardly got started. The pick-up in private residential construction after the war alleviated the national housing shortage that had been the main reason for passage of the program. Nearly three and a half million units were built in the period 1946–1949; an all-time high in residential construction was reached in 1950 when 1,396,000 units were built. This took much of the impetus out of any drive for public housing, which was, moreover, being continually resisted by local interests and also by national trade associations of the building industry. The coming of the Korean War and the conservative bent of Truman's successor, Dwight D. Eisenhower, contributed to the institution of yearly quotas on the number of public housing units that could be built, starting at 50,000 in 1951 and declining to 35,000 units in 1954.

The direction of federal policy from this time on was toward a primary emphasis on slum clearance (under its various changing names) rather than on public housing. But the slum clearance program also moved slowly, partly, of course, because it tended to be associated with the controversial housing program. The newness of the program also caused delay. Procedures were complicated, and it required a great deal of local initiative and organization to get a project going. Moreover, it took time for entrepreneurs to discover that the program could be highly profitable. Accordingly, the amount of slum property eliminated remained relatively small. In the first twenty years that a federal program was in effect, 1934 to 1954, 400,000 substandard units of housing were eliminated, but this constituted only 7 per cent of the substandard units existing in metropolitan areas in 1950. A Presidential committee appointed to look into the matter, and made up primarily of businessmen, reported in 1953: "If we continue only at the present rate of clearance and rely on demolition alone to eliminate slums, it will take us something over two hundred years to do the job."

The Housing Act of 1954, a revision of the 1949 law, represented an attempt to speed up slum clearance through making the federal program more flexible. Ten per cent of the renewal grants, for example, could now be used for nonresidential projects, and this was raised to 35 per cent in later revisions —a procedure that made renewal areas more attractive to developers. The act substituted "urban renewal" for "urban development"; the change in terminology was intended to indicate a new approach, that of restoring property in slum neighborhoods rather than simply leveling an entire area. The destruction of the housing of the poor without providing anything in its place had led to harsh criticism of the program. The act also required that a "workable program for community improvement" (formally termed the Workable Program) be a part of every urban renewal project. The Workable Program imposed seven basic requirements, involving such matters as a land-use plan, zoning measures, provision for the relocation of displaced families, building codes, and citizen participation. By the end of the first year of the new act, seventy-six Workable Programs had been approved. This brought the total number of slum clearance projects under both acts to 340 in 218 cities. Some work had been done on 216 of these, but only nine relatively minor projects had been completed.

Owing in part to the generous mortgage guarantees provided by the FHA for urban renewal projects, there was considerable movement of private real estate interests into the program in the late 1950s. At the same time, the liberal coalition that had supported federal housing, urban reconstruction, and other New and Fair Deal measures began to break apart. Both urban renewal and federal housing came under sharp attack. Spokesmen of the rapidly growing Negro communities in large cities argued that Negro neighborhoods were being destroyed in order to erect upper-class white, high-rise apartments and luxurious shopping centers, and that the program of urban renewal was actually a program of "Negro removal." Some urban reformers argued that model communities in the style of the greenbelt towns should be built away from the central cities, that urban renewal was intensifying the problem of urban congestion. But the few tentative efforts to place public housing in suburbs evoked the most vigorous resistance of all. Others, most notably Jane Jacobs in an influential study, *The Death and Life of Great American Cities*, argued for the wisdom of preserving the character of old big-city neighborhoods. The communities of the planners, with their high-rise apartments, limited lines of movement, and excessive open spaces, inherently led, Jacobs asserted, to a lack of neighborliness and a breakdown of a natural system of order. Spokesmen of the American left began their movement from faith in the good works of government toward distrust of the power of government. Ironically, they tended to accept an old conservative position that the free market might be the best mechanism for supplying housing. The poor could be aided in the free market, they suggested, with direct rent subsidies. Specialized studies of the effects of urban renewal on people demonstrated that slum clearance often destroyed well-functioning neighborhoods, not areas where crime and other social problems flourished. There was concern that many of the early public housing projects, like the succession of model tenements of the nineteenth century, seemed to be rapidly turning into slums themselves. Many reformers in the housing movement began to deliver their farewells to reform. A former public housing official in the late 1950s reflected this disillusion: "Once upon a time we thought that if we could only get our problem families out of those dreadful slums, then papa would stop taking dope, mama would stop chasing around, and Junior would stop carrying a knife. Well we've got them in a nice new apartment with modern kitchens and a recreational center. And they're still the same bunch of bastards they always were." Several critics argued that public housing in effect represented an institutionalization of the slum. Harrison Salisbury of *The New York Times,* used the rhetorical style of a Jacob Riis—perhaps deliberately—to describe Fort Greene, a public housing project in New York. He had been used to seeing shoddy housing in Moscow, he noted:

But, until I visited Fort Greene I had never seen elevators used by children as public toilets. I never imagined that I could find the equivalent of Moscow's newly built slums in the United States. But I have made that unfortunate discovery at Fort Greene and other places. The same shoddy shiftlessness, the broken windows, the missing light bulbs, the plaster cracking from the walls, the pilfered hardware, the cold, drafty corridors, the doors on sagging hinges, the acid smell of sweat and cabbage, the ragged children, the plaintive women, the playgrounds that are seas of muddy clay, the bruised and battered trees, the ragged clumps of grass, the planned absence of art, beauty or taste, the gigantic masses of brick, of concrete, of asphalt, the inhuman genius with which our know-how has been perverted to create human cesspools worse than those of yesterday.

The rhetoric of the 1950s obscured certain realities that did not become apparent until later. Although the statistics are subject to varying interpretations, it is reasonably clear that for the nation as a whole and particularly for metropolitan areas, housing conditions did improve during the decade. The percentage of substandard housing declined, and there was an actual reduction in the number of people living in substandard housing; the number of families in these may have been reduced by about 40 per cent during the decade. Although there was little decline in the number of "dilapidated" housing units standing, which represented about a fourth of all substandard housing (*substandard* being a broader category, which includes unsatisfactory facilities such as plumbing), the number of dilapidated housing units actually occupied by residents decreased from 3,709,000 to 3,485,000. But this was slow progress. Slums still stood. In 1960, one-eighth of the nation's households lived in officially substandard dwellings. The census definition of *substandard* was imprecise and clearly represented a conservative assessment of what was unsatisfactory. Housing experts felt that the figure should be doubled, that at least one-fourth of the American people in 1960 lived in inadequate housing or in housing located in an inadequate environment.

Accordingly, the Democratic presidents of the 1960s, committed more or less to New Deal, Fair Deal principles, once again initiated programs directed toward the problems of the city. John F. Kennedy's statement of aims for his brave New Frontier gave a high priority to the cities. "The scourge of blight must be overcome, and the central cores of our cities, with all their great richness of economic and cultural wealth, must be restored to lasting vitality. . . . We neglect our cities at our peril, for in neglecting them we neglect the nation." In his appeal for the enactment of Kennedy's proposal for a Department of Housing and Urban Development, his successor Lyndon B. Johnson provided an eloquent message on the city as a center of civilization. Its rhetoric evoked so many themes from America's long urban past that it bears quoting at length:

Finance and culture, commerce and government make their home in the city and draw vitality from it. Within the borders of our urban centers can be found the most impressive achievements of man's skill and the highest expression of man's spirit, as well as the worst examples of degradation and cruelty and misery to be found in modern America.

The city is not an assembly of shops and buildings. It is not a collection of goods and services. It is a community for the enrichment of the life of man. It is a place for the satisfaction of man's most urgent needs and his highest aspirations. It is an instrument for the advance of civilization. Our task is to put the highest concerns of our people at the center of urban growth and activity. It is to create and preserve the sense of community with others which gives us significance and security, a sense of belonging and of sharing in the common life.

Aristotle said: "Men come together in cities in order to live. They remain together in order to live the good life."

The modern city can be the most ruthless enemy of the good life, or can be its servant. The choice is up to this generation of Americans. For this is truly the time of decision for the American city.

That Johnson's ideological commitment to the city went very deep is doubtful. In contradiction to the classical view of his message, he was reported as telling someone that he could never understand why anyone would want to cram himself into a place like New York when there were still such great unoccupied spaces in his native Texas. Still, the 1960s, and particularly the period of the Johnson Administration, did see the passage of significant new legislation in regard to the cities. The Housing and Urban Development Act of 1965 finally established a cabinet department of Housing and Urban Development; urban reformers had been voicing a demand for this since at least the turn of the century. Kennedy had proposed the measure, but his insistence that he would appoint a Negro to the post alienated southern Democrats, and it was held up in Congress. In accord with growing liberal opposition to bureaucracy and centralized power, revisions of existing urban programs during this period emphasized local participation and control. A number of new agencies, Volunteers in Service to America (Vista), Neighborhood Youth Corps, and Head Start were intended to foster the participation of local neighborhoods, particularly Negro neighborhoods, in the process of urban reconstruction. The Demonstration Cities and Metropolitan Development Act of 1966 provided for demonstration city projects, later called model cities. These were theoretically to be urban renewal projects that involved social as well as physical reconstruction of cities, projects that applied to whole neighborhoods, not just selective sites. Indicating the legacy of old ideas of urban reform and the contradictions that were always a part of federal urban policy, the act also provided support for the building of greenbelt-type towns; in publicizing this feature of the act, Johnson Administration spokesmen explicitly evoked the early nineteenth-century vision of Ebenezer Howard. The law established procedures, made more generous in 1968 legislation, that permitted the FHA to guarantee loans for land acquisition for these communities, and also for providing such basic physical facilities as streets, water systems, and sewers. The first loan guarantee of $21,000,000 went to developers of the new town of Jonathan, Minnesota, to be located twenty miles southwest of Minneapolis. By early in 1972, a hundred million dollars in loans had been guaranteed on five other projects: near Washington, D. C., Chicago, Little Rock, Dallas-Ft. Worth, and within Minneapolis city limits. It was estimated at that time that the six new towns when fully developed would contain 400,000 residents. This program involved federal response to the growing interest in the mid-1960s in building new towns which private real-estate entrepreneurs had stimulated through such examples as the relatively successful, ambitious city of Columbia, built near Washington in Maryland, and the less successful community of nearby Reston, Virginia.

In the middle of the 1960s, scholars, politicians, and spokesmen of popular opinion expressed optimism and enthusiasm over the possibility that federal programs and new federal relationships with local governments might significantly improve the quality of life in American cities. There was talk of an "urban renaissance" as a number of early urban renewal projects, which dramatically improved the appearance of many downtowns, were finally completed. Considerable private building also seemed to promise the beginning of a dynamic period of city development. Johnson's concept of "creative federalism" indicated the possibility of a more direct, much closer, and more efficient relationship between cities and the federal government. But the large-scale urban riots of the summer of 1966, which followed two summers of lesser rioting, and the nation-wide urban holocaust of 1967 indicated the superficiality of some of the earlier evaluation. The expansion and enlargement of the Viet Nam War diverted resources and interest from the concerns of the city. By 1970 popular magazines and newspapers no longer saw the dawn of a bright new urban era.

Nor was the change in national administration in 1969 beneficial to the cities. Richard M. Nixon owed little politically to a big-city constituency and had seldom expressed direct interest in urban concerns. His administration systematically cut back on urban programs of the past wherever feasible, including completely ending in 1974, by executive order, any new public housing programs. During his abbreviated second term, Nixon took the public position that urban renewal, model cities, and similar programs provided a record of consistent failure. And evidence emerged that the localized, neighborhood renewal approach of the 1960s had added something new to federal urban programs—corruption. The national scandal of Watergate obscured a much more traditional scandal, one which reached into the federal bureaucracy. It involved misappropriation of funds for parts of local model cities programs and, particularly, large-scale dishonesty in the marketing of renovated houses in the poor areas of several cities, made possible through the collusion of FHA officials administering the generous mortgage guarantee provisions of the legislation of the 1960s. The most significant action taken by the Nixon administration was the sponsorship of "revenue sharing," which was established in the State and Local Assistance Act of 1972. The law provided for the dispersal of over $30 billion over a five-year period to state and local governments. Two-thirds of the amount was to go to the latter to be expended in any or all of nine priority areas: public safety, protection of the environment, transportation, health, recreation, libraries, services for the poor and aged, financial administration, and capital expenditures. The one-third for state governments could be used for any legal purpose. The United States Conference of Mayors had vigorously advocated this approach to urban problems, because it allowed the flexibility of expending funds without federal controls other than the requirements of reporting and avoiding discrimination. But despite this advantage, in the light of an administration policy of cutting back on spending, it appeared that the short-range result might be the curtailment of some reasonably well-functioning federal urban programs and a reduction in total resources available. By 1974 an emphasis on local flexibility in the use of broad federal grants had also won considerable support in Congress.

The urban programs of the 1960s and early 1970s did perhaps involve significant innovations and new directions in federal policy, but their effect cannot be predicted. Nor can they yet be judged historically in relation to the programs of the past. Still, one can offer tentative suggestions about this era, that now extends some thirty years into our past, of large-scale federal concern with the city.

First, the programs of urban reconstruction were only a small part of the federal actions that influenced the way cities developed or changed the patterns of life within them. For example, the policy of public school desegregation and its rigorous enforcement accelerated white migration to suburbs, contributed to the higher proportion of blacks in central cities, and intensified resistance to black suburbanization. As it had in World War I, the federal government virtually built whole new cities where a clearly defined national undertaking was involved: Oak Ridge, Tennessee, and other sites for the development of atomic energy; Cape Canaveral, Florida, the space center. Beginning with the Water Pollution Control Act of 1948, which supported research and planning, the federal government became involved with the problem of environmental pollution in cities. Grants-in-aid for the treatment of water pollution were provided in 1956; an Air Pollution Research Act was passed in 1955 and expanded four years later. By the early 1970s control of pollution had become one of the most important federal urban programs, and obviously one that might determine the ultimate fate of American cities. Federal urban programs (the kind that had roots in the nineteenth century) giving aid to transportation projects and to river and harbor improvements were greatly expanded in the post-World War II period. Grants-in-aid for the construction of airports, hospitals, and schools became a standard feature of federal urban policy. A program of federal support of highway construction had particularly important effects, effects that ran counter to the purposes of reconstruction programs. Although the federal government had supported highway construction since 1916, no funds for this purpose were granted to cities until 1944. The support provided then was greatly expanded in the Federal Highway Act of 1956, which established the Interstate System of roads with expressways through cities designed as links in the system. Expressways required enormous amounts of land, and their large-scale construction, particularly in the 1960s, destroyed vast areas of housing and ruthlessly eliminated the neighborhoods of the poor. Assistance in relocating those displaced was authorized in legislation of 1962 and 1968. But assistance was limited, and local authorities, in some instances, simply ignored the laws. The program, of course, accelerated decentralization of cities, contributed to urban sprawl, and intensified the contention between suburb and city. By the 1970s the many critics of the urban highway program had won considerable support for their arguments: that the program was too expensive, that the funds could have been better spent in a large-scale program of renewing cities, that there was more need of public transportation than of additional highways, and that the whole approach had prevented realization of many of the aims of urban renewal programs.

Secondly, it is clear that public housing represented a failure of federal urban policy. This was especially significant, because it was the idealistic aim

of providing decent housing for all that had led to large-scale federal involvement in the cities. Although an unusual figure, such as the powerful New
York planner, Robert Moses, might be able to take advantage of the program
and actually build considerable public housing, in most places vigorous local
resistance sharply limited the extent of the effort. Public housing never escaped
its stigma of charity. In the whole era of public housing, from 1933 to 1970,
only 893,500 units of housing were completed, and a substantial number of
these, 143,400, were for the aged. In fact, the concept of public housing had
become so discredited by 1974 that liberal architect Peter Blake could write,
in probable reflection of the sentiments of many intellectuals: "Housing projects have got to be the very worst way of solving our housing problems."

Thirdly, urban renewal was more successful than public housing, but the
program was still subject to much valid criticism. Over the years, urban
renewal had resulted in the elimination of hundreds of square miles of slums
in cities. But most of the projects had been directed toward central business
districts, and many of them resulted in "city beautiful"-type public centers,
such as Charles Center in Baltimore, Boston's Government Center, and Constitution Plaza in Hartford. These were symbolically important; they contributed to a spirit of urban revival in a number of places. But in a narrow sense,
they tended to benefit a rather small and affluent segment of society. And
this led to harsh judgments of the program. The urban historian and student
of housing, Sam B. Warner, writes, for example: "The refurbished downtowns,
sports stadia, new government and corporate office towers, and slabs of
high-rise luxury apartments which typically characterize big-city urban renewal
stand in shameless witness to the callousness of American class and race relations. The well-to-do have spent ten billion dollars to decorate their central
cities for their own use and benefit while pushing perhaps a comparable
social and economic cost off upon the low-income third of the population.
Urban renewal is now a social and political scandal."

In August 1973, the Department of Housing and Urban Development announced a decision that seemed to have special symbolic importance to the
history of federal urban policy. For the first time, the federal government was
simply abandoning a public housing project, Pruitt-Igoe in St. Louis. Twenty
years earlier, Pruitt-Igoe, which was part of the renewal of some of the country's worst slums, had been widely hailed as a sign of the renaissance of a
fine old American city. Pruitt-Igoe had been widely praised for its progressive
design; its architect, for example, had carefully provided for galleries intended
to serve as play areas for children and places where good neighbors would
convivially gather. But the galleries were soon padlocked; Pruitt-Igoe—for a
number of reasons inherent in the prevailing scheme of public housing—degenerated into a center of crime, violence, and filth. When the decision to
abandon the project was announced, only 340 of 2,800 apartments were
occupied. The dynamiting of the buildings of Pruitt-Igoe perhaps marked the
ending of the hope that American society, at least under its existing values

and social structure, could supply decent housing to the nation's less affluent citizens. The agencies of private enterprise and private philanthropy could not do it in the nineteenth century; if the experience of forty years has been indicative, perhaps the federal government could not do it in the twentieth.

CHAPTER

# 15

# Suburbs and Super-Cities: The Contemporary Era

IN A WORK called *Anticipations* published in 1902 during a stage of world urbanization characterized by great metropolitan growth, H. G. Wells, the popular English historian, novelist, and writer of science-fiction, had prophesied that in the future town and city would no longer have meaning for society, that particularly in America men would live in "urban regions." An area from Washington, D. C. to Albany, for example, would constitute a natural suburb for the resident of New York or Philadelphia. It could not be said with certainty in the mid-1970s whether Wells was right or not, for the contours of a complex, dynamic, rapidly changing urban society could not be drawn with precision. This was not for lack of information; in the period after World War II, the city, as in the late nineteenth century, became a preoccupation of scholars and popular writers, and data accumulated. Congress passed laws regarding cities, and their provisions and effects were reasonably clear. Statistics of housing, urban renewal, and urban crime were carefully gathered. The number of people killed and the amount of property destroyed in another series of urban riots were counted up. But the ideological and political concerns of our own time warped reflections on most urban matters. Accordingly, the larger dimensions of continuity and change in cities, which form the province of the urban historian, could only be dimly sensed, and the shape of things to come, so much the interest of Wells the futurist, could hardly be sensed at all. Still, it appeared that what Wells anticipated might supply a central theme of American urban history in the late twentieth century.

After World War II, as a great urban boom was getting underway, airline pilots observing streams of ground lights began to note that large cities in the northeastern part of the United States were being joined together by ribbons of substantial settlement. Similar development occurred in more compactly settled Europe. By late in the 1950s, students of urbanization had begun to speculate on the emergence of the urban region, the *conurbation*, or more commonly the *megalopolis*. The latter term is a Greek word, meaning simply big city, which had been coined as a name for a cultural and administrative center organized in 371 B.C. to unite a number of smaller cities of Arcadia. The term was popularized by Jean Gottman, a geographer, through a book with that title published in 1961. It was quickly absorbed into the lexicon of social science, but urban students of humanist persuasion occasionally pointed out that the use of the word had suggestive implications. Oswald Spengler had seen the growth of megalopolis as a token of the decline of the West, and the highly influential planner and student of the city, Patrick Geddes, had developed a scheme of stages of city growth, utilized by Lewis Mumford, in which megalopolis represented a preliminary to the final stage of urban development, *necropolis,* the city of the dead. Viewing what seemed to be a major crisis of the city, many critics of society in the 1960s suggested directly or implicitly that necropolis had already arrived in America.

In his influential study, Gottman did not apply the word *megalopolis* in any general sense, but used it precisely as the name for a region of settlement extending from Boston southward to Washington, D. C., which formed a "continuous system of deeply interwoven urban and suburban areas." Not all the area was urbanized of course, nor was much of it densely settled, he pointed out, but there were no traditional rural areas in the region. Many areas that at first might look rural actually contained industrial sites and residences and served as "suburbs in the orbit of some city's downtown." The people living there had little to do with agriculture except in a casual sense; in their work and activities they were tied to the city. Cities within the region functioned not only in relationship to hinterlands but also in relationship to other cities. It was impossible to identify numerous communities in the region as definite suburbs or satellites of any one city. In short, the old conceptions of metropolis and hinterland, of city and country, of rural and urban did not apply to Megalopolis, the "Main street of the nation." In the 1960s it became clear that two similar regions of settlement, and they were generally called megalopolises, were beginning to emerge—one extending from Chicago to Pittsburgh and the other from San Francisco to San Diego. In the same period, Megalopolis itself was observed to be growing, northward to Portland, Maine, and southward to Richmond, Virginia.

The megalopolis represented a change from past physical patterns of urban settlement. Whether or not it represented a change in function from the metropolitan pattern that was central to twentieth-century urbanization was more debatable and depended to a considerable extent on the framework of analysis. There were, for example, a number of special economic characteristics of the megalopolis that could be pointed to: considerable sharing of business among many urban centers; highly specialized economic facilities dispersed through the region; relatively low population densities; and an array of land uses including shopping centers, industrial parks, and varying residential suburbs occupied along class lines. But these characteristics resulted from forces and trends that much earlier had begun to transform the patterns of urban settlement. To some degree megalopolises represented an overlapping of established metropolitan settlements. A 1961 study listed thirteen of these extended metropolitan regions or "strip cities" as they were sometimes called: Boston to Washington, D. C., Albany to Erie, Cleveland to Pittsburgh, Toledo to Cincinnati, Detroit to Muskegon, Chicago-Gary to Milwaukee, St. Louis to Peoria, Seattle to Eugene, San Francisco to San Diego, Kansas City to Sioux Falls, Fort Worth-Dallas-San Antonio-Houston, Miami-Tampa-Jacksonville, and Atlanta to Raleigh. In 1960 they contained half the population of the country, and nearly 55 per cent of the total volume of retail trade was transacted there.

In the most basic sense, these new forms of urban settlement were the result of population changes—of urbanization and suburbanization as demographic concepts. The basic population trends in the period after World War II represented an acceleration or an intensification of the trends that had created the metropolitan pattern of settlement of the first half of the twentieth century: (1) a rapid growth in total population, brought about now by an increase in the birth rate—the familiar postwar "baby boom"—not by foreign immigration as in the past, (2) a tendency for this increase in population to be concentrated in the large metropolitan areas—a result in part of migration from less settled areas as in the past, but also the result now of a natural increase in population in cities themselves, (3) more rapid growth on the periphery than in the centers of metropolitan areas—i.e. suburbanization in a demographic sense.

Again, as in the first half of the century, simple population statistics compiled after the decennial national censuses recorded the broad dimensions of the changes occurring in the post-World War II period. Between 1950 and 1970, the total population of the United States increased from 150.7 million to 179.3 million to 203.2 million. In 1970 the Bureau of the Census still employed the rather arcane device of the Standard Metropolitan Statistical Area to measure metropolitan population and also, to a large extent, to measure suburban population. As has been mentioned, the SMSA includes a city of at least 50,000, the county in which it is located, and any other counties that, on the basis of an elaborate set of criteria, are considered to be "integrated" to the city. (There are slight modifications in New England, Pennsylvania, and New Jersey and in places where there are two cities close together.) In this system, the municipality of 50,000 is called the "central city," the surrounding area the "ring." Although full information on SMSA's were available for the period 1960–1970, there was difficulty in comparing this with data for 1950–1960, because a full reconciliation had not been made between the two census periods. But it is clear that SMSA's grew more rapidly than the over-all population during the whole period, roughly increasing from 89.3 million to 120.2 million to 140.2 million. By 1970 the percentage of the total U.S. population located in SMSA's had risen to 69.

More striking in a statistical sense was the rapid increase of population in the rings of metropolitan areas, particularly between 1960 and 1970, as rings increased by 28.2 per cent in population and central cities increased by only 5.3 per cent. This latter figure was obviously below the total metropolitan increase of 16.6 per cent, but it was also well below the national population increase of 13.3 per cent. The slow growth in the population of central cities, and the fact that many cities actually lost population during the census decade, was widely interpreted as an indication that a wholesale flight from the city was underway. In 1970, for the first time the percentage of total U.S. population in the rings of metropolitan areas (37.6) was higher than in central cities (31.4). This latter percentage was remarkably stable from 1930 to 1970 (31.6, 32.3, 32.6, 31.4) but the ring percentage rose steadily from 18 per cent in 1930 to the 1970 figure. The dynamics of these developments are perhaps best illustrated by "capture" percentages, i.e. what share of the total growth "goes to" or is "captured" by the unit. These have been calculated for a range of categories by Leo F. Schnore and Vivian Zeling Klaff, using slightly different base figures than the foregoing. Between 1950–1960, according to their study, 84.2 per cent of the total population growth of the U.S. occurred in SMSA's; between 1960–1970, 85.3 per cent. Of the total SMSA growth between 1950–1960, 76.3 per cent occurred in rings; between 1960–1970, 84.3 per cent.

Racial considerations were an important part of this pattern. The growth of suburbs in the postwar period represented an increase in white population, and growth of central cities was sustained by an increase in black population. During the decade 1960–1970, the total white population in central cities actually decreased by 1.2 per cent and the number of blacks in central cities increased by 28.2 per cent. More blacks lived in suburbs in 1970 than in 1960 (over 29 per cent more, in fact), but the percentage of the total black population there rose only slightly, from 15.1 to 16.2 per cent. The tendency of metropolitan areas to divide into black cities and white suburbs was one of the most critical developments of postwar American urban society.

Statistics of urbanization revealed the broad dimensions of significant change, but these statistics were to some extent misinterpreted and required qualification and amplification. Commentators sometimes considered the high percentage of population in metropolitan areas as an indication that we were becoming a nation of big-city dwellers. Although over-all a higher percentage of the total population was being concentrated in less of the total land, the megalopolises and metropolitan areas were not densely settled in comparison with urban settlements of the past. Densities in the cities of metropolitan regions were less than in the cities of the nineteenth century; many people in SMSA's lived in small municipalities and many suburban communities were far from compact. Nor was the much publicized notion of the flight from cities to suburbs altogether accurate. In part the increase in population of the rings of metropolitan areas was the result of normal growth; cities simply filled up or were fully developed, and because of political considerations they were unable to annex the surrounding areas as they grew. In the West, central cities showed a much more rapid growth rate because they could more easily annex peripheral areas of development. Census data demonstrated that older cities and larger cities had more of their share of growth in rings than newer and smaller cities. In short, much of the suburban growth was natural growth. "In large measure," writes Norval D. Glenn in a careful study of suburbanization, "the people leaving the central cities are not fleeing the cities but are being pushed out by essentially the same processes of succession which have characterized growing American cities since the nineteenth century and which antedate postwar urbanization." Furthermore, the use of the ring of the SMSA as an indicator of suburbanization perhaps exaggerated its extent. Because the SMSA follows county lines it includes some rural population and some people in small towns that may not really be suburbs of the SMSA's central city. The Bureau of the Census, at the same time it established the Standard Metropolitan Area in 1950, began to organize some of its data on the basis of another conceptual device, the *urbanized area,* but this unit could not be projected back historically as easily as the SMSA, and less data was furnished about it. The urbanized area began with the same central cities, but the outlying areas did not follow county lines. Instead, on the basis of a number of demographic, economic, and political criteria, an enumeration district was laid out around the city, the *urban fringe;* this was intended to represent an area of contiguous settlement naturally tied to the city. The urban fringe provided a substantially smaller suburban population than the ring. In 1970, for example, the urban fringe population was about 54.5 million compared to the ring population of 76.3 million, a difference in percentage of the total U.S. population of 26.8 to 37.6. If the urban fringe were considered the criterion representing suburbanization, then central cities in 1970 would still contain a higher percentage of the nation's total population than suburbs, 31.4 to 26.8.

Still, there are also deficiencies in the use of the urban fringe as a measure of suburbanization, deficiencies chiefly related to the requirement of contiguous settlement. Natural suburbs can be strung out some distance along highways, for example. But regardless of the measurement device used, the trends remain the same. And there is really no questioning the magnitude of this development. The period after World War II did witness a tremendous growth of settlement in the areas outside established cities, and this intensification of suburbanization shaped the urban history of the period.

The rapid suburbanization of the postwar period was of course made possible by a long period of prosperity that permitted a great amount of public highway construction. Although there were no fundamental changes in transportation technology during the period, more powerful automobiles and more spacious highways extended the range of feasible commuting from that of the pre-war period. But of basic importance was a simple increase in the number of roads, and the necessary connecting bridges, as well as improvements in existing highways that allowed faster and easier movement of traffic. Expenditures for highway construction increased to over $2 billion a year in 1949, to over $3 billion in 1953, and to over $4 billion in 1955. Especially important was the interstate highway program authorized in 1956.

The act provided for a 42,500 mile, $60 billion road network that well may be the largest public works program in human history. The potential effects of this program on patterns of urban development, many of which were unfortunate, as we have pointed out, were not considered when the act was passed. It was advocated primarily as a national defense measure; the highways would permit quick movement in case of atomic war. "When the American people, through their Congress," Lewis Mumford observed, "voted a little while ago for a $26 billion highway program, the most charitable thing to assume is that they hadn't the faintest notion of what they were doing."

But the impact of large-scale suburbanization was already evident, and by the late 1950s life in suburbia had become the subject of widespread public attention. In some respects, the inquiry into this strange new world resembled the investigation of the dark jungle of the big cities in, say, the 1880s. The rise of suburbia was viewed as a domestic crisis. The triumph of the suburb would lead to homogeneity, conformity, and the destruction of American diversity; in earlier years, the argument had been that the metropolis would destroy American liberty. The miles upon miles of "little boxes" springing up on the landscape seemed to frighten observers almost as much as had the burgeoning slums of an earlier time. To urban intellectuals, the stock-figure suburbanite, with his allegiance to conservative Republican party principles, the PTA, the station wagon, and the barbecue pit, seemed almost as much an alien intruder in the land as the stock-figure New Immigrant—with his catholicism, his clannishness, and his socialism—had been to the nineteenth century writer of old American stock. At least, those who wrote about suburbia often adopted the supercilious, observer-from-Mars tone that had been characteristic of those who ventured to tour the dark slums of the nineteenth-century city.

The ways of looking at suburbia were as varied as the approaches toward the city in the nineteenth century. The "sins of the cities" had been a favorite topic of sensationalistic writers of the past. Now there were lurid exposés of the sins of the suburbs—some semi-factual, some in the form of the novel, with the motion picture providing an additional vehicle. In these, suburbia was a place where bored housewives practiced prostitution by day, where husbands and wives exchanged sexual partners by night, and where pampered young men engaged in gang rape, and pampered young women turned to lesbianism. There were more serious journalistic investigations whose titles, *The Split-Level Trap* or *The Crack in the Picture Window*, indicated their view. Sociologists began to apply the methods and theories of the Chicago school of urban sociology to the study of this form of community. One book in this vein, William Whyte Jr.'s, *The Organization Man*, which viewed the suburb as part of a society destroying the autonomy of the individual, may not have had the impact on public policy of Jacob Riis's, *How the Other Half Lives*, but it was a highly influential work, and was probably required reading for almost every American college student for at least a decade. "Whyte's negative attitudes toward suburban architecture, life style and politics," Scott Donaldson observes, "were adopted wholesale as official intellectual dogma of the 1950s." The suburbanite could be a figure of fun, as the big-city Irishmen or Jew had been in the nineteenth century. Max Shulman's *Rally Round the Flag, Boys* was a popular, good-natured, amusing satire on suburbia, which was made into a very unhumorous motion picture. Peter De Vries's series of fine suburban novels contained high wit and humor, but his suburbanites also reveal the dark side of the human condition. Two best-selling novels of the period, Sloan Wilson's *The Man in the Gray Flannel Suit* and John P. Marquand's *Point of No Return,* are basically concerned with men in business organizations. But their heroes live in suburbs, and the authors' exploration of community, as a part of a whole set of forces affecting an individual, is comparable to and at least on a level with such turn-of-the-century novelists as Henry B. Fuller and Brander Matthews, who used the city in that fashion.

What took full shape in this period, although it had long been developing, of course, was the myth of the suburb, which now took its place alongside a number of counterparts, the myth of the small town, the myth of the big city, and in a somewhat broader context, the myth of the frontier West. All of these social myths are nourished on the natural perception that varying forms of community settlement produce distinctive patterns of life that can be comprehended through two or three readily evident characteristics. The suburb thereby became the habitat of the white-Anglo-Saxon-Protestant middle class, a dreary land of conformity, dullness, Philistinism, materialism, and quiet desperation. The presence of these social myths in society can be a powerful creative force. The effort to escape the myth, though no one can ever completely do so, and to create sympathetic, realistic studies of life in such places as the small town, the farm, or the city has produced some of the most powerful pieces of American literature—A. B. Guthrie's *The Big Sky* on the West, or Henry Roth's *Call It Sleep* on the metropolis, for example. In the novels and short stories of John Cheever, whose work won widespread public and critical attention in the late 1950s, resulting in a National Book Award, the suburb became a part of serious American literature. Cheever was neither defender nor critic of suburbia; he took the position, in commenting on his writing, that people were people wherever they were found. But particularly in many of his short stories, such as "The Housebreaker of Shady Hill" or "The Swimmer" (the latter rather surprisingly made into an effective motion picture), the suburb becomes an omnipresent setting, a place of power and terror, as artfully conceived as Melville's great ocean or Hawthorne's Puritan village.

Cheever carefully indicates that there are many kinds of suburbs: Remsen Park is brand new, built for workers at a missile installation; Shady Hill is upper class; Maple Hill is a stop-over place for young marrieds, which serves as a kind of spawning ground; Proxmire Manor is old and eminently respectable, but is decaying underneath. This was the simple point ignored in so much contemporary discussion of the suburb. Also completely ignored, of course, was the history of American city growth. In the critique of the suburb there was virtually no recognition of the fact that suburbanization was a part of the natural process of the growth of cities in America. The prevailing view notwithstanding, the suburb was not a post-World War II aberration in the history of human settlement.

Scholars, however, soon began to discover, or to rediscover perhaps, some of these obvious truths. The sociologist Herbert J. Gans in the late 1950s studied and lived in Levittown, New Jersey, and provided a perceptive, scholarly reassessment of the suburban pattern of life. Levittown, New Jersey was a large suburban development of 12,000 houses located seventeen miles outside of Philadelphia. It was the third such community built by Levitt and Sons, Inc., the largest builders in the East, who introduced techniques of mass production into large-scale suburban construction. The Levittowns were highly successful, got considerable attention, and in the attack on suburbia were portrayed as frightening examples of mass homogeneity and conformity. But Gans, who moved into Levittown, New Jersey with his family right at the start, and lived there for two years as part of his project, demonstrated that the suburban community did not differ that much from neighborhoods elsewhere. Gans discovered that those who moved to Levittown, like Bostonians who moved to the streetcar suburbs of the nineteenth century, were not seeking a particular way of life or searching for a special kind of community but were looking for a better house or more living space. Most people were happy with what they had found: Gans asserted "that most new suburbanites are pleased with the community that develops; they enjoy the house and outdoor living and take pleasure from the large supply of compatible people, without experiencing the boredom or malaise ascribed to suburban homogeneity." Moreover, Gans argued, people did not fundamentally change their lives or values to any great extent as a result of moving to suburbs. Many of the changes that did take place were the result of decisions about how one ought to live, decisions made before the move. Levittown was far from being a perfect society. There was conflict in the community along class or generational lines. There was little tolerance of cultural diversity. But many of the antagonisms of Levittown mirrored the antagonisms of American society in general. On the whole, said Gans, Levittown was "a good place to live." A more urgent priority than building more perfect communities (and these certainly could be conceived) would be to make communities like Levittown available to blacks and the poor, who were largely excluded from the new residential suburbs. A second influential sociological study, published in 1960, examined a working-class suburb in California, built when the Ford Motor Company moved a plant from an urban site to a semi-rural community near San Jose, taking virtually all its workers along. The author, Bennett M. Berger, demonstrated the invalidity of much of the "myth of suburbia" when applied to this kind of community, and concluded that "there are no grounds for believing that suburbia has created a distinctive style or a new social character for Americans."

By the 1960s, suburbs—if they are considered in a legal or formal demographic sense—encompassed such a large proportion of the total U. S. population that all of them could not conceivably represent only the traditional middle- to upper-class dormitory community. For one thing, there simply were not that many affluent people in America; for another, suburbs of above twenty-five or thirty thousand population were too large to contain only one or two narrow class groups. Visual observation of any of the older metropolitan areas would reveal a wide range of suburban communities: dismal impoverished manufacturing centers like Hamtramck outside Detroit; large suburbs like Sylvania outside Toledo, with a range of neighborhoods comparable to those of the city itself, from the very wealthiest to a low-density slum sometimes called Dogpatch; or old traditional lake-shore suburbs like Evanston outside Chicago or Shorewood outside Milwaukee, which were once enclaves of the affluent but which, as the years went by, decayed physically, acquired a substantial number of poor people, and shared the problems of the big city. By early in the 1970s, as information from the census became available, this point had become so evident that *Time* magazine could devote a cover story to challenging the myth of suburbia and to demonstrating the wide range of different kinds of suburban communities.

Often lost sight of in the contemporary examination of suburbia were two important historical considerations. One, many of the most notorious slums in the country—Harlem in New York or Bedford-Stuyvesant in Brooklyn—had once been fashionable suburbs. The almost organic process of urban decay did not stop at the city limits. Second, from late in the nineteenth century, the decentralization of manufacturing had led to the creation of manufacturing suburbs that were quite unlike traditional dormitory suburbs. Also overlooked in much of the analysis was the fact that neighborhoods within cities differed sharply from one another, and that many of these had the characteristics of different types of suburbs. Suburbs often tended to be settled on lines of class and ethnicity, but so did neighborhoods in cities. The suburb was sometimes popularly viewed as the twentieth-century version of the nineteenth-century urban melting pot, in which a kind of standard, middle-class American was being forged. But a great deal of sociological and anthropological study of the 1950s and the 1960s (although some of it hardly seemed scientific in its blatant promotion of political and social objectives) demonstrated the cohesiveness and persistence of class and ethnic values in people regardless of where they live or how much they move about. But demonstrating the inaccuracy of a social myth does not, as Bennett Berger and others have suggested, destroy its importance. Its presence in society conditions behavior as a kind of self-fulfilling prophecy. One responds negatively or positively to suburbs and cities partly in terms of the myth of suburbia; how one votes, his views on social issues, and the like are influenced and perhaps transformed as a consequence of its existence.

Moreover, as the move for metropolitan government in this period indicated, characteristics of this central city-independent suburb pattern of urban settlement did lead to many real divisions and to many social and political problems. By 1970 numerous larger suburbs demonstrated pretty much the same range of income as their central cities. But it was still true in general that the well-to-do lived in suburbs and the poor lived in cities. In some newer cities, this was not especially evident because of the possibility of annexation. But in a metropolitan area such as Detroit, with a high percentage of blacks in the central city and a vast suburban region, the disparities in income were striking. In the central city in 1970 the median family income was only three-fourths of that in the urban fringe. The central city had a third of the total families in the metropolitan area, but almost two-thirds of the very poor (less than $1,000 a year income) and less than one-sixth of the very wealthy (income above $50,000). This disproportion was evident at every income level.

A significant cause for the disparity was the continued movement of industry, with its better-paying jobs, from the cities to suburban sites, where land was cheaper, taxes lower, regulation less stringent, and where production and distribution could often be arranged more efficiently. According to census figures for eight representative SMSA's, the percentage of manufacturing jobs in central cities in relation to rings declined significantly from 76.4 per cent in 1939–1958, to 66.7 per cent in 1959–1966, to 60.8 per cent in 1967. By the 1960s, trying to keep manufacturing plants from moving from cities to suburbs had become one of the major concerns of municipal governments. In 1970 Paul Zimmerer, head of Chicago's economic development committee, testified before a U.S. House of Representatives committee: "In Chicago's inner city alone, between 1955 and 1963 there was a net loss of some four hundred manufacturing companies and some seventy thousand manufacturing jobs. . . . Because of discriminatory housing practices, suburban zoning regulations, inadequate mass transit systems . . . most inner-city workers could not continue to work at relocated manufacturing facilities in the suburbs." Kenneth Patton, who had held a similar position in New York City, told the committee that between 1950 and 1970, 200,000 manufacturing jobs had been lost there.

As was frequently noted in popular commentary, the movement of business and industry and of prosperous people to the suburbs cut into the tax base of cities and led to serious financial problems. The concentration of the poor in central cities increased the costs of welfare and of law enforcement. And this development occurred relatively quickly, as there was a large increase in central city-urban fringe income polarization in the period from 1950 to 1960. Statistically, the polarization slowed down markedly in the next decade, mainly as a result of the aging of larger suburbs which now began to experience many of the same problems as the central cities. The basic public cultural institutions that had been identified with urban life—museums, parks, libraries, and zoos—were still largely located in cities; these, along with other public facilities, streets and police for example, were used by suburbanites who did not pay the property taxes that generally supported these agencies. Accordingly, there were efforts to reorganize some of them, particularly park and library systems, along county lines. As a means of requiring suburbanites to support some of the costs of these facilities, users' charges and city income taxes came into increasing use.

By the late 1960s another trend was evident: there was a limited decentralization of the traditional cultural activities of cities as suburban cinema, theater, and even symphony orchestras became common. The suburban dinner-theater became a minor entertainment phenomenon of the late 1960s, and nightclubs were increasingly located away from central cities. Particularly notable was the tendency to build sport facilities—especially stadia for professional football teams such as the Boston Patriots, the Dallas Cowboys, the New York Giants, and the Detroit Lions—some distance from central cities at suburban sites. Even professional ice hockey, the preeminently big-city spectator sport of the thirties through fifties, began to find its way to the suburbs. "The suburbs are beginning to share in the civilizing function, the acculturation, that has traditionally been a central role of cities throughout Western history," noted Donald Canty, editor of *City*, in 1972.

The most significant aspect of the polarization of metropolitan regions in the postwar period was the tendency for them to divide into white suburbs and black cities. The creation of the megalopolis and similar metropolitan regions may constitute the central theme of the post-World War II period of American urban history. A second related theme could well be the growth of the huge black communities of the cities of the North and West and the social conditions these engendered. By 1970, 74.2 per cent of the total U.S. black population of 22,673,000 lived in metropolitan areas, and 58 per cent of that total lived in central cities. Outside the South the black population was almost completely urban, reaching a percentage of 95 as early as 1950. By 1970 there were sixteen cities of over 25,000 with black majorities, including Washington, D. C., at 71 per cent, Newark 54, Gary 53, and Atlanta 51. Two cities by that date, New York and Chicago, had black communities of over a million, and Philadelphia, Washington, D. C., and Los Angeles over half a million.

As it had during World War I, the employment opportunities in northern cities during World War II had stimulated black migration from the South. It followed old pathways—along the Atlantic Coast to Washington, D. C., Baltimore, Philadelphia, and New York; from the Gulf region to St. Louis and the Great Lakes cities; and from Texas and Oklahoma to the Pacific Coast, and especially Los Angeles. "If you took a map of the United States," writes Charles Tilly, "and drew a broad straight line from Tallahassee to

Boston, another heavy line from New Orleans to Chicago, and a spindly one from Houston to Los Angeles, then sketched branching lines leading to the cities along the way—thicker for the bigger cities and the ones farther south —the three trees on your map would represent quite well the main established paths of nonwhite migration." By the 1960s this mass migration from the southern countryside, which had such profound consequences for so long, had largely come to an end; for the first time a majority of migrants to cities, both white and black, came from other urban areas. Also, by this time, of course, much of the growth of cities was the result not of migration as in the past but of a natural increase in population.

In the years since the post-World War I period of violence, there had been considerable change and some improvement in the position of blacks in cities. The struggle for Negro civil rights, a well-chronicled chapter in American history particularly in its later stages, was essentially a national political movement, not really an urban movement or a series of local actions occurring in cities. But it obviously had its urban dimensions, for many of the discriminations black leaders fought against—restrictive covenants; segregated schools, playgrounds, and swimming pools; and exclusionary housing policies —related to the patterns of urban living. Moreover, from the time of the "New Negro" movement and the growth in the 1920s of such organizations as the National Association for the Advancement of Colored People and the National Urban League, the leadership in the civil rights movement within the black community had come from urban lawyers and other professionals, and gained support from a growing black urban-middle-class.

The great civil rights victories of the 1950s and 1960s—the desegregation of transportation, universities, and public facilities; the landmark decision of *Brown v. Board of Education of Topeka,* which overturned the "separate but equal" doctrine; the elimination of discrimination in public housing and other federally supported programs—changed a long-standing public policy toward the black of flagrant discrimination and official segregation. But the proclaimed triumph for the cause of human freedom proved illusory. Legal procedures could alter only parts of the pattern of racial discrimination that was woven into the structure of American society. Moreover, the efforts to enforce these decisions through federal actions in white areas of cities, particularly at a time when black communities were growing rapidly, exacerbated the tensions between races that had always been a part of the American urban community. As had so often occurred in the past, political leaders again boxed the shadows of urban problems but did not confront their substance. The black in cities faced discrimination and hostility because of his color. But along with a good many white people, he also faced the problem of earning a living. Part of the black community might represent the much-publicized "under class" of young hoodlums, drug addicts, "street dudes," and welfare mothers. But the great bulk of blacks were, as Andrew Levison has observed, "blue-collar workers who work in some of the dirtiest, lowest-paying and most dangerous jobs in America." The black worker shared many problems with his white counterpart—a drastically high unemployment rate, hidden to some extent in the way federal statistics were presented, and many jobs with wages too low to support a family. But the black experienced these always in aggravated form. Despite the continual proclamations of victories in the various wars against poverty of the sixties, the struggles had been sham battles for the most part, because a policy of "full employment," which would probably require drastic change in the character of the economy, had never won general acceptance. Accordingly, the tensions created by the fight to survive in the city were added to racial tensions. Most of the efforts that evolved in the 1960s to enforce a policy of racial equality—large-scale moving about of children to achieve racially balanced schools, federally imposed racial job quotas applied to many industries and to numerous occupations such as those in construction, and the location of public housing projects in the poorer sections of cities— affected the lives and fortunes only of those among the poor and lower-middle-class groups of the white communities. The charge could be made, and it was occasionally expressed, that national policy makers of the 1960s and 1970s were not so much concerned with insuring equality for the black as they were with designing programs that would play on white-black antagonisms for the purpose of creating voting constituencies.

Be that as it may, there is little evidence that blacks in cities ever directly identified their interests with those of a white working class. From the beginning, they often experienced the manifestations of prejudice through the actions of the poor. Whites might resent black competition, and being told by the affluent and the intellectuals, "You've got to share with blacks," when it seldom seemed that there was enough to go around. The grievances of blacks were just as valid, and more severely experienced. The harsh economic realities and the dolorous psychological effects of life in the black urban ghettos created in this period have been well chronicled in fact and fiction. Ralph Ellison, for example, probably the best black writer and novelist to emerge in the postwar period, and one of the last permitted by the times to be something other than a pamphleteer in his writing, supplied a large white reading-public insight into the urban ghettos of the North, perhaps for the first time, in his powerful novel *Invisible Man,* published in 1952. Ellison wrote elsewhere of the ghetto that in this period consistently seemed to stand for all others.

Harlem is a ruin—many of its ordinary aspects (its crimes, its casual violence, its crumbling buildings with littered areaways, ill-smelling halls, and vermin-invaded rooms) are indistinguishable from the distorted images that appear in dreams, and which, like muggers haunting a lonely wall, quiver in the waking mind with hidden and threatening significance. Yet this is no dream but the reality of well over four hundred thousand Americans: a reality which for many defines and colors the world.

Fundamental to the problem of the ghetto was the difficulty of escape. During a time when there was a steady decentralization of industry and trade, and, accordingly, jobs, segregationist policies kept blacks from moving where the work was. Blacks who had conformed to the American ethic of self-help and somehow had achieved the success of a rank in the middle classes (and hence had performed as society said they should) found that they were prevented from experiencing a critical part of the American dream—a home in the suburbs with clean surroundings, living space, and good schools for their children. These circumstances of black urban communities led of course to a pervasive lack of incentive and a sense of hopelessness, not only among the old, which was common enough in most American communities, but in this case extending, ominously, to the young. The extensive testimony assembled on civil rights, and also as an aftermath of the later riots, seemed to reveal a theme of profound dislike of ghetto living and a feeling of despair about the future.* A ghetto resident who was asked what she would do if she had sufficient income, observed to the U.S. Commission on Civil Rights in 1967: "The first thing I would do myself is move out of the neighborhood. I feel the entire neighborhood is more or less a trap." But the question Claude Brown posed about the city in his *Manchild in the Promised Land* always had to be in the mind of the ghetto dweller: "Where does one run to when he is already in the promised land?"

Large-scale migration of blacks to cities, the formation of black neighborhoods, policies of segregation and discrimination, and continued animosity between the races again, as in the nineteenth and early twentieth centuries, led to conditions that produced widespread urban violence. In the years 1964 to 1968 there occurred a series of urban riots from which many individual cities have never recovered; and the city, itself, in the symbolic manifestations of its existence as an institution in society, has never recovered. Residual hatreds and tensions contributed to the ungovernability of places like Newark and Detroit; and the city, when perceived abstractively by many who lived in cities and by many who did not, became a place even more fearsome, savage, and mysterious than the cities to be found in the bad dreams of Melville and Poe.

The initial influx of southern blacks into northern cities during World War II led to the kind of racial conflict that had occurred earlier in the century. In 1943, Detroit experienced a riot comparable in intensity to those of 1919. Fifty thousand Negroes had arrived in the city in the fifteen months before the riot, leading to rapid and extensive neighborhood changes and continual tensions on the peripheries of black and white settlements. Fighting broke out in June between blacks and whites on Belle Isle, a park and recreation area. This was followed by skirmishes in the city and widespread looting in business sections of the black neighborhoods. State troops called

---

* This might be questioned, as it has been by later students of community.

in to assist the police proved ineffective, and 6,000 federal troops were eventually necessary to restore order. The riot left thirty-four dead and the customary widespread property damage. It did not, however, arouse public attention because information concerning it was suppressed as part of the war effort. Harlem had a serious riot the same year, and between 1945 and 1964 there were well over a hundred incidents of racial violence. Most of these stemmed from challenges by blacks of the social and economic status quo. For example, there were attempts to use segregated recreational facilities or, most generally, attempts to move into white neighborhoods.

Despite the continued presence of long-standing racial animosities and the frequency of racial incidents, the riots of 1964 to 1968 came as a surprise, for they followed upon the great civil rights victories, which seemed to promise a better day for the black in America. Politicians and shapers of public opinion had expressed the optimistic view that the extension of full civil rights to the black, particularly the passage of the Civil Rights Act of 1964, meant that we were on the way toward solving the problem of race in American society. A sense of shock intensified the impact of the riots and perhaps contributed to the legacy of bitterness, which seemingly had not been an aftermath of earlier episodes of large-scale urban violence. That the riots did occur at the time they did may not be too surprising, for civil rights victories did nothing to alleviate the fundamental problems of the ghetto. To people who lived there, these victories may have raised false hopes or, more likely, had little meaning at all.

It all began, appropriately, in Harlem in July, 1964, the third large-scale riot in that area during the century. This was followed by seven other riots in black ghettos that summer. The next three years resembled a period of a long guerilla war fought only when the weather was right, in the summer, with the battles finally intensifying until the war's climax in 1967. Five cities were hit in 1965, with the most serious riot occurring in the Watts district of Los Angeles, the first time the West Coast had really experienced the traditional urban riot of the East—and in an intense way: the disturbance left thirty-four dead and extensive property damage. Twenty cities had riots during the long hot summer of the following year. The spring of 1967 was ominous as rioting began early in southern cities. The fighting built up in June, and during July and August twenty-two cities had outbreaks with large-scale riots occurring in Toledo, Ohio; Grand Rapids, Michigan; Plainfield, New Jersey; Milwaukee; and especially violent ones in Newark and Detroit. The latter was particularly frightening, leaving forty-three dead and causing at least $50 million in property damage. It was clearly the worst domestic disturbance since the New York Draft Riots of over a hundred years before. The list of casualties for the four years included approximately 142 killed and 4,700 wounded; 20,000 people had been arrested, and property damage ran into the hundreds of millions. Extensive sections of a number of American cities bore the physical marks of serious internal warfare. Although there were further riots in 1968 after the assassination of the black leader Martin Luther King they were not on the same scale, and to many they appeared to mark a winding down of a distinct stage of racial conflict in America.

A national experience this frightening naturally led to the asking of a number of questions: "Why had the riots occurred?" "What would be there effect?" "How could they be prevented in the future?" And as usual the explanations were immediate and wide ranging. Causes were suggested that ranged from riots as part of an international communist conspiracy, to riots as a democratic rebellion led by ennobled freedom fighters. Solutions were offered that ranged from military occupation of the ghettos to the creation of independent black city-states. The President's Advisory Commission on Civil Disorders (the Kerner Commission) presented the most influential interpretation in its report published in March of 1968. The commission was conscientious in its investigation; a large number of scholars were consulted and their views were apparently listened to; a great amount of concrete information about the riots was accumulated; and findings were presented with some observance of the canons of scholarship. Still the report was primarily a political document. Like all such immediate evaluations of catastrophic events it was shaped in its view by political necessity—in this case the necessity of interpreting the events in a way that would conciliate or at least pacify the black community in America. Nor could a Democratic administration endorse any position that went very far in the direction of alienating an important voting bloc of the party. The Kerner report indicated many of the problems of the ghetto rather precisely, and also indicated their complexity. But in formulating a general explanation the commission seized the cliché and in the end blamed the riots on white "racism." The nation was dividing into "two societies, one black, one white—separate and unequal," the report contended. The upheavals represented a natural response by blacks to years of white oppression. The term *racism,* utilized by the Kerner Commission to describe white attitudes and practices, had begun to come into use in ways that bore little relationship to its original rather precise meaning: belief in a systematic theory of racial superiority and inferiority. This doctrine was primarily European in its origins and derived from late nineteenth-century anthropology, biology, and other fields of learning. Twentieth-century science had largely discredited it along with any rigid conception of what constituted a race, but it had won official acceptance in Nazi Germany. "Racism," in this sense, had little to do with the complex and wide-ranging body of sentiments and attitudes that shaped race relations in America—economic fears about job rivalry and property values, a dislike of change among the aging and the old, atavistic fears of the alien intruder, and ordinary ethnocentrism, to name but a few aspects. In the era of mass communication, precise words continually become vague in their meaning and, as George Orwell so effectively demonstrated, in politics this is dangerous, for words can be manipulated as powerful instruments of propaganda.

And "racism" was used to this end. Leaders could now clamor about this "evil in our midst" and demand that society extirpate the heresy. They could thereby avoid the difficult course of trying to deal systematically with a number of quite concrete and specific problems of the city and of race in America. In addition, the attack on "racism" obscured the fact that the various manifestations of prejudice and discrimination required entirely different approaches and policies if their effects were to be alleviated. As a result of the intense feelings stirred up by demagoguery, it appeared in the 1970s that the "racist" might be a successor to a long line of past heretics —from "antinomians," "Freethinkers," and "illuminati" to the "fascists" and "reds" or more recent times—an enemy of orthodoxy to be ceremonially driven from the land. An occasional stoning or hanging of a symbolic demon may provide necessary catharsis for society, but periods of witch hunts have seldom seemed times of achievement to later generations. In American society, witch hunts have frequently interfered drastically with the complex process of accommodating diverse groups and interests so fundamental to the American political and social system. And so it seemed to be during the "anti-racist" movement of the 1970s.

The voluminous body of writing on the riots (although interpretations might differ somewhat) tended to reflect a political view similar to that of the Kerner Commission. Much of it was informed by an effort to justify widespread black violence, arson, and looting. To do this, the riots were sometimes portrayed as an uprising against oppression, a kind of colonial rebellion in the cause of extending human freedom. Some writers embraced the fashionable intellectual melange of neo-primitivism and existentialism which emphasized the individual act of violence as an experience of personal liberation. More generally accepted was the thesis that the riots represented a natural reaction to years of deprivation—or at least relative deprivation, made manifest via television —that led to collective frustration. In these circumstances, an incident could lead to group aggression and especially the satisfying activity of looting. Evidence collected from the riots was mildly tortured to reveal the view that riots represented an upsurge of a substantial part of the black population in cities. They were not the work, it was argued, of small gangs of the young, as had been proven true of so many riots of the American past. There was also an effort to show that a spirit of restraint characterized the riots; mobs attacked private business establishments, sometimes avoiding those that were owned by blacks, and largely left public buildings alone. Moreover, not many whites were deliberately killed. But some of what was characterized as restraint could more cynically be considered as narrow self-interest. As a youthful Detroit rioter observed, "There was nothing to steal in the school. Who wants a book or a desk?"

The Kerner Commission report and subsequent studies, although their polemical parts became tedious, did provide much material of substance about the riots, and several general points seemed substantiated. As the

Kerner Commission pointed out, the circumstances of riots differed from city to city. Ghettos varied in their problems, black communities had different grievances, and there had been a variety of precipitating incidents setting off disturbances. Although no over-all pattern was evident, it was still clear that the riots of the 1960s were unlike those of the past involving blacks. Earlier ones had been race riots fought between blacks and whites on the peripheries of their settlements. But the riots of the 1960s, foreshadowed to a considerable extent by those in Harlem in 1935 and 1943, were outbursts directed against property in the ghetto. Morris Janowitz, in a perceptive interpretative essay, has termed them "commodity riots," directed against the symbols and agencies of the larger society, as contrasted with "communal riots" of earlier times, which involved warfare over terrain contested between the races. Accordingly, there was wider participation by the community than in past riots, but not nearly as wide as was sometimes asserted; perhaps 10 per cent of the total population in a riot area might have been involved in some way, but this calculation was little more than an educated guess. Despite the charges at the time, there was no evidence uncovered that demonstrated the existence of any international, national, or even local conspiracy in the riots. In fact, there was little evidence of direction or leadership at all.

Attempts through sociological methods to find consistent motives among participants in riots that would accord with the broad interpretation of riots as a form of collective protest against oppression yielded few results over the following years. It was even difficult to demonstrate that there was much animosity toward the police or much dissatisfaction with the way they performed their duties in the ghettos. That white police forces were a hated agency of brutality and discriminatory practices had of course long been an article of faith among those sympathetic to black aspirations in America. Edward Banfield in a controversial study of the city argued that much of the rioting was not a matter of protest at all. In a fashion that recalled the tough-minded realism of the nineteenth-century Darwinian sociology of William Graham Sumner, Banfield argued that much of what was termed rioting often involved youth on a rampage or poor people seizing a convenient opportunity to steal something without penalty, "rioting mainly for fun and profit," as he put it. By the mid-1970s the attempt to find protest motives among riot participants and to draw up a profile of a rioter seemed almost to have gone the way of earlier attempts to classify urban- and rural-character and personality types. Clark McPhail, in summarizing a number of sociological studies, concluded that it was impossible to sustain any monolithic conception of civil disorders. Rather than continue the sterile search for motives, it would be more fruitful, he suggested, to try to gain insight into the "assembling process," that led to these disturbances. Many people got into riots not because they were riot-prone or because they had special grievances, but because they were at the right place at the right time. He suggested that scholarly attention should be addressed to two fundamental questions, which he framed in rather technical language: "What settings at what points in time yield large numbers of available persons in general proximity to one another?" "What produces assemblages of persons in a common time-space frame?" But answering these questions seemed to call for a narrative natural history of significant individual city riots. This could be done for the Draft Riots of 1863, but a generation would have to pass before it could be seriously attempted for the Great Ghetto Riots, 1964–1968.

The results of the riots were nearly as uncertain as the causes. Despite extensive local and national attention and a flurry of new programs and approaches, conditions within ghettos did not change that much. Many of the existing programs of urban reconstruction, such as urban renewal, though modified, continued to undermine the stability of black neighborhoods and to intensify ghetto problems. Nevertheless, there were no further significant outbreaks of violence during the next six years, at least none on the scale of those of the 1960s. And no one really knew why. The speculations, as usual, were shaped by ideological considerations. Perhaps, it was suggested, the program of inculcating racial pride through public education and community involvement, and the proclaimed renewed allegiance to equal opportunity and "affirmative action" may have mitigated underlying general resentment in the ghetto of the whole society, if this kind of resentment actually existed. To a large extent, however, many aspects of this approach seemed a convenient way to avoid dealing with the difficult economic and social conditions that produced the poverty of the ghetto. For a time, there was speculation that recognition of the failure of ghetto rioting had shifted black protest in the direction of political terror and deliberate acts of revolutionary violence. But the influence of the movement represented by Black Panthers and similar groups was exaggerated. The latter movement either rather quickly lost its impetus or was suppressed by police action. It was suggested that racial polarization intensified by the riots forced black leaders and the black middle class to identify more closely and more specifically with a black community interest, and this may have led to greater willingness to try to achieve black goals through regular political processes. Big-city police forces seemed to have learned better ways to cope with incidents that might set off group violence; perhaps closer regulation of day-to-day police procedures, and enforcement of standards of courtesy may have reduced hostility. As has often been the case in the history of municipal services, technological responses in the broadest sense—changed patrol patterns, greater mobility of forces, and particularly an improved intelligence apparatus—increased the capability of police departments to deal more efficiently with conditions and circumstances that in the past had led to riots. Maybe, some social scientists asserted, demography told us all. In the mid-sixties there was a particularly high proportion of older adolescents and young adults in American society, and this was the group always most inclined to take part in mass violence. In general, though, it is reasonable to assume that in the period 1968 to 1974 a number of institutional and technological changes taking place, but not yet comprehended, were subtly modifying the circumstances of the urban black community in America, and that these changes had lessened the chances of riots again occurring.

Had the riots then been worthwhile or creative? Many intellectuals, particularly from the left, said they were: They had provided hope and a sense of possibility to the urban black community. They had not been ruthlessly suppressed as they might have been; this had indicated, it was argued, that American society would accept legitimate protest even of a violent kind if the violence was limited. On the other hand, the riots accelerated the movement of whites from the cities to the suburbs, with all the social consequences that this entailed. They also intensified the hatreds and fears of blacks among the white working class of the cities. The terror that the riots produced and its subsequent psychological effects is a subject little explored, although Joyce Carol Oates in her powerful novel *them* captured in fiction the frightening atmosphere of life among the poor in riot-ravaged Detroit. Intellectuals might emphasize the moderation characterizing the riots: there had been no racial blood bath; when it came to killing, this represented a mild episode in the world history of such upheavals. But be that as it may, for many city dwellers, black and white, urban life in America could never again be as civil, stable, and rational as before.

From the perspective of the present, several other themes of contemporary urban history suggested themselves, but these appeared to be outgrowths of the fundamental metropolitan and population trends. A crisis of leadership accompanied the urban governmental problems caused by decay, the migration to the suburbs of the affluent, and a declining tax base. A number of "new style" mayors emerged in the 1950s, and a group of "charismatic" mayors succeeded them in the 1960s, but in the face of the problems they confronted, they usually tried with only limited success to use the office as a stepping stone to higher fortune. Only a decidedly old-style mayor, Richard J. Daley of Chicago, functioning as an old-style boss and using old-style machine techniques could lay much claim to providing effective government in a large city. But his critics were not charitable in describing corruption and authoritarian tactics in his regime. He was seldom portrayed as the man for his times. The process of decay in cities and the formation of ghettos contributed to the increase of crime in cities, but the relationship between crime and social conditions was as dimly understood as it had been in the nineteenth century. It was clear that crime rates, and these were always ambiguous, were influenced by the metropolitan pattern. As the suburbs began to age in the late 1960s, with poor people living there, the suburban crime rate began to rise dramatically; in the 1970s, the city crime rate seemed to be leveling off. Pollution of the urban environment was of course related to suburbanization, the widespread use of the automobile, and largely unrestrained manufacturing development throughout the new urban regions. This seemed the kind of condition that would evoke striking technological response, as in our urban past. But the crisis that had often been necessary before was probably not yet at hand, although it did seem close.

These conditions of late twentieth-century American urban life were usually presented as a series of urban problems. But whether or not these were really problems, or whether or not they were really urban, were matters that could be debated. It was true that there was a good deal of disorder in cities, but there always had been. City dwellers in the 1970s lived longer and healthier lives, had more food, living space, and creature comforts, and probably enjoyed greater personal security than they had in the past, even during the "golden age" of the American city around the turn of the century. The argument for the existence of an overwhelming urban crisis was mainly based on examples from the older cities of the East and parts of the Midwest, and the urban region of California. It tended to overlook the fact that many of the cities of the South, such as Atlanta and Louisville, had alleviated some of the tensions of race in an urban setting and had developed a range of flourishing cultural enterprises. It almost completely ignored the fact that smaller metropolitan areas away from the great industrial regions—Columbia, Missouri, or Fargo-Moorhead on the Minnesota-North Dakota border, or Topeka, Kansas, all alive and doing well—were as much a part of urban America as New York, Newark, Detroit, or Gary, Indiana. It was suggested that perhaps many of the problems that seemed a part of urban life were not related to the fundamental structure of the American city at all, but were simply the temporary result of an unusually large and greatly disproportionate number of young people coming to maturity in the city. As Norman Ryder the demographer put it: "There is a perennial invasion of barbarians who must somehow be civilized and turned into contributors to fulfillment of the various functions requisite to societal survival." In the 1960s, the children born during the baby boom of the postwar years grew up and began to take part in the life of the city. A child born in 1946, when births began to rise dramatically, would have been sixteen in 1962 and seventeen in 1963, years that mark the beginning of the recognition of increasing urban disorder—widespread heroin addiction, mass disturbances, and an increase in many kinds of crime. It could be argued that the patchwork of institutions that accommodate the newcomer broke down, just as it had during the influx of immigrants to cities in the late nineteenth century. The "drug pad," the new types of university-centered communities, and various "counter-culture" and radical groups may have represented the same kind of institutional response as the ethnic saloon, the immigrant-aid organization, and the boss-machine system. It could be surmised that, as this large group of young people matured and found settled places in urban society, the apparent social disorganization would diminish of its own accord. The absence of riots for several years, a possible decrease in drug use, with a corresponding decline in the importance of the "drug culture" offered some support of the view. But all such reflections on the forces of contemporary historical change, no matter how often and how vigorously asserted, were only speculations.

By the mid-1970s some urban leaders had begun to question a fundamental article of the national faith: that growing cities were a sign of progress. They had done so in the past, perhaps, but only as a rationalization when their city had lost out to a rival. Now municipalities, seemingly for the first time in the history of American cities, tried to pass laws that would keep out migrants and would put absolute limits on new residential construction. As in the 1930s, the birth rate was falling, and if the trend were to continue "zero population-growth" would be reached in the United States in the next century. These developments might presage a new era in American urban history. But for several decades into the future, it seemed likely that H. G. Wells's turn-of-the-century prophecy would hold, and great metropolitan regions would continue to grow. In 1972, a Presidential commission on population growth, headed by John D. Rockefeller III, reported that the growth of urban regions was the most significant population trend of the latter part of the twentieth century, and no one disagreed with the view. A few years earlier, in a study for the Hudson Institute, Herman J. Kahn, whose computer-based anticipations of nuclear holocaust had made him a much more frightening prophet of our time than Wells had been of his, had predicted with his collaborator that by the year 2,000 over half the total population of the United States would live in three gargantuan megalopolises, Sansan, Boswash, and Chipitts, which would be filled-in versions of the great metropolitan regions that had begun to emerge at mid-century. By then, like cities in the past, each megalopolis would even have a distinctive culture: Chipitts would retain the lusty vitality of the Midwest of Carl Sandburg; Sansan would combine the culture of the barbecue pit with varieties of Bohemianism; and Boswash would be cosmopolitan, the home of establishment institutions and the center of achievement in letters and arts. This was whimsy of a sort. But the anticipation that American society would soon be the society of the megalopolis was serious, and for the time being irrefutable.

# Epilogue:
# Change and Continuity

N THE middle-1960s two historians who had been studying American cities for a few years tried to assess, in writing the first edition of this book, the significance of American urban history to their own times. They wrote thus, referring to the era from the emergence of cities in the Colonial period to the middle of the twentieth century.

Two-hundred and fifty years of American urban history suggested that a number of viewpoints about the city and contemporary urban life might easily be questioned. Expanding cities were portrayed in vivid metaphors of voraciousness—destroying, swallowing, devouring the countryside. Yet cities at mid-century still represented a spatially concentrated form of human settlement; "urbanized areas" of the United States, which included cities of 50,000 or above and their seemingly vast environs, still occupied less than one per cent of the land in the continental United States. Theorists argued confusingly that the values of the suburb now threatened the values of the city, yet from the beginning the suburb had been an enduring feature of American urban life—a constant in the process of urbanization. As Olmsted and Cleveland had so clearly indicated, the values of the city could not be pitted against the values of the suburb; they were inseparable in American culture. Reformers portrayed the "Negro cores" of great cities as a new dilemma of American society. Yet, for over a hundred years, urban critics, Tuckerman, Riis, and Hunter among them, had portrayed the slums of great cities in precisely the same light; the slum lord was a favorite target of Muhlenberg. Aside from the social tensions engendered by race (and how these might differ from the ethnic tensions of another day was still problematic), it is doubtful that Negro cores represented anything new in urban sordidness and misery. The urban juvenile delinquent became a stock figure of the new era, but a host of nineteenth-century reformers such as Muhlenberg and Brace had been exercised by exactly the same problem. Intellectuals harangued Americans to abandon the myth of the evil city, but if belief in the evil city had ever been important in American life it had always been balanced by belief in the good city as Scott and Gilpin had so clearly demonstrated. And such ambivalences are not the stuff of social myth. Planners denounced the automobile and the expressway as the source of urban problems and insisted upon the return to older systems of transportation. Yet traffic congestion had been a feature of urban life for a hundred years, and the critique of planners missed the point that changes in transportation were not the result of caprice but of response to the almost deterministic necessities of the city. Observing the destruction of old buildings and often whole neighborhoods which lay in the path of urban redevelopment, traditionalists and others with a strong attachment to the past sought to preserve structures which had been historically significant. Yet the thrust of American urbanization has always destroyed the old to make way for the new; urban development has always involved urban redevelopment. Urban politicians demanded renewal of

American cities, yet few of them seemed willing to confront the question of private use of urban land, which had been so fundamental in shaping the whole nature of what they putatively attacked. Change and continuity are both exhibited in the course of American urban history, but too much of the contemporary analysis, through lack of historical understanding, emphasized only the change.

Nearly a decade later, does their evaluation stand? Much of what they wrote was commonplace and hardly arguable. Perhaps a few of their observations were discerning and maybe even prescient. Earlier than most students of the city, they had recognized that suburbanization was a fundamental part of urban growth in America, not just a phenomenon of the post-World War II period or of the twentieth century. The notion that American culture had been consistently "anti-urban," although sometimes still asserted, had frequently been discounted elsewhere. Despite the optimism about the urban future expressed at the time and the roseate predictions of urban politicians, they had understood where others had not that the part played by the city, and particularly the part played by urban land in the American economic system, would not allow any real attack on "urban problems." On other matters, their judgments had been less certain. The city did represent a relatively spatially-concentrated form of settlement, as they had pointed out, and after several years of growth, metropolitan areas, depending on how they are measured, encompassed 2 to 3 per cent of the land area of the continental United States. But this was not insubstantial when one considered the vast amount of uninhabitable land in the country, and their observation obscured the important fact that a spreading out of settlement was a central characteristic of the megalopolitan pattern of development. They had seemed to accept the supercilious argument of the time, that historical urban preservation was often a diversion of the privileged classes. This was partly so, but it had become increasingly clear that rebuilding in cities, judged by whatever set of values or standards one might choose, did not only represent change but also decline in the quality of craftmanship and style in the urban building art.

The authors had also implied that the black ghettos of the twentieth century probably did not differ very much from the ethnic slums of the nineteenth. This was still debatable, as they had indicated, but the evidence of nearly ten years, both historical and contemporary, seemed to indicate that Negro settlements in cities had seldom been much like ethnic neighborhoods and were not conforming to the pattern of transition of the latter. The writers embraced the historians' article of faith that basic social insitutions are stable and in reality always change very slowly despite apparent continual changes in morals and manners. But contemporary evidence, always by its nature deceptive, seemed to suggest that radical ideologies present in American society in the 1960s had significantly modified a number of primary institutions—the law, the church, the family, and the school—that had theretofore served the conservative function of inculcating an acceptance of the order and control essential to the functioning of cities. The consequences of this breakdown were uncertain, and perhaps it was only ephemeral. But if fundamental social institutions ever actually came to be guided by anarchical principles, this would clearly mark the arrival of a strange new era in the history of American cities, one that demonstrated little continuity with the urban past. In their historians' search for pattern, the writers had perhaps suggested too much regularity in the process of urbanization. An elusive quality of disorder, uncertainty, and chaos, suggested in monograph after monograph but not yet captured in synthesis, seemed to inform our urban past.

Finally, writing when they did, they had reflected (though they tried to guard against it) some of the optimism that was part of the urban renaissance of the 1960s. A decade later, there was no difficulty in isolating urban impressions that foreshadowed the oft-predicted coming of necropolis: A journey into the heart of the ghetto of Detroit (to Europeans the "shock city" of the latter twentieth century, as Chicago and Los Angeles had been in other eras) by way of its south industrial environs on a murky January evening; or a drive by automobile through Gary and the Calumet Region on a hot, still July afternoon; or a passage through Newark on almost any occasion; or a walking tour of downtown Toledo; or scrupulous observation of the process of decay in one residential neighborhood of Kansas City would not sustain an individual's faith in an urban ideal—unless perhaps he be a Dante or a Bunyan putting it to the test.

But these journeys would expose a most limited range of urban impressions. As always, the city presented an incredible medley of experiences and possibilities. And if he chose, one could find vitality—and hope. The far lake-shore suburbs of Milwaukee, deep in the luxuriance of a damp May in the North, still evoked the beauty and the power of one great American dream. Wrigley Field and the Chrysler Building still stood as a reflection of the creativity of other urban times. The freeways of Los Angeles still conveyed the force and energy characteristic of the metropolitan era of American urban development. And reflecting the city's historic role as a center of culture, an Edward Hopper exhibition, a Shakespearean company, and even the circus came to town. As so many commentators on American society have noted through the years since the late nineteenth century, the problems of American society have seemed increasingly to be urban problems. And if all the fulminations and harangues of our own time were accepted, American society would represent only problems. But truth and beauty are still to be found in American civilization, and from the beginning, American civilization in large measure has always been a product of the towns, the cities, and new and changing forms of urban settlement.

# Suggestions for Further Reading

THIS list of references is intended to be useful to the student who wishes to extend his knowledge of American urban history; it is also designed to suggest important secondary works upon which we have relied heavily in the preparation of the book. But the list is not intended to be comprehensive. We have, for example, included only a few of the vast number of scholarly articles relating to urban history—those in the main that we have quoted, or from which we have drawn extensive material.

BIBLIOGRAPHY. Blake McKelvey, "American Urban History Today," *American Historical Review* LVII (July, 1952), pp. 919–929; and Charles N. Glaab, "The Historian and the American City: a Bibliographic Survey," in Philip M. Hauser and Leo F. Schnore (eds.), *The Study of Urbanization* (N.Y.: Wiley, 1965), are convenient and thorough guides.

DOCUMENTS. Primary sources are not included here. Many of our important sources—travelers' accounts, novels, census materials and other government documents, and contemporary writings on urban problems are suggested in the text. The following are useful documentary collections: Charles N. Glaab, *The American City: A Documentary History* (Homewood, Ill.: Dorsey, 1963); William Smith, *Cities of Our Past and Present* (N.Y.: Wiley, 1964); David Weimer, *City and Country in America* (N.Y.: Appleton, 1962); Bessie L. Pierce, *As Others See Chicago* (Chicago: U. of Chicago P., 1933); and Bayrd Still, *Mirror for Gotham* (N.Y.: N.Y.U. P., 1956).

THEORY. Contrasting theoretical approaches to urban history are offered in Arthur M. Schlesinger, "The City in American History," *Mississippi Valley Historical Review* XXVII (June, 1940), pp. 43–66, which appears also in Schlesinger's book, *Paths to the Present* (N.Y.: Macmillan, 1949); William Diamond, "On the Dangers of an Urban Interpretation of History," in Eric F. Goldman (ed.), *Historiography and Urbanization: Essays in American History in Honor of W. Stull Holt* (Baltimore: Johns Hopkins U. P., 1941); W. Stull Holt, "Some Consequences of the Urban Movement in American History," *Pacific Historical Review* XXII (November 1953), pp. 337–351; R. Richard Wohl, "Urbanism, Urbanity, and the Historian," *University of Kansas City Review* XXII (Autumn 1955), pp. 53–61; Eric E. Lampard, "American Historians and the Study of Urbanization," *American Historical Review* LXVII (October 1961), pp. 49–61; Charles N. Glaab, "The Historian and the American Urban Tradition," *Wisconsin Magazine of History* XLVII (Autumn 1963), pp. 12–15, reprinted in Abraham S. Eisenstadt (ed.), *The Craft of American History* (Harper Torchbook,

N.Y.: Harper, 1966); and Oscar Handlin and John Burchard (eds.), *The Historian and the City* (Cambridge: M.I.T. and Harvard U. P., 1963).

STANDARD WORKS IN UNITED STATES HISTORY. Some of the series in American history contain useful material on urban development. See John B. McMaster, *A History of the People of the United States from the Revolution to the Civil War* (8 vols., N.Y.: Appleton, 1883–1913); Arthur M. Schlesinger and Dixon Ryan Fox (eds.), *The History of American Life* (13 vols., N.Y.: Macmillan, 1927–1948), which is fundamental for the subject, especially James T. Adams, *Provincial Society* (1927), John Allen Krout and Dixon Ryan Fox, *The Completion of Independence* (1944), Arthur M. Cole, *The Irrepressible Conflict* (1934), Allan Nevins, *The Emergence of Modern America* (1927), Arthur M. Schlesinger, *The Rise of the City* (1933), and Dixon Wecter, *The Age of the Great Depression* (1948); Henry S. Commager and Richard B. Morris (eds.), *The New American Nation Series* (in progress, N.Y.: Harper), especially Russell B. Nye, *The Cultural Life of the New Nation* (1960), Clement Eaton, *The Growth of Southern Civilization* (1961), Harold U. Faulkner, *Politics, Reform and Expansion* (1959), George R. Mowry, *The Era of Theodore Roosevelt* (1958), and John D. Hicks, *Republican Ascendancy: 1921–1933* (1960); Henry David et al. (eds.), *The Economic History of the United States* (10 vols., in progress, N.Y.: Holt), especially George R. Taylor, *The Transportation Revolution* (1951), Harold U. Faulkner, *The Decline of Laissez Faire* (1951), and Edward C. Kirkland, *Industry Comes of Age* (1961).

SURVEYS. Constance McL. Green, *American Cities in the Growth of the Nation* (N.Y.: DeGraff, 1957) contains valuable sketches of several cities' histories; her brief *The Rise of Urban America* (N.Y.: Harper, 1965) is less successful. Adna Ferrin Weber, *The Growth of Cities in the Nineteenth Century* (Ithaca: Cornell U. P., 1963, originally published in 1899) is a pioneering statistical study that has never been superseded.

URBAN BIOGRAPHIES. The preparation of comprehensive histories of individual cities has been the most commonly pursued line of inquiry in American urban history. Urban biographies have been of obvious importance in this study but only a few of the more important and representative titles can be mentioned. Thomas J. Wertenbaker, *Norfolk: Historic Southern Port* (revised edition by Marvin W. Schlegel, Durham, N.C.: Duke U. P., 1962); Constance McL. Green, *Washington: Village and Capital,* and *Washington: Capital City* (Princeton, N.J.: Princeton U. P., 1962 and 1963); Blake McKelvey, *Rochester* (3 vols., Cambridge: Harvard U. P., 1945–1956; 1 vol., Rochester, N.Y.: Christopher, 1961); Bessie L. Pierce, *A History of Chicago* (3 vols., N.Y.: Knopf, 1937–1957); Bayrd Still, *Milwaukee: the History of a City* (Madison: State Historical Society of Wisc., 1948, revised edition, 1965); Constance McL. Green, *Holyoke, Massachusetts* (New Haven: Yale U. P., 1939); Vera Shlakman,

Economic History of a Factory Town: A Study of Chicopee, Massachusetts (Northampton, Mass.: Smith College, 1934–1935); Gerald M. Capers, The Biography of a River Town: Memphis, Its Heroic Age (Chapel Hill, N.C.: U. of N.C. P., 1939); A. Theodore Brown, Frontier Community: a History of Kansas City to 1870 (Columbia, Mo.: U. of Mo. P., 1964); Powell A. Moore, The Calumet Region, Indiana's Last Frontier (Indianapolis: Indiana Historical Bureau, 1959). A sharply etched "urban vignette" is Bernard Mayo's essay on Lexington, "Frontier Metropolis," in Goldman (ed.), Historiography and Urbanization, cited above.

PERIOD STUDIES. Carl Bridenbaugh, Cities in the Wilderness (N.Y.: Ronald, 1938), and Cities in Revolt (N.Y.: Knopf, 1959), both major pieces of scholarship in American urban history; Carl and Jessica Bridenbaugh, Rebels and Gentlemen: Philadelphia in the Age of Franklin (N.Y.: Reynal, 1942); Thomas J. Wertenbaker, Father Knickerbocker Rebels: New York During the Revolution (N.Y.: Scribners, 1948), and The Golden Age of Colonial Culture (Ithaca: Cornell U. P., 1942); Ralph Weld, Brooklyn Village (N.Y.: Columbia U. P., 1938); Sidney I. Pomerantz, New York: An American City, 1783–1803 (N.Y.: Friedman, 1965); Richard C. Wade, The Urban Frontier 1790–1830 (Cambridge: Harvard U. P., 1959), a landmark; and Slavery in the Cities: The South, 1820–1860 (N.Y.: Oxford U. P., 1964); Robert G. Albion, The Rise of New York Port (N.Y.: Scribners, 1939); Blake McKelvey, The Urbanization of America, 1860–1915 (New Brunswick, N.J.: Rutgers U. P., 1963), contains a monumental bibliography; Ray Ginger, Altgeld's America (N.Y.: Funk, 1958), a sensitive portrait of Chicago around the turn of the century.

URBAN RIVALRY AND PROMOTION. These themes from the nineteenth century have produced a considerable body of writing. The following are representative: James W. Livingood, The Philadelphia-Baltimore Trade Rivalry (Harrisburg: Pennsylvania Historical and Museum Commission, 1947); Wyatt W. Belcher, The Economic Rivalry Between St. Louis and Chicago, 1850–1880 (N.Y.: Columbia U. P., 1947); Charles N. Glaab, Kansas City and the Railroads (Madison: State Historical Society of Wisc., 1962); Julius Rubin, Canal or Railroad: Imitation and Innovation in Response to the Erie Canal in Philadelphia, Baltimore, and Boston (Philadelphia: American Philosophical Society, 1961), important also for theoretical considerations; Glen Chesney Quiett, They Built the West: An Epic of Rails and Cities (N.Y.: Appleton, 1934); Richard C. Overton, Burlington West: A Colonization History of the Burlington Railroad (Cambridge: Harvard U. P., 1941) and Paul W. Gates, The Illinois Central Railroad and its Colonization Work (Cambridge: Harvard U. P., 1934) are important for town promotion by railroads; Earl Pomeroy, The Pacific Slope (N.Y.: Knopf, 1965) and C. Vann Woodward, The Origins of the New South (New Orleans: La. State U. P., 1951), contain sections on urban development in the West and South respectively.

INTELLECTUAL HISTORY. Morton and Lucia White, *The Intellectual Versus the City* (Cambridge: Harvard U. P. and M.I.T. U. P., 1962), although we have frequently debated its conclusions, is a pioneering study; R. W. B. Lewis, *The American Adam* (Chicago: U. of Chicago P., 1955); Anselm Strauss, *Images of the American City* (Glencoe, Ill.: Free Press, 1961); Daniel Horowitz, "The Meaning of City Biographies: New Haven in the Nineteenth and Early Twentieth Centuries," *Connecticut Historical Society Bulletin* XXIX (July 1964), pp. 65–75; R. Richard Wohl and A. Theodore Brown, "The Usable Past: a Study of Historical Traditions in Kansas City," *The Huntington Library Quarterly* XXIII (May 1960), pp. 237–259; Daniel Levine, *Varieties of Reform Thought* (Madison: State Historical Society of Wisc., 1964); George Dunlap, *The City in the American Novel, 1789–1900* (N.Y.: Russell, 1965); Blanche H. Gelfant, *The American City Novel* (Norman, Okla.: U. of Okla. P., 1954); Eugene Arden, "The Evil City in American Fiction," *New York History* XXXV (July 1954), pp. 259–279.

GOVERNMENT AND POLITICS. A few citations must suffice to represent the large body of writing in these areas. On colonial cities, see Ernest S. Griffith, *History of American City Government: the Colonial Period* (N.Y.: Oxford U. P., 1938), and Richard B. Morris, *Government and Labor in Early America* (N.Y.: Columbia U. P., 1946). Useful surveys are John Fairlie, *Municipal Administration* (N.Y.: Macmillan, 1901) and Ernest S. Griffith, *The Modern Development of City Government* (London: Oxford U. P., 1927). Seymour Mandelbaum, *Boss Tweed's New York* (N.Y.: Wiley, 1965) makes interesting use of social science concepts. Harold Zink, *City Bosses in the United States* (Durham, N.C.: Duke U. P., 1939) is a comparative study. The following articles will serve to introduce recent thinking on bossism and reform: Eric McKitrick, "The Study of Corruption," *Political Science Quarterly* LXXII (December 1957), pp. 502–514; James Weinstein, "Organized Business and the City Commission and Manager Movements," *Journal of Southern History* XXVIII (May 1962), pp. 167–181; Samuel P. Hays, "The Politics of Reform in Municipal Government in the Progressive Era," *Pacific Northwest Quarterly* LV (October 1964), pp. 157–159; Roy Lubove, "The Twentieth Century City: the Progressive as Municipal Reformer," *Mid-America* XXXI (October 1959), pp. 195–209. Allen F. Davis, "Jane Addams vs. the Ward Boss," *Journal of the Illinois State Historical Society* LIII (Autumn 1960), pp. 247–265, and Louis G. Geiger, "Joseph W. Folk v. Edward Butler: St. Louis, 1902," *Journal of Southern History* XXVIII (November 1962), pp. 438–449, are analytical narratives.

SOCIAL HISTORY, WELFARE, THE URBAN IMMIGRANT. Many sources have been indicated in the text. The following should be specially noted: Roy Lubove, *The Progressive and the Slum* (Pittsburgh: Pittsburgh U. P., 1963); Robert Bremner, *From the Depths: the Discovery of Poverty in the United States* (N.Y.: New York U. P., 1956); Blanche D. Coll, "The Baltimore

Society for the Prevention of Pauperism," *American Historical Review* LXI (October 1955), pp. 77–87; Carroll S. Rosenberg, "Protestants and Five Pointers: the Five Points House of Industry, 1850–1870," *New York Historical Society Quarterly* XLVIII (October 1964), pp. 326–347; Miriam Z. Langsam, *Children West* (Madison: State Historical Society of Wisc., 1964); Charles Rosenberg, *The Cholera Years* (Chicago: U. of Chicago P., 1962); James W. Cassedy, "The Flamboyant Colonel Waring," *Bulletin of the History of Medicine* XXXVI (March–April 1962), pp. 163–176; Maldwyn Allen Jones, *American Immigration* (Chicago: U. of Chicago P., 1960); Robert Ernst, *Immigrant Life in New York City* (N.Y.: King's Crown, 1949); Oscar Handlin, *Boston's Immigrants* (Cambridge: Harvard U. P., 1959); Moses Rischin, *The Promised City: New York's Jews* (Cambridge: Harvard U. P., 1962); Lewis E. Atherton, *Main Street on the Middle Border* (Bloomington: Indiana U. P., 1954); Aaron Abell, *The Urban Impact on American Protestantism* (Cambridge: Harvard U. P., 1962); Allen F. Davis, "The Social Workers and the Progressive Party, 1912–1916," *American Historical Review* LXIX (April 1964), pp. 671–688; Maurice R. Stein, *The Eclipse of Community* (Princeton: Princeton U. P., 1960); Almont Lindsay, *The Pullman Strike* (Chicago: U. of Chicago P., 1942); St. Clair Drake and Horace R. Cayton, *Black Metropolis* (Harper Torchbook, N.Y.: Harper, 1962).

ARCHITECTURE AND URBAN PLANNING. The writing on these subjects is voluminous but much of it is unhistorical. The following are important: John W. Reps, *The Making of Urban America: A History of City Planning in the United States* (Princeton: Princeton U. P., 1965), a magnificent piece of scholarship, beautifully illustrated; Christopher Tunnard and Henry Hope Reed, *American Skyline* (Boston: Houghton, 1955), an incisive survey of American urban development with emphasis on building styles; John Burchard and Albert Bush-Brown, *The Architecture of America: A Social and Cultural History* (Boston: Little, Brown, 1961); Wayne Andrews, *Architecture, Ambition, and Americans* (New York: Harper, 1955); Sigfried Giedion, *Space, Time, and Architecture* (Cambridge: Harvard U. P., 4th ed., 1962); several works by Lewis Mumford, especially *The Brown Decades* (N.Y.: Dover, 1955), *The Culture of Cities* (N.Y.: Harcourt, 1938), and "The City," in Harold Stearns (ed.), *Civilization in the United States* (N.Y.: Harcourt, 1922); John Coolidge, *Mill and Mansion: A Study of Architecture and Society in Lowell, Massachusetts* (N.Y.: Columbia U. P., 1942); Edmund H. Chapman, *Cleveland: Village to Metropolis* (Cleveland, Ohio: Western Reserve U. P., 1965); William H. Wilson, *The City Beautiful Movement in Kansas City* (Columbia, Mo.: U. of Mo. P., 1964); Roy Lubove, *Community Planning in the 1920s: The Contribution of the Regional Planning Association of America* (Pittsburgh: Pittsburgh U. P., 1965); Henry W. S. Cleveland, *Landscape Architecture as Applied to the Wants of the West* (Lubove, ed., Pittsburgh: Pittsburgh U. P., 1965); Paul A. Conkin, *Tomorrow a New World: The New Deal Community Program* (Ithaca: Cornell U. P., 1959).

TECHNOLOGY. This is a relatively undeveloped aspect of American urban history, but the following are valuable: Roger Burlingame, *Engines of Democracy: Inventions and Society in Mature America* (N.Y.: Scribners, 1940); Nelson M. Blake, *Water for the Cities* (Syracuse: Syracuse U. P., 1956); Harold C. Passer, *The Electrical Manufacturers* (Cambridge: Harvard U. P., 1953). Many of the works listed under architecture and planning contain material on building technology.

REAL ESTATE AND URBAN LAND USE. These subjects have not been studied historically to any extent but the following are useful: Aaron M. Sakolski, *The Great American Land Bubble* (N.Y.: Harper, 1932); Eugene Rachlis and John E. Marquesee, *The Landlords* (N.Y.: Random, 1963), a good popular history; Glenn S. Dumke, *The Boom of the Eighties in Southern California* (San Marino, Calif.: The Huntington Library, 1944); Sam B. Warner, Jr., *Streetcar Suburbs: The Process of Growth in Boston* (Cambridge: M.I.T. and Harvard U. P., 1962), an original study, vital for understanding residential suburbanization; M. Mason Gaffney, *Urban Expansion—Will It Ever Stop?* (Yearbook Separate No. 2931, *Yearbook of Agriculture,* 1958) contributed to our understanding of historical urban land use, as did Homer Hoyt, *One Hundred Years of Land Values in Chicago* (Chicago: U. of Chicago P., 1933).

RELATED SOCIAL SCIENCES. Social scientists in other disciplines have much to contribute to the study of urban history. Their work is voluminous, and only a few items can be cited here. Hauser and Schnore, *The Study of Urbanization,* previously cited, is a valuable guide; Paul K. Hatt and Albert Reiss, *Cities and Society: The Revised Reader in Urban Sociology* (Glencoe, Ill.: Free Press, 1957) contains excellent readings. See also Robert K. Merton, *Social Theory and Social Structure* (Glencoe, Ill.: Free Press, 1949), especially for an approach to the subject of bossism; Leo F. Schnore, *The Urban Scene* (N.Y.: Free Press, 1959), a collection of Schnore's essays which has guided our thinking on metropolitan and suburban growth; Donald J. Bogue, *The Population of the United States* (Glencoe, Ill.: Free Press, 1959); Rupert B. Vance and Nicholas J. Demerath (eds.), *The Urban South* (Chapel Hill, N.C.: U. of N. C. P., 1954); N. S. B. Gras, *An Introduction to Economic History* (N.Y.: Harper, 1922); R. D. McKenzie, *The Metropolitan Community* (N.Y.: McGraw-Hill, 1933); Louis Wirth, "The Urban Society and Civilization," *American Journal of Sociology* XLV (March 1940), pp. 743–755; Hope Tisdale, "The Process of Urbanization," *Social Forces* XX (March 1942), pp. 311–316; Jean Gottman, *Megalopolis: The Urbanized Northeastern Seaboard of the United States* (N.Y.: Twentieth Century Fund, 1961).

# Bibliographical Note
# to the Second Edition

THE OUTPOURING of studies in urban history since the first edition of this work would make the preparation of a comprehensive bibliography an arduous task that it did not seem worthwhile to undertake. Changing the original bibliographical essay would obscure for the reader the structure of secondary works that supported the book, and this did not seem proper scholarly practice. Moreover, an effort at this time would probably only duplicate several excellent recent bibliographies. For example, an unannotated but nearly exhaustive listing of fundamental books in urban history is contained in Bayrd Still, *Urban America: A History with Documents* (Boston: Little, Brown, 1974). Several recent anthologies and readers contain interpretative, bibliographical essays. See particularly Kenneth T. Jackson and Stanley K. Schultz (eds.), *Cities in American History* (N.Y.: Knopf, 1972) and Raymond A. Mohl and Neil Betten (eds.), *Urban America in Historical Perspective* (N.Y.: Weybright, 1970). In the following pages, these works will be referred to as *Cities*, and *Urban America*. A number of bibliographical, theoretical, and analytical essays have also surveyed work in the field. A widely reprinted, straightforward article which students find comprehensible is Dwight W. Hoover, "The Diverging Paths of American Urban History," *American Quarterly* XX (Summer 1968), pp. 296–317. An introduction to the "new urban history," with its use of statistics in the study of the plain people in cities, is perhaps best supplied by Stephan Thernstrom, "Reflections on the New Urban History," *Daedalus* C (Spring 1971), pp. 359–375. Richard C. Wade, "An Agenda for Urban History," in Herbert J. Bass (ed.), *The State of American History* (Chicago: Quadrangle, 1970), pp. 43–69, is an assessment by a scholar with much achievement in the field.

The following then is less a guide to general sources than it is a listing of secondary works from which I have gathered ideas, specific information, or quotations. Because of the considerable scholarship of recent years, primary sources have not been used to the extent that they were in the first edition. Those that I have consulted have mainly been in printed form, items like the plan for Chicago, the writings of Frederick Law Olmsted, novels, and the Kerner Commission report. These are identified in the text, and bibliographical citation has therefore not been supplied. Remarks on the aesthetic qualities of bridges, buildings, and paintings are generally based on first-hand observations recorded in personal journals, although several paintings were examined in reproduction. Discussion of these matters is so limited that I have not thought it necessary to supply precise identifying information.

READERS AND ANTHOLOGIES. There have been a number of these in recent years; they all provide good collections of basic articles and, less frequently, key selections from books. I have made particular use of those with original articles. Jackson and Schultz, *Cities* includes in addition to re-printed articles several original essays, all of which are scholarly. Raymond A. Mohl and James F. Richardson (eds.), *The Urban Experience: Themes in American History* (Belmont, Calif.: Wadsworth, 1973), referred to hereafter as *The Urban Experience,* is made up entirely of original articles. The work is uneven, but several of the articles are sound and often supply a synthesis not available elsewhere. I have made specific reference to articles in both these anthologies. Mention should be made of both editions of Alexander B. Callow, Jr., *American Urban History: An Interpretive Reader with Commentaries* (N.Y.: Oxford U. P., 1969; 2nd ed., 1973). This was one of the first readers and one of the most detailed, particularly useful for assembling bibliographical and theoretical articles. In teaching I have long used Allen M. Wakstein (ed.), *The Urbanization of America: An Historical Anthology* (Boston: Houghton, 1970), and I am sure it has influenced my thinking.

GENERAL WORKS. Blake McKelvey's extremely well-researched works are essential to the study of urban history. I have made special use of *The Emergence of Metropolitan America 1915–1966* (New Brunswick, N.J.: Rutgers U. P., 1968). His *American Urbanization: A Comparative History* (Glenview, Ill.: Scott, Foresman, 1973) is fairly brief but original. Still's *Urban America* is a fine achievement by another master craftsman of urban history. His documents are so well chosen that I consulted the collection at numerous points in this study. Zane L. Miller, *The Urbanization of Modern America: A Brief History* (N.Y.: Harcourt, 1973) contains good material on Negroes and on urban politics. Sam Bass Warner, Jr., *The Urban Wilderness: A History of the America City* (N.Y.: Harper, 1972) has been widely praised as a seminal work in the study of American urban history. It represents the new style of history as personal polemic, which some find congenial. I agreed with little of the advocacy but found much of the history original and in-structive.

COLONIAL. In recent years, in part owing to a continuing interest in Puritanism, there has been an extensive body of writing on early new England towns, villages, and cities. The class structure of Colonial America and its effect on urban society has also received considerable investigation. I have made specific use of the following: James A. Henretta, "Economic Develop-ment and Social Structure in Colonial Boston," *William and Mary Quarterly* XXII (January 1965), pp. 75–92; Kenneth A. Lockridge, *A New England Town, The First Hundred Years: Dedham, Massachusetts, 1636–1736* (N.Y.: Norton, 1970); Raymond A. Mohl, "Poverty in the Cities: A History of Social Welfare," in Mohl and Richardson, *The Urban Experience,* pp. 99–126; Raymond A.

Mohl, "Poverty in Early America, a Reappraisal: The Case of Eighteenth-Century New York City," *New York History* L (January 1969) pp. 5–27; Gary B. Nash, "The Transformation of Urban Politics, 1700–1765," *The Journal of American History* LX (December 1973), pp. 605–632; Sumner Chilton Powell, *Puritan Village: The Formation of a New England Town* (Wesleyan, Conn.: Wesleyan U. P., 1963); John C. Rainbolt, "The Absence of Towns in Seventeenth-Century Virginia," *Journal of Southern History* XXXV (August 1969), pp. 343–360; Darrett B. Rutman, *Winthrop's Boston: Portrait of a Puritan Town* (Chapel Hill, N.C.: U. of N. C. P., 1965); Michael Zuckerman, *Peaceable Kingdoms: New England Towns in the Eighteenth Century* (N.Y.: Knopf, 1970).

URBAN GROWTH AND DEVELOPMENT (NINETEENTH CENTURY). Allan R. Pred, *The Spatial Dynamics of U.S. Urban-Industrial Growth, 1800–1914* (Cambridge: M.I.T. U. P., 1966) is a difficult but important theoretical work. See also Blaine A. Brownell, "Urbanization in the South: A Unique Experience?" *Mississippi Quarterly* XXVI (Spring 1973), pp. 105–120; Robert William Fogel and Stanley L. Engerman, *Time on the Cross: The Economics of American Negro Slavery* (Boston: Little Brown, 1974); Charles N. Glaab and Lawrence H. Larsen, "Neenah-Menasha in the 1870's," *Wisconsin Magazine of History* LII (Autumn 1968), pp. 19–34; Eric E. Lampard, "The Evolving System of Cities in the United States: Urbanization and Economic Development," in Harvey S. Perloff and Lowdon Wingo, Jr. (eds.), *Issues in Urban Economics* (Baltimore: Resources for the Future, 1968), pp. 81–139; Roger W. Lotchin, *San Francisco, 1846–1856: From Hamlet to City* (N.Y.: Oxford U. P., 1974); Allan R. Pred, *Urban Growth and the Circulation of Information: The United States System of Cities 1790–1840* (Cambridge: Harvard U. P., 1973); Julius Rubin, "Urban Growth and Regional Development," in David T. Gilchrist (ed.), *The Growth of the Seaport Cities: 1790–1825* (Charlottesville, Va.: U. of Va. P., 1967), pp. 3–21; Harry N. Scheiber, "Urban Rivalry and Internal Improvements in the Old Northwest, 1820–1860," *Ohio History* LXXI (October 1962), pp. 227–239, 290–292; J. Christopher Schnell and Patrick E. McLear, "Why the Cities Grew: A Historiographical Essay on Western Urban Growth 1850–1880," *Missouri Historical Society Bulletin* XXVIII (April 1972), pp. 162–177; Kenneth W. Wheeler, *To Wear a City's Crown: The Beginnings of Urban Growth in Texas, 1836–1865* (Cambridge: Harvard U. P., 1968).

SOCIAL HISTORY: CLASS, MINORITIES, AND PROBLEMS (NINETEENTH CENTURY). Studies in the "new urban history" have greatly enlarged understanding of the class structure and character of life in nineteenth-century cities. Material from the following is referred to in the text. Howard Chudacoff, *Mobile Americans: Residential and Social Mobility in Omaha, 1880–1920* (N.Y.: Oxford U. P.: 1972); Richard J. Hopkins, "Status, Mobility, and the Dimensions of Change in a Southern City: Atlanta, 1870–1910," in Jackson and Schultz, *Cities*, pp. 216–231; Peter R. Knights, *The Plain*

*People of Boston, 1830–1860: A Study in City Growth* (N.Y.: Oxford U. P., 1971); Stephan Thernstrom, *The Other Bostonians: Poverty and Progress in the American Metropolis, 1880–1970* (Cambridge: Harvard U. P., 1973). Rowland Berthoff, *An Unsettled People: Social Order and Disorder in American History* (N.Y.: Harper, 1971) is a general social history which embodies recent conceptions and contains considerable material on cities. Philip Taylor, *The Distant Magnet: Foreign Emigration to the U.S.A.* (N.Y.: Harper, 1971) and David Ward, *Cities and Immigrants: A Geography of Change in Nineteenth-Century America* (N.Y.: Oxford U. P., 1971) supply excellent general information on the immigrant in cities. Despite the flourishing of black history, there is nothing comparable on the Negro in cities. The following have been useful: David R. Goldfield and James B. Lane (eds.), *The Enduring Ghetto: Sources and Readings* (Philadelphia: Lippincott, 1973); Leon F. Litwack, *North of Slavery: The Negro in the Free States, 1790–1860* (Chicago: U. of Chicago P., 1961), a landmark study; Richard J. Meister (ed.), *The Black Ghetto: Promised Land or Colony* (Lexington, Mass.: Heath, 1972); Zane L. Miller, "The Black Experience in the Modern American City," in Mohl and Richardson, *The Urban Experience,* pp. 44–60; Humbert S. Nelli, *Italians in Chicago, 1880–1930: A Study in Ethnic Mobility* (N.Y.: Oxford U. P., 1970); Gilbert Osofsky, *Harlem: The Making of a Ghetto, Negro New York, 1890–1930* (N.Y.: Harper, 1966); Robert Rockaway, "Ethnic Conflict and Self-Help in Detroit's Jewish Ghetto, 1881–1914," *American Jewish Historical Quarterly* XL (December 1970), pp. 133–150; Allan H. Spear, *Black Chicago: The Making of a Negro Ghetto, 1890–1920* (Chicago: U. of Chicago P., 1967). On nineteenth-century urban violence, see Ray Allen Billington, *The Protestant Crusade, 1800–1860* (N.Y.: Macmillan, 1938); Adrian Cook, *The Armies of the Streets: The New York City Draft Riots of 1863* (Lexington, Ky.: U. of Ky. P., 1974); Richard Hofstadter and Michael Wallace (eds.), *American Violence: A Documentary History* (N.Y.: Vintage, 1970). On services, see John K. Alexander, "The City of Brotherly Fear: The Poor in Late-Eighteenth Century Philadelphia," in Jackson and Schultz, *Cities,* pp. 79–97; James H. Cassedy, *Charles V. Chapin and the Public Health Movement* (Cambridge: Harvard U. P., 1962); John Duffy, *A History of Public Health in New York City, 1625–1866* (N.Y.: Russell Sage Foundation, 1968); Joseph M. Hawes, *Children in Urban Society: Juvenile Delinquency in Nineteenth-Century America* (N.Y.: Oxford U. P., 1971); Roger Lane, *Policing the City: Boston, 1822–1885* (Cambridge: Harvard U.P., 1967); Lawrence H. Larsen, "Nineteenth-Century Street Sanitation, A Study of Filth and Frustration," *Wisconsin Magazine of History* LII (Spring 1969), pp. 239–247; Raymond A. Mohl, "Poverty, Pauperism, and Social Order in the Preindustrial American City, 1780–1840," *Social Science Quarterly* (March 1972), pp. 934–948; Raymond A. Mohl, *Poverty in New York, 1783–1825* (N.Y.: Oxford U. P., 1971); James F. Richardson, "The Police in the City: A History," in Mohl and Richardson, *The Urban Experience,* pp. 164–181; James F. Richardson, *The New York Police: Colonial Times to 1901* (N.Y.: Oxford U. P., 1970);

David J. Rothman, *The Discovery of the Asylum: Social Order and Disorder in the New Republic* (Boston: Little, Brown, 1971); Joel A. Tarr, "Urban Pollution—Many Long Years Ago," *American Heritage* XXII (October 1971), pp. 65–69, 106. Other studies include Lois W. Banner, "Religious Benevolence as Social Control: A Critique of an Interpretation," *Journal of American History* LX (June 1973), pp. 23–41; Carroll Smith Rosenberg, *Religion and the Rise of the American City: The New York City Mission Movement, 1812–1870* (Ithaca: Cornell U. P., 1971); Timothy L. Smith, "Immigrant Social Aspirations and American Education, 1880–1930," *American Quarterly* XXI (Fall 1969), pp. 523–543; Dale A. Somers, *The Rise of Sports in New Orleans, 1850–1900* (Baton Rouge: La. State U. P., 1972); and Selwyn K. Troen, "Education in the City," in Mohl and Richardson, *The Urban Experience,* pp. 127–143.

URBAN CULTURE, ART, AND ARCHITECTURE. The studies of urban elites by Edward Pessen are valuable. I have made particular use of "The Egalitarian Myth and the American Social Reality: Wealth, Mobility, and Equality in the 'Era of the Common Man'," *American Historical Review* LXXVI (October 1971), pp. 989–1034, and "The Lifestyle of the Antebellum Urban Elite," *Mid-America* LV (July 1973), pp. 163–183. Martin Green, *The Problem of Boston: Some Readings in Cultural History* (N.Y.: Norton, 1966) and Neil Harris, *The Artist in American Society: The Formative Years, 1790–1860* (N.Y.: Braziller, 1966) are important interpretative studies. See also Paul Goodman, "Ethics and Enterprise: The Values of a Boston Elite, 1800–1860," *American Quarterly* XVIII (Fall 1966), pp. 437–451; James Marston Fitch, *American Building: The Historical Forces That Shaped It* (Boston: Houghton, 2nd ed., 1966); William Ransom Hogan and Edwin Adams Davis (eds.), *William Johnson's Natchez: The Ante-Bellum Diary of a Free Negro* (Baton Rouge: La. State U. P., 1951); Ada Louise Huxtable, "The Skyscraper Style," *The New York Times Magazine* (April 14, 1974), Huxtable's regular columns on urban architecture in *The New York Times* are perceptive and informed by historical understanding; D. Clayton James, *Antebellum Natchez* (Baton Rouge: La. State U.P., 1968); Helen M. Morgan (ed.), *A Season in New York, 1801: Letters of Harriet and Maria Trumbull* (Pittsburgh: Pittsburgh U. P., 1969); Jules David Prown, *American Painting: From Its Beginning to the Armory Show* (Cleveland, Ohio: World, n.d.); Vincent Scully, *American Architecture and Urbanism* (N.Y.: Prager, 1969); Alan Trachtenberg, *Brooklyn Bridge: Fact and Symbol* (N.Y.: Oxford U.P., 1965).

GOVERNMENT AND POLITICS. Blaine A. Brownell and Warren E. Stickle (eds.), *Bosses and Reformers: Urban Politics in America, 1880–1920* (Boston: Houghton, 1973) and Bruce M. Stave (ed.), *Urban Bosses, Machines, and Progressive Reformers* (Lexington, Mass.: Heath, 1972) are convenient readers. Lyle W. Dorsett, "The City Boss and the Reformer," *Pacific North-*

*west Quarterly* LXIII (October 1972), pp. 150–154 surveys recent interpretations. See also Lyle W. Dorsett, *The Pendergast Machine* (N.Y.: Oxford U. P., 1968); Scott Greer, *Governing the Metropolis* (N.Y.: Wiley, 1962); Melvin G. Holli, *Reform in Detroit: Hazen S. Pingree and Urban Politics* (N.Y.: Oxford U. P., 1969); John W. Pratt, "Boss Tweed's Public Welfare Program," *New York Historical Society Quarterly* XLV (October 1961), pp. 396–411; Zane Miller, *Boss Cox's Cincinnati: Urban Politics in the Progressive Era* (N.Y.: Oxford U. P., 1968); Kenneth T. Jackson, "Metropolitan Government Versus Political Autonomy: Politics on the Crabgrass Frontier," in Jackson and Schultz, *Cities,* pp. 442–462.

URBAN TECHNOLOGY. Daniel J. Boorstin's two splendid volumes on American social history *The Americans: The National Experience* (N.Y.: Random, 1965) and *The Americans: The Democratic Experience* (N.Y.: Random, 1973) contain excellent material on inventions and other technological aspects of urban development. Howard Mumford Jones, *The Age of Energy: Varieties of American Experience, 1865–1915* (N.Y.: Viking, 1971) is a masterwork that contains some valuable material on cities. I have also drawn material from William D. Middleton, " 'Gems of Symmetry and Convenience,' " *American Heritage* XXIV (February 1973), pp. 23–37, 99, on street railways, and David McCullough, *The Great Bridge* (N.Y.: Simon and Schuster, 1972) on Brooklyn Bridge.

PLANNING. Despite considerable scholarship in recent years, there is no comprehensive history that relates the topic to broad social, economic, and cultural themes. However, Mel Scott, *American City Planning Since 1890* (Berkeley: U. of Calif. P., 1969) is a good technical history of the modern era of planning. Other studies include Stanley Buder, *Pullman: An Experiment in Industrial Order and Community Planning 1880–1930* (N.Y.: Oxford U. P., 1970); Henry S. Churchill, *The City Is the People* (N.Y., Norton, 1962, first ed., 1945); Albert Fein, *Frederick Law Olmsted and the American Environmental Tradition* (N.Y.: Braziller, 1972); Albert Fein (ed.), *Landscape into Cityscape: Frederick Law Olmsted's Plans for a Greater New York City* (Ithaca: Cornell U. P., 1967); Park Dixon Goist, "Lewis Mumford and 'Anti-Urbanism,' " *Journal of the American Institute of Planners* XXXV (September 1969), pp. 340–347; Henry-Russell Hitchcock et al., *The Rise of an American Architecture* (N.Y.: Praeger, 1970); Roy Lubove, *The Urban Community: Housing and Planning in the Progressive Era* (Englewood Cliffs, N.J.: Prentice-Hall, 1967), mainly documents, but contains an excellent long introductory essay; Roy Lubove, "Urban Planning and Development," in Melvin Kransberg and Carroll W. Pursell, Jr. (eds.), *Technology in Western Civilization* (Madison: U. of Wisc. P., 1967); Raymond A. Mohl and Neil Betten, "The Failure of Industrial City Planning: Gary, Indiana, 1906–1910," *Journal of the American Institute of*

*Planners* XXXVII (July 1972), pp. 203–215; Christopher Tunnard, *The Modern American City* (Princeton: D. Van Nostrand, 1968), includes well-chosen documents.

FEDERAL POLICY.   Useful collections of essays include Jewel Bellush and Murray Hausknecht (eds.), *Urban Renewal: People, Politics, and Planning* (Garden City, N.Y.: Anchor, 1967), a comprehensive collection on the subject; Melvin I. Urofsky (ed.), *Perspectives on Urban America* (Garden City, N.Y.: Anchor, 1973), especially Betty D. Hawkins, "Cities and the Environmental Crisis," pp. 161–185; Shirley S. Passow, "Urban Planning: Old Realities and New Directions," pp. 209–241, and Anona Teska, "The Federal Impact on the Cities," pp. 267–294; James Q. Wilson (ed.), *The Metropolitan Enigma* (Garden City, N.Y.: Anchor, 1970), especially Bernard J. Frieden, "Housing and National Urban Goals: Old Policies and New Realities," pp. 170–225. Other studies used include Charles Abrams, *The City Is The Frontier* (N.Y.: Harper, 1965); Joseph L. Arnold, *The New Deal in the Suburbs: A History of the Greenbelt Town Program, 1935–1954* (Columbus: Ohio State U. P., 1971); Richard O. Davies, *Housing Reform During the Truman Administration* (Columbia, Mo.: U. of Mo. P., 1966), an excellent monograph greatly broadened in scope through introductory and concluding chapters; Scott Greer, *Urban Renewal and American Cities* (Indianapolis: Bobbs, 1965); William H. Wilson, "A Great Impact, a Gingerly Investigation: Historians and the Federal Effect on Urban Development," in Jerome Finster (ed.), *The National Archives and Urban Research* (Athens: Ohio U. P., 1974), pp. 113–123.

RECENT URBAN HISTORY (SINCE 1915).   Many of the studies cited in the aforementioned topical categories, "Planning" and "Federal Policy" in particular, are useful here. For material on the last twenty years, I have also used a variety of newspaper and magazine articles assembled for teaching and writing, but these are too diffuse and ephemeral to be usefully cited here. William H. Wilson, *Coming of Age: Urban America, 1915–1945* (N.Y.: Wiley, 1974) is a reasonably detailed, well written, interpretative chronological study of a kind that is lacking for many periods of American urban history. Of the flood of books on contemporary urban problems, the best, despite the attacks against its political point of view, is Edward C. Banfield, *The Unheavenly City: The Nature and Future of Our Urban Crisis* (Boston: Little, Brown, 1968). It is one of the few such books grounded in a firm knowledge of urban history. H. Wentworth Eldredge (ed.), *Taming Megalopolis* (Garden City, N.Y.: Anchor, 2 vols., 1967) contains particularly well-chosen readings and articles. See also Robert Gutman and David Popenoe (eds.), *Neighborhood, City, and Metropolis* (N.Y.: Random, 1970) especially William M. Dobriner, "The Growth and Structure of Metropolitan Areas," pp. 190–201; James W. Hughes (ed.), *Suburbanization Dynamics and the Future of the City* (New Brunswick, N.J.: Center for Urban Policy Research, 1974), especially

Leo F. Schnore and Vivian Zelig Klaff, "Suburbanization in the Sixties: A Preliminary Analysis," pp. 43–53 and Herman Kahn and Anthony J. Wiener, "Urbanization and (soon) the Growth of Megalopolises," pp. 65–66; and Seymour I. Toll, *Zoned American* (N.Y.: Grossman, 1969). On suburbanization, see Bennett M. Berger, *Working-Class Suburb: A Study of Auto Workers in Suburbia* (Berkeley: U. of Calif. P., 1968); Scott Donaldson, *The Suburban Myth* (N.Y.: Columbia U. P., 1969); Herbert J. Gans, *The Levittowners: Ways of Life and Politics in a New Suburban Community* (N.Y.: Vintage, 1969); Kenneth T. Jackson, "The Crabgrass Frontier: 150 Years of Suburban Growth in America," in Mohl and Richardson, *The Urban Experience*, pp. 196–221; Louis H. Masotti and Jeffrey K. Hadden (eds.), *Suburbia in Transition* (N.Y.: New Viewpoints, 1974); Louis H. Masotti and Jeffrey K. Hadden (eds.), *The Urbanization of the Suburbs* (Beverly Hills, Calif.: Sage, 1973), especially Norval D. Glenn, "Suburbanization in the United States Since World War II," pp. 51–78. On urban violence, see Richard A. Berk and Howard E. Aldrich, "Patterns of Vandalism During Civil Disorders As an Indicator of Selection of Targets," *American Sociological Review* XXVII (October 1972), pp. 535–547; Nathan S. Caplan and Jeffrey M. Paige, "A Study of Ghetto Rioters," *Scientific American* CCXIX (August 1968), pp. 15–21; Peter K. Eisinger, "The Urban Crisis As a Failure of Community: Some Data," *Urban Affairs Quarterly* IX (June 1974), pp. 437–461; Lawrence B. De Graaf, "The City of Black Angels: Emergence of the Los Angeles Ghetto, 1890–1930," *Pacific Historical Review* XXXIX (August 1970), pp. 323–352; Robert M. Fogelson, *Violence as Protest: A Study of Riots and Ghettos* (Garden City, N.Y.: Doubleday, 1971); Hugh Davis Graham and Ted Robert Gurr (eds.), *Violence in America: Historical and Comparative Perspectives* (N.Y.: Bantam, 1969), especially Morris Janowitz, "Patterns of Collective Racial Violence," pp. 412–444; Andrew Levison, "The Working-Class Majority," *The New Yorker* (September 2, 1974), pp. 36–61; Clark McPhail, "Civil Disorder Participation: A Critical Examination of Recent Research," *American Sociological Review* XXXVI (December 1971), pp. 1058–1073; J. Paul Mitchell (ed.), *Race Riots in Black and White* (Englewood Cliffs, N.J.: Prentice-Hall, 1970), documents; Elliott Rudwick, *Race Riot at East St. Louis, July 2, 1917* (N.Y.: Atheneum, 1972); Charles Tilly, "Race and Migration to the American City," in Wilson (ed.), *The Metropolitan Enigma*, pp. 144–169; William M. Tuttle, Jr., "Contested Neighborhoods and Racial Violence: Chicago in 1919," in Jackson and Schultz, *Cities*, pp. 232–248; Richard C. Wade, "Violence in the Cities: A Historical View," in Jackson and Schultz, *Cities*, pp. 475–491.

# Index